THE
SACRED BOOKS OF THE EAST

Translated by

VARIOUS ORIENTAL SCHOLARS

Edited by

F. MAX MÜLLER

Vol. 18

SACRED BOOKS OF THE EAST

(50 VOLUMES)

Series Editor : *F. Max-Müller*

ISBN: 978-81-208-0101-1 (Set) Rs. 15000 (Each Vol. Rs. 350)

These volumes of the Sacred Books of the East series include translations of all the most important works of the seven non-Christian religions that have exercised a profound influence on the civilisations of the continent of Asia. The Vedic Brahmanic system claims 21 volumes, Buddhism 10, and Jainism 2; 8 volumes comprise Sacred Books of the Parsis; 2 volumes represent Islam; and 6 the two main indigenous systems of China. Translated by twenty leading authorities in their respective fields, the volumes have been edited by the late F. Max Müller. The inception, publication and the compilation of these books cover almost 34 years.

I. BUDDHISM

Vol. 49: Buddhist Mahayana Texts (2 Parts)
Vol. 11: Buddhist Suttas
Vol. 10: The Dhammapada and Sutta Nipata
Vols. 35 & 36: The Questions of King Milinda (2 Parts)
Vol. 21: The Saddharma Pundarika or the Lotus of the True Law
Vols. 13, 17 & 20: Vinaya Texts (3 Parts)

II. CHINESE

Vol. 19: The Fo-Sho-Hing-Tsan-King
Vols. 3, 16, 27, 28, 39 & 40: The Sacred Books of China (6 Parts)

III. A GENERAL INDEX

Vol. 50: A General Index to the Names and Subject-matter of the Sacred Books of the East

IV. ISLAM

Vols. 6 & 9: The Qur'an (2 Parts)

V. JAINISM

Vols. 22 & 45: The Jaina Sutras (2 Parts)

VI. PARSIS

Vols. 5, 18, 24, 37 & 47: Pahlavi Texts (5 Parts)
Vols. 4, 23 & 31: The Zend-Avesta (3 Parts)

VII. VEDIC-BRAHMANIC SYSTEM

Vol. 8: The Bhagavadgita with the Sanatsujatiya and the Anugita
Vols. 29 & 30: The Grihya-Sutras: Rules of Vedic Domestic Ceremonies (2 Parts)
Vol. 42: Hymns of the Atharva Veda together with Extracts from the Ritual Books and the Commentaries
Vol. 7: The Institutes of Vishnu
Vol. 25: The Laws of Manu
Vol. 33: The Minor Law Books
Vols. 2 & 14: The Sacred Laws of the Aryas as Taught in the Schools of Apastamba, Gautama, Vasishtha and Baudhayana (2 Parts)
Vols. 12, 26, 41, 43 & 44: The Satapatha Brahmana According to the Text of the Madhyandina School (5 Parts)
Vols. 1 & 15: The Upanishads (2 Parts)
Vols. 34 & 38: The Vedanta Sutras (2 Parts)
Vol. 48: The Vedanta-Sutras (with the commentary by Ramanuja)
Vols. 32 & 46: Vedic Hymns (2 Parts)

PAHLAVI TEXTS

THE DÂ*D*ISTÂN-Î DÎNÎK AND THE EPISTLES OF MÂNÛ*SK*ÎHAR

Translated by
E.W. WEST

PART II

MOTILAL BANARSIDASS PUBLISHERS
PRIVATE LIMITED • DELHI

7th Reprint: Delhi, 2013
First Published by the Oxford University Press, 1882

ISBN: 978-81-208-0119-6

MOTILAL BANARSIDASS
41 U.A. Bungalow Road, Jawahar Nagar, Delhi 110 007
8 Mahalaxmi Chamber, 22 Bhulabhai Desai Road, Mumbai 400 026
203 Royapettah High Road, Mylapore, Chennai 600 004
236, 9th Main III Block, Jayanagar, Bangaluru 560 011
Sanas Plaza, 1302 Baji Rao Road, Pune 411 002
8 Camac Street, Kolkata 700 017
Ashok Rajpath, Patna 800 004
Chowk, Varanasi 221 001

UNESCO COLLECTION OF REPRESENTATIVE WORKS— Indian Series
This book has been accepted in the Indian Translation Series of the UNESCO Collection of Representative Works, jointly sponsored by the United Nations Educational Scientific and Cultural Organization (UNESCO) and the Government of India

Printed in India

by RP Jain at NAB Printing Unit,
A-44, Naraina Industrial Area, Phase I, New Delhi–110028
and published by JP Jain for Motilal Banarsidass Publishers (P) Ltd,
41 U.A. Bungalow Road, Jawahar Nagar, Delhi-110007

RASHTRAPATI BHAVAN,
NEW DELHI-4
June 10, 1962

I am very glad to know that the Sacred Books of the East, published years ago by the Clarendon Press, Oxford, which have been out-of-print for a number of years, will now be available to all students of religion and philosophy. The enterprise of the publishers is commendable and I hope the books will be widely read.

S. RADHAKRISHNAN

PUBLISHER'S NOTE

First, the man distinguished between eternal and perishable. Later he discovered within himself the germ of the Eternal. This discovery was an epoch in the history of the human mind and the *East was the first to discover it.*

To watch in the Sacred Books of the East the dawn of this religious consciousness of man, must always remain one of the most inspiring and hallowing sights in the whole history of the world. In order to have a solid foundation for a comparative study of the Religions of the East, we must have before all things, complete and thoroughly faithful translation of their Sacred Books in which some of the ancient sayings were preserved because they were so true and so striking that they could not be forgotten. They contained eternal truths, expressed for the first time in human language.

With profoundest reverence for Dr. S. Radhakrishnan, President of India, who inspired us for the task; our deep sense of gratitude for Dr. C. D. Deshmukh & Dr. D. S. Kothari, for encouraging assistance; esteemed appreciation of UNESCO for the warm endorsement of the cause ; and finally with indebtedness to Dr. H. Rau, Director, Max Müller Bhawan, New Delhi, in procuring us the texts of the Series for reprint, we humbly conclude.

CONTENTS.

INTRODUCTION.

TRANSLATIONS.

INTRODUCTION.

1. General Remarks.

The Pahlavi texts selected for translation in this volume are distinguished from all others by the peculiarity that both the name and station of their author and the time in which he lived are distinctly recorded.

His name, Mânûs*k*îhar, son of Yûdân-Yim (or Gûs*n*-dam), is mentioned in each of the headings and colophons to the Dâ*d*istân-î Dînîk and the three Epistles attributed to him. He is styled simply aêrpat, or 'priest,' in the headings of Eps. I and II, and aêrpat khû*d*âî, or 'priestly lordship,' in that of Ep. III; but he is called the ra*d*, 'pontiff, or executive high-priest,' of Pârs and Kirmân, and the farmâ*d*âr, 'director,' of the profession of priests, in the colophons to Dd. and Ep. II; and we learn from Dd. XLV, 5 that the farmâ*d*âr was also the pes*s*ûpâî, or 'leader' of the religion, the supreme high-priest of the Ma*zd*a-worshipping faith.

Regarding his family we learn, from Ep. I, iii, 10, vii, 5, that his father, Yûdân-Yim, son of Shahpûhar, had been the leader of the religion before him; and his own succession to this dignity indicates that he was the eldest surviving son of his father, who, in his declining years, seems to have been assisted by his advice (Ep. I, iii, 11). We also learn, from the heading of his second epistle, that Zâ*d*-sparam was his brother, and this is confirmed by the language used in Ep. II, vi, 1, ix, 6, and by Zâ*d*-sparam being a son of the same father (Eps. I, heading, III, 2); that he was a younger brother appears from the general tone of authority over him adopted by Mânûs*k*îhar in his epistles. Shortly before these epistles were written, Zâ*d*-sparam appears to have been at Sarakhs (Ep. II, v, 3), in the extreme north-east of Khurâsân, where he probably came in contact with the Tughazghuz (Ep. II, i, 12) and adopted some of their heretical opinions, and whence he may have travelled through Nîvshahpûhar (Ep. II, i, 2, note) and Shîrâ*z* (Ep. II, v, 3, 4) on his way to Sîrkân to take up his appointment as high-priest of the south (Eps. I, heading, II, i, 4, v, 9, vii, 1, viii, 1, Zs. I, 0). Soon after his arrival at Sîrkân he issued a decree, regarding the ceremonies of purification, which led to complaints from the people of that place, and compelled his brother to interfere by writing epistles, threatening him with deprivation of office (Ep. I, xi, 7) and the fate of a heretic (Eps. II, viii, 2, 3, III, 17–19). That Zâ*d*-sparam finally submitted, so far as not to be deprived of his office, appears from his still retaining his position in the south while writing his Selections (Zs. I, 0), which must have been compiled at some later period, free from the excitement of active and hazardous controversy.

The age in which Mânû*sk*îhar lived is decided by the date attached to his third epistle, or public notification, to the Ma*zd*a-worshippers of Irân; which date is the third month of the year 250 of Ya*zd*aka*rd* (Ep. III, 21), corresponding to the interval between the 14th June and 13th July A.D. 881; at which time, we learn, he was an old man (Ep. II, ix, 1), but not too old to travel (Eps. I, iii, 13, xi, 4, II, v, 5, vi, 4, 6, vii, 3, viii, 4, 5).

His writings, therefore, represent the state of the Zoroastrian religion a thousand years ago; and it may be presumed, from the importance and influentialness of his position, that his representations can be implicitly relied upon. To detect any differences there may be between the tenets and religious customs he describes, and those upheld by Zoroastrians of the present time, would require all the learning and experience of a Parsi priest; but, so far as a European can judge, from these writings and his own limited knowledge of existing religious customs among the Parsis, the change has been less than in any other form of religion during the same period.

The manuscripts containing the writings of Mânû*sk*îhar

are of two classes, one represented in Europe by the codex No. 35 of the collection of Avesta and Pahlavi manuscripts in the University Library at Kopenhagen, the other represented by No. 14 of the Haug Collection of similar manuscripts in the State Library at Munich, which two manuscripts are called K35 and M14, respectively, in this volume. In the former of these classes, represented by K35, the Dâ*d*istân-î Dînîk occupies the central third of the codex; being preceded by a nearly equal extent of other miscellaneous religious writings of rather later date, resembling a Pahlavi Rivâyat; and being followed by a third series of similar writings of about the same age and extent as the Dâ*d*istân-î Dînîk, which includes the Epistles of Mânû*sk*îhar and the Selections of Zâ*d*-sparam. In the latter class of manuscripts, from which M14 is descended, the text of the Dâ*d*istân-î Dînîk contains many variations from that in the former class, as if it had been revised by some one whose knowledge of Pahlavi was insufficient to decipher difficult passages, and who had freely exercised his editorial license in altering and mutilating the text to suit his own limited comprehension of it.

The codex K35, which was brought from Persia by the late Professor Westergaard in 1843, is one of the most important manuscripts of the former class, and now consists of 181 folios; but it is incomplete at both ends, having lost seventy-one folios at the beginning and about thirty-five at the end. It still includes, however, the whole of the Dâ*d*istân-î Dînîk and the Epistles of Mânû*sk*îhar; though its date has been lost with its last folios. But this date can be recovered from an old copy of this codex existing in India (here called BK) and still containing a colophon, probably copied from K35[1], which states that the manuscript was

[1] One reason for supposing that this colophon was so copied is that K35 does not seem older than the date mentioned in it. Another reason is that the loss of the end of this colophon in BK allows us to assume that it was followed by another colophon, as is often the case in copies of old MSS. A colophon that extends to the end of the last folio of a manuscript can never be safely assumed to belong to that manuscript, because it may have been followed by others on further folios.

completed by Mar*z*apân Frê*d*ûn Vâhrôm Rûstâm Bôndâr Malkâ-mar*d*ân Dîn-ayâr, on the day Âsmân of the month Ame*r*ôda*d* A.Y. 941 (19th March, 1572), in the district of the Dahîkân in the land of Kirmân. The end of this colophon is lost with the last folio of BK, which renders it possible that the last folio contained the further colophon of this copy.

That BK is descended from K35 is proved by its containing several false readings, which are clearly due to mis-shapen letters and accidental marks in K35. And that it was copied direct from that codex is proved by the last words of thirty-two of its pages being marked with interlined circles in K35, which circles must have been the copyist's marks for finding his place, when beginning a fresh page after turning over his folios. This copy of K35 has lost many of its folios, in various parts, but most of the missing text has been recently restored from the modern manuscript J, mentioned below; there are still, however, eleven folios of text missing, near the end of the codex, part of which can be hereafter recovered from TK, described below. The independent value of BK is that it supplies the contents of the seventy-one folios lost at the beginning of K35, and of about nineteen of the folios missing at the end of that codex.

A third manuscript of the first class, which may be even more important than K35, was brought to Bombay from Persia about fifteen years ago, and belongs to Mr. Tehmuras Dinshawji Anklesaria, of Bombay, but it has not been available for settling the texts translated in this volume. It is here called TK, and is described as still consisting of 227 folios, though seventy folios are missing at the beginning and about fourteen at the end. In its present state, therefore, it must begin very near the same place as K35, but it extends much further, so as even to supply nearly half the contents of the eleven folios missing from BK; it does not, however, include the contents of the last three folios of BK. According to a colophon appended in this manuscript to the 'Sayings of Zâ*d*-sparam, son of Yûdân-Yim, about the formation of men out of body, life, and soul' (see Zs. XI, 10, note), some copy of these 'sayings' was written by Gôpatshah Rûstôm Bândâr Malkâ-mar*d*ân in the land of Kirmân. This Gôpatshah was evidently a brother of Vâhrôm, the grandfather of the Mar*z*apân who wrote the colophon found in BK and supposed to have been copied from K35 (see pp. xv, xvi). If, therefore, this colophon in TK has not been copied from some older MS., it would indicate that TK is two generations older than K35.

A recent copy of TK exists in the library of the high-priest of the Parsis in Bombay, to whom I am indebted for the information that its text does not differ from that of K35, at the two points (Dd. XCIII, 17 and Ep. III, 11) where some omission of text may be suspected.

The manuscripts of the second class appear to be all descended from an old, undated codex brought to Bombay from Persia about sixty-five years ago[1], and recently in the library of Mr. Dhanjibhâî Frâmji Pâtel of Bombay. From what is stated, concerning the contents of this codex, it appears to commence with about three-fourths of the miscellaneous religious writings, found at the beginning of BK; and these are followed by the altered text of the Dâ*d*istân-î Dînîk, as appears from the copies described below, but how the codex concludes is not stated. It may, however, be supposed that it contains as much of the third series of writings as is found in the manuscript J, a copy of this codex which ends in Ep. II, vi, 2.

This manuscript J belongs to the library of Dastûr Jâmâspji Minochiharji in Bombay; it commenced originally at the same point as the codex just described, and, so far as it has been examined, it contains the same altered text of the Dâ*d*istân-î Dînîk. There is, therefore little doubt that it was originally copied from that codex, but a considerable

[1] There is some doubt about this period. Dastûr Peshotanji mentions thirty or forty years, but in the MS. J, which appears to have been copied chiefly from this codex in Bombay, the date noted by the copyist of the older part of that MS. is 'the day Rashn of the month Khûrdâd, A.Y. 1188' (21st December 1818, according to the calendar of the Indian Parsis), showing that the codex must have been at least sixty-four years in Bombay.

portion of the additional matter at the beginning of BK has been prefixed to it at a later date. The oldest portion of this copy, extending to Ep. I, vii, 4, bears a date corresponding to 21st December 1818; the date of a further portion, extending to Ep. II, vi, 2, corresponds to 12th February 1841; and a third portion copied from BK, at the beginning of the manuscript, is still more recent.

Another copy of this codex, or of the Dâ*d*istân-î Dînîk contained in it, exists in the library of the high-priest of the Parsis in Bombay; and from this copy the text of the Dâ*d*istân-î Dînîk contained in M14 was transcribed.

This latter manuscript consists of two volumes, written in 1865 and 1868, respectively; the first volume containing Chaps. I, 1–XXXVII, 9, and the second volume Chaps. XXXVI, 1–XCIV, 15 of the altered text of the Dâ*d*istân-î Dînîk.

Other copies of the Dâ*d*istân-î Dînîk, which have not been examined, are to be found in India, but, unless descended from other manuscripts than K35 and the above-mentioned codex recently belonging to Mr. Dhanjibhâi Frâmji, they would be of no further use for settling the text.

Of the manuscripts above described the following have been available for the translations in this volume:—K35 for the whole of the Dâ*d*istân-î Dînîk and the Epistles; M14 for the whole of the Dâ*d*istân-î Dînîk alone; BK for Dd. I, 1–VI, 3[1], X, 2–XIV, 3[2], LXXXVIII, 9–XCIV, 15, the whole of the Epistles, the legend about the soul of Kerêsâsp (see pp. 373–381), and the extracts from the Pahlavi Rivâyat in these codices relating to Khvêtûk-das (see pp. 415–423); and J for Dd. I, 1–XXXIX, 10[3]; LXXXVIII, 9–LXXXIX, 1[4], XCI, 7–XCIV, 15, Ep. I, i, 1–II, ix, 7[5], the

[1] The text of Chaps. VI, 3–X, 2 has been lost, and recently supplied from J.

[2] No copy of the intermediate chapters obtained by the present translator, and several of the original folios have been lost.

[3] No copy of the intermediate chapters taken by the present translator.

[4] Chaps. LXXXIX, 1–XCI, 7 omitted.

[5] Ep. II, vi, 2–ix, 7 being copied from BK and wrongly inserted in Dd. XXXVII, 33 (see p. 89, note 5).

legend about Keresâsp, and the extracts relating to Khvêtûk-das. Other manuscripts, used for the remaining extracts translated in the Appendix, will be mentioned in § 4 of this introduction.

The existence of two versions of the text of the Dâ*d*istân-î Dînîk would have been a source of much perplexity to the translator, had it not been soon apparent that the version represented by M14 was merely a revision of that in K35, attempted by some editor who had found much difficulty in understanding the involved phraseology of Mânûs*k*îhar. There are, undoubtedly, some corrupt words and passages in K35, where the revised version may be followed with advantage, but nine-tenths of the alterations, introduced by the reviser, are wholly unnecessary, and in many cases they are quite inconsistent with the context.

Under these circumstances it has been the duty of the translator to follow the text given in K35, wherever it is not wholly unintelligible after prolonged study, to note all deviations of the translation from that text (which are usually small), and merely to mention the variations of the revised text, so far as they are intelligible, in the notes.

The writings of Mânûs*k*îhar are certainly difficult to translate, not only from the involved and obscure style he affects, but also from the numerous compound epithets he uses, which are not easy either to understand with certainty, or to express clearly in English. The only other Pahlavi writings that approach them in difficulty are those of his brother, Zâ*d*-sparam, and those of the author of the third book of the Dînka*rd*, who seems to have also been a contemporary writer. To a certain extent, therefore, an involved style of writing may have been a failing of the age in which he lived; and his works, being of an epistolary and hortatory character, would naturally be more abstruse and idiomatic than simple narrative; but much of the obscurity of his style must still be attributed to his own want of clear arrangement of thought and inadequate, though wordy, expression of ideas, the usual sources of all obscure and rambling writing.

When to the difficulty of tracing the thread of an argument

through the involved obscurity of the text is added the perplexity occasioned by the ambiguity of many Pahlavi words, it can be readily understood that no translation is likely to be even approximately accurate, unless it be as literal as possible. The translator has to avoid enough pitfals, in the shape of false constructions and incorrect readings, without risking the innumerable sources of error offered by the alluring by-paths of free translation. If, therefore, the reader should sometimes meet with strange idioms, or uncouth phrases, he must attribute them to a straining after correctness of translation, however little that correctness may be really attained.

For the purpose of more effectually keeping a curb upon the imagination of the translator, and indicating where he has been compelled to introduce his own ideas, all words not expressed or fully understood in the original text are italicised in the translation. Occasionally, also, the original word is appended to its translation, where either the reading or meaning adopted is unusual, or where a scholar might wish to know the particular Pahlavi word translated.

Some endeavour has likewise been made to introduce greater precision than has hitherto been attempted, in the transliteration of Pahlavi words and names, by taking advantage of the italic system, adopted for this series of Sacred Books of the East, not only for distinguishing variations of sound (as in the use of *g*, *k*, and *s* for the sounds of j, soft ch, and sh, respectively, in English), but also to indicate the use of particular Pahlavi letters, when there are more than one of nearly the same sound. Thus, *d* is used where its sound is represented by [Pahlavi] t; *l* and *r* where they are represented by [Pahlavi] n, v, û, or by [Pahlavi] Av. o; *v* and *z* where they are represented by [Pahlavi] *k*; and *zd* where those letters are represented by [Pahlavi] â. If, in addition to these particulars, the Pahlavi scholar will remember that the uncircumflexed vowels are not expressed in Pahlavi characters, and the vowel ŏ is expressed, he will find no particular difficulty in restoring any of the transliterated words to their original character, by merely following the ordinary rules of Pahlavi writing. Without some such mode[1] of distinguishing the different Pahlavi letters used for the same sound, it would be practically impossible to restore the transliteration of any word, new to the reader, to its original Pahlavi form. And even the system here adopted requires the addition of *a* and *â* to represent the vowel a, â when one of its turns is omitted in writing (as in *a*p, *â*v, used for ap, af; *a*dîn used for adîn, &c.), and of j or *j* to represent y when it has the sound of *g* or English j, in order to distinguish it from *k*, *g*.

The general reader should, however, observe that these niceties of transliteration are merely matters of writing, as the exact pronunciation of Pahlavi cannot now be fully ascertained in all its details. There is every reason to suppose that the Semitic portion of the Pahlavi was never pronounced by the Persians as it was written (unless, indeed, in the earliest times); but to transliterate these Semitic words by their Persian equivalents, as the Persians certainly pronounced them, would produce a Pâzand text, instead of a Pahlavi one. If, therefore, we really want the transliteration to represent the Pahlavi text correctly, we must transliterate the Semitic words as they are written, without reference to the mode in which we suppose that the Persians used to read them. With regard to the Persian words, if we call to mind the fact that Pahlavi was the immediate parent of modern Persian, we shall naturally accept the modern Persian pronunciation (stripped of its Arabic corruptions) as a guide, so far as Pahlavi orthography permits, in preference to tracing the sounds of these words downwards from their remote ancestors in ancient Persian or the Avesta. But the pronunciation of words evidently derived directly from the Avesta, as is the case with many religious terms, must clearly depend upon the

[1] Dotted letters might be used, if available, instead of italics; but they are liable to the objection that, independent of the usual blunders due to the ordinary fallibility of human eyesight, it has been found by the translator that a dot, which was invisible on the proofs, will sometimes appear under a wrong letter in the course of printing.

Avesta orthography, so far as the alteration in spelling permits. These are the general rules here adopted, but many uncertainties arise in their practical application, which have to be settled in a somewhat arbitrary manner.

2. THE DÂ*D*ISTÂN-Î DÎNÎK.

The term Dâ*d*istân-î Dînîk, 'religious opinions or decisions,' is a comparatively modern name applied to ninety-two questions, on religious subjects, put to the high-priest Mânû*sk*îhar, and his answers to the same. These questions appear to have been sent in an epistle from Mit*r*ô-khûrshê*d*, son of Âtû*r*ŏ-mahân, and other Ma*zd*a-worshippers (Dd. heading and I, 2), and were received by Mânû*sk*îhar, who was the leader of the religion (Dd. I, 10, note), in the month of July or August (Dd. I, 17); but it was not till September or October, after he had returned to Shîrâ*z* from a tour in the provinces, that he found time to begin his reply which, when completed, was sent by a courier (Dd. I, 26) to his correspondents, but at what date is not recorded.

Regarding the residence of these correspondents, and the year in which these transactions took place, we have no positive information. The correspondents seem to have thanked Mânû*sk*îhar for sending them one of his disciples (Dd. I, 3, 4) to act probably as their high-priest; and, from the mode in which the land of Pârs is mentioned in Dd. LXVI, 28, LXXXIX, 1, it seems likely that they were not inhabitants of that province; but this conclusion is hardly confirmed, though not altogether contradicted, by the further allusions to Pârs in Dd. LXVI, 3, 15, 21, LXXXVIII, 1. With regard to the date of this correspondence we may conclude, from the less authoritative tone assumed by Mânû*sk*îhar in his reply (Dd. I, 5–7, 11), as compared with that adopted in his epistles (Ep. III, 17–19), that he was a younger man when he composed the Dâ*d*istân-î Dînîk than when he wrote his epistles; we may, therefore, probably assume that the Dâ*d*istân-î Dînîk was written several years before A.D. 881.

Although the subjects discussed in the Dâ*d*istân-î Dînîk cover a wide range of religious doctrines, legends, and duties, they cannot be expected to give a complete view of the Ma*zd*a-worshipping religion, as they are merely those matters on which Mit*r*ô-khûrshê*d* and his friends entertained doubts, or wished for further information. It is also somewhat doubtful whether the whole of the questions have been preserved, on account of the abrupt transition from the last reply, at the end of Dd. XCIII, to the peroration in Dd. XCIV, and also from the fact that a chapter is alluded to, in Dd. XVII, 20, XVIII, 2, which is no longer extant in the text.

The questions, although very miscellaneous in their character, are arranged, to some extent, according to the subjects they refer to, which are taken in the following order:—The righteous and their characteristics; the temporal distress of the good; why mankind was created; good works and their effects; the account of sin and good works to be rendered; the exposure of corpses and reasons for it; the paths, destinations, and fate of departed souls, with the ceremonies to be performed after a death; the contributors to the renovation of the universe; the contest between the good and evil spirits from the creation till the resurrection; works of supererogation; the sacred shirt and thread-girdle; apostasy and its prevention; the use of fire at ceremonies, and other details; duties, payment, and position of priests; details regarding ceremonies; lawful and unlawful trading in corn, wine, and cattle, with a definition of drunkenness; adoption, guardianship, and inheritance; rights of foreigners and infidels; the origin of mankind and next-of-kin marriage; the cost of religious rites; the causes of the rainbow, phases of the moon, eclipses, and river-beds; things acquired through destiny and exertion; the sins of unnatural intercourse and adultery; imperfect prayer before drinking; ceremonies and payments for them; the seven immortal rulers before Zaratû*s*t; the sky, the source of pure water, and the cause of rain and storms.

In his replies to these questions Mânû*sk*îhar displays

much intelligence and wisdom, the morality he teaches is of a high standard for the age in which he lived, and, while anxious to uphold the power and privileges of the priesthood, he is widely tolerant of all deficiencies in the conduct of the laity that do not arise from wilful persistence in sin. The reader will search in vain for any confirmation of the foreign notion that Ma*zd*a-worship is decidedly more dualistic than Christianity is usually shown to be by orthodox writers, or for any allusion to the descent of the good and evil spirits from a personification of 'boundless time,' as asserted by strangers to the faith. No attempt is made to account for the origin of either spirit, but the temporary character of the power of the evil one, and of the punishment in hell, is distinctly asserted.

Although Mânû*sk*îhar does not mention, in his writings, any of the lost Nasks or sacred books of the Ma*zd*a-worshippers, except the Hûspârûm (Dd. LXI, 3) and the Sakâ*d*ûm (Ep. I, viii, 1, 6, 7), he certainly had access to many Pahlavi books which are now no longer extant; hence he is able to give us more information than we find elsewhere regarding some of the legendary personages mentioned in Dd. II, 10, XXXVI, 4, 5, XLVIII, 33, XC, 3; he hints that the second month of the year (April–May) was called Zaremaya in the Avesta (Dd. XXXI, 14); and he mentions two places, instead of one, intermediate between heaven and hell, one for the souls of those not quite good enough for heaven, and one for those not quite bad enough for hell (Dd. XXIV, 6, XXXIII, 2).

The present translation of this work is not the first that has been attempted. Shortly before the late Professor Haug left India he delivered a lecture on the Parsi religion to a large assemblage of Parsis in Bombay, at their request, and at his desire the sum of 900 rûpîs, out of the net proceeds of the entrance-tickets sold, was offered as a prize for an edition of the Pahlavi text of the Dâ*d*istân-î Dînîk with a Gu*g*arâti translation and glossary. Some years afterwards this prize was awarded to Mr. Shehriarji Dadabhoy and Mr. Tehmuras Dinshawji Anklesaria, for their joint Gu*g*arâti translation of the work, which still, however, remains unpublished for want of funds, and has, therefore, been inaccessible to the present translator.

3. THE EPISTLES OF MÂNÛSKÎHAR.

It has been already stated (see pp. xiii, xiv) that Zâd-sparam, a younger brother of Mânûs*k*îhar, after having been at Sarakhs, in the extreme north-east of Khurâsân, where he seems to have associated with the heretical Tughazghuz, was appointed high-priest of Sîrkân, south or south-west of Kirmân[1]. Shortly after his arrival there he issued a decree, regarding the ceremonies of purification and other matters, which was so unpalatable to the Ma*zd*a-worshippers of that place that they wrote an epistle to Mânûs*k*îhar, complaining of the conduct of his brother (Ep. I, i, 2, ii, 1).

In reply to this complaint, which was sent by a special courier (Ep. I, i, 2), and after going to Shîrâ*z* and holding a general assembly of the priests and elders (Ep. II, i, 11), Mânûs*k*îhar wrote his first epistle, completed on the 15th March 881 (Ep. I, xi, 12), in which he condemned the practices decreed by Zâ*d*-sparam, to whom he sent a confidential agent, named Ya*zd*ân-pânak (Ep. I, xi, 1, 2, 6, 10, II, vii, 2), with a copy of this epistle and a further one to himself, which has not been preserved, for the purpose of inducing his brother to withdraw his decree and conform to the usual customs.

It would appear that Ya*zd*ân-pânak was not very successful in his mission, as we find Mânûs*k*îhar writing a general epistle (Ep. III) to all the Ma*zd*a-worshippers in Irân, in the following June or July (Ep. III, 21), denouncing as heretical the mode of purification decreed by Zâ*d*-sparam, and ordering an immediate return to former customs. At the same time (Ep. II, vii, 2, viii, 1) he wrote a second epistle (Ep. II) to his brother, as he had already

[1] The city of Kirmân was itself called Sîr*g*ân, or Sîrgân, in the middle ages, and is evidently mentioned by that name in Ouseley's Oriental Geography, pp. 139, 143, though the Sîrgân of pp. 138, 141 of the same work was clearly further south. Which of these two towns was the Sîrkân of these epistles, may, therefore, be doubtful.

promised in Ep. I, xi, 2, and, after referring to an epistle (now lost) which he had received from Zâ*d*-sparam in the previous November or December, he proceeded to enforce his views by a judicious intermingling of argument, entreaty, and threats. He also contemplated making preparations (Ep. I, xi, 4, II, vii, 3) for travelling himself to Sîrkân, notwithstanding his age (Ep. II, ix, 1), to arrange the matters in dispute upon a satisfactory basis. Whether he actually undertook this journey is unknown, but that his brother must have finally submitted to his authority appears from Zâ*d*-sparam retaining his position in the south, as has been already noticed (p. xiv).

The matter in dispute between Zâ*d*-sparam and the orthodox Ma*zd*a-worshippers may seem a trivial one to people of other religions, but, inasmuch as the ceremonial uncleanness of a person insufficiently purified after contact with the dead would contaminate every one he associated with, the sufficiency of the mode of purification was quite as important to the community, both priests and laity, as avoidance of breach of caste-rules is to the Hindû, or refraining from sacrifices to heathen gods was to the Jew, the early Christian, or the Muhammadan. And much more important than any disputes about sacraments, infallibility, apostolic succession, ritual, or observance of the Sabbath can possibly be to any modern Romanist or Protestant.

In his mode of dealing with this matter Mânû*sk*îhar displays at once the moderation and tact of a statesman accustomed to responsibility, the learning and zeal of a well-informed priest, and the kindly affection of a brother. That he was not without rivals and enemies appears from his casual allusions to Zaratû*s*t, the club-footed, and Âtû*r*ŏ-pâ*d* in Ep. II, i, 13, v, 14, ix, 11; but in all such allusions, as well as in his denunciation of heretical opinions, he refrains from coarse invective, and avoids the use of exaggerated language, such as too often disfigures and weakens the arguments in polemical discussions.

Indirectly these epistles throw some light upon the condition of the Ma*zd*a-worshippers after more than two centuries of ceaseless struggle with the ever-advancing flood of Muhammadanism which was destined to submerge them. Shîrâz, Sîrkân, Kirmân, Râî, and Saraḳhs are still mentioned as head-quarters of the old faith; and we are told of assemblies at Shîrâz and among the Tughazghuz, the former of which appears to have had the chief control of religious matters in Pârs, Kirmân, and the south, acting as a council to the high-priest of Pârs and Kirmân, who was recognised as the leader of the religion (Dd. XLV, 5). We also learn, from Ep. I, iii, 11, II, v, 14, that the leaders of the Mazda-worshippers, if not their high-priests, were still in the habit of maintaining troops; and, from Ep. II, i, 9, that when a high-priest became very old his worldly duties were performed by four of the most learned priests, forming a committee, which had full authority to deliberate and act for him in all worldly matters. Mânûskîhar even speaks of emigrating by sea to China, or by land to Asia Minor (Ep. II, viii, 5), in order to escape from the annoyances of his position.

But the statements which are most important to the Pahlavi scholar, in these epistles, are the date attached to the third epistle, corresponding to A.D. 881, and the mention of Nîshahpûhar in Ep. I, iv, 15, 17 as the supreme officiating priest and councillor of king Khûsrô Nôshirvân (A.D. 531–579), engaged apparently in writing commentaries on the Avesta. The date of these epistles not only limits that of the Dâdistân-î Dînîk to the latter half of the ninth century, but also fixes those of the larger recension of the Bundahis and of the latest revision of the Dinkard within the same period, because it is stated in Bd. XXXIII, 10, 11 that the writer of that chapter was a contemporary of Zâd-sparam, son of Yûdân-Yim, and Âtûr-pâd, son of Hêmîd, the former of whom was evidently the brother of Mânûskîhar, and the latter is mentioned in Dînkard III, ccccxiii as the latest editor of that work. The actual compiler of a great part of the Dînkard (especially of the fourth and fifth books) was, however, the somewhat earlier writer Âtûr-frôbag, son of Farukhûzâd (Dd. LXXXVIII, 8, Ep. I, iii, 9). The name of Nîshahpûhar is also mentioned as that of a commentator in the Pahlavi Vendidâ*d* and Nîrangistân, which works must, therefore, have been revised since the middle of the sixth century. And as we are informed in the book of Ar*d*â-Vîrâf (I, 35) that 'there are *some* who call *him by* the name of Nikhshahpûr,' we ought probably to refer that book to the same age. These epistles, therefore, enable us, for the first time, to fix the probable dates of the latest extensive revisions of six of the most important Pahlavi works that are still extant; and from the relationship of these to others we can readily arrive at safer conclusions, regarding the age of Pahlavi literature in general, than have been hitherto possible.

4. The Appendix.

For the sake of elucidating certain matters, mentioned in the writings of Mânûs*k*îhar, further information than could be given in the foot-notes has been added in the shape of an appendix.

To a brief summary of the Avesta legends, relating to the ancient hero Keresâsp, has been added a translation of a Pahlavi legend regarding the fate of his soul, in which several of his more famous exploits are detailed. This legend is found in the Pahlavi Rivâyat preceding the Dâ*d*istân-î Dînîk in the manuscripts BK and J, and is evidently derived from the fourteenth fargar*d* of the Sû*d*kar Nask, whose contents, as described in the ninth book of the Dînka*rd*, are also given. It is likewise found in the later Persian Rivâyats, with several modifications which are duly noticed.

The Nîrang-i Kustî, or ceremony of tying the sacred thread-girdle, is also described in detail, with a translation of the ritual accompanying it, partly from actual observation, and partly from Gu*g*arâti accounts of the rite.

It having become necessary to ascertain with certainty whether the term 'next-of-kin marriage' was a justifiable translation of khvêtûk-das, as used by Pahlavi writers, an extensive examination of all accessible passages, which throw any light upon the meaning of the word, has been made. The result of this enquiry can be best understood from the details collected, but it may be stated in general terms that, though 'marriage among kinsfolk' might fairly represent the varying meaning of khvêtûk-das in different ages, its usual signification in Pahlavi literature is more accurately indicated by 'next-of-kin marriage.'

Some apology is perhaps due to the Parsi community for directing attention to a subject which they consider disagreeable. But, by the publication of a portion of the Dînka*rd*, they have themselves placed the most important passage, bearing on the subject, within the reach of every European Orientalist; thus rendering it easy for any prejudiced translator to represent the practice of such marriages as having been general, instead of their being so distasteful to the laity as to require a constant exertion of all the influence that the priesthood possessed, in order to recommend them, even in the darkest ages of the faith. To avoid such one-sided views of the matter, as well as to hinder them in others, has been the special aim of the present translator in trying to ascertain the exact meaning of the obscure texts he had to deal with.

The translations from the Pahlavi Vendidâ*d*, regarding the Bareshnûm ceremony and the purifications requisite after finding a corpse in the wilderness, will be found necessary for explaining many allusions and assertions in the Epistles of Mânû*sk*îhar.

The text followed in all passages translated from the Dînka*rd* is that contained in the manuscript now in the library of Dastûr Sohrâbji Rustamji, the high-priest of the Kadmi sect of Parsis in Bombay. It was written A. D. 1669, and was brought from Persia to Surat by Mullâ Bahman in 1783. All other known copies of the Dînka*rd* are descended from this manuscript, except a codex, brought from Persia by the late Professor Westergaard in 1843, which contains one-fifth of the Dînka*rd* mostly written in 1574, and is now in the University Library at Kopenhagen.

For translations from the Pahlavi Vendidâ*d* the text adopted, wherever available and not evidently defective, has been that of L4, a manuscript of the Vendidâ*d* with

Pahlavi, Z. and P. IV, in the India Office Library in London. The date of this manuscript has been lost with its last folio, but its text is in the same handwriting as that of three others, in Kopenhagen and Bombay, which were written A.D. 1323–4. A considerable portion of the beginning of this manuscript has also been lost, and is replaced by modern folios of no particular value.

In conclusion, the translator must take the opportunity of thankfully acknowledging the kindness and readiness with which Dastûr Peshotanji Behrâmji Sanjânâ, the high-priest of the Parsis in Bombay, and Dastûr Jâmâspji Minochiharji Jâmâsp-Âsâ-nâ, of the same city, have always furnished him with any information he applied for, not only on those matters specially mentioned in the foot-notes, but also on many other occasions.

E. W. WEST.

MUNICH,
September, 1882.

ABBREVIATIONS USED IN THIS VOLUME.

Acc. for accusative case; Âf. Zarat. for Âfrîngân-i Zaratûst; anc. Pers. for ancient Persian; App. for Appendix to this volume; Ar. for Arabic; AV. for the Book of Ardâ-Vîrâf, ed. Hoshangji and Haug; Av. for Avesta; B29 for Persian Rivâyat MS. No. 29 of the University Library in Bombay; Bd. and Byt. for Bundahis and Bahman Yast, as translated in vol. v of this series; BK for an old imperfect copy of K35 written in Kirmân, but now in Bombay; Chald. for Chaldee; comp. for compare; Dd. for Dâdistân-î Dinîk, as translated in this volume; Dk. for Dînkard; Ep. for Epistles of Mânûskîhar, as translated in this volume; Farh. Okh. for Farhang-i Oîm-khadûk, ed. Hoshangji and Haug; Gen. for Genesis; Haug's Essays for Essays on the Sacred Language, Writings, and Religion of the Parsis, by M. Haug, 2nd edition; Hn. for Hâdôkht Nask, as published with AV.; Huz. for Huzvâris; Introd. for Introduction; J. for Dd. MS. belonging to Dastûr Jâmâspji Minochiharji in Bombay; K35 for Dd. MS. No. 35 of the University Library in Kopenhagen; L4 for Vend. MS. No. 4 of the India Office Library in London; Lev. for Leviticus; M5, M7, M10, M14 for MSS. Nos. 5, 7, 10, 14 of the Haug Collection in the State Library in Munich; Mkh. for Mainyô-i-khard, ed. West; n. for foot-note; nom. for nominative case; p. for page; Pahl. for Pahlavi; Pâz. for Pâzand; Pers. for Persian; p. p. for past participle; Sîr. for Sîrozah, ed. Westergaard; Sls. for Shâyast-lâ-shâyast, as translated in vol. v of this series; TD for Bd. MS. belonging to Mr. Tehmuras Dinshawji in Bombay; TK for Dd. MS. belonging to the same; trans. D. for translated by Darmesteter, in vol. iv of this series; Vend., Visp., and Yas. for Vendidâd, Visparad, and Yasna, ed. Spiegel; Yt. for Yast, ed. Westergaard; Z.D.M.G. for Zeitschrift der deutschen morgenländischen Gesellschaft; Zs. for Selections of Zâd-sparam, as translated in vol. v of this series.

DÂ*D*ISTÂN-Î DÎNÎK

OR

THE RELIGIOUS OPINIONS

OF

MÂNÛ*SK*ÎHAR, SON OF YÛDÂN-YIM,

DASTÛR OF

PÂRS AND KIRMÂN,

A. D. 881.

OBSERVATIONS.

1. For all divisions into chapters and sections the translator is responsible, as the manuscripts merely indicate the beginning of each question and reply.

2. Italics are used for any English words which are not expressed, or fully understood, in the original text, but are added to complete the sense of the translation.

3. Italics occurring in Oriental words, or names, represent certain peculiar Oriental letters (see the 'Transliteration of Oriental Alphabets' at the end of this volume). The italic *d*, *l*, *n*, *r*, *v* may be pronounced as in English; but *g* should be sounded like j, *hv* like wh, *k* like ch in 'church,' *s* like sh, and *z* like French j.

4. In Pahlavi words the only vowels expressed in the original text are those circumflexed, initial a, and the letter ŏ; italic *d* is written like t, *r* and *l* like n or the Avesta o, *v* and *z* like *g*, and *zd* like â in the Pahlavi character (see the latter part of § 1 of the Introduction).

5. In the translation, words in parentheses are merely explanatory of those which precede them.

6. For the meaning of the abbreviations used in the notes, see the end of the Introduction.

7. The manuscripts mentioned are:—

BK, an old imperfect copy of K35 written in Kirmân, but now in Bombay.

J (about 60 years old), belonging to Dastûr Jâmâspji Minochiharji in Bombay.

K35 (probably written A. D. 1572), No. 35 in the University Library at Kopenhagen; upon the text of which this translation is based.

M5 (written A.D. 1723), a MS. of miscellaneous texts in Persian letters, No. 5 of the Haug Collection in the State Library at Munich.

M14 (a modern copy of a MS. in the library of the Parsi high-priest in Bombay), No. 14 in the same Collection.

TD, a MS. of the Bundahi*s* belonging to Môbad Tehmuras Dinshawji in Bombay.

DÂ*D*ISTÂN-Î DÎNÎK.

SOME chapters of the enquiries which Mit*r*ô-khûrshê*d*, son of Âtû*r*ŏ-mahân[1], and others of the good religion made of the glorified (anoshakŏ-rûbân) Mân-ûs*k*îhar[2], son of Yûdân-Yim, and the replies given by him in explanation.

CHAPTER I.

0. Through the name and power and assistance of the creator Aûha*r*ma*zd* *and* all good *beings*, all the heavenly and earthly angels, and every creature and creation that Aûha*r*ma*zd* set going for his own angels and all pertaining to the *celestial* spheres.

---

[1] The name Âtû*r*-mâhân occurs in a Pahlavi inscription, dated A.Y. 378 (A.D. 1009), in one of the Kanheri caves, near Bombay (see Indian Antiquary, vol. ix, pp. 266, 267), and Adharmâh is mentioned in Hoffmann's Auszüge aus syrischen Akten persischer Märtyrer (Leipzig, 1880), p. 203; so that this name must have been commonly used by Parsis in former times, though unknown now.

[2] He calls himself pontiff and director of the priests of Pârs and Kirmân in A.Y. 250=A.D. 881, and was, therefore, the leader of the religion (see Chaps. XLV, 5, XCIV, 13, and Ep. III, 21). Besides these titles of pê*s*ûpâî, 'leader,' farmâ*d*âr, 'director,' and ra*d*, 'pontiff or executive high-priest,' he is also called aêrpat khû*d*âî, 'priestly lordship,' in the heading to Ep. III, and has the general title aêrpat, 'priest,' in those of Ep. I and II. The reading of the name of his father, Yûdân-Yim (Pers. *G*uvân-*G*am, 'the youthful *G*amshêd'), is merely a guess; the Parsis read either Gôshna-*g*am or *G*ôdân-dam; and, perhaps, Gûshna-dam, 'breathing virility,' is a likely alternative reading.

1. *To* those of the good religion, who are these enquirers owing to devout force of demeanour and strength of character, the type of wisdom and standard of ability—and of whom, moreover, the questions, seeking wisdom, contemplating good works, and investigating religion, are specified—the blessing *and* reply of Mânûskîhar, son of Yûdân-Yim, are these:—2. That is, forasmuch as with full affection, great dignity, and grandeur you *have* blessed me in this enquiring epistle[1], so much as you *have* blessed, *and* just as you *have* blessed, with full measure *and* perfect profusion, may it happen fully likewise unto you, in the first place, and *to your* connections, separately for yourselves and dependents; may it come upon *you* for a long period, and may it be connected with a happy end.

3. *As to* that which you ordered to write about wishes for an interview and conversation *with* me, and the friendliness and regard for religion of yourselves *and* our former *disciple*[2] (lanmanak kâdmôn) —who is a servant of the sacred beings (yazdânŏ)[3] and a fellow-soldier in struggling with the fiend, alike persistent in reliance upon the good religion of Mazda-worship—I am equally desirous of that one path of righteousness when *its* extension is to a place in the best existence[4], *and* equally hopeful

[1] Regarding this epistle, nothing further is known that can be gathered from the text of this reply to it, which gives the substance of the questions it contained.

[2] This disciple appears to have been previously sent by Mânûskîhar to the community he is addressing, most probably to serve as their high-priest.

[3] The word is plural, like Elohim in the book of Genesis, but it means 'God' in Persian.

[4] Another name for Garôdmân, the highest heaven, or dwelling of Aûharmazd (see Sls. VI, 3, 4).

of resurrection (âkhezisnŏ) at the renovation of the best existence[1]. 4. *As to* the interview and important conversation of that *disciple* of ours (mânak), and his going, and that also which he expounded of the religion—that of him who is intimate in interview and conversation with him who is wise and righteous the stunted[2] good works are then more developing[3]—and *as to* the degree of praise which you ordered to write concerning me, much greater than reason, and the important statements full of the observations of friendship as to kind regards, my course about these is also *that* which *leads* to gratitude.

5. That which you ordered to write about the way of knowing and understanding not being for any one else but for *your* servant, *was* owing to your affection, and for the sake of kind regard; but on account of the importance of truth *it* is more expressly to be regarded *as* being proper to write also to other spiritual[4] men, as to the learning which is more fully studied by them. 6. For even with the perplexing struggle of the fiend, *and* the grievous devastation and collapse (nizôrîh) which have happened to religious people, after all, through the persistence (khvâparîh) of the sacred beings even

[1] That is, when this transitory world is purified and made permanent, so as to form a part of heaven, which is expected to take place at the resurrection.

[2] Pahl. kazd, which may be compared with Pers. kaz, 'distorted,' or may be a miswriting of Pahl. kas, 'small.'

[3] The modern MSS., M14 and J, add 'and those which are great are more attainable.'

[4] The word is maînôk (mînavad), but the omission of one stroke would make it magôg, 'priestly,' which was probably the original reading.

now *there are* pontiffs (ra*d*ânŏ), priests, high-priests, judges, and also other religious leaders of those of the religion in various quarters. 7. Moreover, the other priests *and* spiritual[1] men *here* enumerated *have* well considered the commentary (zand) of the text (mânsar) which is muttered, are acquainted with opinions explaining the religion, *and* are, in many places, the cause of preferring good works; with whom also, on account of *their* understanding *and* knowing about such opinions, the sacred beings are pleased.

8. The desires expressed, and. the good wishes as to what is mine and *has* happened *to me*, which you ordered to write, are likewise marks of friendship and kind regard, and owing to them a like measure of friendship and kind regard becomes your[2] own.

9. *As to* that which you ordered to write in much friendship *and* commendation and profusely about me—as regards the administration of the realm (kêshvar dastôbarîh), *of* the unity without counterpart (da*d*îgarîh), and the singleness co-extensive with any duality—if the writing of that, too, *were* owing to your friendship, even then it seemed *to* me disquieting, owing to this *being* so much praise. 10. If in these times and countries *there be* an understanding of the time and a boasting about any one, if *it be* graceful as regards him who is a leader of the religion (dînô pê*s*ûpâî) of long-continued faith, I consider it not suitable for myself[3]. 11. Though

[1] See p. 5, note 4.

[2] All MSS. have 'thy.'

[3] Although he was himself the 'director of the profession of priests' of Pârs (see Chap. XCIV, 13), an office which was then equivalent to that of 'leader of the religion' (see Chap. XLV, 5).

the praise of a leader (sardâr), raised by agreeable voices[1], is uttered about me, yet I am not pleased when they extol my greatness *more* than *that of* their own leader; for my wish is *for* that praise which is *due* to my own rank and similar limits, and seems suitable to me; and humility in oneself is as correct as grandeur among inferiors.

12. That which is about the lengthy writing of questions, *as to* your worldly circumstances (stihâ-nîhâ) and worldly affairs, *has* also shown this, that I should write a reply at a time in which I have leisure. 13. That is more important on account of your well-expressed questions *and* boldness about ambiguous answers, and *your* ardent desire for the setting aside of time; for the setting aside, or not beginning, of a reply is implied. 14. *But* owing to the perplexing[2] struggle on account of the fiend there is little leisure for quick *and* searching thought, and owing to that which is undecided[3] *there is little* for indispensable (frêzvânîkŏ) work.

15. As to a reply *at* a period of leisure time, the occurrence of the time appointed is manifested in everything, apart even from the kind regards of friendship, and the collection of information whereby, owing to my little leisure, it is declared unto you. 16. And I have, too, this confidence, that your questions are written with religious faith *and* desiring religious decision; *and* in the reply the statement of reasons from revelation (dînô) is manifold, for

[1] This translation of mânŏ-advâzîkŏ-âkhezakŏ is somewhat doubtful.

[2] Or 'prodigious.'

[3] That is, awaiting the high-priest's judicial and ecclesiastical decision.

guidance which is not destitute of wisdom and *which* is without risk from every kind of importunity[1].

17. And *this* same epistle[2] came in the month Tîr[3], at such season as, owing to entreaties for three years from the country-folk (dêsîkânŏ), and the burden of troubles of the offspring (sarakŏ) of those of the good religion, the much importunity for arranging *what was* undecided among them—which, inasmuch as I had no power about investigating that trouble and suffering, *was* the more indispensable—the arrangements for the preservation and education of disciples[4], *and* many private *matters* which had accumulated, I obtained no *opportunity* for properly looking *over these* same questions till the month Shatvaîrô[5], when I came to Shirâz[6] and had *at* various times a little leisure.

18. And I looked *over these* same questions; and when I saw the compact writing (ham-dâdakîhâ-yektîbûnisnîh) it then seemed to me more important to make each chapter of the questions separate and more explanatory. 19. And I gave the questions to a writer, in the same copy which you ordered to write, *and* instructed *him* to write the various chapters, every single question in one chapter; and the several opinions, both due to my acquaintance with the religion and my remembrance in perfection,

[1] Or 'over-persuasion.'

[2] See § 2.

[3] The fourth month of the Parsi year, which corresponded to July–August in the time of Mânûskîhar.

[4] That is, candidates for the priesthood and young priests.

[5] The sixth month of the Parsi year, which then corresponded to September–October.

[6] From this it would appear that the Dâdistân-î Dînîk was written at Shîrâz which, being the principal city of Pârs, was probably the high-priest's usual residence.

both of the decisions (dastôbarîh) of the ancients and as regards wisdom, are the replies I intend to write below the questions.

20. When there is nothing in such as you ask, concerning which I consider such otherwise, as I write, than what is like that which was once advisedly our different opinion from those high-priests of the ancients who *were* better and wiser, and have become our lord (ahvô), master (ra*d*ŏ), and high-priest, I *have* written that[1], even though the *usual* decision on the same subject is such as our high-priests, who are of our family, *have* maintained in particular. 21. Afterwards, moreover, about the sayings of that high-priest whose custom is otherwise there is no difference of opinion *expressed*[2]; and if there be *any one* for whose opinion I *have* acquired perfect reverence, a priestly man acquainted with the religion, who understands *and* who manages intelligently, by holding in reverence the ancient treatises and truth, and the sayings of the high-priests, whatever *of his* is to the purpose, as regards the reply, this also is written as successful illustration.

22. If owing to such cause it be not fully perceived, or regarding the decision *it be not* clear, *it* is chiefly not owing to the incompleteness of the decision of revelation in clearness of demonstration and correctness of meaning, but owing to our incomplete attainment to understanding the authoritative decrees (nikê*z*ak fragûftŏ)[3] of the religion. 23. From the

---

[1] That is, his own different opinion apparently, but the writer's sentences are often so involved as to confuse the reader.

[2] Meaning, apparently, that he does not propose to mention the opinions of others unless he approves of them.

[3] The MSS. have fragûtŏ, possibly Pers. far*g*ûd, 'miracle.'

imperfection (avêhîh) of that also which is asked of us the hasty thinking, notably therein, owing to the grievousness of the times, is even till now devoid of a distinct knowledge, interpreting the texts *about* the compassion of the good spirits, and *regarding* a clearer demonstration of the exposition of revelation which is thereby[1] more fully declared, as regards religious practice, from two sources, one is from the treatises which are an exposition of the rules *and* wisdom of the leader of the religion, and one—which is more descriptively expressed (mâ*d*î-gânŏtar hankhetûntô)—is the writings (vutakŏ) of various glorified ancients, those who *were* the great leaders of those of the primitive faith[2]. 24. Owing to that[3], as their writings (nipîkân) about the demonstration of reasons, on account of depth *and* minute wording, are not well known, even to minute observers *and* penetrative (vêhramakŏ) understandings, and through the little diffusion (f*r*â*g*ŏ-pa*d*îkhûîh), likewise, of difficult words, *there* may be doubts *among* the less intelligent, so, about the purport of *these* same questions, if there be *anything* which is wanted by you more clear and more plain in meaning, *or* a nearer way to a true interpretation, not without clearness, of *any* decision of a learned leader of the religion, I *will* give a reply, whenever you ask and I am able, so far as my knowledge and want of power *permit*.

25. When *one has* to observe the nature of the attributes (gôhârânŏ) of the sacred beings the

[1] That is, revelation is declared by the exposition.

[2] The true Maz*d*a-worshipping religion in all ages, both before and after the time of Zaratû*s*t (see Sls. I, 3).

[3] Want of knowledge referred to in § 23.

investigator's great advantage is the perfection, peace, equipment with righteousness, and fiend-destroying power of his own people; *and* since you are made aware of the result of wishes and actions, and are directed by me, many new blessings also *arise* from you.

26. That which is written to you yourselves and unto all, in the beginning and even the end, is completely adapted to your own several wants; may it have an exalted end, with one courier (aê-barî*d*ŏ) and continuously from beginning to end, and also perpetually!

27. A fair copy (bûr*z*is*n*îkŏ pa*k*înŏ) of the questions, as well as the replies, is this; so that, when there is nothing in it which owing to that cause[1] is different, I am of opinion as is *here* written.

CHAPTER II.

1. First you ask thus: Why is a righteous man created better than the stars and moon *and* sun and fire of Aûha*r*ma*zd*, and is called in revelation greater and better than the spiritual creation, *and* also than that which is worldly?

2. The reply is this, that the greatness and goodness of advance in wisdom and just judgment over the creatures arise from proficiency (hûnar). 3. Justice is the one good proficiency over the creatures, the means of wisdom are great, and praise bestowed is the most effectual performance

[1] Owing to the copying. The sentence is equivalent to the modern phrase, 'errors excepted.'

of what is desirable (kâmisn-karîh). 4. For all three are mutually connected together; since the manifestation of justice is through wisdom, and its advantage is the performance of what is desirable for the creator; wisdom is the performance of what is desirable for the requirements of the creator, and its weapon (zênô) is justice; and the desire of the creator, which is progress, is in wisdom with justice. 5. All three are great among the creatures, and their lodgment in the superior beings and righteous men is spiritual, in the spirit which is the pure guardian angel[1], *in* the understanding for encountering, averting, smiting, and prostrating (khvâpâk) the fiend, *in* the army of angels, and *in* the sovereignty of the far-seeing (dûr-vênâkŏ)[2] spirit, Aûharmazd; and, materially, in the worldly equipment and mutual connection of body *and* life. 6. And their appliances are the wisdom and worldly efficacy of treatises on the wise adoption of good thoughts, good words, *and* good deeds, *and* the relinquishment *and* discontinuance of evil thoughts, evil words, *and* evil deeds. 7. And their acquirer is the worldly ruler who is providing for Aûharmazd, and approving and stimulating the pure religion, a praiser of the good and pure creator, and a director of persistence in destruction of the fiend. 8. And in the pro-

[1] The fravâhar or fravashi, which is the prototype or spiritual counterpart supposed to have been created in the beginning for each good creature and creation afterwards produced, whether material or immaterial, and whose duty is to represent the creature and watch over its interests in the spiritual world.

[2] This word is badly written in K35, so that it has become zôrînâk in later MSS., which might perhaps mean 'strength-exerting.'

mulgation (rûbâkŏ-dahi*s*nîh) of the good and religious liturgy (mânsar), the coming of the good cause of the resurrection, and the production of the renovation *of the universe*[1] are *his* cöoperation and his own thanksgiving; and over the creatures of *this* prior world *he* is a guardian, defender, and manager.

9. And *such rulers* are great and pre-eminent; yet every man is not for that greatness, but it is mentioned as to superior beings *and* concerning righteous men, in whom it *has* arisen, and the best are the three who are the beginning, middle, *and* end of the creation. 10. One is the pure man, Gâyômar*d*, who was its first rational praiser; he in whose keeping *was* the whole creation of the sacred beings, from *its* beginning and immaturity unto the final completion of the worldly creatures, over which *was* the exercise of goodness of his well-destined progeny, suçh as Hôshâng, Tâkhmôrup, Yim, and Frê*d*ûn[2], such as the apostles of the religion, like Zaratû*s*t, Hûshê*d*ar, and Hûshê*d*ar-mâh[3], and the producers of the renovation *of the universe*, like Sôshâns[4], Rôshanô-*k*ashm, and

---

[1] Which is expected to take place about the time of the resurrection (see Bd. XXX, 32).

[2] The first four rulers of the world (omitting the usurper Dahâk) after Gâyômar*d* (see Bd. XXXI, 1–3, 7). The five names of these primeval sovereigns are corruptions of the Avesta names, Gaya-maretan, Haoshyangha, Takhmô-urupa, Yima, and Thraêtaona. The third name is always written Tâkhmôrî*d*ŏ in Dd.

[3] Corruptions of Av. Zarathu*s*tra, Ukhshya*d*-ereta, and Ukhshya*d*-nemangh. The last two are future apostles still expected by the Parsis to restore their religion to its original purity, in preparation for the resurrection (see Bd. XXXII, 2–10, Byt. III, 13, 43–48, 52, 53).

[4] Av. Saoshyãs. The last of the future apostles, in whose

Khûr-*k*ashm[1]. 11. The approver[2] of the enterprises (rûbâk-dahisnîhâ) of cöoperators, the purely-praising and just worshipper of the sacred beings through the strength of the spirit, the disabler of the worldly activity of the fiend as regards worldly bodies, and the one of pure religion—which is his charge (spôr)[3], the revelation of the place of the beneficent spirit and of the destruction of the depravity of the evil spirit[4], the subjugation (khvâpisnŏ) of the fiend, the completion of the triumph of the creator, and the unlimited progress of the creatures—is the upholder of Ma*zd*a-worship. 12. And likewise through the goodness of Gâyômar*d*, which is the begetting of Zaratûst, *he* is also just; likewise through the goodness of Sôshâns, by which he is the progeny of Zaratûst, *he* is also progressive in every good thought, good word, *and* good deed, *more* than the creatures which are produced with a hope of the religion, and equally thankful. 13. And one is the producer of bodies[5],

time the universe is expected to be renovated and the resurrection to take place (see Bd. XXX, 4–27, XXXII, 8, Byt. III, 62).

[1] These two names, which mean 'bright-eyed' and 'sunny-eyed,' are the Av. Rao*k*as-*k*aêshman and Hvare-*k*aêshman of Fravardîn Yt. 128 (see also Chap. XXXVI, 4).

[2] This is Zaratûst (see § 12), the righteous apostle of the middle portion of the history of creation referred to in § 9.

[3] Or 'which is wholly his.'

[4] These two spirits are supposed to be the authors of all the good and evil, respectively, that exists in creation. They appear, originally, to have been both supposed to spring from Aûharmazd, who speaks of 'the more beneficent of my two spirits' in Yas. XIX, 21; but in later times, and throughout the Pahlavi literature, the beneficent spirit is identified with Aûharmazd, and the origin of the evil spirit is left in obscurity.

[5] The renovated bodies of the future existence which are prepared for mankind at the resurrection (see Bd. XXX, 4, 7, 25–27).

the renovator (frashagar) Sôshâns, who is the putter down, with complete subjugation from the world, of the glorification of fiends *and* demons, and of the contention with angels in apostasy and heterodoxy of various kinds and unatoned for; and the completer of the renovation through the full continuance of the glorification of the angels, and the perfect continuance of the pure religion.

14. And through that excellent, unblemished, brotherly work[1] *such a ruler* may be seen above the sun with swift horses, the primeval luminaries, and all removal of darkness, the advance of illumination which is the display (tô*g*is*n*ŏ) of the days *and* nights of the world[2]. 15. Regarding the same completion of the renovation *of the universe* it is said in the revelation of the Ma*zd*a-worshippers, that this great light is the vesture of the like righteous men.

Chapter III.

1. The second is that which you ask thus: For what purpose is a righteous man created for the world, and in what manner is it necessary for him to exist in the world?

2. The reply is this, that the creator created the creatures for progress, which is his wish; and

---

[1] Mentioned in §§ 7, 8.

[2] M14 and J have '*such rulers*' own praise is above the sun with swift horses, the primeval luminaries, and all good creatures; for that, too, which may be seen when the light of the sun is owing to the removal of darkness, and the removal is the advance of illumination of the world, is the display of days *and* nights.'

it is necessary for us to promote whatever is his wish, so that we may obtain whatever is our wish. 3. And, since that persistent creator is powerful, whatever is our wish, and so far as we remain very faithful, such is as *it were* deserving of his wish, which is for our obtainment of whatever is our wish[1].

4. The miracle of these creatures was fully achieved (âvôrîdŏ) not unequally, and the gain (gûâftâkŏ) also from the achievement of the same miracle is manifest; that is, achieving, and knowing[2] that his achievement is with design (kîm) and his desire is goodness, when the designed achievement, which is his creature, and also the goodness, which is his wish, are certain, and likewise, owing to the perfect ability which is due to the creator, the wish is achieved, *it* is manifest. 5. And, afterwards, it is decided by wisdom that *he has* achieved it, and the creatures, as perfected for the complete progress which is his wish, lapse into evil; and since when evil exists good becomes the subjugation of evil—for when evil is not complete, and after it is expressly said that his creatures are created for his own will, the progress due to subjugations of evil is on account of the good completed—it is similarly testified, *in accordance* with the will aforesaid, that it[3] is achieved.

6. The creatures are for the performance of what is desirable for the creator, and the performance of what is desirable for the creator is necessary

---

[1] Reading kâmakŏ instead of the dâmakŏ of the MSS., which was, no doubt, originally gâmakŏ.

[2] M14 has 'knowing perfectly.'

[3] The subjugation of evil apparently.

for two *purposes*, which are the practice of worship *and* contention. 7. As the worship is that of the persistent creator, who is a friend to his own creatures, *and* the contention is that with the fiend —the contender who is an enemy to the creation of the creator—that great worship is a pledge, most intimate to one's self, of the utmost contention also, and a pledge for the prosperity owing to the friend subjugating by a look which is a contender with the enemy, the great endeavour of the acquirers of reliance upon any mortals whatever[1]. 8. For when the persistent *one* accomplished that most perfect and wholly miraculous creation of the lord, and his unwavering look—which *was* upon the coming on of the wandering evil spirit, the erratic, unobservant spirit—*was* unmingled with the sight of an eye[2], he made a spirit of observant temperament, which *was* the necessary soul, the virtuous lord of the body moving into the world. 9. And the animating life, the preserving guardian spirit, the acquiring intellect, the protecting understanding, the deciding wisdom, the demeanour which is itself a physician, the impelling strength, the eye for *what* is seen, the ear for *what* is heard, the nose for *what* is smelt, the mouth for recognising flavour, the body for approaching the assembly (pi*d*râm) of the righteous, the heart for

[1] Referring probably to the strong influence of a steady eye upon all living creatures.

[2] This appears to be the meaning of agûmê*g*i*s*nŏ-î va*l* vênâftâkŏ dî*d*ag; which phrase is followed by the conjunction 'and,' so that the original text means that when the creator had done as in §§ 8, 9, he proceeded to act as in § 10. This conjunction, for the sake of clearness, is here transferred to the beginning of § 10.

thinking, the tongue for speaking, the hand for working, the foot for walking, these which make life comfortable, these which are developments in creating, these which are to join the body, these which are to be considered perfected, are urged on by him continuously, and the means of industry of the original body are arranged advisedly. 10. *And* by proper regulation, and the recompense of good thoughts, good words, and good deeds, he announced and adorned conspicuous, patient, and virtuous conduct; *and* that procurer of the indispensable did not forget to keep men *in* his own true service and proper bounds, the supreme sovereignty of the creator.

11. And *man* became a pure glorifier and pure praiser of that all-good friend, through the progress which is his wish. 12. Because pure friendship is owing to sure meditation on every virtue, and from its existence no harm whatever arose; pure glorifying is owing to glorifying every goodness, and from its existence no vileness whatever arose; and pure praising is owing to all prosperity, and from its existence no distress whatever arose. 13. And pronouncing the benedictions he is steadfast *in* the same pure friendship, just glorifying, and expressive praising, *which* are performed even as though Vohûman were kept lodging in the thoughts, Srôsh in the words, and Ar*d* in the actions[1]. 14. That, moreover, which is owing to the lodgment of Vohûman in the thoughts is virtu-

[1] These three angels are personifications of the Avesta terms vohû-manô, 'good thought,' sraosha, 'listening, obedience,' and areta, 'righteous.' The coming of Vohûman ('the good spirit' of § 17) and of Srôsh is mentioned in the Gâthas (Yas. XLIII, 16, c d).

ously rushing unto true propitiation from the heart, and keeping selfishness away from the desires; the lodgment of Srôsh in the words is owing to him who is intelligent *being* a true speaker, *and* him who is unintelligent being a listener to *what is* true and *to* the high-priests; *and* the lodgment of Ar*d* in the actions is declared to be owing to promoting that which is known *as* goodness, *and* abstaining *from* that which *one* does not know. 15. And these three benefits[1] which *have been* recited are sent down (farôstakŏ) in two ways that the ancients *have* mentioned, which are *that* deliberately taken and *that* they should deliberately leave[2], whose means are wisdom and proper exertion.

16. And his (man's) high-priest is he whose instigation is to keep him truly *in accordance* with the revelation (dînô) of the sacred beings, and is the origin of his pure meditation which is truly through goodness like Vohûman's. 17. As the religious of the ancients *have* religiously said, that of him who keeps the goodness of Vohûman lodging in the thoughts the true way is then that of the good spirit. 18. The Maz*d*a-worshipper understands the will of the creator in the true way, and grows and acquires by performing what is desirable for the creator, which obtains the benefit of the renovation.

19. A more concise reply is this, that a righteous man is the creature by whom is accepted that occupation which is provided for him, and is fully

[1] The lodgments of the three angels.

[2] Meaning, probably, the deliberate adoption of good conduct and relinquishment of evil (compare Chap. VII, 7).

watchful in the world as to his not being deceived by the rapacious fiend. 20. And as a determiner, by wisdom, of the will of the creator—*one* who is himself a propitiator and understander, and a promoter of the understanding of goodness—and of whatever *pertains* to him (the creator), *he* is a giver of heed thereto; and it is necessary for him to be thus, so that such greatness *and* goodness may also be his more securely in the spiritual *existence*.

CHAPTER IV.

1. The third question is that you ask thus: For what reason does this greatness[1] of a righteous man exist?

2. The reply is this, that *it* is for the performance of what is desirable for the creator by the Ma*zd*a-worshipper; because he strives unhesitatingly that the way for the performance of what is desirable for the creator *may* be the propitiation[2] which is his desire, and that desired propitiation[2] becomes perfect through sound wisdom. 3. The wisdom by which he understands about the desire of the heavenly angels is not appointed (vakht), but is the true, pure religion which is knowledge of[3] the spirits, the science of sciences, the teacher of the

---

[1] Referring to Chap. II, 1, and not to Chap. III, 20; otherwise it might be supposed that the questions were contrived to suit the replies.

[2] Or, perhaps, 'understanding.'

[3] K35 has 'obedience to' by inserting a medial stroke in dânisnô, which converts it into sinvisnô, but is probably a mistake.

teaching of the angels, and the source of all knowledge.

4. And the progress, too, of the pure religion of the Mazda-worshippers is through the righteous man, as is shown of him in revelation thus: 'I created, O Zaratûst the Spîtamân! the righteous man who is very active[1], and I will guard his hands from evil deeds; I *will* also have him conveyed unto those who are afterwards righteous and more actively wise[2]. 5. And *at* the same time the religion of me who created him is his desire, *and* it is the obtainment of a ruler which is to be changed by the well-organised renovation *of the universe*[3].'

6. As through wisdom is created the world of righteousness, through wisdom is subjugated every evil, and through wisdom is perfected every good; and the best wisdom is the pure religion whose progress is that achieved by the upholders of religion, the greatness of the best men of the righteous, in whose destiny *it is*, such as that which *was* shown about Gâyômard, Zaratûst, and Sôshâns[4].

---

[1] M14 and J here insert 'I will guard his mind from evil thoughts, *his* tongue from evil-speaking.'

[2] In the future existence.

[3] M14 and J have '*and* it is the obtainment of a ruler who is a wise upholder of religion, from time to time, even unto the change of the last existences by the well-organised renovation *of the universe*.' But the additional words appear to have been suggested by the word 'ruler' being taken literally, whereas it seems to have been figuratively applied to the religion which is to rule the righteous till the future existence.

[4] In Chap. II, 9–13.

CHAPTER V.

1. The fourth question is that which you ask thus: Of this destruction (zadam) and terror which ever happen to us from the retribution[1] of the period, and are a cause of the other evils and defects of the good religion, what kind of opinion exists? And is there a good opinion of us among the spirits, or not?

2. The reply is this, that it is said in the revelation of the Mazda-worshippers that the impediments (râs-bandîh), through which *there* is vexation in righteousness, are because its doctrine is this, that, regarding the difficulty, anxiety, and discomfort which occur through good works set going, it is not desirable to account *them* as much difficulty, trouble, and discomfort. 3. Whereas it is not desirable to account *them* as anxiety and difficulty, it is then declared by it[2] thereof, that, as its recompense, so much comfort *and* pleasure will come to the soul, as that no one is to think of that difficulty and discomfort which came upon him through so many such good works, because he is steadfast to maintain the good religion, and utters thanksgivings (va stâyedŏ). 4. And as regards the discomfort[3], which the same good religion of ours *has* had, it comes on from the opponents of the religion.

---

[1] Reading pâdâsân, but by a slight alteration M14 and J have pâdakhshahân, 'monarchs,' which is equally suitable.

[2] By revelation.

[3] M14 and J have 'and he remains thereby certain that his good works are in the statement (mâdîgânŏ) of good works, *and* as regards all that terror, anxiety (vayâdŏ), and discomfort,' &c.

5. Through the coming of religion we have full enjoyment (ba*r*â gûkârêm), and owing to religion, unlike bondsmen (abûr*d*ŏgânvâr), we do not become changeable among the angels; our spiritual life (ahvôîh) of praise then arrives in readiness, and owing to the angels *there* are joyous salutation, spiritual life, and glory for the soul.

CHAPTER VI.

1. The fifth question is that you ask thus: Why does evil always happen more *to* the good than to the bad?

2. The reply is this, that not *at* every time and every place, *and* not *to* all the good, does evil happen more—for the spiritual welfare of the good is certainly more—but in the world it is very much more manifest[1]. 3. And the reasons for it are many; one which is conclusive is even this, that the modes

[1] M14 and J have 'but the worldly evil and bondage are incalculably more manifest about the good, much more in the season (zêmânîh) of Srôsh.' The 'season of Srôsh' may perhaps mean the night-time, or the three nights after death, when the protection of the angel Srôsh is most wanted; but Dastûr Peshotanji Behramji, the high-priest of the Parsis in Bombay, prefers reading zîmânash (with a double pronominal suffix), and has favoured me with the following free translation of the whole passage:—'At every time and every place much evil does not happen *to* all the good; for the good, after having been separated from this world, receive (as a reward for their suffering evil) much goodness in the next world, which goodness is (regarded as) of a very high degree in religious doctrines (srôsh).' Perhaps, after all, Srôsh is a miswriting of saryâ, 'bad, evil.'

and causes of *its* occurrence are more; for the occurrence of evil is more particularly appointed (vakhtŏ) by two modes, one by the demons, the appointers of evil, *and* one by the vile, the doers of evil; even to the vileness of creation and the vile they cause vexation. 4. Moreover, incalculable is the evil which happens to the vile from the demons, and that to the good from the demons and also from the vile, and the mode of its occurrence is in the same way without a demon.

5. This, too, is more particularly such as the ancients *have* said, that the labour and trouble of the good are much more in the world, and their reward *and* recompense are more certain in the spiritual *existence;* and the comfort and pleasure of the vile are more in the world, and their pain *and* punishment in the spiritual *existence* are more severe. 6. And this, too, is *the case*, that the good, through fear of the pain and punishment of hell, should forsake the comfort and ease in the world, and should not think, speak, *or* do anything improper whatever. 7. And through hope for the comfort and pleasure in heaven they should accept willingly, for the neck[1], much trouble *and* fear in the practice of virtue in thought, word, *and* deed.

8. The vile, through provision with temporary enjoyment[2]—even that enjoyment of improprieties for which eventually there is hell—then enjoy them-

[1] The word can be read either garêvan, 'collar,' or gardûn, 'neck,' and is the usual Pâz. of the Huz. *k*avarman (Chald. צַוְּרָא), 'the neck,' though 'neck' is often expressed by gar*d*ûn. The meaning is that the yoke of trouble and fear should be accepted.

[2] M14 and J have 'through provision with the enjoyment of improprieties which is temporarily theirs.'

selves therein temporarily, and lustfully on account of selfishness; those various actions also, through which *there* would be a way to heaven, they do not trouble themselves with.

9. And in this way, in the world, the comfort and pleasure of the vile are more, and the anxiety, vexation, despondency, and distress of the good *have* become more; the reason is revealed by the stars[1].

Chapter VII.

1. The sixth question is that which you ask thus: Why are we men produced for the world, and what is it necessary for us to do therein?

2. The reply is this, that even in the reply to an accompanying question[2] *it* is written that the creatures are achieved for[3] justice and the performance of what is desirable for the creator; and to prepare thoroughly well that which is unlimited and the virtuous progress of the creatures, whose distress is like fear, there is the unparalleled (abrâ*d*arvatô) renovation *of the universe.*

3. And that preparation arises from the complete predominance of the creator *and* the non-predominance of the fiend, as is said of it in revelation thus: 'In that time I become completely predominant, I who am Aûha*r*ma*z*d; in nothing whatever

[1] That is, it is dependent upon destiny.

[2] See Chap. III.

[3] Reading pavan instead of ba*r*â, two words which are often confounded by the copyists of MSS. because their Persian equivalents are nearly identical.

is the evil spirit predominant.' 4. And also about the good procedure of the creature-creation *it* is recounted thus: 'Happy *am* I when the creatures are so created by me, and according to any wish whatever of mine they give the sovereignty to me, and also come *to* the sovereignty when I have created *it* for the performance of what is desirable for the expression of what sovereignty is.'

5. And it is necessary for us to become so in the world as that the supreme sovereignty of the creator may be kept more friendly to us, its own true servants. 6. The way to that true service is known through wisdom, is believed (vâvarî-aîtŏ) through truth, *and* is utilized through goodness; and the path of excellence more particularly *leads to* it. 7. And to set the good spirit rightly in the place of thought *it is* deliberately taken *and* they should deliberately leave *it*[1], as it is said in revelation that Aûharmazd spoke out to Zaratûst thus: 'Thou shouldst assist Vohûman with thy pure spiritual faculties (ahvô), so that they may make him fully welcome; for when thou assistest Vohûman with thy pure spiritual faculties, so that they make him fully welcome, thou shalt thus fully understand the two ways, *that* which is good conduct, and *that* also which is bad conduct.'

Chapter VIII.

1. The seventh question is that you ask thus: When a man is passing *away*, *and* after the occurrence of his passing *away*, how does the good work

[1] Compare Chap. III, 15. The 'good spirit' is Vohûman.

then go to him *and* assist him, which any others may do for him who has gone out from the world, on the third night in the dawn[1], *at* which he goes out to the balance[2]? *And is its* greatness such as though it be done by his own hand, or otherwise?

2. The reply is this:—When any others do a good work for him who *has* passed away, after the passing away, and if he who *has* passed away did not order that good work in *his* lifetime, and did not bequeath it, nor *was its* originator, and it was not even his by design (dâ*d*ŏ), then it does not go and does not reach him out at the balance. 3. Even at the time for being proceeded with, when that good work does not assist it is not appropriated, for that which is appropriated as the design of some one is appropriated by acceptance from some one; when it is not his by design it is then not accepted *as* his.

4. If he who *has* passed *away* did not order that good work, and did not even bequeath *it*, but was consenting to it by design, that which shall be done in *his* life*time* then reaches out in the three *nights* (satûîh) for the aggrandizement of his position; *but* that which shall be done after *his* passing *away* is not in the account of the three *nights* and the balance, but reaches out, at the time the good work is proceeded with, for the enjoyment of the soul.

5. And if he who *has* passed *away* ordered that

[1] The soul of a dead person is supposed to hover about the corpse for three nights, and not to depart for the other world till the dawn after the third night; that is, at dawn of the fourth day, including the day of death (see Chap. XX, 2, 3, Sls. XVII, 2–6).

[2] Where the soul's good works are balanced against its sins, to determine its fate till the resurrection.

good work in his own life*time*, or bequeathed it, or was the originator and cause of the soul's employment, although it is proceeded with after *his* passing away, it then reaches out to him for the happiness of his soul, since the origin of the thanksgiving (sipâs)[1], and the orderer and ownership of the good work are certain.

6. Any good work whatever which is proceeded with is clearly a like good work as regards those who account for *it as* with him who is the doer *of it;* also in the account of his soul the good work is as much with him who did *it*, but the soul of him by whom the good work is done by his own hand, is handsomer and stronger than of him by whom it is ordered. 7. And its similitude is such as when a man's handsome and seemly suit of clothes is his own, and he wears *it* on *his* body *and* is handsomer, more splendid, and more seemly *than* another man *who* wears a suit of clothes, *in* like manner, *which* is his own by theft.

Chapter IX.

1. The eighth question is that which you ask thus: Of him who, out of his *own* wealth, himself directed others thus: 'Let them act advantageously (khan*g*înakŏ) for my soul,' is it so that what others may do for him out of that wealth *and that* done by his own toil are very different, one from the other, or not?

---

[1] The good works mentioned in this chapter would chiefly consist of prayers and ceremonies for which priests have to be remunerated, and gifts to holy men and the poor; such actions as are most highly appreciated by priests.

2. The reply is this, that *they* are very different, one from the other; for that which he orders out of his own wealth is more effectual than that which others may do for him without order. 3. And among the kinds of good work, that is more effectual which *one* practises himself and with his own toil; then that *which one* sets going out of whatever is his own by his own order, regarding which he[1] afterwards bequeaths *and* orders out of his own *property and* it comes into progress; and, lastly, that which others may do for him.

4. Since thus his own *and* that which is his by design, when any one manages for him and in his life*time*, aggrandize his position then, *and his* soul is preserved, when he manages for him thereafter the enjoyment then reaches unto his soul. 5. When not consenting as to the good work, and *it is* not his by design, even though others may do *it* for him it does not then come into his possession.

CHAPTER X.

1. The ninth question is that which you ask thus: How much does the growth[2] of his good works increase, from the *time* when the good works are done, so long as *he* is living?

2. The reply is this, that from the *time* when a good work comes into progress *its* growth remains on the increase so long as *he* is living; moreover,

---

[1] M14 and J make this an additional kind of good work by reading 'after which is that regarding which he himself,' &c.

[2] Reading vakhsh instead of the vê*s*, 'more,' of the MSS.

when he is distressed by that good work[1], while the increase does not desist *from* increase, it grows just as a child becomes enlarged in the womb of a mother.

CHAPTER XI.

1. The tenth question is that which you ask thus: Does the growth which increases become as commendable in the fourth night[2] as the original good work[3] in *his* possession, or does it become otherwise?

2. The reply is this, that *it* is otherwise; for the original good work stands up opposing sin, and the growing good work[4] stands up opposed to the growth of sin.

CHAPTER XII.

1. The eleventh question is that you ask thus: Does the growth of a good work eradicate sin just like the original good work, or not?

2. The reply is this, that the growth does eradicate *it*, as happens *with* the good work which is for atonement for sin; it shall be done as retribution for sin, *and* it eradicates the sin, which is specially mentioned in revelation[5]. 3. 'Then the place of his

---

[1] The good work being more meritorious when more troublesome.

[2] After death, when all the immediate ceremonies for the dead have been completed (see Sls. XVII, 5 note).

[3] Literally 'the good work of the beginning.' That bûn kirfakŏ does not here stand for bûn-î kirfakŏ, 'the origin or root of the good work,' appears from Chap. XII, 1, where it is written kirfakŏ-î bûn.

[4] Literally 'the good work of growth.'

[5] See Pahl. Vend. VII, 136, where the matter is mentioned, but

other good work is evidently the soul; and, in order to be with the sin at *its* origin, it remains *and* is taken into account.' 4. 'Through good works and the growth of good works is the recompense of the soul, so that they should do those good works in atonement for sin.' 5. And concerning the sin eradicated it is said: 'An original good work eradicates original sin[1], and the growth of a good work *eradicates* the growth of a sin.'

CHAPTER XIII.

1. The twelfth question is that which you ask thus: In the fourth night do they score off (ba*r*â angârênd) the sin by the good works, and does he go by the residue (bôn); or do they inflict punishment on him for the sin which *has* happened to him, and give reward *and* recompense for the good works which he *has* done?

2. The reply is this, that at dawn of the third night the account is prepared it is said, and about the sin which he *has* atoned for, *and* the good work which is its equivalent (â*v*âr) *there* is no need for account, since the account is about the good works which may be appropriated by him *as* his own, and about the sin which may remain *in* him as *its* origin. 3. Because the origin of it (the sin atoned for) remains distinct, and it is cancelled (astar*d*ŏ)

---

the passages which seem to be quoted here must be from some other source.

[1] Literally 'sinning of the beginning' (bûn-vinâsîh). It must mean the first commission of any particular sin, and has no connection with the 'original sin' of Christian writers.

by it (the good work), they balance it therewith; and they weigh the excess and deficiency, as it may be, of the *other* good works *and* sin.

4. Of those living, at the just, impartial (akafsisnŏ) balance the *man* of proper habits (dâdŏ), whose good works are more, when sin *has* happened to him, undergoes a temporary (vidanâîk) punishment and becomes eternally cleansed by the good works; and he of improper habits, of much sin and little good works, attains temporary enjoyment by those good works, *but* through the sin which they perceive *in* him he is suffering punishment unto the resurrection.

CHAPTER XIV.

1. The thirteenth question is that which you ask thus: Who should prepare the account of the soul as to sin and good works, and in what place should they make it up? *And* when punishment is inflicted by them, where is their place then?

2. The reply is this, that the account about the doers of actions, as to good works *and* sin, three times every day whilst the doer of the actions is living, Vohûman the archangel should prepare; because taking account of the thoughts, words, and deeds of all material existences is among his duties. 3. And about the sin which *affects* accusers[1], which

[1] Sins are divided into two classes, hamêmâlân or those which affect 'accusers,' and rûbânîk or those which affect only one's own soul. In the first class are included all evil actions which injure our fellow-creatures or any good animal or thing, and for which the injured party (the 'accuser') must receive satisfaction before the sinner can be pardoned (see Sls. VIII, 1).

is committed by (va*l*) breakers of promises, even in the world Mit*r*ô[1] is said *to be* over the bodies, words, and fortunes (hû-bakhtakŏ) of the promise-breakers; *and* as to the amount, and also as to *being* more than the stipulation when *there is* a period of time[2], Mit*r*ô is the account-keeper. 4. In the three *nights' account* (satûîh) Srôsh the righteous *and* Rashnû the just[3] are over the estimate of the limits of the good works *and* sin of righteousness and wickedness. 5. In the future existence, on the completion of every account, the creator Aûha*r*ma*zd* himself takes account[4], by whom both the former account of the three *nights* and all the thoughts, words, and deeds of the creatures are known through his omniscient wisdom.

6. The punishment for a soul of the sinners comes from that spirit[5] with *whom* the sin, which *was* committed by it, is connected; fostered by the iniquity practised, that punishment comes upon the souls of the sinful and wicked, first on earth, afterwards in hell, *and* lastly at the organisation of the

[1] The angel of the sun's light; he is a personification of friendship and good faith, and is, therefore, specially aggrieved by breaches of promise and fraudulent debtors, but assists righteous souls in their passage to the other world (see AV. V, 3, Mkh. II, 118).

[2] Referring to debts and promises to pay.

[3] The angels of obedience and justice; the duty of the former is to protect the righteous, and that of the latter is to weigh the good works and sins in his golden scales, when the soul's account is balanced after the third night after death (see AV. V, 2–5, Mkh. II, 115–122).

[4] Referring, perhaps, to the future temporary separation of the wicked from the righteous, after the assembly of the Sa*d*vâstarân (see Bd. XXX, 10–16).

[5] The demon who is supposed to have occasioned the sin.

future existence[1]. 7. When the punishment of the three *nights* is undergone[2] the soul of the righteous attains to heaven *and* the best existence, *and* the soul of the wicked to hell and the worst existence. 8. When they have undergone their punishment at the renovation *of the universe* they attain, by complete purification from every sin, unto the everlasting progress, happy progress, *and* perfect progress of the best *and* undisturbed existence.

CHAPTER XV.

1. The fourteenth question is that which you ask thus: Is the eradication of life the gnawing of dogs and birds upon the corpse? And does the sin of those who suppose *it*[3] a sin proceed from *that* origin, or not?

2. The reply is this, that the decrease of sin and increase of good works, owing to good thoughts, good words, *and* good deeds, arise really from the effort and disquietude which come on by means of the religion the soul practises, *and* through the strength in effort, steadfastness of religion, and

---

[1] The three days and nights of final punishment, after the resurrection and before the final purification in melted metal (see Bd. XXX, 13, 16, 20), which is mentioned again in § 8.

[2] This does not refer to the final punishment of §§ 6 and 8, but to the previous three nights' tribulation just after death, and to the fate of the soul before the resurrection (see Chaps. XXIV, XXV).

[3] The exposure of the dead, apparently; but the construction of this question and its relation to the reply are by no means clear at first sight. From §§ 2, 5, 6 we have to infer that the exposure is a meritorious action rather than a sin; and from §§ 3, 4 we have to gather that as loss of life occurs to every one, and exposure of the corpse only to some, the former cannot be caused by the latter.

protection of soul *which* the faithful possess. 3. That evil which *occurs* when doing good works, which is the one (hanâ) when doing iniquity, and when one strives *it* is the one when he does not strive, the one when content and the one when not content, and after *it is* undesired, and no cause of good works is with it, it occurs just as undesired, for the sake of favour and reward, is the certain eradication of life. 4. It happens once only (aêtûm) unto the righteous and the wicked, every one *who* may have received the reward—that reward is living until the time of passing *away*—but the gnawing of dogs and birds does not happen unto every one and every body. 5. It is necessary *for those* to act very differently[1] whose understanding of good works is owing to proper heed of dead matter; and, on account of the rapid change (var*d*î-hastanŏ) of that pollution, and a desire of atonement for sin, they should carry the body of *one* passed *away* out to a mountain-spur (kôf vakhsh), *or* a place of *that* description, enjoining unanimously that the dogs and birds may gnaw it, owing to the position of the appointed place[2]. 6. Therefore, as owing to that fear[3], the commands of religion, and progressive

[1] Differently from others.

[2] The dead must be deposited upon some dry and barren spot, remote from habitations and water, and, if possible, upon the summit of a hill (see Chap. XVII, 17, and Vend. VI, 93). From the mention of dogs gnawing the corpse it would appear that the depositories for the dead were less enclosed when this work was written than they are at present; and in ancient times both enclosed and unenclosed depositories seem to have been used (see Vend. VI, 92–106). For a description of the present form of such depositories see Sls. II, 6, note.

[3] Fear of pollution from the dead.

desire *it* is accepted strenuously for the wicked himself, his own recompense is therein, and it happens to him in that way for the removal (narafsisnŏ) of sin *and* for the gratification of *his* soul.

CHAPTER XVI.

1. The fifteenth question is that which you ask thus: When the dogs and birds tear it (the corpse) does the soul know *it*, and does it occur uncomfortably *for* it, or how is it?

2. The reply is this, that the pain *occasioned* by the tearing and gnawing so galls (mâlêdŏ) the body of men that, though the soul *were* abiding with the body, such soul, which *one* knows is happy and immortal, *would* then depart from the body, *along* with the animating life, the informing (sinâyinâkŏ) consciousness, *and* the remaining resources of life. 3. The body is inert, unmoving, and not to be galled; and at last no pain whatever galls *it*, nor is it perceived; and the soul, with the life, is outside of the body, and is not unsafe as regards its gnawing, but through the spiritual perception[1] it sees *and* knows *it*.

4. That which is wicked is then again desirous of its bodily existence[2], when it sees them thus: the wonderfully-constructed body which was its

[1] Supposing that sinâsnŏ stands for sinâyisnŏ; otherwise we must read 'in the spiritual places (dîvâgânŏ).'

[2] This section is made still more complicated in the Pahlavi text by the division of this first phrase; half of it being placed at the beginning, and the other half at the extreme end of the sentence.

vesture, *and* is dispersed, and that spiritual life (hûkŏ) which was with its heart, and is even on account of this—that is: 'Because in my bodily existence and worldly progress *there was* no atonement for sin and no accumulation of righteousness'—also in mourning about it thus: 'In the prosperity which this body of mine had, it would have been possible for me to atone for sin *and* to save the soul, *but* now I am separated from every one and *from* the joy of the world, which is great hope of spiritual *life*; and I have attained to the perplexing account and more serious danger.' 5. And the gnawing becomes as grievous to it, on account of that body, as a closely-shut arsenal (afzâr bêtâ-î badtûm) and a concealed innermost garment are useless among those with limbs *provided* with weapons and accoutrements, and are destroyed.

6. And of that, too, which is righteous and *filled* with the great joy that *arises* from *being* really certain of the best existence, then also the spiritual life which was with its body, on account of the great righteousness, *fit* for the exalted (fîrâkhtagânîk), which *was* ever accumulated by it with the body, is well developed (madam hû-tâshî*d*ŏ), *and* the wonderfully-constructed body is destroyed in the manner of a garment, particularly when its dispersion (apâ*s*is*n*ŏ) occurs thereby.

7. And the consciousness of men, as it sits three nights outside of the body, in the vicinity of the body, *has* to remember and expect that *which* is truly fear and trouble (khâr) unto the demons, *and* reward, peace, and glad tidings (nôvîk) unto the spirits of the good; and, on account of the dispersion and injuring of the body, it utters a cry spiritually,

thus: 'Why do the dogs and birds gnaw this organised body, when still at last the body and life unite together at the raising of the dead?' 8. And this is the reminding of the resurrection *and* liberation, and it becomes the happiness and hope of the spirit of the body *and* the other good spirits, and the fear *and* vexation of the demons and fiends.

Chapter XVII.

1. The sixteenth question is that which you ask thus: What is the purpose[1] of giving up a corpse to the birds?

2. The reply is this, that the construction of the body of those passed *away* is so wonderful that two co-existences have come together for *it*, one which is to occasion endurance (dêr pa*d*âyînî*d*anŏ) *and* one which is to cause conflict (nipôr*d*înî*d*anŏ), and their natures are these, for watching the angels *and* averting the demons. 3. After appertaining *to it* the life—so long as *it is* in the locality of the place of the body—and the demons of dull intellects, *who* are frightened by the body, are just like a sheep startled by wolves when they shall further frighten *it* by a wolf[2]. 4. The spirit of the body, on account of being the spiritual life (hûkŏ) for the heart in the body, is indestructible; so is the will which resided therein, even when they shall release it from *its* abode.

5. In the same way the body of those who are

[1] Assuming that âhan stands for âhang.

[2] This last clause is a quotation, slightly altered, from Pahl. Vend. XIX, 108, 109.

passed *away* is so much the more innocently worthy of the rights (sânŏ) of *one* properly passed *away*, and *what it* is therein provided with, as it has uttered thanksgivings. 6. *For* those guardian spirits who keep watch over the body of Keresâsp[1] the Sâmân are also such praises from the life and body, for that reason, moreover, when they unite.

7. The injury of the destroyer to the body of those passed *away* is contaminating; the Nasû*s* ('corruption')[2] rushes on it and, owing to its violence when it becomes triumphant over the life of the righteous man, and frightens it from the place of the catastrophe (hanka*rd*îkîh), and puts itself into the place of the body, that body is then, for that reason, called Nasâî ('dead matter'). 8. And, on account of the co-existence of rapid changing and the mode of attacking of the same Nasû*s*, even when it is necessary for the disintegration of the body, this is also then to lie and change sanatorily.

---

[1] An ancient hero, mentioned both in the Avesta and Shâhnâmah, who, owing to his disregard of religion, is said to be lying asleep on the plain of Pê*s*yânsaî (probably the Pi*s*în valley near Qandahâr), watched by a myriad guardian spirits of the righteous, until he shall be hereafter aroused by the angels to kill the revived usurper A*z*-i Dahâk (see Bd. XXIX, 7, 8, Byt. III, 59–61). Regarding his soul a legend is related in the Pahlavi tracts which precede Dd. in some MSS., of which a translation will be found in Appendix I.

[2] Supposed to be a fiend who enters and pervades every corpse immediately after death, except in certain cases of violent death, when its arrival is delayed till the next period of the day (see Sls. X, 32). This exception is made in Vend. VII, 5, 6, and was probably intended, in most cases, to prevent a person who had met with a serious accident being left to perish, through fear of his death contaminating any one coming to his relief; not from any idea of the fiend being taken unawares by the suddenness of the death. This fiend is the Av. nasu (nom. nasu*s*).

9. Hence, as the body of men is formed out of hard bone and soft fat, that *which* is established is the expulsion of the bone from the fat. 10. For the bone through its hardness, when no damp fat is with it, and it does not become a holder of its damp, is itself essentially dry; and it becomes unconsumable and attaining durability, through dryness, out of the dead matter even for perpetuity. 11. And the sun is provided to make rotten, dispersed, *and* useless the fat that is around the bone, which on the decay of the animating life is to become increasingly damp, and, after the departure of life through terror and disgust (adôstîh), it comes to rottenness and stench; and the noxious creatures in *it* alike afflict it and the hard *part* such as bone.

12. As regards the shrinking away of those who are sinners, the nearer way to a remedy is the gnawer away from men[1]; the fat becomes separate from the bone, and is seized and digested, as by the separation of the fat from the dead matter for digestion, moreover, the permanent matter (asarîh) and bone attain more fully unto their own nature (*s*ânŏ), *and* the body (kâlpû*d*ŏ) to emptiness. 13. Because there is no *other* way to consume that fat of men, since *it* is most grievous to them (the sinners), and the pollution and contamination are made a blessing unto it (the gnawer). 14. The dispersers (astâr*d*ŏ-garân) completely disperse from it[2]; they are ap-

[1] That is, in the case of those who neglect the proper exposure of corpses, there is a natural remedy in the worms produced for consuming them. Perhaps the word khastâr, 'cutter or gnawer,' stands for khastar, 'noxious creature.'

[2] The consumers of the corpse disperse when their work is done, and carry contamination with them unless purified by the sun's heat, as described in § 15.

pointed and produced, a production not worthy, for its defilement of those purified *and* animals is contaminating, through contact again with men. 15. The crow (galâg) and such-like, through scorching away by the fire of the luminaries, become worthy; moreover, the affliction of that which is completely pure fire arises therefrom, as it is not able itself to come unto the scorched *one, for* then the defilement (darvâkh) of the scorcher by the most grievous gnawer *would* be possible.

16. But it is not proper to recount (angâstanŏ) the devouring of the noxious creatures, for the spirit of the body is troubled when it observes the alarmed (vazî*d*) spirituality which *was* in the body of those destroyed, the noxious creatures upon the goodly forms, and the mode and strangeness of *their* disintegration and spoliation. 17. And so it then becomes the more remedial way[1] when, as it is ordered in revelation[2], the body fraught with corruption is placed on the ground of a clear mountain-spur (kôf vakhsh); *and*, in order not to convey *it* to the water, plants, and men of the plain, it is fastened[3] in the customary manner, so that the corpse-eating dogs and corpse-eating birds, which are not subject to the hand (dastô-âmûkŏ) of men, and are likewise not entertained as food, shall yet not drag *any* of it away for man's eating of dead matter.

18. For streams and waters go themselves[4] *and*

---

[1] That is, it is better to adopt the customary mode of removing the corpse.

[2] See Vend. VI, 93–97.

[3] This is ordered only when the corpse is not placed in any enclosure.

[4] Or, as Vend. V, 49–62 describes it, the water is rained down by

consume that fat, and are digested by the vital fire[1] which is in the life of the creatures of Aûharmazd; *and* from fat the corpses and dead matter are reduced unto dregs of clay[2] and permanent matter, even with the dust they are mingled *and* become scattered about. 19. Likewise to those dogs, flying creatures, *and* birds they themselves (the waters) have given the corpse-eating quality *and* habit[3], and on account of dull intellect they (the creatures) are not overwhelmed even by that sin.

20. From that fat which is mingled with the living body of a creature of Aûharmazd then *arises* also the assault[4] of the demons, as is shown in the chapter[5] on the reason for showing a dog to a dead *person*, so that the body of those passed *away*, when the gnawers away are mingled with the living body of a creature of Aûharmazd, exhibits a partial resurrection and the tokens *of it*, and thereby the demons keep in it (the living body), and give pain[6] by the will of the sacred beings.

Aûharmazd, purified in the Pûtîk sea, and conveyed through the wide-formed ocean to the well-watered tree of all seeds, whence the falling seeds are brought back, with the misty clouds, and rained upon the earth, to grow there and yield food for cattle and men.

[1] The vital heat, or Vohu-fryãn fire (see Bd. XVII, 1, 2).

[2] Reading gîl-valîgîh (compare Pers. kalîk, 'sediment,' or galîz, 'saliva').

[3] Which they have imbibed by contact with dead matter.

[4] Or 'weapon.'

[5] No such chapter is now extant in Dd., and, therefore, this remark favours the supposition that some chapters are lost between Chaps. XCIII and XCIV. A corpse must be shown to a dog in order that the demon, Nasûs, may be driven out of it by the look, or touch, of the dog (see Sls. II, 1–4, X, 33).

[6] A recognition of the fact that the drinking of impure water, or eating of tainted food, is apt to produce disease.

Chapter XVIII.

1. The seventeenth question is that you ask thus: Is it better when they give *it* to the birds, or what mode is better?

2. The reply is this, that after showing the dog—the reason of which is as declared[1] in its own chapter—they shall carry the corpse at once to the hills and rising ground (vakhsh bûm); and, for the reason that the dogs *and* birds should not bring that dead matter away to a watered, cultivated, *or* inhabited place, *one* is to fasten *it in* the manner of a thief[2]. 3. When the corpse-eating birds have eaten the fat, that fat which, when it is not possible to eat *it*, becomes rotten, offensive, and fraught with noxious creatures, then *men* shall properly convey the bones away to the bone-receptacle (astôdânŏ), which[3] *one* is to elevate so from the ground, *and* over which[4] a roof (â*s*kûpŏ) so stands, that in no way does the rain fall upon the dead matter, nor the water reach up to it therein, nor the damp make up to it therein, nor are the dog and fox able to go to it, and for the sake of light coming to it a hole is made therein.

4. More authoritatively (dastôbarîhâ) it is said that bone-receptacle is a vault (ka*d*akŏ) of solid stone[5], and its covering (nihûmbakŏ) *one* is to

[1] Literally 'as the reason of it is declared.' This is another allusion to the missing chapter mentioned in Chap. XVII, 20.

[2] Reading âhûn khadûînŏ, but this is very likely a corruption of khadûînŏ khadûînŏ, '*in* various modes.'

[3] The MSS. have mûnam, 'which by me.'

[4] The MSS. have min madam, 'from above.'

[5] Whether khadûkŏ-sagakŏ means 'solid rock' or 'solid ashlar' is doubtful.

construct also of a single stone which is cut perforated (sûlâk-hômand), and around it *one* is to fill in with stone and mortar [1].

Chapter XIX.

1. The eighteenth question is that which you ask thus: When the souls of the righteous *and* the souls of the wicked go out to the spirits, will it then be possible for them to see Aûharmazd and Aharman [2], or not?

2. The reply is this, that concerning Aharman it is said that his is no material existence (stîs); *and* Aûharmazd, as a spirit among the spirits, is to be heard by those who are material and those also who are spiritual, *but his* form (kerpô) is not completely visible except through wisdom. 3. And a semblance of *his* power is seen, as *was* told unto Zaratûst the Spîtamân when he saw the result (zah) of his handiwork, and he (Aûharmazd) spoke thus: 'Grasp the hand of a righteous man! for the kindly operation of my religion through [3] thee thyself is as

---

[1] Perhaps the single stone is not to cover the whole space, but merely to contain the opening for light, and to be set in a vaulted roof of ashlar or rubble; otherwise it is not clear where the filling with stone and mortar is to be placed. This bone-receptacle was to be provided for the bones of those corpses which were deposited on the open ground. In the enclosed depositories, used in India, the bone-receptacle is a circular well in the centre, from which the rain does not appear to be excluded (see Sls. II, 6, note).

[2] The evil spirit (see Chap. II, 11), whose nature and powers differ very little from those ascribed to the devil by most Christian writers.

[3] Or 'on;' or, perhaps, it 'is as much as he shall grasp at thee thyself.'

much as he shall grasp, and thou mayst see him whose reception (mâhmânîh) of my wisdom and glory is the most.'

4. And about the souls of the righteous and wicked, in the spiritual places they see the throne (gâs), which they deem a sight of Aûha*r*ma*zd*. 5. And so also those who are domiciled with (hamnemân) Aharman, through that wisdom with reference to whose creator they shall suffer, will understand minutely as regards Aûha*r*ma*zd* and the nature of Aharman (Aharmanîh). 6. And he who is of the righteous is delighted at escaping from Aharman *and* coming to the existence pertaining to Aûha*r*ma*zd*; and they shall offer homage to the glory[1] of Aûha*r*ma*zd*. 7. And he who is wicked, through being deceived by Aharman, and turning from the direction (pe*l*ag) of Aûha*r*ma*zd*, becomes more vexed *and* more penitent; the hope (zahî*s*nŏ) and forgiveness which he possesses, and the retribution *and* manacling which are his among the fiends *and* spirits through his own handiwork, are *by* the permission which comes from the most persistent of the persistent[2] at the period of the resurrection.

---

[1] The word 'glory' is always to be understood in its material sense of 'radiance, effulgence.'

[2] That is, from Aûha*r*ma*zd*. The epithet khvâpar, here translated 'persistent,' appears to mean 'self-sustaining' in the Avesta (see Sls. XXII, 21); traditionally it is supposed to mean 'protecting, cherishing,' but this is merely a guess, though it seems related to Pers. khapârah, 'active,' and may, therefore, often mean 'persevering.'

CHAPTER XX.

1. The nineteenth question is that you ask thus: To what place do the righteous and wicked[1] go?

2. The reply is this, that it is thus said that the souls of those passed *away and* of the dead[2] are three nights on earth; and the first night satisfaction comes to them from *their* good thoughts *and* vexation from *their* evil thoughts, the second night *come* pleasure from *their* good words *and* discomfort and punishment[3] from *their* evil words, *and* the third night *come* exaltation from *their* good deeds *and* punishment from *their* evil deeds[4]. 3. And that third night, in the dawn, they go to the place of account *on* Albûrz[5]; the account *being* rendered they proceed to the bridge[6], and he who is righteous

[1] As K35 inserts the relative î here, some such phrase as 'who are dead' has probably dropped out of the Pahlavi text.

[2] The Parsi books speak of the righteous dead as 'departed,' a term very rarely applied to the wicked (see Chap. XXXII, 4), who are nearly always said 'to die;' the latter verb is, however, occasionally used when speaking of the righteous. This distinction is made even in the Huzvâris logograms, which express the death of the righteous by forms allied to Chald. עֲבַר 'he passed over,' and the death of the wicked by forms allied to Chald. מִית 'he died.'

[3] So in all MSS., but the 'punishment' seems superfluous here.

[4] The Avesta merely states that the soul remains three nights near the body, chanting a particular hymn, and experiencing as much pleasure or uneasiness as it had in the world (see Hn. II, 3-17, III, 3-16); and much the same account is given in AV. IV, 9-14, XVII, 2-9, Mkh. II, 114, 158-160.

[5] The mountain chain which is supposed to surround the world (see Bd. XII, 3); the Av. Hara-berezaiti.

[6] The *K*invad bridge (see Chap. XXI, 2-7), which is said to

passes over the bridge on the ascent (lâlâîh), and if belonging to the ever-stationary (hamîstânîkŏ)[1] he goes thither where their place is, if *along* with an excess of good works *his* habits are correct (frârûn-dâ*d*) *he goes* even unto heaven (vahi*s*tô), and if *along* with an excess of good works *and* correct habits *he has* chanted the sacred hymns (gâsânŏ) *he goes* even unto the supreme heaven (garô*d*mânŏ). 4. He who is of the wicked falls from the lower end (tîh) of the bridge, or from the middle of the bridge; he falls head-foremost to hell, *and* is precipitated (nikûnî-aîtŏ) unto that grade[2] which is *suitable for* his wickedness.

CHAPTER XXI.

1. The twentieth question is that which you ask thus: How are the *K*invad bridge, the Dâîtih peak (*k*akâ*d*), and the path of the righteous and wicked;

---

rest upon the Dâîtih ('judicial') peak, and to pass over to Albûrz (see Bd. XII, 7). According to the Avesta (Vend. XIX, 100, 101, trans. D.) his conscience, in the form of a maiden, 'makes the soul of the righteous one go up above the Hara-berezaiti (Albûrz); above the *K*invad bridge she places it in the presence of the heavenly gods (angels) themselves.' See also AV. V, 1, 2, Mkh. II, 115.

[1] The intermediate place for those not good enough for heaven and not bad enough for hell, where such souls remain in a passive, immovable state till the resurrection (see Sls. VI, 2). It is divided into two parts, according to the author, one for those nearly righteous (see Chap. XXIV, 6), and one for those nearly wicked (see Chap. XXXIII, 2).

[2] Four grades of heaven and four of hell are mentioned in AV. and Mkh. (see Sls. VI, 3, note).

how *are they* when *one* is righteous, and how when *one* is wicked?

2. The reply is this, that thus the high-priests *have* said, that the Dâîtih peak[1] is in Aîrân-vê*g*[2], in the middle of the world; reaching unto the vicinity of that peak is that beam-shaped (dâr-kerpô) spirit, the *K*inva*d* bridge[3], which is thrown *across* from the Albûr*z* enclosure (var) back to the Dâîtih peak. 3. As *it were* that bridge is like a beam of many sides, of whose edges (pôstŏ) there are *some* which are broad, and there are *some* which are thin *and* sharp; its broad sides (sûkîhâ) are so large that its width is twenty-seven reeds (nâî), and its sharp sides are so contracted (tang) that in thinness *it* is just like the edge of a razor. 4. And when the souls of the righteous and wicked arrive it turns to that side which is *suitable to* their necessities, through the great glory of the creator and the command of him who *takes* the just account[4].

5. Moreover, the bridge becomes a broad bridge for the righteous, as much as the height of nine spears (nîzakŏ)—and the length of those which they carry is each separately three reeds[5]—; and

---

[1] The *K*akâ*d*-î Dâîtîk of Bd. XII, 7.

[2] The primeval home of Mazda-worship (see Vend. I, 5, 6), which the Bundahi*s* places 'in the direction of Âdarbî*g*ân;' it is also stated to contain the Dâîtîk or Dâîtih river (which must not be confounded with the Dâîtih peak) and the Dâra*g*a river (on whose bank Zaratû*s*t's father is said to have dwelt), and to have been the scene of Zaratû*s*t's first promulgation of the religion (Bd. XX, 13, 32, XXIX, 12, XXXII, 3). Its winter is likewise described as both long and cold (Vend. I, 8–12, Bd. XXV, 11, 16), which is the case in Âdarbî*g*ân.

[3] See Chap. XX, 3.

[4] The angel Rashnû.

[5] The nine spears of three reeds each, in length, making up the

it becomes a narrow bridge *for* the wicked, even unto a resemblance to the edge of a razor. 6. And he who is of the righteous passes over the bridge, and a worldly similitude of the pleasantness of his path upon it is when thou shalt eagerly and unweariedly walk in the golden-coloured spring, and *with* the gallant (hû-*k*îr[1]) body and sweet-scented blossom in the pleasant skin of that maiden[2] spirit, the price of goodness. 7. He who is of the wicked, as he places a footstep *on* to the bridge, on account of affliction (siparîh) and *its* sharpness, falls from the middle of the bridge, and rolls *over* head-foremost. 8. And the unpleasantness of his path to hell is in similitude such as the worldly *one* in the midst of that stinking *and* dying existence (hastân), there where numbers of the sharp-pointed darts (têzŏ mûk dû*g*ŏ) are planted[3] out inverted and point upwards, and they come unwillingly running; they shall not allow *them* to stay behind, *or* to make delay. 9. So much greater *than* the worldly similitude is that pleasantness and unpleasantness unto the souls, as such as is fit for the spirit is greater than *that* fit for the world.

---

twenty-seven reeds mentioned in § 3. As the reed appears to have been about 4 feet 8 inches (see Chap. XLIII, 5, note), the width of the bridge is supposed to be about 126 feet, and the length of a spear is taken as 14 feet.

[1] So in the MSS., but hû-*k*îhar, 'handsome,' is more probable.

[2] Reading kanîkŏ, instead of the kanâkŏ of the MSS., as there can be no allusion to the evil spirit here. The reference is to a good conscience, which is symbolised by the handsome maiden who is supposed to meet the righteous soul on its way to heaven (see Chap. XXIV, 5).

[3] Assuming that â*g*zast is equivalent to Pers. â*g*ast. The allusion seems to be to a form of torturing punishment (running upon ground studded with sharp points) well known to the author.

Chapter XXII.

1. The twenty-first question is that which you ask thus: When he who is righteous passes away, who has performed much worship of the sacred beings, and many duties and good works, do the spirit of creation, the spirit of the *sacred* ceremony (yazisnŏ) and religion of the Mazda-worshippers, the water, earth, plants, and animals, make complaint unto Aûharmazd, owing to the passing away of him who is righteous, and is it distressing to them when he goes out from the world, or how is it?

2. The reply is this, that *as to* him who is of the righteous, in *his* transit of worldly pain in passing away, and also after passing away to the passage onwards[1] which is his limit (stâr) still in the perplexing account, and, after the account, in his own joy, and in what *occurs* when his gossips (hamvâkân) in the world—by whom the spiritual beings are also not unrecognised, *nor* his position unknown—are in worldly demeanour downcast and grieving, *on all these occasions*[2] *his* thoughts, procuring forgiveness, are about the sacred beings. 3. And the spirit of creation, *and* the good spirit of the religion of the Mazda-worshippers, which are in the worldly *existence*—of which[3] also, in the world, that righteous *one* is a praiser, an employer, a manager, a protection, and a forbearing friend—shall make an outcry to

---

[1] The *K*invad bridge, near which the soul's account is rendered.

[2] The sentence is clear enough in Pahlavi, but too involved to be readily understood in English without these extra words.

[3] The worldly existences which those spirits represent.

the creator about him who is righteous, who is *away* from worldly protection, *also* for the granting of a promoter of forbearance, and *for* a restorer (àvôr*d*âr) of *what* is extorted[1]; *likewise* a petition about the compensatory concomitants as to his new protection and disposer.

4. And the almighty creator responds, *and* allots a teacher[2] for smiting the fiend, for the satisfaction of the righteous, *and* for the protection of the good creatures. 5. As it is said, that in every age a high-priest of the religion and *his* managing of the creatures are made manifest, in whom, in that age, the protection of the creatures and the will of the sacred beings are progressing.

CHAPTER XXIII.

1. The twenty-second question is that which you ask thus: When they shall snatch forth the life from the body of man how does it depart?

2. The reply is this, that *it* is said *to be* in resemblance such as when the redness is drawn up out of a fire; for when the inflammable *material* of a fire is burnt, *and has* remained without glowing[3],

[1] These latter clauses of the outcry refer to their own wants, and the necessity of providing some one to take the place of the deceased; but the final petition seems to be for the deceased himself.

[2] The word may be either farhakhtâkŏ, 'preparing, educating,' or firî*s*tâkŏ, 'sending, deputing,' and must be used as a substantive.

[3] Reading abarî*s* (compare Pers. bar*z*, 'splendour'), or it may be abarâkh, 'sparkless,' if barkh, 'a spark,' be a pure Persian word, which is doubtful.

and when it does not obtain new inflammable *material*, or extinguishing *matter* (nîzâyisnîk) comes upon *it*, its redness *and* heat then depart from it[1]; the life, too, on the departure of the breath (vâdŏ vasakîh), does not stay in the body, *but in* like manner departs.

3. *To* a like purport the high-priests of the religion *have* also said this, that mortals *and* men by listening[2] perceive the time when the spirits shall put a noose (band) on the neck[3]; when his time *has* fully come *one* then conducts him with a companion (pavan ham-bar)[4], and at his falling are the place of death[5] and cause of death; and *having* made lethargy (bûshâsp) deliver him up, and terrified his fever (tapŏ), death (aôsh) seizes decrepitude (zarmân) *away* from him[6].

4. The strength in those intrusted *with him*, and the good proceedings *and* pursuit of means which remain behind[7], giving them strength, are the deter-

---

[1] M14 and J omit the remainder of the sentence.

[2] Reading sinvisnŏ, but by omitting a stroke we should have dânisnŏ, 'knowledge.'

[3] Of a person at the point of death. The demon of death, Astô-vîdâd, is supposed to cast a noose around the necks of the dead to drag them to hell, which only the righteous can throw off (see Bd. III, 21, 22).

[4] That is, the dying man must be conveyed by more than one person, for fear of such contamination by the demon of corruption (at the time of death) as would require the tedious Bareshnûm ceremonial of purification (see Sls. II, 1, 6–8).

[5] And, therefore, the place where his body will rise again at the resurrection (see Sls. XVII, 11–14).

[6] Lethargy, fever, and decrepitude are considered as fiends, but are dispossessed by the mightier demon of death. M14 and J mention 'lethargy,' but omit the after part of the sentence.

[7] Alluding probably to the ceremonies to be ordered and performed by the survivors (see Chap. XXVIII, 6, Sls. XVII, 2–6).

mination (vi*k*îr) which is their own inward physician. 5. And should it be a passing *away* (vi*d*arg) which obtains no light, and on account of their disquietudes *they have* gone to the understanders of remedies for strength for the remedial duties, and the way is closed, he proceeds with insufficiency of means[1]. 6. And the soul of the body, which is the master of *its* house (ka*d*ak khû*d*âî), *along* with the animating life, *goes* out of the impotent body to the immortal souls[2], as a wise master of a house *goes* out of a foreign (anîrânŏ) house to a residence of the good worship.

7. *It was* also told to the ancient learned that life (khayâ) is where there is a living spirit within the soul's body, which is connected with the soul[3], as much as a development (*s*arîtûntanŏ) of the body, and is the life (zîvandakîh) of the soul of a body of *one* passed *away*.

Chapter XXIV.

1. The twenty-third question is that which you ask thus: When he who is righteous passes away, where is the place the soul sits the first night, the second, and the third; and what does it do?

2. The reply is this, that thus it is said, that the

---

[1] That is, when there are doubts about the fate of the soul, and the survivors can obtain no satisfactory assurances from the priesthood, the soul has to proceed to the other world without suitable provision for its happiness.

[2] The MSS. have 'soul.'

[3] M14 and J have 'which is the soul,' and omit the remainder of the sentence.

soul of man, itself the spirit of the body[1], after passing away, is three nights upon earth, doubtful about its own position (gâs)[2], and in fear of the account; and it experiences terror, distress (dahyakŏ), and fear through anxiety about the *K*inva*d* bridge[3]; and as it sits it notices about its own good works *and* sin. 3. And the soul, which in a manner *belongs* to *that* same spirit of the body which is alike experiencing and alike touching it, becomes acquainted by sight with the sin which it *has* committed, and the good works which it *has* scantily done.

4. And the first night from its own good thoughts, the second night from *its* good words, and the third night from *its* good deeds it obtains pleasure for the soul; and if also, with the righteousness, there be sin which remains *in it* as its origin, the first punishment in retribution for the evil deed occurs *that* same third night. 5. The same third night, on the fresh arrival of a dawn[4], the treasurer of good works, like a handsome maiden (kanîkŏ)[5], comes out to meet *it* with the store of its own good works; and, collected by witches (parîkŏ-*k*ind), the sin and crime unatoned for (atôkhtŏ) come on to the account *and* are justly accounted for[6].

[1] The 'spirit of the body' which is to some extent distinguished from the 'soul,' both in this chapter and the next, is probably the life, as described in Chap. XXIII, 7.

[2] That is, its future position, or 'destination.'

[3] See Chap. XXI, 2–7.

[4] Reading dên bâm-1 nuk ayâftŏ.

[5] Fully described in Hn. II, 22–32, AV. IV, 18–35, Mkh. II, 125–139.

[6] The author is more practical than most other writers on the same subject, as he assumes that the righteous soul is not absolutely righteous, nor the wicked soul absolutely wicked.

6. For the remaining (ketrûnd) sin it undergoes punishment *at* the bridge, and the evil thoughts, evil words, and evil deeds are atoned for; and with the good thoughts, good words, and good deeds of its own commendable and pleasing spirit it steps forward unto the supreme heaven (garôdmânô)[1], or to heaven (vahistô), or to the ever-stationary (hamîstânagânŏ) of the righteous[2], there where there is a place for it in righteousness.

Chapter XXV.

1. The twenty-fourth question is that which you ask thus: When he who is wicked shall die, where is the place the soul sits the first night, the second, and the third; and what does it say and do?

2. The reply is this, that those three nights the soul is upon earth, *and* notices about the thoughts, words, and deeds of its own body; *it* is doubtful about its own position, and experiences grievous fear of the account, great terror of the bridge, and perplexing fear on account of hell. 3. Thought is oppressive as an indicator of fear, and the soul, in a manner the spirit of the body, is a computer[3] and acquirer of acquaintance by sight about the good works which it *has* not done, and the sin which it *has* committed.

4. And the first night *it* is hastening *away* from

---

[1] See Chap. XX, 3.

[2] There is another place for the ever-stationary of the wicked (see Chap. XXXIII, 2).

[3] Assuming that angrâîdâr stands for angârîdâr.

its own evil thoughts, the second night from its own evil words, and the third night from its own evil deeds; but, owing to the good works which it has done in the world, the first night the spirit of *its* good thoughts, the second night the spirit of *its* good words, and the third night the spirit of *its* good deeds, come unto the soul, and become pleasing and commendable to it.

5. And the third night, on the fresh arrival of a dawn, its sin, in the frightful, polluted shape of a maiden (*k*aratîk) who is an injurer, comes to meet *it* with the store of its sin; and a stinking northerly[1] wind comes out to meet *it*, and it comes on shudderingly, quiveringly[2], and unwillingly running to the account. 6. And through being deceived and deceiving, heresy (a*v*ârûn-dînôîh), unrelenting and false[3] accusation of constant companions, and the wide-*spread* sinfulness of a fiend-like existence (drû*g*-stihîh) it is ruined, falls from the bridge, *and* is precipitated to hell.

Chapter XXVI.

1. The twenty-fifth question is that which you ask thus: How are the nature of heaven (vahi*s*tô), *and* the comfort and pleasure which are in heaven?

2. The reply is this, that *it is* lofty, exalted, and

[1] The demons are supposed to come from the north, where the gates of hell are situated (see Sls. X, 7).

[2] Reading astô-sîstîhâ nafô-*g*umdânîhâ, which may be, literally, 'with bones started *and* with shaking navel;' but the reading is doubtful.

[3] Literally 'not allowing to hear and false-speaking.'

supreme, most brilliant, most fragrant, and most pure, most *supplied with* beautiful existences, most desirable, and most good, and the place *and* abode of the sacred beings (yazdânŏ). 3. And in it are all comfort, pleasure, joy, happiness (vasîdâgîh), and welfare, more *and* better even than the greatest *and* supremest welfare *and* pleasure in the world; and there is no want, pain, distress, *or* discomfort whatever *in* it; and its pleasantness and the welfare of the angels are from that constantly-beneficial place (gâs), the full *and* undiminishable space (gûng)[1], the good and boundless world.

4. And the freedom of the heavenly from danger from evil in heaven is like unto *their* freedom from disturbance, and the coming of the good angels is like unto *the heavenly ones'* own good works provided. 5. This prosperity (freh-hastŏ) and welfare of the spiritual *existence* is *more* than that of the world, as much as that which is unlimited *and* everlasting is *more* than that which is limited and demoniacal (sêdânîkŏ).

CHAPTER XXVII.

1. The twenty-sixth question is that which you ask thus: How are the nature of hell, *and* the pain, discomfort[2], punishment, and stench of hell?

2. The reply is this, that *it is* sunken, deep, and descending, most dark, most stinking, and most terrible, most *supplied with* wretched existences (anâzîdântûm), and most bad, the place and cave

[1] See Chap. XXXI, 24.

[2] Or 'ingloriousness.'

(grêstakŏ) of the demons and fiends. 3. And in it is no comfort, pleasantness, *or* joy whatever; *but* in it are all stench, filth, pain, punishment, distress, profound evil, and discomfort; and *there* is no resemblance of it whatever *to* worldly stench, filthiness, pain, and evil. 4. And since *there* is no resemblance of the mixed evil of the world to that which is its sole-indicating (aê-numâî) good, *there* is also a deviation (gumisnŏ) of it from the origin and abode of evil[1].

5. And so much more grievous is the evil in hell than even the most grievous evil on earth, as the greatness of the spiritual *existence* is *more* than *that of* the world; and more grievous is the terror of the punishment on the soul than that of the vileness of the demons on the body. 6. And the punishment on the soul is from those whose abode *it has* become[2], from the demons and darkness—a likeness of that evil to hell—the head (kamârakŏ) of whom is Aharman the deadly.

7. And the words of the expressive utterance of the high-priests are these, that where *there* is a fear of every other thing *it* is more than the thing itself, *but* hell is a thing worse than the fear *of it*.

Chapter XXVIII.

1. The twenty-seventh question is that which you ask thus: Why and what is *the ceremony of*

[1] Meaning, probably, that the mixture of good and evil in the world is as far removed from heaven as it is from hell. But the words aê-numâî and gumisnŏ are doubtful both in reading and meaning.

[2] That is, hell has become; reading mân gastŏ.

the three *nights* (satûîh), when during three days they order and perform the sacred-cake ceremony (yazisnŏ drônô) of Srôsh[1]?

2. The reply is this, that the life and soul, when from the realm of the spirit of air[2] they attain unto worldly attire, and have passed into its pain and misfortune, are more sensitive (nâzûktar); owing to their nurture, birth, *and* mission, protection and defence are more desirable and more suitable for the discreet (hû-kîragânîktar); and milk food, and renewed (navagûnak) and constant attention to the fire are requisite[3]. 3. So also when they are ousted from bodily existence, and pain and the eradication of life have come upon them, *they* are *in* like manner more sensitive, and sending them protection and defence from spirits *and* worldly existences is more desirable. 4. And on account of their spiritual character the offering (firîstisnŏ) of gifts *for* the angels, fit for the ritual of a spirit (maînôk nîrangîk), is more presentable; and also a fire newly tended (nôgônd) is that which is more the custom in the *sacred* ceremony (yazisnŏ).

5. *For* the same reason *in* the three days when in connection with the soul the *sacred* ceremony, the burning of fire, *its* cleanly clearance (gôndisnŏ),

---

[1] See Chap. XIV, 4.

[2] Reading min maînôk vâyîh, and assuming that 'the good Vâê' (the Vayô of the Râm Yt.), who is often called the angel Râm, is alluded to (see Chap. XXX, 4, Sls. XI, 4, XVII, 4). The life and soul are treated as one being in this chapter, as all the verbs and pronouns referring to them are in the singular number in the Pahlavi text.

[3] Referring to the proper care of new-born infants, for whose protection from the demons a bright fire is to be kept constantly burning for three days (see Sls. XII, 11, 12).

and other religious *and* ritualistic defence, feeding on milk *and* eating with a spoon[1] are ordered, because—as the *sacred* ceremony, the defence and protection of the worldly existences, is, by order of the creator, the business of Srôsh the righteous[2], and *he* is also one of *those* taking the account in the three *nights*[3]—Srôsh the righteous gives the soul, *for* three days and nights, the place of the spirit of air in the world, and protection. 6. And because of the protectiveness of Srôsh, and *that one* is assisted likewise by Srôsh's taking the account, and for that purpose, are the manifest reasons for performing *and* ordering the ceremony of Srôsh *for* three days and nights[4].

7. And the fourth day the ordering and performing the ceremony of the righteous guardian spirit (ar*d*âî fravar*d*ŏ)[5] are *for* the same soul and the remaining righteous guardian spirits of those who are *and* were *and will* be, from Gâyômar*d* the propitious to Sôshâns the triumphant[6].

Chapter XXIX.

1. The twenty-eighth question is that you ask thus: For what reason is it not allowable to perform

---

[1] No meat is to be eaten by the survivors until the third night has passed away (see Sls. XVII, 2).

[2] The angel Srôsh is said to have been the first creature who performed the sacred ceremony (see Yas. LVI, i, 2–7, ii, 2–4, iii, 2–4), of which the spiritual counterpart was produced by Aûha*r*ma*zd* during the creation (see Bd. II, 9).

[3] See Chap. XIV, 4.

[4] See Sls. XVII, 3.

[5] See Sls. XVII, 5.

[6] That is, from the first man to the last; the phrase is quoted from Yas. XXVI, 33.

the ceremony of Srôsh, the living spirit (ahvô)[1], *along* with other propitiations (shnûmanŏ)[2], when they reverence him separately?

2. The reply is this, that the lord of all *things* is the creator who is persistent over his own creatures, and a precious work is his own true service[3] which is given by him to Srôsh the righteous whom, for this reason, *one* is to reverence separately when even his name is not frequently mentioned, and *one* is not even to reverence the names of the archangels with him.

CHAPTER XXX.

1. The twenty-ninth question is that which you ask thus: The third night, in the light of dawn, what is the reason for consecrating separately the three sacred cakes[4] with three dedications (shnûman)?

2. The reply is this, that one sacred cake, whose dedication is *to* Rashnû *and* Â*s*tâ*d*[5], is for[6] satisfying

---

[1] Probably a miswriting of ashôk, 'righteous.'

[2] Short formulas of praise, reciting all the usual titles of the spirits intended to be propitiated by them, which are introduced into a particular part of the liturgy to dedicate the ceremony to the particular spirit in whose honour it is being performed (see Sls. VII, 8).

[3] Reading bôndakîh; but it may be bûndakîh, 'completeness, perfection.'

[4] The drôn, or sacred cake, is a small flexible pancake which is consecrated in the ceremonies, and dedicated to some particular spirit by means of the shnûman, or propitiatory dedication (see Sls. III, 32).

[5] See Sls. XVII, 4. These two angels are supposed to be present when the soul renders its account; Rashnû weighs its actions in his golden balance, and Â*s*tâ*d* assists it (see AV. V, 3, 5).

[6] Reading râî, instead of lâ, 'not.'

the light of dawn and the period of Aûshahîn[1], because the mountain Aûshdâ*s*târ[2] is mentioned in the propitiation of the angel Â*s*tâ*d*. 3. With Â*s*tâ*d* is the propitiation of the period of Aûshahîn[3], and *she* is the ruler of glory[4] of that time when the account occurs; the souls are in the light of the dawn of Aûshahîn when they go to the account; their passage (vi*d*âr) is through the bright dawn.

4. One sacred cake, which is in propitiation of the good Vâê[5], is, moreover, on this account: whereas the bad Vâê[6] is a despoiler and destroyer, even so the good Vâê is a resister (kûkhshî*d*âr), and likewise encountering the bad Vâê; *he* is also a diminisher (vizû*d*âr) of his abstraction of life,

[1] One of the five periods of the day and night, extending from midnight until the stars disappear in the dawn, or, as some say, until all the fixed stars disappear except four of the first magnitude (see Bd. XXV, 9, Sls. XIV, 4–6).

[2] Called Ushi-dare*n*a in the Avesta, and identified with some mountain in Sagastân in Bd. XII, 15. It is mentioned in the dedicatory formula of Â*s*tâ*d* (see Sîr. 26), and its name is evidently here supposed to mean 'the holder of dawn,' an appropriate term for a lofty mountain to the eastward.

[3] Both Rashnû and Â*s*tâ*d* are blessed in the prayers appointed for the Aûshahîn period of the day.

[4] The 'glory of the Aryans' is lauded in the Â*s*tâ*d* Ya*s*t.

[5] The spirit of air, or angel Râm, who receives and protects the good soul on its way to the other world (see Chap. XXVIII, 2, 5).

[6] Identified with Astô-vîdâ*d*, the demon of death, in Bd. XXVIII, 35, but Pahl. Vend. V, 25, 31 makes him a separate demon, who conveys away the bound soul, which would identify him with the demon Vîzarêsh of Vend. XIX, 94, Bd. XXVIII, 18. There is very little doubt, however, that the Pahlavi translator of Vend. V misunderstood the Avesta, which merely says that 'Astô-vîdhôtu binds him, Vayô conveys him bound,' referring probably to the good Vâê who receives the parting soul; and Pahl. Vend. V, 31 admits that this was the opinion of some.

and a receiver and protection of life, on account of the sacred cake[1].

Chapter XXXI.

1. The thirtieth question is that which you ask thus: When a soul of the righteous goes on to heaven, in what manner does it go; also, who receives it, who leads[2] *it*, and who makes it a household attendant[3] of Aûha*r*ma*zd*? Also, does any one of the righteous in heaven come out to meet it, and shall any thereof make enquiry of it, or how? 2. Shall they also make up an account as to its sin *and* good works, and how is the comfort and pleasantness in heaven shown to it; also, what is its food? 3. *Is it* also their assistance which

[1] Nothing is here said about the third sacred cake, but Sls. XVII, 4 states that this is to be dedicated to the righteous guardian spirit (see Chap. XXVIII, 7).

[2] It is doubtful whether the verb be yezrûn (a corruption of yezderûn) or dezrûn (a corruption of dedrûn), but both forms are traceable to the same Semitic root (דבר), one with and the other without the prefix 'ye,' and both, therefore, have nearly the same meaning.

[3] Reading khavág-î-mân, 'servant of the house' (see also §§ 5, 8, Chaps. XXXII, 7, XXXVII, 16, 17, 21, XLIII, 1, XLVIII, 41). This word occurs in Pahl. Vend. XIX, 102, in a compound which is doubtfully read avîdamânkarânŏ, 'those acting without time, eternal ones,' in Haug's Essays, p. 388 (it should be 'those acting as household attendants'). It also occurs in the Pâzand tract called Aogemadaê*k*â, from its initial word (see Geiger's ed. p. 23, § 11), where it is read a*ñ*dimânî, and translated by Sans. pratîhâra, 'doorkeeper;' but in a Pahlavi version of this tract (which seems to form part of the Âfrîn-i Dahmân, and differs considerably from the Pâzand text) this word is replaced by bôndak mânîk-ı, 'a household servant,' which confirms the reading adopted here.

reaches unto the world, or not? And is the limit (sâmânŏ) of heaven manifest, or what way *is it*?

4. The reply is this, that a soul of the righteous steps forth unto heaven through the strength of the spirit of good works, *along* with the good spirit[1] which is the escort (parvânakŏ) of the soul, into *its* allotted station and the uppermost (tâyîkŏ) which is *for* its own good works; *along* with the spiritual good works, without *those* for the world, and a crown and coronet[2], a turban-sash and a fourfold fillet-pendant[3], a decorated robe (*g*âmakŏ) and suitable equipments, spiritually flying unto heaven (vahis*t*ô), or to the supreme heaven (garô*d*mân), there where its place is. 5. And Vohûman[4], the archangel, makes it a household attendant (khavag-î-mânî-nê*d*ŏ) to Aûha*r*ma*zd* the creator, *and* by order of Aûha*r*ma*zd* announces *its* position (gâs) and reward; *and* it becomes glad to beg for the position of household attendant of Aûha*r*ma*zd*, through what it sees and knows.

6. Aûha*r*ma*zd* the creator of good producers

[1] Probably the good Vâê, the spirit of air (see Chaps. XXVIII, 2, 5, XXIX, 4).

[2] Reading rukhŏ var*d*îvanŏ, which words also occur in AV. XII, 16, XIV, 9. A most elaborate account of heaven and hell will be found in the Book of Ar*d*â Vîrâf with an English Translation, ed. Hôshangji and Haug, 1872.

[3] Reading vâ*s* va *k*ahârakŏ bâlak.

[4] Vend. XIX, 102–107 (trans. D.) states as follows: 'Up rises Vohu-manô from his golden seat; Vohu-manô exclaims: "How hast thou come to us, thou holy one, from that decaying world into this undecaying one?" Gladly pass the souls of the righteous to the golden seat of Ahura Mazda, to the golden seat of the Amesha-spe*n*tas, to the Garô-nmânem, the abode of Ahura Mazda, the abode of the Amesha-spe*n*tas, the abode of all the other holy beings.'

(dahâkân) is a spirit even among spirits, and spirits even *have* looked for a sight of him; which spirits are manifestly above worldly existences[1]. 7. But when, through the majesty[2] of the creator, spirits put on worldly appearances (vênisnŏîhâ), or are attending (sinâyânîkŏ) to the world and spirit, and put away appearance (vênisnŏ apadô*g*ênd), then he whose patron spirit (ahvô)[3] is in the world is able to see the attending spirits, in such similitude as when they see bodies in which is a soul[4], or when they see a fire in which is Varahrân[5], or see water in which is its own spirit[6]. 8. Moreover, in that household attendance, *that* Aûha*r*ma*zd has* seen the soul is certain, for Aûha*r*ma*zd* sees all *things;* and many even of the fiend's souls[7], who are put away from those of Aûha*r*ma*zd* in spiritual understanding, are delighted by the appearance (numû*d*anŏ) of those of Aûha*r*ma*zd.*

9. And the righteous in heaven, who have been

---

[1] Implying that Aûha*r*ma*zd* can hardly be considered visible, except by the eye of faith (see Chap. XIX, 2).

[2] Assuming that rabâ-vânagîh is equivalent to Pers. buzurgânagî, 'magnificence.'

[3] The ahvô (Av. ahû) seems to be a spiritual protector, somewhat similar to a patron saint; as, according to the Ahunavar, the most sacred formula of the Parsis (see Bd. I, 21, Zs. I, 12-19), both an ahû and a ratu are to be chosen, that is, both a patron spirit and a high-priest.

[4] That is, he sees the spirits by means of their material manifestations.

[5] The old Pahl. form of Vâhrâm, the angel whose name is applied to the sacred fire (see Bd. XVII, 1, 2, 9); he is the Av. Verethraghna of the Bahrâm Yt.

[6] The female angel of water is the Av. ardvî sûra Anâhita of the Âbân Yt.

[7] The souls in hell.

his intimate friends, of the same religion and like goodness, speak to him *of* the display of affection, the courteous enquiry, and the suitable eminence from coming to heaven, and his everlasting well-being in heaven.

10. And the account as to sin and good works does not occur unto the heavenly *ones; it is* itself among the perplexing questions of this treatise, for the taking of the account and the atonement for the sins of a soul of those passed *away and* appointed unto heaven happen so [1], although its place (gâs) is there [2] until the renovation *of the universe,* and *it has* no need for a new account. 11. And that account is at the time the account occurs; *those* taking the account are Aûharmazd, Vohûman, Mitrô, Srôsh, and Rashnû, and they shall make up the account of all with justice, each one at his own time, as the reply is written in its own chapter [3].

12. *As to* that which you ask concerning food, the meals of the world are *taken* in two ways: one is the distribution of water in haste, and one is with enjoyment (aûrvâzisnŏ) to the end; *but* in heaven there is no haste as to water, and rejoicing with much delight *they* are like unto those who, as worldly beings, make an end of a meal of luxury (aûrvâzisnîkîh). 13. To that also *which* is the spiritual completion of the soul's pleasure *it* is attaining in like proportion [4], and in its appearance to worldly beings *it* is a butter of the name of Maîdyôk-zarem [5]. 14. And the reason of

[1] As in Chap. XXIV, 5, 6.
[2] In heaven.
[3] See Chap. XIV, 2–5.
[4] This sentence is rather ambiguous in the original.
[5] Said to be the food of the souls in heaven (see Hn. II, 38,

that name of it is this, that of the material food in the world that which is the product of cattle is said *to be* the best (pâshûm), among the products of cattle *in use* as food is the butter of milk, and among butters that is extolled as to goodness which they shall make *in* the second month of the year[1], and when Mitrô[2] is in the constellation Taurus; as that month is scripturally (dînôîkŏ) called Zaremêyâ[3], the explanation of the name to be accounted *for* is this, that its worldly representative (andâzakŏ) is the best food in the world.

15. And *there* is no giving out of assistance *by* the soul of the righteous from heaven and the supreme heaven[4]; for, *as to* that existence full

Mkh. II, 152); it is to be distinguished from the draught of immortality, called Hûsh, which is prepared from the fat of the ox Hadhayôs and the white Hôm at the time of the resurrection (see Bd. XXX, 25).

[1] If the writer refers to the correct solar year of Bd. XXV, 21, beginning at the vernal equinox, the second month would be 19th April–19th May when the sun is in the conventional sign of Taurus; but the ordinary Parsi year in his time commenced in the middle of April, and its second month would be May–June when the sun (about A.D. 880) would be in the actual constellation of Taurus. So that the statements in the text afford no certain indication of the particular calendar used by the author.

[2] The angel of the sun's light, here used for the sun itself.

[3] The fifteenth day of the second month of the Parsi year is the season festival called Maidhyô-zaremaya, 'mid-verdure,' in the Avesta; being also the middle of the second month, the author assumes that the name of that month was originally Zaremaya. The Pahl. word can also be read Zar-mâh, 'the month of gold, or the green month.'

[4] That is, there is no intercession of saints for those still in the world. The only interceders are the angels and guardian spirits, and they go no further than to obtain strict justice for every one according to his worldly merits.

of joy, *there* is then no deserving of it for *any* one unless each one is fully worthy of it. 16. But the soul has a remembrance of the world and worldly people, *its* relations *and* gossips; and he who is unremembered and unexpecting (abarmarva*d*) is undisturbed, and enjoys in his own time all the pleasure of the world as it occurs in the renovation *of the universe*, and wishes to attain to it. 17. And, in like manner, of the comfort, pleasure, and joy of the soul, which, *being* attained in proportion, they cause to produce in heaven and the supreme heaven, its own good works of every kind are a comfort and pleasure such as *there* are in the world from a man who is a wise friend—he who is a reverent worshipper—and other educated men, to her who is a beautiful, modest, *and* husband-loving woman — she who is a manager (ârâstâr) under protection—and other women who are clever producers of advantage[1]. 18. This[2], too, *which arises* from beasts of burden, cattle, wild beasts, birds, fish, and other species of animals; this, too, from luminaries, fires, streams (hû-ta*g*is-nân), winds, decorations, metals, and coloured earths; this, too, which is from the fences (pardakânŏ) of grounds, houses, *and* the primitive lands of the well-yielding *cattle;* this[3], too, which is from rivers, fountains, wells, *and* the primary species of water; this, too, which is from trees and shrubs, fruits, grain, and fodder salads, aromatic herbs, *and* other plants; this, too, which is

[1] Reading sû*d* â*z* kârânŏ, and identifying the second word with Pers. â*z*.

[2] That is, the pleasure.

[3] This clause is omitted in M14 and J.

the preparation of the land for these[1] creatures *and* primitive creations; this, too, from the species of pleasant tastes, smells, and colours of all natures, the producers of protections[2], the patron spirits (ahûân), and the appliances of the patron spirits, can come unto mortals.

19. And what the spirit of good works is in similitude is expressly a likeness of stars and males, females and cattle, fires and sacred fires, metals of every kind, dogs, lands, waters, *and* plants[3]. 20. The spiritual good works are attached (a*v*a-yûkhtô) to the soul, and in the degree and proportion which are their strength, due to the advancement of good works by him who is righteous, *they* are suitable as enjoyment for him who is righteous. 21. He obtains durability thereby[4] and necessarily preparation, conjointly *with* constant pleasure and without a single day's vexation (ayôm-aê-bêshîhâ).

22. There is also an abundant joyfulness, of which no example is appointed (vakhtô) in the world from the beginning, but it comes thus to those who are heavenly ones *and* those of the supreme heaven; and of which even the highest worldly happiness and pleasure are no similitude, except through the possession of knowledge which is said *to be* a sample *of it* for worldly beings.

---

[1] It is doubtful whether we should read le-denmanshânŏ, a rare plural form of denman, 'this,' or whether it should be le-denman yaz*d*ânŏ; in the latter case the translation would be 'for these creatures of the sacred beings.'

[2] Assuming that zinharânŏ stands for zinhârânŏ, otherwise we must read zôharânŏ, 'holy-waters.'

[3] The chief objects benefited by good works.

[4] Reading hangâmîh-ash, but the construction is unusual.

23. And of *its* indications by the world the limited with the unlimited, the imperishable with perishableness, the consumable with inconsumableness are then no equivalent similitudes of it[1]. 24. And *it is* the limited, perishable, and consumable *things* of the world's existence which are the imperishable *and* inconsumable *ones* of the existence of endless light[2], the indestructible *ones* of the all-beneficial and ever-beneficial space (gûn*g*)[3], and the all-joyful *ones*—without a single day's vexation—of the radiant supreme heaven (garô*d*mânô). 25. And the throne (gâs) of the righteous in heaven and the supreme heaven is the reward he obtains first, and is his until the resurrection, when even the world becomes pure *and* undisturbed; *he* is himself unchangeable thereby, *but* through the resurrection he obtains what is great and good and perfect, *and* is eternally glorious.

Chapter XXXII.

1. The thirty-first question is that which you ask thus: When he who is wicked goes to hell, how

---

[1] Meaning that no adequate conception can be obtained of the enjoyments of heaven by contrasting the earthly objects which most resemble it with those most opposed to it.

[2] The place of Aûha*r*ma*zd*, or heaven in general (see Bd. I, 2), where things which are perishable on earth become everlasting.

[3] The 'constantly-beneficial place' of Pahl. Vend. XIX, 122, 'which is self-sustained, (its constant beneficialness is this, that, when it once became *so*, all of it became thereby ever-beneficial).' The Avesta version (trans. D.) merely calls it 'the sovereign place of eternal weal;' and it appears from Chap. XXXVII, 22, 24 that it is here understood as the unlimited space of heaven, contained in the 'endless light.'

does he go, *and in* what manner does he go; also, who comes to meet him, and who leads him[1] to hell; also, does any one of the infernal ones (dû*s*a-h̦ûîkânŏ) come to meet him, or how is it? 2. Shall they also inflict punishment upon him, for the sin which he *has* committed, at once, or is his punishment the same until the future existence? 3. Also, what is their food in hell, and of what description are their pain *and* discomfort; *and* is the limit of hell manifest, or how is it?

4. The reply is this, that a soul of the wicked, the fourth night after passing away[2], *its* account *being* rendered, rolls head-foremost and totters (kapînê*d*ŏ) from the *K*inva*d* bridge[3]; and Vîzarâsh[4], the demon, conveys (nâye*d*ŏ)[5] him cruelly bound therefrom, and leads him unto hell. 5. And with him are the spirits *and* demons connected with the sin of that *soul*, watching in many guises, resembling the very producers of doubt (vîman-dâ*d*ârân-i*k*), the wounders, slayers, destroyers, deadly ones, monsters (dû*s*-gerpânŏ), and criminals,

[1] M14 and J omit the words from 'also' to 'leads him.'

[2] The term 'passing away' is here used with reference to the death of a wicked person, contrary to the general rule (see Chap. XX, 2).

[3] See Chap. XX, 3.

[4] 'Then the fiend, named Vîzaresha, carries off in bonds the souls of the wicked Daêva-worshippers who live in sin' (Vend. XIX, 94, trans. D.); see also Bd. XXVIII, 18, where the name is Vîza-rêsh, but it is always Vîzarâsh in Dd. Here it has been first miswritten in K35, and afterwards corrected, so that later copyists have read Vîrâsh, as in M14 and J.

[5] Identifying the verb with Av. nayêiti of Vend. V, 25, 31; or it may be read vâye*d*ŏ, and identified with Av. vayêiti of Vend. XV, 17, or Av. vâdhayêiti of Vend. XIX, 94, without much change of meaning.

those *who* are unseemly, those, too, *who* are diseased *and* polluted, biters and tearers, noxious creatures, windy stenches, glooms, fiery stenches, thirsty ones, those of evil habits, disturbers of sleep (khvâp-khârân), and other special causers of sin and kinds of perverting, with whom, in worldly semblance, are the spiritual causers of distress. 6. And proportional *to* the strength *and* power which *have* become theirs, owing to his sin, they surround him uncomfortably, and make him experience vexation, even unto the time of the renovation *of the universe*. 7. And through the leading of Vîzarâsh[1] he comes unwillingly unto hell, becomes a household attendant (khavag-î-mânôî-aîtŏ) of the fiend and evil *one*, is repentant of the delusion of a desire for fables (vardakîhâ), is a longer for *getting* away from hell to the world, and *has* a wonderful desire for good works.

8. And his food is as a sample of those which are among the most fetid, most putrid, most polluted, and most thoroughly unpleasant; and *there* is no enjoyment and completeness *in* his eating, but he shall devour (*g*a*l*â*d*) with a craving which keeps him hungry and thirsty, due to water *which* is hastily *sipped*[2]. 9. Owing to that vicious habit *there* is no satisfaction therefrom, but it increases his haste and the punishment, rapidity, and tediousness of his anguish.

10. The locality[3] in hell is not limited (sâmânî-

---

[1] See § 4.

[2] Referring to the fact that a person who is both hungry and thirsty cannot quench his thirst, for more than a few minutes, by drinking water without eating.

[3] Or, perhaps, 'his position,' if we read dîvâk-a*s* instead of

aît) before the resurrection, *and* until the time of the renovation *of the universe he* is in hell. 11. Also out of his sin is the punishment connected *with it*, and that punishment comes upon him, from the fiend *and* spirit of his own sin, in that manner and proportion with which he *has* harassed and vexed *others*[1], and *has* reverenced, praised, and served that which is vile.

12. And at the time of the renovation, when the fiend perishes, the souls of the wicked pass into melted metal (ayênô)[2] *for* three days; and all fiends and evil thoughts, which are owing to their sin, have anguish effectually, and are hurried *away* by the cutting and breaking *away* of the accumulation (ham-dâ*d*akîh) of sin of the wicked souls. 13. And by that pre-eminent (a*v*artûm) ablution in the melted metal they are thoroughly purified from guilt and infamy (dastŏ va raspakŏ), and through the perseverance (khvâparîh)[3] and mercifulness of the pre-eminent persistent ones they are pardoned, and become most saintly (môgtûm) pure ones; as it is said in metaphor that the pure are *of* two kinds, one which is glorious (khvârvatô), *and* one which is metallic (ayênavatô)[4].

dîvâkîh, but the former reading would be more of a modern Persian idiom than a Pahlavi one.

[1] Or, '*the good;*' the word is not expressed in the Pahlavi text.

[2] Bd. XXX, 20 states that both the righteous and wicked are finally purified by melted metal which is a torment to the latter, but only like a bath in warm milk to the former.

[3] See Chap. XIX, 7 n.

[4] This is probably a misapplication of a Pahlavi phrase which contained the word âsnavatô, 'indestructible,' and was the translation of an Avesta passage containing the words *hv*âthrava*nd*, 'brilliant, glorious,' and âsna, 'stony, indestructible, enduring' (often translated 'heavenly'), which words are sometimes used together

14. And after that purification *there* are no demons, no punishment, *and* no hell as regards the wicked, and their disposal (vîrâstakŏ) also is just; they become righteous, painless, deathless, fearless, and free from harm. 15. And with them comes the spirit of the good works which were done *and* instigated by them in the world, and procures them pleasure and joy in the degree and proportion of those good works. 16. But the recompense of a soul of the righteous is a better formation (vêh-dâdîh) and more[1].

Chapter XXXIII.

1. *As to* the thirty-second question and reply, that which you ask is thus: In which direction and which land is hell, and how is it?

2. The reply is this, that the place of a soul of the wicked, after the dying off[2] of the body, is in three districts (vîmand): one of them is called *that* of the ever-stationary[3] of the wicked, and it is a

as in Yas. LIX, 14. As the Pahl. âsnavatô and ayênavatô are written alike they are easily confounded, but that 'metal' is meant here appears from Yas. L, 9, b, Bd. XXX, 20.

[1] M14 has 'and the position of more good works is better, the rank is greater, and the pleasure *and* delight more.'

[2] Literally 'dying down.'

[3] Assuming that ham-hastakân, 'co-existences, associates,' is meant for hamîstakân (see the hamîstânîkŏ of Chap. XX, 3). From this it would appear that the place of the Hamîstakân, intermediate between heaven and h ll, was itself supposed by the author to be divided into two widely separated regions, one for the slightly righteous (see Chap. XXIV, 6), and one for the slightly wicked, as here described. No such separation is mentioned in AV. and Mkh., and the passage is omitted in M14.

chaos (gûmêzakŏ), but the evil is abundantly and considerably more than the good; and the place is terrible, dark, stinking, and grievous *with* evil. 3. And one is that which is called the worst existence, and it is there the first tormentors (vîkhrunîgânŏ) and demons have *their* abode; it is full of evil and punishment, and there is no comfort and pleasure whatever. 4. And one is called Drûgâskân[1], and is at the bottom of the gloomy existence, where the head (kamârâkŏ) of the demons rushes; there is the populous abode of all darkness and all evil.

5. These three places, collectively, are called hell, *which* is northerly, descending, and underneath this earth, even unto the utmost declivity of the sky; and its gate is in the earth, a place of the northern quarter, and is called the Arezûr ridge[2], a mountain which, among its fellow mountains of the name of Arezûr[3] that are amid the rugged (kôfîk) mountains, is said in revelation[4] *to have* a great fame with the demons, and the rushing together and assembly of the demons in the world are on the summit of that mountain, *or* as it is called 'the head of Arezûr.'

[1] The Av. drugaskanãm of Vend. XIX. 139, which is translated 'the slothful ones of the Drug' by Darmesteter, 'the servants of the Drug' by Harlez, and 'wizards' in Haug's Essays, p. 336. Drûgâskân is said to be a son of the evil spirit in Bd. XXXI, 6.

[2] See Bd. XII, 8.

[3] Bd. XII, 16 mentions another Arezûr 'in the direction of Arûm.'

[4] Vend. XIX, 142 (trans. D.) says 'they run away casting the evil eye, the wicked, evil-doing Daêvas: "Let us gather together at the head of Arezûra!"'

CHAPTER XXXIV.

1. *As to* the thirty-third question and reply, that which you ask is thus: In what manner is there one way of the righteous from the Dâîtih peak[1] to heaven, and one of the wicked to hell; and *what is* their nature?

2. The reply is this, that one is for ascent, and one for descent; and on account of both being of one appearance I write thus much for understanding and full explanation, that is to say:—3 The righteous souls pass over on the *K*invad bridge[2] by spiritual flight and the power of good works; *and* they step forth up to the star, or to the moon, or to the sun station, or to the endless light[3]. 4. The soul of the wicked, owing to *its* falling *from* the bridge, its lying demon, and the pollution collected by its sin, they shall lead therefrom to the descent into the earth, as both ways *lead* from that bridge on the Dâîtih peak.

CHAPTER XXXV.

1. The thirty-fourth question is that which you ask thus: Does this world become quite without men[4], so that *there* is no bodily existence in *it* what-

---

[1] See Chap. XXI, 2. [2] See Chap. XXI, 2–7.

[3] These are the four grades of heaven, as described in AV. VII–X, Mkh. VII, 9–11.

[4] Reading a*v*îk (or a*v*ih) anshûtâ, but it may possibly be a*v*î-1 anshûtâ, 'without a single man.'

ever, and then shall they produce the resurrection, cr how is it?

2. The reply is this, that this world, continuously from *its* immaturity even unto *its* pure renovation, *has* never been, and also *will* not be, without men; and *in* the evil spirit, the worthless (as*a*pîr), no stirring desire of this arises. 3. And near to the time of the renovation the bodily existences desist from eating, and live without food (pavan akhûris-nîh)[1]; and the offspring who are born from them are those of an immortal, for they possess durable and blood-exhausted (khûn-girâî) bodies. 4. Such are *they* who are the bodily-existing men that are in the world when there are men, passed *away*, who rise again and live again.

Chapter XXXVI.

1. The thirty-fifth question is that which you ask thus: Who are they who are requisite in producing the renovation *of the universe*, who were they, *and* how are they?

2. The reply is this, that of those assignable for that most perfect work the statements recited are lengthy, for even Gâyômar*d*, Yim the splendid, Zaratûst the Spîtamân[2], the *spiritual* chief (ra*d*ŏ) of the righteous, and many great thanksgivers *were*

---

[1] Bd. XXX, 3 states that men first abstain from meat, afterwards from vegetables and milk, and, finally, from water.

[2] See Chap. II, 10. His title, which is nearly always written Spîtamân in K35 (rarely Spîtâmân), is Av. spitama or spitâma, but is usually understood to mean 'descendant of Spitama,' his ancestor in the ninth generation (see Bd. XXXII, 1).

appointed for completing the appliances of the renovation; and their great miracles and successful (a*v*a*k*îragânîk) management *have* moved on, which works for the production of the renovation[1]. 3. Likewise, on the approach of the renovation, Keresâsp[2] the Sâmân who smites Dahâk, Kaî-Khûsrôî[3] who *was* made to pass *away* by Vâê the long-continuing lord[4], Tûs and Vêvan[5] the allies (a*v*âkânŏ), *and* many other mighty doers are aiding the production of the renovation.

4. But those who are the producers of the renovation more *renowned* throughout the spheres (vâspôharakânîktar) are said *to be* seven, whose names are Rôshanô-*k*ashm[6], Khûr-*k*ashm, Frâda*d*-gadman,

---

[1] That is, even these ancient rulers and legislators have contributed to the final renovation of the universe by their wise actions and laws.

[2] See Chap. XVII, 6.

[3] Av. Kavi Husravangh, the third king of the Kayânian dynasty (see Bd. XXXI, 25, XXXIV, 7), whose mysterious disappearance, as related in the Shâhnâmah, is evidently alluded to here.

[4] The Av. vayãm dareghô-*hv*adhâitîm of Khûrshêd Nyâyish, 1, that seems to be identified here with the good Vâê (see Chap. XXX, 4), who conducts the soul to the other world.

[5] The Tûs and Gîw of Bd. XXIX, 6 and the Shâhnâmah, where they are said to have been frozen in the mountain snow, with other warriors, after the disappearance of Kaî-Khûsrôî. They are the Av. Tusa of Âbân Yt. 53, 58, and, perhaps, Gaêvani of Fravardîn Yt. 115, but the Pahlavi form Vêvan (or Vîvô) of our text is inconsistent with the latter identification; the form Gîw of Bd. XXIX, 6 is merely Pâzand.

[6] These names are the Av. Rao*k*as-*k*aêshman, Hvare-*k*aêshman, Frâda*d*-*hv*arenô, Vareda*d*-*hv*arenô, Vouru-nemô, Vouru-savô, and Saoshyãs of Fravardîn Yt. 128, 129, partly transcribed, partly translated, and partly corrupted into Pahlavi. The corruptions are easily explained thus: Av. vouru, 'wide,' when written in Pahlavi is often identical with varen, 'desire,' and has been so read by a later copyist and then translated by its synonym kâmak; Av.

Vâredad-gadman, Kâmak-vakhshisn, Kâmak-sûd, and Sôshâns. 5. As it is said that in the fifty-seven years[1], which are the period of the raising of the dead, Rôshanô-kashm in Arzâh[2], Khûr-kashm in Savâh, Frâdad-gadman in Fradadâfsh, Vâredad-gadman in Vîdadâfsh, Kâmak-vakhshisn in Vôrûbarst, *and* Kâmak-sûd in Vôrûgarst, while Sôshâns in the illustrious *and* pure Khvanîras is connected with them, are immortal. 6. The completely good sense, perfect hearing, and full glory of those seven producers of the renovation are so miraculous that they converse from region unto region, every one together with the six *others*, just as now men at an interview utter words of conference and co-operation with the tongue, one to the other, and can hold a conversation[3].

7. The same perfect deeds for six[4] years in the six *other* regions, and for fifty years in the illustrious Khvanîras[5], prepare immortality, and set going ever-

nemô is translated by Pahl. nîyâyisn, 'homage, praise,' which is written very much like vakhshisn, 'increase,' and has been so read by a later copyist. For the first two names and the last see Chap. II, 10.

[1] The same period is mentioned in Bd. XXX, 7.

[2] That is, there is one of the seven producers of the renovation in each of the seven Kêshvars, or regions of the earth, of which Arzâh is the western, Savâh the eastern, Fradadâfsh and Vîdadâfsh the two southern, Vôrûbarst and Vôrûgarst the two northern, and Khvanîras the central one (see Bd. V, 8, 9, XI, 2-4).

[3] If this passage were found in the Christian scriptures, it would very probably be considered as a prophetical allusion to the electric telegraph and telephone.

[4] So in all MSS., but one would expect it to be 'seven,' so as to complete the fifty-seven years of § 5. The number being written in ciphers the difference between 'six' and 'seven' is very slight.

[5] This central region of the earth is that which contains Irân and all lands well known to the Irânians.

lasting life and everlasting weal (sûdîh) through the help and power and glory of the omniscient *and* beneficent spirit, the creator Aûharmazd.

Chapter XXXVII.

1. *As to* the thirty-sixth question and reply, that which you ask is thus: How shall they produce the resurrection, how do they prepare the dead, and when the dead are prepared by them, how are they? 2. When it is produced by them, is an increase in the brilliance of the stars, moon, and sun necessary, *and* does it arise, or not? are *there* seas, rivers, *and* mountains, or not? and is the world just as large as this, or does it become more *so* and wider?

3. The reply is this, that the preparation and production of the resurrection are an achievement *connected* with miracle, a sublimity (rabâîh), and, afterwards, also a wondrous appearance unto the creatures who are uninformed. 4. The secrets and affairs of the persistent creator are like every mystery and secret; excepting himself—he who is *capable* of all knowledge, the fully-informed, and all in all (vispânŏ vispô)—no one of the worldly beings and imperfect spirits *has* known them.

5. A true proverb (gôbisnŏ-gô) of the intelligent *and* worldly, which is obvious, is that as it is easier in teaching to teach again learning *already* taught *and* forgotten than that which *was* untaught, and easier to repair again a well-built house, given gratuitously, than that *which* is not *so* given, so also the formation *again* of that which *was* formed is more excellent (hunîrtar), and the wonder is

less, than the creation of creatures. 6. And through the wisdom and glory *of* the omniscient and omnipotent creator, by whom the saddened (âlîkhtŏ) creatures *were* created, that which *was* to perish is produced again anew, *and that which was* not to perish, except a little, is produced handsome even for a creation of the creator[1].

7. He who is a pure, spiritual creature is made unblemished; he, also, who is a worldly creature is immortal and undecaying, hungerless and thirstless, undistressed and painless; while, though he moves (*g*undê*d*ŏ) in a gloomy, evil existence, the fiend is rightly judging from *its* arrangement (min nivâr*d*ŏ) *that it* is not the place of a beneficent *being*, but the place of an existence *which* is deadly, ignorant, deceiving, full of malice, seducing, destroying, causing disgrace, making unobservant (aûbêngar), and full of envy. 8. And his existence is so full of malice, deceit, seductiveness, unobservance, destructiveness, and destruction that *he has* no voice except for accomplices (ham-bû*d*îkân) and antagonists, except also for his own *creatures and* gossips when *their* hearts are desirous of evil, seducing, destroying, making unobservant, causing malice, *and* bearing envy. 9. And *he* is disclosed (vishâ*d*) from his own origin and abyss full of darkness, unto the limits of darkness *and* confines of the luminaries; and in his terribleness and demoniacal deliberation he gazes at the unblemished light and creatures of the beneficent Aûha*r*ma*z*d. 10. And through abundant envy and complete maliciousness is his lying; and he mounts (sûbârê*d*ŏ) to seize, destroy,

[1] This last clause is omitted in M14 and J.

render unobservant, and cause to perish *these* same well-formed creatures of the sacred beings. 11. And owing to his observance of falsehood he directed falsehood *and* lies with avidity (varenô), which were necessary for obtaining his success in his own rendering *others* unobservant (aûbênŏ); even in the nine thousand winters (hazangrôk zîm)[1] of falsehood that which is disregarded therein is his own falsity.

12. He who is the most lordly of the lords of the pre-eminent luminaries, and the most spiritual of spirits, and all *the beings* of Aûharmazd the creator—who was himself capable of an effectual (tûbânŏ) gain for every scheme of his[2]—do not allow that fiend into the interior, into the radiance (farôgîd) of the luminaries. 13. And *they*[3] understood through *their* own universal wisdom that fiend's thoughts[4] of vileness, *and* meditation of falsehood

---

[1] The interval between the first appearance and the final disappearance of the evil spirit. Twelve thousand years are supposed to elapse between the first creation and the resurrection; during the first three (about B.C. 8400–5400) the creation remains undisturbed in a spiritual state, during the next three (B.C. 5400–2400) the evil spirit appears, but flies back to hell in confusion, during the next three (B.C. 2400–A.D. 600) he attacks the creation and keeps it in a constant state of tribulation, and during the last three (A.D. 600–3600) his power, having attained its maximum, is gradually weakened till it is finally destroyed at the resurrection (see Bd. I, 8, 18, 20, 22, III, 1, XXXIV, 1–9, Byt. III, 11, 44, 52, 61, 62).

[2] Probably 'the fiend,' but the sentence is by no means clear.

[3] As the verbs 'allow' in § 12 and 'accept' in § 13 are both plural we must understand that the opposition to the fiend arises from the spiritual creatures of Aûharmazd, and not from Aûharmazd alone.

[4] Reading mînishnŏ instead of maînôgânŏ, 'spirits;' the difference between these words in Pahlavi being only a single stroke.

and lies, and became aware *of them* by themselves and through their own intuition, and shall not accept the perdition (aôshîh) of the fiend, *but* are to be rightly listening to the commands of him[1] who is worthy. 14. For his[2] is not the nature of him who is good, *nor* the wisdom of him who is propitious; and he does not turn from the confines of the shining ones, and the developments pertaining to those of the good *being*[3], until he arrives at the creatures; and he struggles in an attempt (aûzmânŏ), spreads forth into the sky, is mobbed (garôhagî-aît) in combats, is completely surrounded, *and* is tested *with* perfect appliances. 15. His resources, also, are destroyed, *his* internal[4] vigour is subdued, *his* weapons of falsehood are disregarded, and *his* means of deceiving shall perish; and with completeness of experience, thorough painfulness, routed troops, broken battle-array, and disarranged means he enjoys on the outside the radiance of the luminaries with the impotence (anaîyyâragîh) of a desire which again returns to him.

16. And the same well-shining light of all kinds of the creator, when they shall not let in him who is Aharman, shall remain an unlimited time, *while* the fiend is in household attendance on those of the frontier through not being let in, *and* constantly troubled at the everlasting creatures. 17. The household attendance of the fiend seemed to it[5] perpetually afflicting; and also the previous struggle

[1] Aûha*r*ma*z*d. [2] The fiend's.

[3] Reading vêhîkânakŏ vakhshi*s*nŏ.

[4] Assuming that andarmûnîh is a form analogous to pîrâmûnîh, and with the meaning of andarûnîh.

[5] The light.

of the fiend when the celestial spirit (ahvô) *pertaining* to the luminaries *was* not contended *with* by him, *his* defeat (makhîtûntanŏ) when the luminaries *were* not defeated by him, *his* infliction of punishment before sin, and *his* causing hatred before hatred *exists* are all recounted by it to the justice and judiciousness whose unchangeableness, will, persistence, and freedom from hatred—which is the character of its faithful ones—are not so[1], to him who is the primeval (pê*s*akŏ) creator.

18. The fiend, after *his* falsity, the struggle—on account of the fighting of the shining ones *and* the decreed keeping *him* away which *was* due to the fighter for the luminaries—*and* the ill-success of the struggle of himself and army, ordered the beating back of the worthy fighter *against* destruction, the malicious avenging again of the causer of hatred, *and* the destroyer's internal vileness and disorganisation anew of his own place. 19. He saw the beneficent actions by which, through the wisdom of Aûha*r*ma*zd*, the spiritual wisdom[2], within the allotted (burîn-hômônd) time, the limited space, the restricted conflict, the moderate trouble, *and* the definite (far*g*âm-hômand) labour *existing*, struggles against the fiend, who is the unlawful establisher *of* the wizard; and he returned inside to fall disarmed (asâmânŏ) *and* alive, *and* until he shall be fully tormented (pûr-dar*d*ag-hâe) and shall be thoroughly experienced, they shall not[3] let *him* out again in the allotted time that the fiend ordered *for* the success of falsehood *and* lies. 20.

---

[1] That is, they are altogether different from the faults of the fiend, just recounted.

[2] Perhaps the same as 'the spirit of wisdom' of Mkh.

[3] Reading lâ, 'not,' instead of râî, 'on account of.'

And the same fiend *and* the primeval (kâdmôn) demons are cast out confusedly, irreverently, sorrowfully, disconcertedly, fully afflicting *their* friends, thoroughly experienced, even with their falsehoods and not inordinate means[1], with lengthy slumbers, with broken-down (a*v*asîst) deceits and dissipated resources, confounded and impotent, into the perdition of Aharman, the disappearance of the fiend, the annihilation of the demons, and the non-existence of antagonism.

21. To make the good creatures again fresh and pure, *and* to keep *them* constant and forward in pure and virtuous conduct is to render *them* immortal; and the not letting in of the co-existent *one*[2], owing to the many new assaults (pa*dg*astŏîh) that *occur* in his perpetual household attendance[3] of falsity—through which *there* would have been a constant terror of light for the creatures of the sacred beings—is to maintain a greater advantage. 22. And his (Aûha*r*ma*zd*'s) means are not the not letting in *of the fiend*, but the triumph arranged for him*self* in the end—the endless[4], unlimited light *being* also produced by him, and the constantly-beneficial space[5]

---

[1] The words va avi*g*âftŏ afzârîhâ are omitted in M14 and J.

[2] The evil spirit. As the co-existent spirits of good and evil are antagonistic the word ham-bu*d*îkŏ, 'co-existent,' is often supposed to mean 'antagonistic.'

[3] See § 16. M14 and J have only 'that *occur* through his falsity *and* the constant terror of light *which* would have arisen from him.'

[4] That the term asar has only its etymological meaning 'endless,' and not the wider sense of 'eternal,' is clear from this phrase. The 'endless light' is the phrase used in Pahlavi to express Av. anaghra rao*k*au, a term implying 'the fixed stars,' so the passage in the text is very suggestive of the phrase, '*he made* the stars also' (Gen. i. 16).

[5] Instead of gun*g*, 'space,' we might read gan*g*, 'treasury,'

that is self-sustained—which (triumph) is the resource of all natures, races, characters, powers, *and* duties from the beginning and maturing of those of the good religion and the rushing of the liar and destroyer on to the creatures, which are requisite *for* the final, legitimate triumph of the well-directing creator, and *for* the termination of the struggles of all by the protection and recompense of the praises and propitiation performed, which are the healing of the righteous *and* the restoration of the wicked *at* the renovation. 23. Even these developments, even these established habits (da*d*-*s*ânîhâ), even these emissions of strength, even these births, even these races, even these townspeople (dihîkŏîhâ), even these characters, even these sciences [1], even these manageable and managing ones [2], and even these other, many, special species and manners which at various periods (anbânŏ) of time are in the hope that the quantity and nature of their auxiliaries *may be* complete, and their coming accomplished and not deficient in success (vakhtŏ), are distributed and made happy by him.

24. The sky is in three thirds, of which the one at the top is joined to the endless light, in which is the constantly-beneficial space; the one at the

---

but it is written gûn*g* in Chap. XXXI, 24, according to K35, and the meaning 'space' is more appropriate to the gâtu*s* *hv*adhâtô, 'self-sustained place,' of Vend. XIX, 122. The epithet 'constantly-beneficial' is a Pahl. translation of Av. misvâna, and is evidently applied here to the unlimited heavenly space contained in the 'endless light' (see § 24) and including the supreme heaven, as appears from the order in which these three existences (the earliest creations of Aûha*r*maz*d*) are mentioned in Chap. XXXI, 24.

[1] M14 and J have 'separate doers.'

[2] M14 and J have 'doers at different times.'

bottom reached to the gloomy abyss, in which is the fiend full of evil; and one is between those two thirds *which are* below and above. 25. And the uppermost third, *which* is called 'the rampart of the supreme heaven' (garô*d*mânô drupû*s*tŏ)[1], *was* made by him with purity, all splendour, and every pleasure, and no access to it for the fiend. 26. And he provided that third for undisturbedly convoking the pure, the archangels, *and* the righteous *that have* offered praises who, as *it were* unarmed (azenâvar), struggle unprepared *and* thoroughly in contest *with* the champions of the co-existent *one*, and they smite the co-existent *one* and his own progeny (gôhârakŏ) *already* described, and afford support to the imperishable state[2], through the help of the archangels and the glory of the creator. 27. And, again also, in their[3] fearlessness they seek for the destruction of the demons and for the perfection of the creatures of the good *beings*; as *one* who is fearless, owing to some rampart which is inaccessible *to* arrows and blows, and shoots arrows at the expanse below, is troubled (bakhsê*d*ŏ) for friends below.

28. And he made a distinction in the prescribed splendour and glory for the lowermost third of the sky; and the difference is *that* it is liable to injury (pavan resh), so that the fiend, who is void of goodness, comes *and* makes that third full of darkness and full of demons, *and* shall be able to perplex in that difficulty when the thousand winters occur, and the five detested (lakhsî*d*akŏ) kinds of the

---

[1] Bd. III, 26 says that 'the rampart of the sky was formed so that the adversary should not be able to mingle with it.'

[2] Reading âgûrazênd va*l* aseg gûn.

[3] Assuming that va*l* stands for valman or valman*s*ân.

demons of life[1] have also overwhelmed with sin those of the wicked who are deceived by the demons and *have* fled from the contest. 29. *But* they shall not let the fiend fully in, owing to the luminaries of the resplendent *one*, during the allotted time when the demons' punishing and the repentance of the wicked are accomplished.

30. And he appointed for the middle third the creatures of the world separated[2] from the world and the spiritual *existence;* and among those creatures[3] *were* produced for them the managing man *as* a guardian of the creatures, and the deciding wisdom *as* an appliance of man; *and* the true religion, the best of knowledge *was* prepared by him. 31. And that third is for the place of combat and the contest of the two different natures[4]; and in the uppermost part of the same third is stationed by him the light *of* the brilliant sun and moon and glorious stars, and *they* are provided by him that they may watch[5] the coming of the adversary, and revolve around the creatures. 32. All the *sacred* ceremonies of the distant earth (bûm), the light, the abundant rains, and the good angels vanquish

---

[1] Probably referring to the five fiends, or demonesses, which are the special embodiments of each man's evil passions, and are thus detailed in Mkh. XLI, 9–11:—'That man is the stronger who is able to contend with his own fiends, and who keeps these five fiends, in particular, far from *his* body, which are such as avarice, wrath, lust, disgrace, and discontent.'

[2] Reading fî*s*ar*d*akŏ, but the word is doubtful. This central region of the sky would seem to be the place of the 'ever-stationary,' if it do not include the earth itself, which is not quite clear, owing to the obscure style of the author.

[3] While in the world.

[4] The beneficent and evil spirits.

[5] Reading venâpênd, but the word is doubtful.

and smite the wizards *and* witches who rush *about* below them[1], *and* struggle to perplex by injury to the creatures; they make all such assailants become fugitives[2]. 33. And through their revolution the ascents and descents, the increase and diminution (narafsisnŏ), of the creatures[3] shall occur, the flow and ebb of the seas, and the increase of the dye-like[4] blood of the inferior creatures[5]; also owing to them *and* through *them have* elapsed the divisions of the days, nights, months, years, periods, *and* all the millenniums (hazagrôk zîmân) of time.

34. He also appointed unto *our fore*fathers the equipment which is their own, a material vesture, a sturdy bravery, and the guardian spirits of the righteous; and he provided that they *should* remain *at* various times in their own nature[6], and come into worldly vesture. 35. And those for great hosts *and* many slaves are born, for the duties of the period, into *some* tribe; he who has plenty of offspring is like Fravâk[7], he who is of the early law

[1] Below the sun, moon, and stars which protect the creatures.

[2] Literally 'springers back.'

[3] Reading dâmîkŏ, but the word is unusual; it might be read dahmîkô, 'of the holy man,' or be considered a corruption of damîkŏ, 'earth.'

[4] Reading rangmânŏ, but the word is doubtful.

[5] Five folios of text are here interpolated in J, of which four contain the passage (Ep. II, vi, 4—ix, 7) omitted at the end of that MS., and the fifth contains a passage on the same subject as Ep. III, and which may possibly be part of the text missing in Ep. III, 11.

[6] Meaning that the unembodied spirits of men should enter upon their worldly existence.

[7] The great-grandson of the primeval man, Gâyômar*d*, and the forefather of the fifteen races of undeformed human beings (see Bd. XV, 25-31, XXXI, 1).

(pês*dâd*ŏ) like Hôshâng[1], he who is a smiter of the demon like Tâkhmôrup[2], he who is full of glory like Yim[3], he who is full of healing like Frê*d*ûn, he who has both wisdoms[4] like the righteous Mânûs*k*îhar[5], he who is full of strength like Keresâsp[6], he who is of a glorious race like Kaî-Kavâ*d*[7], he who is full of wisdom like Aôshânar[8]. 36. He who is noble is like Sîyâvash[9], he who is an eminent doer (a*v*arkâr) like Kaî-Khûsrôî[10], he who is exalted like Kaî-Vi*s*tâsp[11], he who is completely good like the righteous Zaratû*s*t[12], he who arranges the world like Peshyôtanû[13], he who is over the religion (dînô-

[1] See Chap. II, 10 for this and the following three names.

[2] He is said to have kept the evil spirit thirty years as a steed (see Râm Yt. 12, Zamyâd Yt. 29, Mkh. XXVII, 22).

[3] Here written *G*îm.

[4] Instinctive wisdom and that acquired by experience (see Chap. XL, 3).

[5] Av. Manu*s**k*ithra; the descendant of Frê*d*ûn, in the eleventh generation, who overthrew the usurpation of the collateral branches of his family, and restored the Irânian line of the Pê*s*dâdian dynasty in his own person (see Bd. XXXI, 12–14, XXXIV, 6).

[6] See Chap. XVII, 6.

[7] Av. Kavi Kavâta; the first king of the Kayânian dynasty (see Bd. XXXI, 24, 25, XXXIV, 7).

[8] Probably the Av. Aoshnara, mentioned in Âf. Zarat., along with several of the other names, in a passage somewhat similar to that in our text. The name here can also be read Aûsh-khûr.

[9] Av. Kavi Syâvarshân; the son of king Kaî-Kâûs and father of king Kaî-Khûsrôî, but he did not reign himself. He is said to have formed the settlement of Kangdez (see Chap. XC, 5, Bd. XXXI, 25, Byt. III, 25, 26).

[10] See Chap. XXXVI, 3.

[11] Av. Kavî Vî*s*tâspa, Pers. Gu*s*tâsp; the fifth king of the Kayânian dynasty, who received the religion from Zaratû*s*t. His father, the fourth king, was of collateral descent from the first king (see Bd. XXXI, 28, 29, XXXIV, 7).

[12] The great apostle of the Parsis (see Chap. II, 10).

[13] Av. Peshôtanu; a son of Kaî-Vi*s*tâsp, who is said to be

a*v*arag) like Âtûr*ŏ*-pâ*d*[1], he who is liturgical like Hûshê*d*ar[2], he who is legal like Hûshê*d*ar-mâh, and he who is metrical and concluding like Sôshâns. 37. Among them are many illustrious ones, glorious doers, supporters of the religion, and good managers, who are completely (âpûr) for the smiting of the fiend and the will of the creator.

38. He also produced the creatures as contenders, and granted assistance (vê*d*varîh), through the great, in the struggle for the perfect happiness from heaven at the renovation[3] *of the universe;* and he made *them* universally (vâspôharakânîhâ) contented. 39. A vitiated thought *of* a living, well-disposed *being* is a stumble (nisî*v*ŏ) which is owing to evil; and these are even those[4] contented with death, because they know their limit, *and* it shall be definite (burînŏ-hômônd) and terminable; the evil of the world, in life, is definite, and they shall not make *one* exist unlimitedly *and* indefinitely in the evil of the world, through an eternal life with pain.

40. And through a great mystery, wholly miraculous, he produced a durable immortality for the living; a perplexity so long as the best and utmost of it is such an immortality of adversity, for *it* is

immortal and to live in Kangdez, whence he is to come to restore the religion in the millennium of Hûshê*d*ar (see Chap. XC, 3, 5, Bd. XXIX, 5, Byt. III, 25–32, 36–38, 41, 42).

[1] Probably the supreme high-priest and prime minister of the ninth Sasanian king, Shâpûr II (A.D. 309–379; see Bd. XXXIII, 3).

[2] See Chap. II, 10 for these last three names. The terms mânsarîk, 'liturgical,' dâ*d*îk, 'legal,' and gâsânîk, 'metrical,' are those applied to the three divisions of the twenty-one Nasks, or books of the complete literature of the Maz*d*a-worshippers.

[3] M14 and J have merely 'granted assistance in the struggle at the renovation.'

[4] Assuming that gha*l* stands for valman, as it sometimes does.

ever living molested and eternally suffering. 41. And their development, the strength of lineage obtained, is ever young in succession, and the tender, well-destined *ones*, who are good, are in adversity and perpetuity of life, so that there is a succession of life through their own well-destined offspring[1]. 42. They become eternally famous, so that they obtain, every one, an old age which is renewed, *free* from sickness and decay, visibly in their own offspring and family (gôharakŏ) whenever they become complete; and any one of the combative, whose struggle is through the smiting that his fellow-combatant obtains, is of a comfortable disposition at the balance[2]. 43. This *one*, too, is for stepping forth to heaven, even as that pre-eminent *one* of the righteous, the greatest of the apostles and the most fortunate of those born, the chief of worldly beings, the righteous Zaratûst the Spîtamân, when the omniscient wisdom, *as* a trance (gîp), came upon him from Aûharmazd, and he saw him who *was* immortal *and* childless, and also him *who was* mortal *and provided* with children; that perpetual life of the childless then seemed to him terrible, and that succession of mortals *seemed* commendable[3]; so that

[1] M14 and J have merely: 'are a succession in adversity and perpetuity of life.'

[2] Assuming that tarâz stands for tarâzûk. The meaning is that any one who has successfully struggled with sin in the world, and leaves offspring behind him, goes to his account, at the balance of the angel Rashnû, with cheerfulness.

[3] This seems to be a variation of the statement in Byt. II, 13, where Zaratûst, after asking for immortality, and having had the omniscient wisdom infused into him for a week, describes what he had seen, and amongst other things says: 'I saw a wealthy *man* without children, and it did not seem to me commendable; and I

the coming of *his* assured offspring[1], Hûshê*d*ar, Hûshê*d*ar-mâh, *and* Sôshâns[2], became more longed for and more desired, *and* death *more* than the perpetual life of his own body.

44. And when he[3] who is all-watchful and all-knowing had arranged the means of opposing the fiend, *there* came for destroying, like a general leader (vispvar), that fiend of deceiving nature, the harassing, rushing, evil-wishing, primeval (pê*s*) contender, *together* with the demons Akômanô ('evil thought')[4], Aêshm ('wrath'), Zarmân ('decrepitude'), Bûshasp ('lethargy'), craving distress, bygone luck[5], Vâê[6], Varenô ('lust')[7], Astô-vîdâ*d*[8], and Vîzarâsh[9], and the original, innumerable demons and fiends of Mâzendarân[10]. 45. And his darkness *and* gloom, scorpions (kadzûnŏ), porcupines, and vermin, poison

saw a pauper with many children, and it seemed to me commendable.'

[1] The Av. âsna frazai*n*ti*s*, 'inherent or natural offspring,' of Yas. LIX, 14, &c. The Pahl. equivalents âsnû*d*ak and âsnî*d*ak can hardly be mere transliterations of âsna, but are more probably translations, formed of â + *s*unu*d*ak and *s*inî*d*ak, with some such meaning as 'assured.'

[2] These three future apostles (see Chap. II, 10) are considered to be sons of Zaratû*s*t (see Bd. XXXII, 8).

[3] Aûha*r*ma*zd*.

[4] These first four demons are described in Bd. XXVIII, 7, 15-17, 23, 26.

[5] The words nîyâ*z*înâkŏ tangîh bû*d*ŏ bakhtŏ, here translated, may possibly be a miswriting of five names of demons.

[6] The bad Vâê (see Chap. XXX, 4).

[7] See Bd. XXVIII, 25.

[8] A demon of death (see Chap. XXIII, 3, note, Bd. XXVIII, 35).

[9] Another demon of death (see Chap. XXXII, 4, 7).

[10] The mountainous country south of the Caspian, said to be full of demons, the Mâzainya daêva of the Avesta (see Bd. III, 20, XV, 28). These demons were, no doubt, merely idolators.

and venom, and the mischief originally in the lower-*most* third *of the sky*[1], issue upwards, astute in evil, into the middle third, in which are the agreeable[2] creatures which Aûha*r*ma*zd* created.

46. And he smote the ox[3], he made Gâyômar*d* mortal, and he shook the earth; and the land was shattered, creation became dark, and the demons rushed below, above, *and on all* sides, and they mounted even to the uppermost third *of the sky*[4]. 47. And there the barricade (band) and rampart fortifying (vakhshîkŏ) the spiritual *world* is approached, for which the safeguard (nigâs) of all barricades[5], that is itself the great glory of the pure religion, solving doubts—which is the safeguard of all barricades—is arrayed. 48. And the splendid, belt-bearing Pleiades[6], like the star-studded girdle of the spirit-fashioned, good religion of the Ma*zd*a-worshippers, are so arrayed *as* luminaries of the fully-glorious *ones*. 49. And there was no possibility (aîtŏkîh) of any demon *or* fiend, nor yet even of

---

[1] See § 28.

[2] By omitting a stroke nô*s*, 'agreeable,' would become vêh, 'good.'

[3] The sole-created, or primeval ox, whence all animals are said to have sprung. For an account of this incursion of the fiend, see Bd. III, 12–20, VIII, 1, Zs. II, 1–11.

[4] M14 and J have 'even to the upper sky of the middle third,' which means the same thing, as the author's words imply that the demons did not enter the upper third, but only reached its borders (see § 49).

[5] M14 and J conclude the sentence as follows: 'the pure religion, solving doubts, is arrayed.'

[6] Reading vandvar Pêrvakŏ. The author seems to have been thinking of Yas. IX, 81: 'Mazda brought to thee the star-studded, spirit-fashioned girdle (the belt of Orion) leading the Pleiades; the good Mazda-worshipping religion' (Haug's Essays, p. 182).

the demon of demons, the mightiest (mazvantûm) in valour, rushing up across that boundary; they are beaten back now, when *they have* not reached *it* from the gloom, at once *and* finally (yak-vayô akha*r*).

50. And the fiend *of* gloomy race, accustomed to destruction (aôsh-âyin), changed into causes of death the position (gâs) of the brilliant, supreme heaven of the pure, heavenly angels—which he ordained through the power *of*[1] Mîtôkht ('falsehood')—and the triumph of the glory of the world's creatures, *as ordained* through two decrees (zîkŏ):—one, the destruction of the living by the power[2] of death; and one causing the manacling of souls by a course of wickedness. 51. And he made *as* leaders therein that *one* astute in evil who is *already* named[3], and Astô-vîdâ*d*[4] *who* is explained *as* 'the disintegration of material beings;' he also intrusted the demon Bûshasp ('lethargy')[4] with the weakening of the breath, the demon Tap ('fever')[5] with stupefying and disordering the understanding, and the demon Â*z* ('greediness')[6] with suggesting cravings and causing drinking before *having* the thirst of a dog[7]. 52. Also the demon Zarmân ('decrepitude')[8] for injuring the body and abstract-

[1] Or, zôharakŏ may mean 'venomous.' Mîtôkht was the first demon produced by the evil spirit (see Bd. I, 24, XXVIII, 14, 16) who is supposed to be as much 'the father of lies' as his counterpart, the devil of the Christians.

[2] Or, zôhar may mean 'venom.'

[3] Mîtôkht.

[4] See § 44.

[5] See Chap. XXIII, 3.

[6] See Bd. XXVIII, 27.

[7] Reading pê*s* ti*s*nŏ-î sagak nô*s*ânînî*d*anŏ, but we might read pê*s* ti*s*nŏg sedkûni*s*nînî*d*anŏ, 'causing gnawing before *being* thirsty.'

[8] See § 44 for this demon and the next two.

ing the strength; the bad Vâê's tearing away the life by stupefying the body; the demon Aêshm ('wrath') for occasioning trouble by contests, *and* causing an increase of slaughter; the noxious creatures of gloomy *places* for producing stinging and causing injury; the demon Zâîrîk[1] for poisoning eatables and producing causes of death; with Nîyâz ('want')[2] the stealthily-moving and dreading the light[3], the fearfulness of Nihîv ('terror') chilling the warmth, and many injurious powers and demons of the destroyers *were* made by him constant assistants of Astô-vîdâd in causing death.

53. Also, for rendering wicked *and* making *fit* for hell those whose souls are under the sway of[4] falsehood (kadbâ), which in religious language is called Mîtôkht—since it is said in revelation that that is as much an evil as all the demons with the demons of demons—*there* is Akômanô ('evil thought')[5], who is with the evil spirit owing to the speaking of Mîtôkht ('falsehood')[6]. 54. And for his doctrine (dînôîh) of falsehood, and winning the creatures, slander the deceiver, lust the selfish, hatred, and envy, besides the overpowering progress of disgrace (nang), the improper desires of the creatures, indolence in seeking wisdom, quarrelling about that

[1] One of the seven arch-fiends, the Av. Zairika, which probably means 'decay,' but from the resemblance of his name to zâhar, 'poison,' he is called 'the maker of poison' (see Bd. I, 27, XXVIII, 11).

[2] See Bd. XXVIII, 26.

[3] Reading gadman bîm, but it may be yadman bîm, 'dreading the hand;' and it is doubtful whether the epithet be applied to Nîyâz, or to Nihîv.

[4] Reading î instead of the va, 'and,' of the MSS.

[5] See § 44.

[6] See § 50.

which is no indication of learning, disputing (sitôg) about the nature of a righteous *one*, and many other seductive powers *and* demons helping to win, *were* made auxiliary to the doctrine of falsehood in deceiving the creatures.

55. Also, to turn his disturbance[1] to creatures of even other kinds, *there* are demons *and* fiends of further descriptions (freh-aîtân); and for the assistance of those combatants he established also *those* afflictions (nîvakân) of many, the witches of natures for gloomy *places*, whose vesture is the radiance of the lights[2] that fall, *and* rush, and turn below the luminaries which have to soar (vâzisnî-kânŏ) in stopping the way of *any* little concealment of the spirits *and* worldly *beings*[3]. 56. And they (the witches) overspread the light and glory of those *luminaries*, of whose bestowal of glory and their own diminution *of it*, moreover, for seizing the creatures, consist the pain, death, and original evil of the abode for the demon of demons[4].

57. And those demons *and* original fiends, who are the heads and mighty *ones* of the demons, injudiciously, prematurely moving, prematurely speaking, not for their own disciplined advantage,

---

[1] Reading paîtîyârakŏ, but K35 and J have paîtâzârakŏ, which, if it be a real word, would have nearly the same meaning.

[2] Shooting stars, meteors, and comets, the last of which are apparently intended by the term Mûspar (Av. Mûs pairika, 'the Mûs witch') of Bd. V, 1, XXVIII, 44.

[3] That is, the luminaries which have to prevent these beings from becoming obscured by the darkness produced by the evil spirits.

[4] By the omission of one loop the MSS. have yazdânŏ, 'angels,' instead of shêdânŏ, 'demons;' the difference between the two words being very slight in Pahlavi characters.

but with unbecoming hatred, lawless manner[1], envy, *and* spears exposing the body[2], undesirably struggle together—a perplexing contention of troublers—about the destruction of the luminaries. 58. The army of angels, judiciously and leisurely fighting for the good creatures of the sacred beings, not with premature hatred and forward spears (pês-nîzahîh), but by keeping harm away *from* themselves—the champions' customary mode[3] of wounding —valiantly, strongly, properly, and completely triumphantly struggle *for* a victory triumphantly fought. 59. For Aharman the demons are procurers (vashîkânŏ) of success *in* the contests till the end, when the fiend becomes invisible *and* the creatures become pure.

60. Since worldly *beings* observe, explain, *and* declare among worldly *beings* the work of the spirits and knowledge of customs (rîstakŏ), by true observation, through wisdom, *that* that life (zîk) is proper when *it is* in the similitude of the true power of wisdom, *and* the visible life is undiscerning of that which is to come *and* that which is provided, so also the evidence of a knowledge of the end of the contention is certain *and* clearly visible. 61. And tokens are discernible and signs apparent which, to the wisdom of the ancients—if it extended, indeed, to a knowledge about this pre-eminent subject—*were* hidden by the fiends, who are concealers *of them* from the perception (hâzisnŏ) of worldly *beings*, and also from *their* coming to the perception of worldly *beings*.

---

[1] Reading an-âyin gun, but this is uncertain.

[2] Reading *k*ihar-tanû nîzah; the last word is usually spelt nîzak, but occurs in § 58 in the same form as here.

[3] Reading nîvikân mank gûn, but this is uncertain.

62. The learned high-priests who *were* founders (pâyînîkânŏ) *of the religion* knew *it* (*the evidence*), and those portions of it *were* transmitted by them to the ancients which the successive realisers of it, for the ages before me (levînam), *have* possessed. 63. The deceivers[1] of the transmitters, who have existed *at* various times, even among those who are blessed[2], *have* remained a mass of knowledge for me, by *being* my reminder of the mature *and* proper duty of those truly wise (hû-*k*îragânîkŏ), through the directions issuable by even worldly decision, and of so many of which I have a remembrance[3], for the writing of which *there would be* no end. 64. Then the manifest power of the fiend among us below, and the way provided by the creator for *his* becoming invisible *and his* impotence are clear; so also the full power of the creator of the army of angels, assuredly the procurers of success *in* the end, and[4] the accomplishment all-powerfully—which is his own advantage—of the completely-happy progress, for ever, of all creations which are his creatures, are thereby visible *and* manifest; *and* many tokens and signs *thereof* are manifestly clear.

65. One is this, that the creator is *in* his own predestined (bagdâ*d*akŏ) abode, and the fiend is

[1] The unorthodox, or those holding erroneous views regarding the traditions handed down by them.

[2] Reading âf*r*înî*d*ŏ, which K 35 has converted into afgônê*d*ŏ, 'casts,' by inverting the order of the two central characters.

[3] M14 and J omit the words from 'through' to 'remembrance.' The author means that he has acquired much information on the subject even from the opinions of the unorthodox judiciously studied.

[4] M14 has merely the words: 'and the completely-happy progress,' &c.

advancing *and has* rushed in, and his advancing is for the subjugation of the creation[1].

66. One, that the creatures of Aûha*r*ma*zd* are spiritual *and* also worldly, and that is no world of the fiend, but he gathers an evil spiritual state into the world; *and* as among so many the greed of success is *only* in one[2], so the triumph is manifest of the good spirits *and* worldly beings over the evil spirits.

67. One is this, that *his* defeat in the end is manifest from his contention and aggression (pê*s*-za*d*ârîh); for the fiend is an aggressor *in* an unlawful struggle, and leaving the army of Aûha*r*ma*zd*—subsequently the lawful defender (lakhvâr-za*d*âr)—the fiend of violence is a cause of power among those wholly unrequiting the creator *in* the world[3]. 68. If, also, every time that he smites the creatures he is equally *and* lawfully beaten once again, it is assuredly evident therefrom that, when their beating *and* being beaten are *on* an equality together, *at* first he whose hand *was* foremost *was* the smiter, and the backward fighter was beaten; *but at* last that backward fighter is the smiter, and the foremost fighter becomes beaten[4]; for when he is

---

[1] K35 has altered dakhshakŏ, 'token,' into dahi*s*nŏ, 'creation,' by changing one letter, and M14 and J have adopted the wrong reading.

[2] Reading *k*igûn dên hâvandîh *k*îr âz dên khadûkŏ. The drift of these two first reasons seems to be that the fiend, being an invader and outnumbered, must be vanquished in the end.

[3] Reading zak-î zôr drû*g*ô dên-î dâ*d*âr ba*r*â-atô*g*îgânŏ-î stî*s* vahânŏ-î nîrûkŏ-hômandîh. This phrase seems to have been generally misunderstood by copyists, as both M14 and J have altered it into something like: 'when the violence of the fiend is in the hand of the creator, yet even if the motive of the army is so much power.'

[4] M14 and J omit this clause, from '*but*' to 'beaten.'

beaten *in* the former combat, *there* is then a combat again, and his enemy is beaten.

69. One is this, that when the supply of weapons[1], the fighting, and the ability of the contenders are equal, the supply of weapons of him who is the beginner (pêsî*d*âr) has always sooner disappeared, and, *at* last, he is unarmed and his opponent remains armed; *and* an armed *man* is known *to be*[2] victorious over him *who is* unarmed, just as *one* fighting is triumphant over *one* not fighting[3]. 70. And a similitude of it, which is *derived* from the world, is even such as when each one of two furious *ones* (âr*d*ŏ) of equal strength, in a fight together, has an arrow, and each one is in fear of the other's possession of an arrow; *and* one of them alone shoots *his* arrow, and makes *it* reach *his* opponent; then he is without an arrow, and his opponent, fully mindful *of it*, has an arrow, and becomes fearless through possession of the arrow, his own intrepidity, *and* the lack of arrows and complete terror of that earlier shooter. 71. And as regards mighty deeds he is successful; *and* though *there be* as much strength for the earlier fighter a successful termination is undiscoverable *for him;* despoiled of possession *by* him who is later, *and* ruined in that which is all-powerful, *his* end *and* disappearance are undoubted, clear, *and* manifest[4].

---

[1] The term zênô afzâr evidently refers here to the warrior's stock of arrows and other missiles which were to be expended in battle, so that it is analogous to the modern term 'ammunition.'

[2] M14 has yehevûnê*d*, 'becomes,' instead of dânôstŏ, 'known.'

[3] M14 and J omit these last four words.

[4] The argument, both in this case and the preceding one, is that even when two combatants are equal in power and resources the hasty aggressor is likely to be beaten in the end, and, therefore,

72. One is this, that owing to the previous non appearance of the fiend, the coming forward of sickness and death unto the creatures of the sacred beings *occurred* when the fiend rushed *in*, and he rendered the existence of men sickly; he also destroyed *and* put to death the progeny of animals. 73. Afterwards, through lawfully driving *him* away, sickness and death *come* in turn (bârîkîhâ) unto the demons, *and* the healthiness[1] of the righteous *and* perfect life unto the creatures of the sacred beings, as its counterpart is the great healthiness *which* comes, more rightly rising, unto the creatures advised by the sacred beings, through united arrangement[2]. 74. And, in the end, a worldly similitude of the sickness and grievous, complete death for the fiends[3], and of the healthiness *and* intrinsic (benaf-*s*man-*k*îgûnîh) life for the creatures of the sacred beings, is that which *occurs* when one of two litigants (ham-patkâr), prematurely revengeful, gives to *his* fellow-litigant an irritating poison, *and* himself eats wholesome flour before the later litigant gives a poison, as an antidote, to the earlier litigant, *and* himself eats the poison-subduing flour; after which he is cured *by* the poison, and his enemy is dead through the poison of the later flour[4].

the inferiority of the fiend is still more likely to lead to his final defeat.

[1] M14 begins a fresh argument here, owing to some misunderstanding of the meaning of the sentence.

[2] That is, the advantage of driving away the fiend in this life is a counterpart of the blessings attained at the resurrection.

[3] The word drû*g*ânŏ, 'fiends,' is omitted in K35, but is evidently necessary to complete the sentence.

[4] This appears to be a description of ordeal by poison and the two usual modes of evading its operation. The hasty evader relies upon deceitfully substituting a wholesome powder for the

75. One is this, that Aûharmazd, the creator, is a manager with omniscient wisdom, *and* the contention of the fiend of scornful looks (tar nigîrisn) is through lust of defilement; of united power is the management of that creator, as existing with (hamzîk)[1] all the vigilance in the wisdom which is in everything; and that united power is the strength of the management of heaven. 76. And of much power is the contention of the fiend, as *his* manifold changing of will—which is hostile to the will of even his own creatures, and is through the weakness and exhausted[2] strength of an evil nature—is the contending power which forms his visible strength[3].

77. One is this, that is, on account of the fiend's contending ill-advisedly, however strongly the contest is adapted for the damage of his own fiendishness, and regret and bad consequences therefrom are perceptible. 78. Such as the very paralyzing[4] affliction which *was* appointed (nîhâdŏ) by him

---

poison he has to take; while the more cautious evader trusts to recognising his adversary's poison by its taste, and selecting another poison as an antidote for both to take, so that the hasty evader suffers through his own deceit in not taking the first poison. Similarly, the fiend is supposed to suffer in the end from the death and destruction which he was the first to introduce into the world.

[1] By omitting a phrase M14 and J have: 'and the management of the fiend of scornful looks is as *it were* existing with,' &c.

[2] This is little more than a guess at the meaning of a word which can be read vashakîdŏ (compare Pers. gas and kasîdan). The whole sentence is rather uncertain.

[3] The argument is that this unstable power of the fiend cannot permanently stand against the consolidated strength of the creator.

[4] Adopting J's reading samakgûntar, but K35 has vasmakgûntar, which may be 'very troublesome,' and M14 has samkîntar, probably for sahmgîntar, 'very terrible.'

for the creatures of the world in putting the living to death, which he ordered with violence and the hope that it *would* be *his* greatest triumph. 79. Even that is what is so self-damaging to the same fiend that, when he puts to death him who is wicked, and he who is wicked, who is performing what is desirable for him (the fiend)—that performance of what is desirable *being* the practice of sin—is useless *and* goes thither where he is penitent of that seduction, the spirit[1] of the owner (shah) of the sin, whose soul is wicked[2], is righteous, in whose worldly body exist the fetters of pain and darkness; and owing to the unfettering of *its* hands *from* that pain it (the spirit) is far *away*, and goes to heaven, which is the most fortified of fortresses. 80. Fearlessly it fights for it, even as the guardian spirit of Yim the splendid[3] kept away all trouble (vê*s*am), the guardian spirit of Frê*d*ûn kept away even those active in vexing[4], *and* other guardian spirits of those passed *away* are enumerated as *engaged* in the defeat of many fiends.

---

[1] That is, the guardian spirit (see Chap. II, 5) which is not rendered wicked by the sin of the soul.

[2] The phrase mûn rûbân-î zak darvand is ambiguous, as it might mean 'which is the soul of that wicked one,' but this is not reconcileable with the context.

[3] See Chap. II, 10. Yim-î shê*d*ô is the Yimô khshaêtô of Vend. II, 43, 45, the Jamshêd of the Shâhnâmah. The legends here referred to are mentioned in Fravar*d*în Yt. 130–138, where the guardian spirit of Yima is said to withstand the misfortune brought on by the demons, while that of Thraêtaona (Frê*d*ûn) withstands various diseases, and those of other heroes withstand various other evils and demons.

[4] Reading pavan bêsh-i*k* kar*d*ârân, but for i*k* we ought probably to read az, so as to make the phrase correspond to the Av. azi-kar*s*tahê *d*baêshanghô of Fravar*d*în Yt. 131.

81. One is this, that the most grievous severance that is owing to him (the fiend)[1] is the production of the mortality of the creatures, in which the afflicting (nîzgûn) demon Astô-vîdâ*d*[2] is the head *of* the many Mâzînîkân *demons*[3]. 82. And the propitious creator's developers *were* thus unprovoked (anârgônd) when the only person, who is called Gâyômar*d*[4], *was* destroyed by him, and came back to the world *as* a man and a woman whose names were Marhayâ *and* Marhîyôih[5]; and the propagation *and* connection of races *were* through their next-of-kin marriage of a sister[6]. 83. The unlucky[7] fiend, while he

---

[1] Instead of zî*s* madam, 'that is owing to him,' we ought probably to read zî*s* bar, 'that is his production;' the Huz. madam, which is the proper equivalent of the preposition bar, 'on, according to,' being wrongly used for the noun bar, 'produce.'

[2] See § 44.

[3] The Mâzainya daêva of the Avesta (see § 44, note).

[4] The sole-created, or primeval, man from whom the whole human race is said to have sprung (see Chap. II, 10, Bd. III, 14, 17, 19-23, XV, 1, 31).

[5] The progenitors of the undeformed human race, who are said to have grown up, in the manner of a plant, from the seed of the dead Gâyômar*d* (see Bd. XV, 2-5). Their names are derived from Av. mashya mashyôi, 'the man and woman,' but the latter form is no longer extant in the Avesta. From Av. mashya we have the Mashya of Bd. XV, 6, and the Mâshya of Bd. XV, 11, 19, 20, 30. From its dialectical variant martiya in ancient Pers., which would be marethya in the Avesta (compare Av. mareta, Pers. mard), we have the Marhayâ of our text. And by transposition of the letters rt=reth=rha in these latter forms, we have the Matrô of Bd. XV, 2 and the Maharîh or Maharyâ of Bd. XV, 22, note. Other forms of these names also occur (see Chaps. LXIV, 2, LXV, 2, LXXVII, 4).

[6] M14 has 'of brother and sister,' but the insertion of the extra word is unnecessary. Regarding khvêtudâ*d*, or next-of-kin marriage, see Chap. LXV.

[7] Reading lâ-khâ*g*astŏ; the fiend is certainly 'unlucky' here,

increased offspring and fortune for them through death, so uplifted *his* voice in *their* presence, about the death of the living *ones* of their offspring and lineage, that *together* with the unmeasured destructiveness of the deadly evil spirit, and the unjust contention of his through death and the conveyer of death[1], the sting also of birth *was* owing to death. 84. The repetitions of the cry *were* many, so that the issue (bâr) of thousands and thousands *of* myriads from those two persons, and the multitude passed *away*, from a number *which* is limited and a counterpart (aê*d*ûnŏîh) of the living people in the world, are apparent; and for the annihilation of many fiends, through death, the propitiousness of the contending power of the creator is clear *and* manifest.

85. One is this, that the most steadfast quality of the demon himself is darkness, the evil of which is so complete that they shall call the demons also those of a gloomy race. 86. *But* such is the power in the arms *and* resources of the angels, that even the first gloomy darkness in the world is perpetually subdued by the one power really originating with the sun *and* suitable *thereto*, *and* the world is illuminated[2].

87. One is this, that the most mischievous weapon of the demons is the habit of self-deception which,

---

as by introducing death into the world he merely increases the number of beings who pass into the other world to join his opponents in the end; but the text probably means that he is 'inauspicious' and wishes to bring misfortune on mankind.

[1] Astô-vîdâ*d* (see § 81).

[2] The argument is that, as the sun is able to subdue darkness, the most constant quality of the fiend, every day, it is probable that the fiend himself will be entirely subdued in the end.

on account of rendering the soul wicked thereby, seemed to them as the greatest triumph for themselves, *and* a complete disaster for the angels. 88. In the great glory of the pure, true religion of the sacred beings is as much strength as is adapted to the full power of the lawlessness and much opposition of falsehood, *and* also to the fully accurate (a r *s* î *d* ŏ) speaking which is in itself an evidence of the true speaking of every proper truth; and no truth whatever is perverted by it. 89. And the false sayings are many, and good sayings—*their* opponents through good statement—do not escape from their imperfect truth[1]; since a similitude of them is that which *occurs* when, concerning that which is white-coloured, the whole of the truthful speak about *its* white colour, *but as to* the liars there are *some* who *speak of* its black colour, some of *its* mud colour, some of *its* blue colour, some of *its* bran[2] colour, some of *its* red colour, and some of *its* yellow colour. 90. And every single statement of each of the truthful is as much evidence, about those several colours of those who are liars, as even the compiled sayings of the Abraham of the Christians[3], which are the word of *him* who is also called their Messiah[4], about the

---

[1] Assuming that apûrâstîh stands for apûr râstîh; it may, however, be intended for a*v*î-râstîh, 'want of truth.' The meaning is that even true statements become perverted by inaccurate speakers.

[2] Perhaps sapû*s*ag, 'bran,' may have originally been sapzag, 'green.'

[3] Written Abrêhâm-î Tarsâkîgân.

[4] The letter *s* in Ma*s*îkhâ is here written like âî, but the word is correctly written in § 91.

Son of the *Supreme* Being[1]; thus, they recount that the Son, who is not less than the Father, is himself He, the Being whom they consider undying. 91. One falsehood they tell about the same Messiah is that he died, and one falsehood they tell is that he did not die; it is a falsehood for those who say he did not die, *and* for those who say he did die; wherefore did he not die, when *he is* not dead? *and* wherefore is it said he did not die, when he is mentioned as dead[2]? 92. Even the compilation itself is an opponent to its own words, for, though it said *he* is dead, it spoke unto *one* not dead; and though *he* is not dead, it spoke unto *one* dead. 93. The proper office (gâs) of a compiler and mutilator[3]—through whose complete attainments the demons of like power as to the force of truth are strengthened, *and* the pure, good religion of the Maz*d*a-worshippers is itself dissipated and rendered useless for itself—is a habit (dâ*d*ŏ) growing with

[1] The phrase is ba*r*manŏ-î dâ*d*, literally 'son of the created *one*,' unless we assume that dâ*d* is taken as a name of God. It is, however, quite conceivable that a priest would be reluctant to admit that a strange god could be anything better than a created being. That dâ*d* is here used as a noun, and not with the meaning of 'gift' or 'law,' appears from the subsequent phrase dâ*d*ŏ-î amîrâkŏ yakhsenund, 'the created *one* whom they consider undying.'

[2] Owing to the frequent repetitions of the same words in these phrases they are specially liable to corruption by copyists, but as they stand in K35 they can hardly be translated otherwise than as questions. M14 and J have an altered text which may be translated as follows:—'for whomever he did not die, when dead, *he is* as dead; for whomever it is said he died, *he is so* when he is mentioned as dead;' but this seems no improvement of the text.

[3] Referring to those who compile commentaries and mutilate texts to suit their own views.

the fiend; and, as he is seen *to be* victorious who overturns reliance on changeableness and similar powers, the final disruption of forces is a disruption of peculiarities (khû*d*îh vishôpi*s*nŏ)[1].

94. One is this, that is, even that prodigious devastation *of* which it is declared that it happens through the rain of Malkôs[2], when, through snow, immoderate cold, *and* the unproductiveness of the world, most mortals die; *and* even the *things* attainable by mortals are *attended* with threatenings of scarcity. 95. Afterwards—*as* among the all-wise, preconcerted remedies (pê*s* *k*ârîh) of the beneficent spirit[3] such a remedy *was* established (and nihâ*d* *k*âr) that *there is* one of the species of lands, that is called 'the enclosure formed by

[1] The argument is that even heterodoxy, 'the most mischievous weapon' of the fiend (see § 87), must fail in the end, because, like other revolutions, it relies on constant change, which implies want of permanency.

[2] Malkôsânŏ, 'of Malkôs,' is a denominative adjective derived from Chald. מַלְקוֹשׁ 'autumnal rain.' The deluging rain of Malkôs is supposed to usher in the dreadful winter foretold to Yima in Vend. II, 46–56, when all, or nearly all, living creatures were to perish, a truly glacial epoch. In a Persian paraphrase of the Bahman Ya*s*t (see Byt. Introd. p. lix) this period of Malkôs is described as follows:—'As three hundred years have elapsed from the time of Hûshê*d*ar (Byt. III, 44–49), the period of Malkôs comes on; and the winter of Malkôs is such that, owing to the cold and snow which occur, out of a myriad of men in the world only one will remain, and the trees and shrubs all become withered, and the quadrupeds, whether carrying, walking, leaping, or grazing, will all utterly die. Then, by command of God, they will come from the enclosure formed by Yim, and the men and quadrupeds from that place spread over Irân, and make the world populous a second time, and it is the beginning of the millennium of Hûshê*d*ar(-mâh).'

[3] The formation of the enclosure was ordered, as a precaution, by Aûha*r*ma*z*d (see Vend. II, 61–92).

Yim[1],' through which, by orders issued by Yim the splendid *and* rich in flocks, the son of Vîvangha[2], the world is again filled—men of the best races, animals of good breeds, the loftiest trees, *and* most savoury (kharegistânŏ) foods, *in* that manner came back miraculously *for* the restoration of the world; which new men are *substituted* for the former created beings, which is an upraising of the dead[3]. 96. Likewise from that miracle is manifested the non-attainment of the evil spirit to the universal control of the glory of the creator for every purpose.

97. One is this, that—when the heterodox (dûs-dînô) Dahâk[4], on whom most powerful demons and fiends in the shape of serpents are winged[5], escapes from the fetters of Frêdûn, and, through witchcraft, remains a demon even to the demons[6] *and*

---

[1] Reading Yim-kard var, but these words are corrupted in three different ways in the three MSS. consulted. This enclosure is said to have been in the middle of Pârs in Bd. XXIX, 14.

[2] Av. Vîvanghau (see Bd. XXXI, 2).

[3] That is, a type of the resurrection.

[4] The Av. Azi Dahâka, 'destructive serpent,' slain by Thraêtaona. In later times he was converted into a usurping king, or dynasty, the Dha'h'hâk of the Shâhnâmah, who conquered Yim (Jamshêd) and, after a reign of a thousand years, was defeated by Frêdûn (Thraêtaona) and fettered under Mount Dimâvand; whence he is to escape during the millennium of Hûshêdar-mâh to devastate the world, till he is finally slain by the hero Keresâsp, who is revived for the purpose (see Bd. XXIX, 8, 9, XXXI, 6, Byt. III, 56–61).

[5] That is, attached to the shoulders like wings; referring to the serpents said to have grown from the shoulders of Dahâk.

[6] M14 alters shêdân, 'demons,' into gêhân, 'world,' so as to read 'through the demon of witchcraft remains a destroyer unto the world.' The alteration in the Pahlavi text is small, but seems unnecessary.

a destroyer—a mighty man *who* is roused[1] up beforehand from the dead, *and* is called Keresâsp the Sâmân[2], crushes that fiendishness with a club *consisting* of a cypress tree, *and* brings that Dahâk through wholesome fear to the just law of the sacred beings[3].

98. One is this, that these, which are *distinct* from those born *and* the men who have laboured together, Astô-vîdâ*d*[4] *has* not obtained, nor even *will* obtain, for death; and through the power of immortals, and the action of the good discourses (hû-sakhunagânîh)[5], they urge on to the sacred beings *those* who are inquiring (kâv-hômand), even to the immortality which is the renovation of the other creatures. 99. One, *which is* where the mingled conflict of the meeting *of good and evil occurs*[6], is the glorious good-yielding *one* of the creator which is guarded by purity, so that the fiend *has* not attained to injuring *it*, since it is pronounced *to be* the uninjured ox which is called Hadhayã*s*[7]. 100. Also the long life which

[1] Reading angê*z*ôî-aîtô, instead of the unintelligible angî*d*î-aîtô.

[2] See Chap. XVII, 6.

[3] Dahâk and all other heinous offenders are said to undergo a special punishment for three nights at the resurrection, and are then finally purified by passing through molten metal like the rest of mankind (see Bd. XXX, 16, 20).

[4] See § 44.

[5] Perhaps referring to the liturgical recitations.

[6] In the atmosphere apparently (see Bd. I, 4).

[7] Written Hadhayãm here, but Hadhayã*s* in § 119, Chaps. XLVIII, 34, XC, 4, and Hadhayô*s* or Hadhayâv*s* in Bd. XIX, 13, XXX, 25, though always in Pâzand. It is also called Sarsaok, or Srisaok, in Bd. XV, 27, XVII, 4, XIX, 13, always in Pâzand, and this name is converted into Pahl. Srûvô in Zs. XI, 10.

is through its all-controlling power[1] until they cause the end to occur, and the devourers of fires are subdued by it—*besides* the whole strength of the unboasting (a*k*ûm) creatures of the beneficent spirit, after they live even without eating[2]—is because of the Hôm that is white[3] and the promoter (frâshm) of perfect glory, which possesses the wholesomeness of the elixir of immortality, and through it the living become ever-living. 101. And also as many more specially pure glorious *ones* whose enumeration *would* be tedious[4].

102. One is this, that the struggle of the evil *one* and the demons *with* the creatures is not precisely the existence of *various* kinds of contest, but

---

It is said to be an ox which never dies till it is slaughtered at the resurrection, so that its fat may form one of the ingredients of the elixir of immortality which all men have then to taste; it is also said that mankind, in ancient times, crossed the ocean on its back, when going to settle in the other regions of the earth. From what is stated in the text it may be supposed to be some form of cloud myth, but it is not mentioned in the extant portion of the Avesta, unless 'the ox Hadhayô*s*' be taken as a corruption of gâu*s* hudh*a*u, 'the well-yielding ox,' and Sarsaok as connected with Pers. sri*s*k, 'a drop,' and referring to showers of rain; but this is very uncertain.

[1] The power of the white Hôm mentioned below.

[2] As, it is said, they will do for ten years before Sôshâns, the last apostle, appears to prepare for the resurrection (see Chap. XXXV, 3, Bd. XXX, 3).

[3] A tree said to grow in the ocean, the juice of which is the other ingredient of the elixir of immortality; it is also called Gôkarn, or Gôkar*d*, Av. gaokerena, and is guarded by ten enormous fish (see Bd. XVIII, 1–3, XXVII, 4, XXX, 25).

[4] The existence of such immortal creatures, said to be intended for special use at the resurrection, is here taken as a proof of the reality of the resurrection itself. Whether the seven immortals described in Chap. XC are to be included among them is uncertain.

by natural operation and through desire of deceit[1]. 103. And the demon of slander (spazg), whose nature it is to make the indignation (zôhar) of the creatures pour out, one upon the other, about nothing, as he does not succeed in making *it* pour out among the righteous[2], he makes the wicked even pour *it* out upon the wicked; *and* as he does not succeed even in making *it* pour out among the wicked, he makes a demon pour *it* out upon a demon. 104. The impetuous assailant, Wrath (Aeshm), as he does not succeed in causing strife *among* the righteous, flings discord *and* strife amid the wicked; *and* when he does not succeed *as* to the strife even of the wicked, he makes the demons *and* fiends fight together. 105. So also the demon of greediness (â*z*ŏ), when he does not attain, in devouring, to that of the good, mounts[3] by his own nature unto devouring that of the demons. 106. So also the deadly Astô-vîdâ*d*[4] is ever an antagonistic operator; when *there* is no righteous *one* who is mortal, nor any creatures in the world, the wicked dying *one* (mîrâk) rides to the fiends through a death which is an antagonism of himself[5].

[1] That is, the demons do not come into personal conflict with material creatures, but are supposed to influence their evil passions and to pervert the original laws of nature.

[2] M14 omits the passage from this word to the same word in § 104.

[3] The word sôbârê*d*ŏ, 'rides, mounts,' both here and in § 106, is possibly only a miswriting of the very similar word dûbârê*d*ŏ, 'runs, rushes.' Several words in this sentence are accidentally omitted in M14.

[4] See § 44.

[5] As it is uncertain whether the 'dying *one*' is a human being or the demon himself, it is doubtful which of them is here supposed to commit suicide. M14 and J have merely: 'nor even among the

107. The means of the united forces[1] are means such as the wise and the high-priests *have* proclaimed, that is, at the time of the renovation *of the universe*[2] *being* nigh, when completion *has* come to generation—those who *were* provided *being* born —and after they occasion freedom from generation (azerkhûnisnîh), they cause men *and* animals to exist, though passed *away and* dead. 108. All men, righteous and wicked, who continue in the world *become* immortal, the men are righteous whom Astôvîdâd does not obtain for death by evil noosing (dûs-vadisnŏ)[3] from behind, and *who have* completely attained to the rules of the sacred beings (yang-î yazdân); *and* the soul of the wicked, which is repentant of deceit, turns back upon the demons and fiends themselves all that previous violence of destruction and perversion, contention and blinding[4] which is natural to a demon, and they fight, and strike, and tear, and cause to tear, and destroy among themselves (benafsman val

creatures of the sacred beings those which are an antagonism of himself;' apparently connecting this section with the next. This final argument is that, as the demons by their very nature must injure their friends if they fail with their enemies, they contain within themselves the source of their own final destruction. In other words: 'if Satan rise up against himself, and be divided, he cannot stand, but hath an end' (Mark iii. 26).

[1] The army of angels of §§ 58, 64. The author, having exhausted his arguments in favour of the final triumph of the good creation, now returns to his description of the issue of the contest, which he was about to commence in § 64.

[2] M14 and J omit the following words as far as 'provided.'

[3] See Chap. XXIII, 3.

[4] Or, perhaps, 'concealment,' as there is some doubt whether aûbênîdârîh means 'making unseeing, or making unseen.'

benafsman) so long as they are in hell and numerous.

109. The wicked who are penitent become courageous anew as to the demon who perverts, the living occasion strength[1], *and* the retribution of the hellish existence of the wicked is completed, because the increase of sins[2], owing to the sin which they committed, ceases. 110. They are let out from hell, though their sins are thus accumulated by the demons; they have also prepared[3] the spirit of sin by the three days *in* molten metal[4], which drives away tears, as its name is owing to the lessening of tears[5], which is all[6] in that which *occurs* when all the doers of actions for the demon of falsehood[7] pass through that preparation. 111. And *he* who, *for* three days, thus bathes (vushakê*d*ŏ) his sins which are owing to the fiend, and *has* destroyed the filth (*k*akhû) of the accumulated sins, is like *those who* have passed off *and* turned over a burden.

112. And the impotence of sin is owing to the destroyer *of* the fiend by the perception of light,

---

[1] That is, the wicked who are still living, being penitent, reinforce the host of the righteous.

[2] Referring probably to the 'growth of sin' mentioned in Chaps. XI, 2, XII, 5.

[3] That is, 'purified.'

[4] All men are said to be purified, at the time of the resurrection, by passing through melted metal, which seems like warm milk to the righteous, but is a final torment to the wicked (see Chap. XXXII, 12, 13, Bd. XXX, 19, 20).

[5] This would seem to allude to some Avesta name of this molten metal, which is no longer extant.

[6] We should probably read hamâî, 'ever,' instead of hamâk, 'all.'

[7] Reading zûr, but it may be zôr, 'violence.'

who was their creator[1]; they (men) all see all, they all forgive, and they all are powerful as regards all *things* for the creator. 113. And, moreover, after the three days, when they occur, all the creatures of the good creator are purified *and* pure by the perfect washing passed through, by the most amazing preparation ordained (bakhtŏ), *and* by the most complete account they render complete. 114. And they are triumphant *over* the fiend through their own weapons, through their own driving away *of* their own littleness (kâsvî*d*ârîh), and the glory of the creator and that of the angels; and since he becomes exhausted in resources (dên *k*âr) they make *him* become extinct.

115. *But* previously[2] they are attacked, and dispersed, and subdued, and this even fully painfully and with complete experience; and they aid, through backward goodness, in the antagonism of means which are separated divergently, through scattered resources and subdued strength, like the life from the body of worldly mortals, and this, moreover, confusedly, uselessly, and unmovingly. 116. *But* the abode[3] for the essential material existence (stî-î *k*îharîkŏ), about which *there* is a seeking for interment[4], is not powerless, and on enquiring the wishes of such numbers[5] they have

[1] That is, the destroyer of the fiend was the creator of the men mentioned in § 108. The reading sinâ*s*nŏ, 'perception,' is uncertain; perhaps we ought to read 'in the regions (dîvâgânŏ) of light.'

[2] That is, before the purification in molten metal.

[3] The 'body,' apparently, but this section is by no means clear.

[4] This must be on the part of the fiend, as burial is unlawful.

[5] Perhaps the meaning is that the fiend is at length overcome by the constantly accumulating numbers of the penitent wicked.

cast *him* out; and no share whatever, *nor* fragment of a share, of fiendishness, *nor* even so much as some morsel of unpardonableness sent by fiendishness, remains in this light.

117. Those who are righteous, intelligent through their own glory of religion—which is a spirit[1] in the form of light—are scattered (parvandag-aîtŏ) equally around the sky of skies, when from every single side of it *there* arises, for the sake of margin, three *times* as much *space* as the earth created by Aûha*r*ma*zd*, in the preparation of the creatures which *were* created by him. 118. Through his own will he again constructs the bodies of the evil creation, unlaboriously, easily, and full-gloriously, though their construction is even from the clay of Aûshdâ*s*târ[2], and their moisture is from the purified water of Arekdvisûr[3] the undefiled. 119. And from that which is a good protector *through* him, and which is also connected *with*

---

[1] The handsome maiden who is supposed to meet the departed soul, and whose form is an embodiment of its own deeds and religion (see Chaps. XXIV, 5, XLIV, 20). Or, perhaps, the angel of religion (Dîn) itself, which is reverenced for its radiance and glory in Dîn Yt. 4.

[2] A mythical mountain (see Chap. XXX, 2).

[3] The mythical source of pure water which is said to flow from Mount Albûr*z* into Lake Urvis on the summit of Mount Hûgar, and thence to Mount Aûsîndôm in the wide-formed ocean, whence it partly flows into the ocean, and partly rains upon the earth (see Bd. XIII, 1, 3–5). Much the same account of it is given in Chap. XCII, 5, only the lake is said to be on the summit of Mount Aûsîndôm. It is the Av. Ardvî sûra of the Âbân Yt., and the Pahl. form Arekdvisûr = Aregdvisûr may be explained as a transposition of Aredgvisûr, an ordinary mispronunciation of Ardvî sûra. Modern Parsis, who consider the Pahl. k as silent (or merely a soft aspirate) after a vowel, would pronounce Aredvisûr.

him, even from the Hadhayãs ox[1], is the strength of everlasting welfare (vêhgarîh) *and* immortality; and the living are again produced for the body, they have immortal life, *and* they become hungerless *and* thirstless, undecaying *and* undying, undistressed and undiseased, ever-living *and* ever-beneficial.

120. After the renovation *of the universe there* is no demon, because *there* is no deceit; and no fiend, because there is no falsity; *there* is no evil spirit (angraminô), because there is no destruction; *there* is no hell, because there is no wickedness; *there* is no strife, because there is no anger; *there* is no hatred, because there is no ill-temper (dazîh); *there* is no pain, because there is no disease. 121. *There* is also no Dahâk[2], because there is no fear; *there* is no want, because there is no greediness; *there* is no shame, because there is no deformity; *there* is no falsehood[3], because there is no desire of falsehood; *there* is no heterodoxy, because there are no false statements; and *there* is no tardiness, because *it speaks* of a dilatory (sustŏ) race in that which is said thus: '*They are* all those of evil thoughts, of evil words, of evil deeds, a race of all evils to be made to tear by the evil spirit.'

122. And on his (the demon's) disappearance every evil has disappeared, on the disappearance of evil every good is perfected, and in the time of complete goodness it is not possible to occasion (andâkhtanŏ) any pain *or* distress whatever, by any means, to any creature. 123. Those who are present (nunak) sufferers[4], when *there* is a blow of

[1] See § 99. [2] See § 97.

[3] M14 and J omit what follows, as far as 'heterodoxy.'

[4] Literally 'attainers to endurance.'

a fist on the body, or the point of a nail (têkh bûrâk) is driven into a limb, are pained on account of the combination (ham-dâ*d*akîh) of a different nature for the purposes of the fiend in the body. 124. *But* at that time of no complication (aham-yâkhtîh), when a limb is struck upon a limb, or even such *a thing* as a knife, *or* sword, *or* club, *or* stone, *or* arrow reaches the body, *there* is no pain *or* discomfort whatever corresponding to that present pain. 125. And at that time one consideration (vu*s*î*d*-aê) occurs, for now the pain from that beating *and* striking is always owing to that different nature, and on account of *their being* suitable *to it*, but at that time everything *being* of like nature and like formation *there* is never *any* distress.

126. And in that most happy time they let the sun, moon, and luminaries exist, but *there* is no need for a return of the day and a removal of *its going* forth (frâshm)[1], for the world is a dispenser (vakhtâr) of all light, and all creatures, too, are brilliant; those luminaries also become as it were perfectly splendid *for* them. 127. And every creature, too, is of like will and like power; whichever *were* mortals, unenvious of the welfare of all creatures, are alike joyous, and that *share* of their position and pleasure rejoices *them* which has come to them from the glory of all *the existences and* capabilities of him, the all-good, who is aware of all of everything through his own perfect persistence *and* complete resources.

128. And he allots, to the doers of good works

[1] The 'going forth' of the day or the sun means its disappearance or going away, and is an Avesta phrase. The sun is supposed to be 'forth' when it is absent, not when it appears.

and the suitable ranks, the power of a judge (da*d*akŏ), wealthiness, goodness, and the directorship (ra*d*îh) of *what* is intended. 129. *He is* the designer of *what* is intended, as it is said about his creatures and capability that fire is producing wind, fire is producing water, and fire is producing earth; wind is producing fire, wind is producing water, and wind is producing earth; water is producing fire, water is producing wind, and water is producing earth; earth is producing fire, earth is producing wind, and earth is producing water. 130. The spirit is both the cause of spirit and the cause of matter (stî*s*); and the cause of matter, too, is also the cause of spirit, through that perpetual capability.

131. And, moreover, all the angels, the souls, and the guardian spirits are attending to the wishes *of* the glory of the creator and the commands of the creator, without trouble *and* fully rejoicing, in likeness unto the forms of seas, rivers, mountains, trees, and waters[1]; and they have comforted and decorated the creation. 132. And the angels, souls, and guardian spirits, themselves also the constituted spirits of a former contact with life, are thereby pleased *and* rejoiced; eternal *and* thoroughly prepared they are naturalised in that complete joy.

Chapter XXXVIII.

1. *As to* the thirty-seventh question and reply, that which you ask is thus: The measure that they

[1] All objects being supposed to be represented by guardian spirits in the other world.

measure good works *with being* revealed[1], how is it then *when* there is more, or not, done by us?

2. The reply is this, that every thought, word, and deed whose result is joy, happiness, and commendable recompense—when a happy result is obtainable, and the exuberance (afzûnŏ) of thought, word, and deed is important—is well-thought, well-said, and well-done[2]. 3. And for him the result of whose wish for good works is conclusively joy and exaltation of soul—which are his attainment of recompense from the constantly-beneficial space[3], the immortal *and* unlimited, which shall never perish—there is no measure of the multitude of good works. 4. For every one by whom many are performed, and *who* engages in still more, appropriates the result more fully, and is more worthy; *but* it is not obtained for the completion of that which is a *definite* measure, therefore he does not obtain still more, and it is not necessary *he should;* and it is, moreover, not obtained even for the completion of a limit of unlimitedness[4].

---

[1] They are balanced against the sins committed (see Chaps. XIII, 2–4, XXIV, 5, 6); if the good works exceed the sins by a very small quantity the soul is supposed to go to the ordinary heaven (vahistô), but if by a quantity sufficient to balance one unatonable sin it goes to the best existence, or supreme heaven (garôdmânô, see Sls. VI, 3, 4). M14 and J have merely: 'The measure for good works *being* revealed.'

[2] The three characteristics of good works.

[3] See Chaps. XXVI, 3, XXXI, 24, XXXVII, 22.

[4] The good works in excess of the quantity necessary for admitting the soul into the supreme heaven cannot affect the destination of the soul, but they add to its future enjoyment (see Chap. VIII, 4), and no limit can be assigned to the quantity that can be thus absorbed.

Chapter XXXIX.

1. *As to* the thirty-eighth question and reply, that which you ask is thus: What are the reason and cause of tying *on* the *sacred thread*-girdle (kûstîkŏ)[1] which, when they shall tie *it* on is said *to be* so greatly valuable, and when they shall not tie *it* the sin is so grievous?

2. The reply is this, that the all-good, most spiritual of spirits, and most ruling of rulers is the creator, and there is no need of troubles for men of the poor as to any wealth *or* anything, for all are his own. 3. And through his will *as* ruler, and all-powerful, he demands this of men, to remain properly

[1] The Kûstîk (Pers. kustî) consists of a string, about the size of a stay-lace, which is first passed twice round the waist very loosely, over the sacred shirt (see Chap. XL, 2), and tied in front with a loose double knot (right-handed and left-handed), and the long ends are then passed a third time round the waist and tied again behind with a similar double knot. This string contains six strands, each consisting of twelve very fine, white, woollen threads twisted together, or seventy-two threads in all. Near each end the six strands are braided together, instead of being twisted, and for the last inch they are braided into three separate string-ends of two strands each; these string-ends, therefore, contain twenty-four threads each, and form a kind of fringed end to the string. This fringe is a sort of remembrancer, as its six strands are supposed to symbolize the six Gâhanbârs or season-festivals, the twelve threads in each strand symbolize the twelve months, the twenty-four threads in each string-end symbolize the twenty-four kar*d*aks or sections of the Vispara*d*, and the seventy-two threads in the whole string symbolize the seventy-two hâs or chapters of the Yasna. The girdle has to be re-tied every time the hands have been washed, which, in order to comply with the ceremonial laws, occurs many times in the day; and each time it has to be done with ceremony and a particular formula of prayer (see § 27).

skirted[1] as a true servant not even bound—which is due to that service, and also the indication of a servant—as is seen *and* clearly declared in the ever-fixed (hamâî-dâ*d*ŏ) religion and belief.

4. Formerly men paid homage through the will and worship, as *it were* more effectually, more essentially, *and* more suitably for the discreet; and every day *spent* in worship offered and homage paid they account as *of* the greatest use, particularly for observing the world, and understanding *its* character. 5. And *as to him* of whose offering of homage no worldly advantage whatever is apparent—as fruit is apparent from trees, flavour from foods, fragrance from aromatic herbs, tint (bâm) from colours, the good quality of spears from the forest, health from the patient (môlvarakân), and decision from words—but, audibly speaking, *his* head is lowered in sign of humility—as though the head, which is uppermost in the body and in the most pre-eminent *position*, and is lowered as far even as the sole of the foot, which is lowermost in the body, salutes[2] *and* is placed on the ground in thought about worship *and* desire of paying homage—and the appearance which exists as regards himself through *that* lowliest (kî-hastŏ) servitude is *in accordance* with that which is apparent from trees, food, and the many other worldly advantages *before* recited—whoever *has* offered homage and such advantageous (vê*s*i*s*nakŏ) appearance

[1] That is, fully clad, as going about uncovered is a sin (see Chap. XL, 4). On occasions of ceremony, and for the purpose of showing extraordinary respect, the Parsis wear an extra long-skirted robe.

[2] Reading d*r*û*d*ŏê*d*, but the orthography is unusual and the word, therefore, uncertain.

is manifest—even then that sign of humility *and* servitude is *what* great multitudes consider the offering of homage of a man more essential for hypocrisy (shêdŏ)[1].

6. *But* owing to that which *happens* when they plant a tree in the name of a sacred being[2] and eat the produce, and practise other worldly labour of worldly advantage, owing also to work of this kind through the doing of which they preserve all the growing *crops* of the whole world, and through tillage and multitudinous cultivated plots (khûstakîhâ) *it* is manifest that they should meditate inwardly (dên mînŏyên)[3]. 7. A token *and* sign of worship is *of* great use, and a great assistance (ban*g*i*s*nŏ) therein is this belt (band), which is called the Kûstîk, that is tied on the middle of the body.

8. The reasons of the assistance are numerous; and its first assistance is this, that *as to* him who—*as* a worshipper of the sacred beings, owing to the undeceitful (akadbâ) religion whose indication is sagaciously propitiating with the *purifying* cup[4]—wears upon the body that spiritual, customary, and

[1] The author is here adopting his most involved style of writing, which, in the original Pahlavi, is often hardly intelligible, and particularly apt to be misunderstood; but the object of this section seems to be to deprecate the Muhammadan practice of frequent prostrations during prayer, which are in marked contrast to the slight obeisances made by the Parsis.

[2] Whether yêdatô means 'an angel,' or 'God,' is here uncertain.

[3] The argument is that the growth of plants is so obviously occasioned by some unseen power that it naturally leads to meditation, and then to prayer.

[4] The words dâni*s*nîkŏ levatman-tâ*s*tîk-shnâyîn seem to refer to the Bareshnûm ceremony of purification, described in Vend. IX, 1–145 (see App. IV), which is a rite eminently characteristic of Maz*d*a-worship.

doctrinal indication of the sacred beings with a wisdom which is truly religion, *his* steadfastness and religious service of the sacred beings are audibly spoken thereby; even for the religious *it* is commanded, because *it* is an assisting motive of beneficial high-priests and such-like submitters *to* the commands of the religion of the sacred beings.

9. One is this, that, as the lowliest servant and greatest lord are steadily agreed, and *it is* beneficial[1] when they (the servants) wear a belt upon the body *as* a sign of service—because *it* is not the custom to grant that little at any time without guardianship —the lapse of which service is also not a beneficial lapse, then those unbound are without a token of the lord's service.

10. One is this, that it is commanded in revelation to keep thought, word, and deed confined from sin by a belt, and just like a servant; for the sake of confinement of sins from purity of thought, whose dwelling is the heart, *one* is to wear the same belt, which is the token of a servant, *on* the middle of the body and before the heart; and the periodical (hangâmîkânŏ) sight of the token and sign of confined sins, and of the constant reminder for *one's* own mind, is the necessity of wearing *it* as a belt which is very restraining from the sin in thought, word, and deed that is manifest even in experience; which wearing of the same belt is as a reason and cause of much remembrance of much sin, that in the same way is therefore a restraint of it.

11. One is this, that the ancients acquainted with religion *have* communicated these tidings (srôbŏ)

[1] Reading spenâk, but it may be sazŏâk, 'seemly.'

unto our ancestors *and* to us :—'When the destroyer came upon the creatures, the demons and witches (parîkŏ) especially rushed up in the earth and atmosphere, and even to *just* below the position of the stars; and they saw multitudes of luminaries, and also the barricade *and* rampart[1] of the glory of the religion, and the girdle (parvand)[2] of the wishes *and* good works of all, when[3] it is arrayed like a brilliant *thread*-girdle (kûstîk), and all its luminaries are girded (parvastŏ) by the girdle as the girdle of the omniscient wisdom has girded the all-intelligent angels.' 12. That great glory of the pure religion, solving doubts, became as beautiful and far-adorning as is stated in the liturgy (mânsar) thus: 'The star-studded girdle (ayîvyahângânŏ) of the spirit-fashioned, good religion of the Mazda-worshippers[4].' 13. All the demons and fiends *were* terrified by the great glory of the religion, *and it is* said that, by the recital, practice, *and* promulgation of the whole routine of the enlightened religion, all those fiends are subdued, *and* the renovation *of the universe* is produced by the will of the patron spirits (ahvân). 14. Likewise, on account of that terror, none of the demons and fiends, who are the mightiest of the demons, rushed upon the creatures of that uppermost third *of the sky*[5], who are in purity and inde-

---

[1] See Chap. XXXVII, 47.

[2] It is not certain that parvand signifies 'a girdle,' or that parvastanŏ means 'to gird,' but they seem to be used in that sense here. The former word translates Av. paurvanîm, 'leading the Pleiades' (Haug's Essays, p. 182), in Yas. IX, 81, an epithet applied to the belt of Orion.

[3] M14 has 'which.'

[4] Quoted from Pahl. Yas. IX, 81 (see Chap. XXXVII, 48).

[5] See Chap. XXXVII, 24-27.

structictibility. 15. And it (the girdle) is commanded in revelation for men, more particularly for upholders of the religion[1], *to be* within the middle third *and* near to the uppermost third of the body[2].

16. *One is* this, that Yim the splendid, *son* of Vîvangha[3], who in *his* worldly career was most prosperous in worldly affairs, a keeper away of all agitations of temper[4] *and* all death, *and* a provider of freedom from decay *and* exemption from death, when he was deceived by the fiend *was* thereby made eager for supreme sovereignty instead of the service of Aûharmazd. 17. And about his administration (dâdârîh) of the creatures *it* is said he himself became cut[5] away from radiant glory by that fiendishness[6], and their cause of wandering

[1] M14 continues as follows:—'through that girdle (parvand) of the religion, *and* a *thread*-girdle (kûstîkŏ), from the region of the world and religious *in character*, is put on within the middle third,' &c.

[2] Some words are evidently here missing in the Pahl. text, including the first word of the next section. The reason here given for the girdle being worn round the waist, just below the uppermost third of the body, is that the impregnable barrier of heaven (of which the girdle is a counterpart) is said to be just below the uppermost third of the sky.

[3] See Chap. XXXVII, 80, 95.

[4] Reading vispŏ khôî-*s*ôrân, but we might perhaps read vispŏân sahôrân, 'all oppressors,' assuming that sahôr stands for Av. sâthra, a term applied to some particular tribe of another religion which was under the rule of Yim and his two predecessors (see Zamyâd Yt. 26, 28, 31). Another possible reading is vispŏân yêkhvarân, 'all frosts.'

[5] Assuming that khvû*d*akŏ stands for khû*d*akŏ, but the word is uncertain.

[6] The particular kind of fiendishness that led Yim astray in his old age (like Solomon) was lying, that is, denial of the truth of his religion. In consequence of this apostasy the royal glory departed from him, and he allied himself to the demons in the

(garînisnŏ) is the demon, and mankind perishes in that wandering from plain and hill-side[1]. 18. And his pardon originated from the fully-persistent creator; therefore he spoke *and* gave advice unto his successors as to the retribution of those *who* shall abandon the service of the creator; and therein is explained about the fortress of the angels[2], with the many proper actions which are the strength of the fortress, and about the proportional way it is strengthened when a belt worn on the waist is ordered for men *by* him—the fully glorious ruler who *was* lord of the world, and also in gloriousness well-betokening the good creation—*and* they[3] likewise order *it*.

19. One is this, that just as through that reason[4], which is an appointment (padŏ-dahisnŏ) that the sacred beings decreed, the *sacred thread*-girdle *was* worn even before the coming of Zaratûst the Spîtamân, *so* after *the coming of* that messenger (vakhsvar) of the sacred beings, the righteous Zaratûst—who enjoined the commands of the good spirits *and* the exposition of the religion, with discourse praising the sacred beings and scriptures (avîstâkŏ) about steadfastness in the good religion—the same religious girdle is put on, with a religious formula[5], around

---

617th year of his reign, and remained in their power for most of the remaining century of his life (see Zamyâd Yt. 31–38, Bd. XXIII, 1, XXXIV, 4).

[1] Assuming that dastŏ stands for Pers. dast, and varîvakŏ for Pers. garîvah; otherwise, we may read 'from dignity and the hovel (varîkakŏ),' meaning that they perish from all ranks, instead of all places.

[2] The rampart of heaven (see § 11).

[3] His successors.

[4] As detailed in § 18.

[5] The Nîrang-i Kustî (see § 27).

the body, over the garment of Vohûman[1]. 20. Because the same intimation, relative to girding (parvandisnîk) is wisdom for which the race of the religion is so justly famed that innumerable people, with the same customs *and* equally proper girding, wear the *sacred thread*-girdle, the ceremonial belt of the religion *and* indication of the creator, on the middle of the body; *and* it becomes more destructive of the power of destruction[2], more obstructive of the way to sin, and more contesting (kastaktar) the will of the demons.

21. One is this, that *he* is unwise that *has* not worn *it* when that *man has* arrived in whose law no belting and no girdling[3] are ordered, and more perplexing and more grievous destruction is so manifested at the time, that *it* is similar evidence to that exposition of revelation, the purport (aêvâz) of *whose* question *and* reply is spoken thus[4]:—'"O creator! in whom is the manifestation of secretly-progressing destruction, that is, in whom is its progress[5]?" And Aûharmazd spoke thus: "In him who is the guide of a vile religion; whoever it is who puts on a girdle

---

[1] The sacred shirt (see Chap. XL, 2). The garment of a purified man is called Vohûman in Vend. XIX, 76–78, 81–83 (trans. D.).

[2] The term seg or sêg, used for 'destruction' here and in §§ 21–23, is the name of 'the fiend who causes annihilation' (see Bd. XXVIII, 26).

[3] It is possible that an-ayîvyâgânîh may mean 'no garmenting,' and refer to the sacred shirt, as the previous term avîbandîh, 'no belting,' refers to the sacred thread-girdle.

[4] In Pahl. Vend. XVIII, 21–23, with some variations (see Haug's Essays, p. 367).

[5] Instead of rûbâkîh, 'progress,' K35 has rûbânîh, which might mean 'soul-state,' but is probably a clerical blunder.

at most thrice (3-tûmak) in a year[1], that is, he does not wear a *sacred* shirt and *thread*-girdle, and his law also is this, that it is not necessary to wear *them*"'—and when the law of no belting is so grievous that, when that law shall be accepted, it is observed *that* destruction is strengthened.

22. The same belt, kept on after the command of Yim, *was* the first token as regards which an annihilator of destruction is mentioned *and* established by law; *and on* both occasions[2] destruction is more grievously manifest. 23. That which is more particularly important is such as the destroyer of destruction, Yim the splendid, advised, which the high-priest of the good, Zaratûst the Spîtamân, mentioned thus:—'The *sacred thread*-girdle is as a sign of the service of the sacred beings, a token of sin ended, and a presage of beneficence; *and one is* to put *it* on *and* to gird *it*, in the neighbourhood of the heart and *on* the middle of the body, with the religious formula accompanying the glorious scripture.' 24. That is also betokened by *its* equally-dividing (hambûr) position and determining fashion; for, as a wise man becomes a discriminator between benefit *and* injury, between good and evil, so also the place of the *sacred thread*-girdle is between below and above. 25. With a low *sacred* girdle there is a passage for one's want of openness (avîshô*d*anŏ) and secret ruin, and also a shutting up[3] of life; with a high *sacred*

---

[1] In the Vendidad it is he who does not put one on for three years.

[2] Both when ordered by Yim and when confirmed by Zaratûst.

[3] Reading a*v*ar-vadi*s*nŏîh (the first nasal in bandi*s*n=vandi*s*n being often omitted); it can hardly be afrandi*s*nŏîh, 'magnificence,' because the latter abstract suffix, -îh, would be

girdle there is a way *for* thought, word, and deed, and no confinement (agîrisnŏkârîh) of life; and tying the *sacred* girdle with a religious rite (hamdînŏ) is like a glory amid the glories *of* the angels, for it is itself through the aid of the patron spirit (ahvô). 26. And from the heart, which is the place of thought and dwelling of life, on the upper side (lâlâîh) are the eye, ear, tongue, *and* brain, which are the dwellings of sight, hearing, speech, understanding, and intellect; and on its lower side (frôdîh)[1] is the abode of a father's generativeness.

27. When this *sacred thread*-girdle, whose token, sign, and presage are such[2], is tied, it is girded on with this glorious rite[3] of the glorious ones, the custom of the learned, the command of rulers, and the decree of apostles.

28. That secretly-progressing destruction[4], which *arises* from the fiend of insubordination (asardârîh)[5] who *was* much afraid of Yim, *and* which is averse to the labour of men *and* the service of Aûharmazd, is a demon and irreligious (dûs-dînô), who is full of fear of the girdles (parvandîhâ) of the glory of

ungrammatical after the former, -isnŏ, in an uncompounded verbal noun. Some of the other words are also uncertain.

[1] The MSS. have merely rôdîh. [2] As stated in § 23.

[3] This is the Nîrang-i Kustî, or girdle formula, that has to be performed every time the girdle is re-tied, which happens several times a day. It is fully detailed in Appendix II, at the end of this volume.

[4] See § 21; the first letter of nîhân, 'secretly,' is omitted by K35 in both places.

[5] Sêg, the fiend of destruction, is connected with the demon Bût in Vend. XIX, 4, 6; but the characteristic of 'insubordination' is more applicable to the demon Tarômat, 'the disobedient' (see Bd. XXVIII, 14, 26, 34).

religion, *with* which both angels *and* also worldlings *have* become belted *and* diligent.

29. Then, because the glory for this belt of ours, which is called the Kûstîk and is worn on the middle of the body, remains unreleased (a*v*î-vûkht) from the angels, who are givers of glory, *and from* men who are glorious—which is explained as a similitude *and* sample of fortunes (bâharakŏîhâ) among worldlings, even those *who are* actually primitive creatures likewise[1]—it *has*, therefore, seemed comely and desirable. 30. And their heart, will, knowledge, and purpose are as much for it as that which is perceptible where, even apart from those of the good religion who shall tie the *sacred thread*-girdle with the scripture formula, *some* of the faiths of all countries, except those who are unbelted, possess the religious custom[2]. 31. Also outside the seat of the existence of faith[3] all men have the waist, or the palms of the hands[4], or similar joints for a girdle (kûstîkŏ); *and* it is deemed comely, desirable, and convenient for work to wear *it*. 32. And *it* is manifestly the lot (dakŏ) of the thoroughly-praising one whose own desire is truth and the enjoyment of welfare, *it is* a token of the service of the sacred beings, and a sign of walking *in* the commands of religion,

---

[1] The precise meaning is not very clear.

[2] Alluding probably to the Brahmanical thread which is worn by the higher castes of Hindus diagonally, over one shoulder and below the other arm, and is so far analogous to the Parsi thread-girdle that it is a religious symbol put on with a religious rite.

[3] Reading varôyi*s*nŏ ahû gâs, but K35 has rôyi*s*nŏ, 'growth,' instead of 'faith.'

[4] Reading kafihâ, or kafagîh. Perhaps the allusion is to a rosary which is held in the hands, or worn on the wrists, by people of many religions.

which they shall tie on account of the superior beings (pâshûmân) with the proper formula, more particularly *with* that which *one* utters when *there is* reliance *upon* the scripture itself.

CHAPTER XL.

1. *As to* the thirty-ninth question *and* reply, that which you ask is thus: What kind of goodness and want of goodness can there be *in* the *sacred thread-*girdle and shirt; *and* what are the sin of running about uncovered, of prayer offered and prayer not offered, and the purpose of cleansing (mîsn)?

2. The reply is this, that it (the shirt)[1] is needful *to be* perfectly pure white *and* single, which one fold is because Vohûman also is thus the one creature who *was* first[2], and afterwards from him the garment which is innermost and concealed is called in revelation[3].

3. Proper girdling is double[4], which two folds are because he also who is in the course of the twofold religious wisdom is intelligent, and the duties *due to* the sacred beings are themselves *in* two divisions

---

[1] The sacred shirt, constantly worn by Parsis of both sexes (young children excepted), is a very loose tunic of white muslin, with very short loose sleeves covering part of the upper arm (see Sls. IV, 4–8).

[2] The archangel Vohûman (see Chap. III, 13) is said to have been the first creation of the creator (see Bd. I, 23).

[3] The garment of Vohûman (see Chap. XXXIX, 19).

[4] That is, it is passed twice round the waist before it is tied the first time, but then it is passed a third time round the waist (see Chap. XXXIX, 1).

which are called the instinctive *and that* heard by the ears[1].

4. After a man is in the girding they shall tie on, the symptoms of *any* sins of the belted body are *free* from sin which is condemned (vigîrînîdŏ); and when he walks uncovered, or naked, or with a twofold garment, there is then no root of *the sin of* running about uncovered[2] in him. 5. Moreover, on hymns *being* chanted during a meal an *inward* prayer is not also necessary[3].

6. The purpose[4] of a cleansing (mîsn-aê) is this, that the suitableness of men for eating is due to worship of the sacred beings and glorification of the sacred beings. 7. And *as to* their necessary recommendation (siparîh)[5] of any food for eating, the

[1] The twofold wisdom of the Avesta comprises the two intellects, the âsnô khratus, 'the durable or instinctive wisdom,' and the gaoshô-srûtô khratus, 'the ear-heard or acquired wisdom,' which are the terms used here.

[2] The sin of vishâd-dûbârisnîh, which would have been incurred in any of these cases if no girdle had been worn, is a venial sin of one Farmân for each of the three first steps, but becomes a Tanâpûhar sin (equivalent to 75 or 400 Farmâns) at the fourth step (see Sls. IV, 8–10).

[3] This is mentioned as a further illustration of a greater religious duty superseding a lesser one. When the Gâthas, or hymns, are being chanted, the reciter is already under the protection of the inward prayer (vâg) with which all acts of worship must commence; it is, therefore, unnecessary to take another prayer inwardly before eating. Inward prayer is a short formula which is said to be 'taken' and 'retained' inwardly, as a protective spell, by muttering its commencement before certain necessary acts, and after the completion of the act the remainder of the formula is 'spoken out' aloud, and the spell is dissipated, before the person can converse (see Sls. III, 6).

[4] The MSS. have pêm, 'milk,' instead of *k*îm, 'purpose,' but see § 1; the Pahl. letters p and *k* are often much alike.

[5] M14 has sipâsîh, 'praise;' but this and several other emenda-

glorifying of the sacred beings, and the true usages about recounting *it*, it is commanded, before eating, when the mouth is not soiled with food, *that* the mouth (dahân) *should* proceed with the utterance of the pure glorification[1]. 8. Being thereupon suitably seated, and *having* properly eaten the food, *one* is to make the mouth clean with a tooth-pick and water; and after eating, before all words, the praise of the sacred beings is glorified by the mouth cleansed by washing. 9. And between the glorifying before eating and the after glorification *one* is not[2] to speak other words, and when during a meal a word is spoken by the mouth, that kind of glorification which *it* is the custom to utter before and after eating is offered by its own organ (andâm)[3].

10. And every single organ *has* one function, *but* two special functions are connected with the mouth, which are speaking *and* eating; *and* because *they are* together *they* are mutually opposed, for speaking connects that which is an inward possession with outside teachings (*k*âshîhâ), *and* through eating, the outside food comes for the inward further vitality of life. 11. As the ancients *have* sáid, where one operation is appointed unto two operators, *it is* more

---

tions in the same MS. are probably nothing but unsuccessful attempts to render an obscure text intelligible, without taking the trouble to understand it.

[1] This glorification (stâyi*s*nŏ) must refer to the inward prayer of § 5, which commences by praising Aûha*r*ma*zd* (see Chap. LXXIX, 2, note).

[2] Reading lâ, 'not,' instead of râî, 'on account of.' M14 has altered the passage.

[3] That is, when the spell of the inward prayer is broken by speaking before the proper time (see § 5, note), the spell must be renewed before proceeding with the meal.

expressly so that during eating two operations may not both at once (ayag-i*k*-gûn) be produced, by speaking *and* by eating.

12. To keep those two operations distinct, one from the other, the custom of uttering the praise of sacred beings *and* the glorification of sacred beings when the mouth remains in the act of eating, until the mouth becomes clean from food, is decreed as inconsistent with goodness (aham-vêhîh). 13. And that *which* remains from the outpouring (rîkh) at the time of a cleansing is called 'a cleansing (mîsn-aê).'

14. One means for the retention of knowledge is through not having that retention of knowledge exhausted, but when *one* thus speaks during that cleansing the words are really originating with the mouth, for he does not retain *them*; and whenever (maman) he does not speak anything whatever with the tongue, that religious glorification which *it* is the custom to utter before and after eating is then offered by him from his own limited resources (sâmânŏ-î vîmônd), and it will be offered from his own limited resources.

Chapter XLI.

1. *As to* the fortieth question and reply, that which you ask is thus: Of those whose decision is this, that it is not necessary to be steadfast in the religion of the Maz*d*a-worshippers—by *which* decision this is asserted, *that* they should abandon the religion of the Maz*d*a-worshippers—*some one* disparages the religion *and* goes over to a foreign faith (an-aîrîh), then of what nature is his sin

owing thereto, *and* what does the sin owing thereto, as regards those of the same foreign religion, amount to? 2. Or order *some one* then to tell us clearly concerning it, how it is, and how is the disobedience due to this sin.

3. The reply is this, that an adult is worthy of death[1] on account of the good religion they[2] would abandon, on account also of the adopted law of the foreign faith *he* is worthy of death, in whose reliance upon the improper law is also the sin which they[3] maintain *and* practise by law, and through *being* in the same law *he* is equally sinful with them. 4. And also when any one is on that course, and his wish is *for* the same protection, of which a similitude is *in* the enduring words of that good law they would forsake, and he adopts that which is vile[4], even through that impropriety *he* is equally sinful.

5. When he dies, without renunciation[5] *of that sin* and impenitently, in that improperly-constituted law, the position of his soul is then in the worst

[1] That is, he commits a mortal sin, for which he could have formerly been condemned to death by the high-priest (see Sls. VIII, 2, 5–7, 21).

[2] The teachers of infidelity.

[3] The foreigners.

[4] The probable meaning is that if he conforms to the foreign faith merely from politic motives, while retaining a belief in his own religion, he is still equally sinful.

[5] This renunciation is effected by the recitation of a particular formula called the Patit, in which every imaginable sin is mentioned with a declaration of repentance of any such sins as the reciter may have committed. But this formal renunciation must be accompanied by atonement and true repentance; and in order to ascertain the proper atonement all serious sins must be confessed to the high-priest (see Sls. IV, 14, VIII, 1, 2, 8–10).

existence[1], and his punishment is that of many *sins* worthy of death; from the demons also *there* come grievously, hand in hand, pain and suffering, gnawing and stench of many kinds, stinging, tearing, and lacerating, primary evil and discomfort. 6. And through their[2] law and faith his distress in that worst existence is thus until the last change of existence, when the renovation *of the universe* is produced by will among living beings.

7. But reality (aîtŏîh), as regards living, arises from renunciation of that disobedience; it makes those attract to the good law who seduced him to that evil law, that which established him improperly in the law it eradicates from *his* conduct (rûbâkîh), advancing sins it again restrains, and whatever *has* advanced it repairs again anew through the religion of the Maz*d*a-worshippers, *and* he becomes thoughtful, constant, and steadfast. 8. The sin which he set going he restrains and atones for by wealth, trouble, and authorising[3] commands; even in the body he also undergoes punishment in the three *nights* (satûîh)[4]; he then obtains forgiveness, and his soul is saved.

9. And as *it* is said in the persistent law of the sacred beings[5], that 'the good religion of the sacred beings, who are the Maz*d*a-worshipping superiors,

---

[1] See Chap. XXXIII, 3. [2] The foreigners'.

[3] Or, tûbânkâr may mean 'lavish.' The ordering of religious ceremonies, as good works in atonement for sin, is probably intended; and these always imply a lavish expenditure upon the priesthood.

[4] Referring to the three nights' punishment after the resurrection of the body, which is specially reserved for mortal sinners (see Bd. XXX, 16).

[5] Quoting, with some alteration, from Pahl. Vend. III, 151.

ordains *it* as retribution,' so that the sin it takes away (spayêiti)[1] may not exist in him, his retribution is declared by revelation. 10. And by the same witness *it* is said, that all of the primitive faith have been quite of the same opinion about this, that from the good religion except by[2] the way of renunciation *of sin* there is none unless to hell; but that renunciation *should* be during life, for it is said that 'whoever *when* living does not become righteous, that is, does not fully atone for sin, *for* him *when* dead *there* is no grant of[3] the best existence.' 11. To commit no sin is better than retribution *and* renunciation of sin.

CHAPTER XLII.

1. *As to* the forty-first question and reply, that which you ask is thus: *As to* him who remains in the good religion of the Ma*zd*a-worshippers, *whom* men shall make the protection and assistance of the good religion[4], *who* shall save men from a foreign faith and irreligion (akdînôîh), and then holds back *some* of those who have the idea that they should go over to a foreign faith and irreligion, *and* they do not go over to the foreign faith, *but* become steadfast in the religion of the Ma*zd*a-worshippers, what is then[5] the

[1] The Avesta verb spayêiti, here used as a technical term, occurs frequently in Vend. III, 142–148.

[2] Assuming that ba*r*â, 'indeed,' stands for pavan, 'by,' (see Chap. VII, 2 n.)

[3] Reading bakhshi*s*n-î, but it may be a corruption of bakhshând, 'they shall grant,' as assumed in M14. This passage is quoted from Pahl. Vend. V, 173.

[4] Some one placed in authority, such as a high-priest or judge, is evidently meant.

[5] Reading êdîna*s*, 'then of him,' instead of ayûf, 'or;' the

nature of the decision of the angels *about* him, and what is the nature of their (the men's) good works *and* sin?

2. The reply is this, that *he* is much extolled, happy, exalted, of great good works *and* abundant recompense, and the path to the best existence, prepared (frârâstŏ) by his righteousness, is wide[1]; the delight of *his* soul becomes complete, *and its* hope[2] is great. 3. And every good work that is manifested in the good religion by those who are transferred by him from a foreign faith and irreligion, and *which* they shall do thereafter—when, through the perseverance *and* praise exercised by him who is protected by the religion, they are saved *from* irreligion—becomes his as much as though it had been set going by him himself, and *he has* the same praise and the same good works with them. 4. Of the extent (sâmânŏ) *and* amount of such good works *there* is no writing a second time, unless *his* acquaintance with the full computation of the good works due to *their* number is continuous[3]; but when *in* the same way they are practising and steadfast in sin it shall not be assigned *to him*[4]. 5. Then his position in

two words being alike in Pahlavi except in the latter part of the last letter.

[1] That is, his path to heaven over the *K*invad bridge is rendered wide and easy by his good deeds (see Chap. XXI, 5).

[2] Reading aîmê*d*; M14 has khîm, 'disposition,' and K35 has khîmâ*d*, which suggests 'shall be greatly celebrated' as a possible translation.

[3] The meaning appears to be that their good works are imputed to him only so long as he continues to exercise some control over them.

[4] That is, their sins will not be imputed to him in the same way as their good works.

righteousness[1] is very grand, and in the world he has himself great eminence, applause, *and* dignity.

6. And as much as that which is an improper law *and* a law worthy of death is a punishing of the soul, and the disconnected[2] words and perversion (vas*takîh), due also to the perfidy (rangis*nŏ) of the fiend *who has* come, are such that in his time the religious rites (dînô) performed are rites of grievous vexation *and* fear, *so* that which is a proper law, like the great glorification in spirit and the connected words of the high-priests, is the arrival of the good spirit as much as a virtue worthy of recompense *and* full of hope. 7. Even as that which is said thus: 'Of men who are practisers of good deeds the manifestation is then in their children.'

CHAPTER XLIII.

1. *As to* the forty-second question and reply, that which you ask is thus: *Regarding* a man who is consecrating a sacred cake[3], and the fire is his household attendant (khavag-î mânô) from afar, when he sees *it*, at how many steps is it improper? 2. When they consecrate a sacred cake by *light of* a lamp, why do they not say *the words* 'tava âthrô (for thee, the fire),' as *by* another fire? 3. And of the propitiatory dedications (shnûmanŏîhâ)[4] to the period of the day (gâh), the day, and the month of the consecration of the sacred cake, which is that

[1] Or, perhaps, aharûbŏîh may here mean 'the righteous existence' or heaven.

[2] Reading apa*d*vand, instead of va pa*d*vand.

[3] See Chap. XXX, 1.

[4] See Chap. XXIX, 1.

which when earlier *or* later is also then not proper, *and* which is that which is proper? 4. When they shall accomplish the consecration of a sacred cake *with* one more dedication *than those* of the thirty days of the months in the year, how is it necessary to act so that it may not enter *too* early; and which is the one more dedication which, when they shall make *it*, is proper, which is that which is not proper, and which is that which is earlier and later?

5. The reply is this, that at forty-eight[1] feet from the sacred twigs[2] to the fire—which would be about nine reeds, *if* of a medium man—even though *one*

---

[1] K35 has 'forty-seven.' Taking the foot at 10½ English inches (see Bd. XXVI, 3 n) the 48 feet would be 42 English feet, and the nâî or reed would be 4 feet 8 inches.

[2] The baresôm (Av. baresma), or bundle of sacred twigs, is an indispensable part of the ceremonial apparatus; it is held in the hand of the officiating priest while reciting many parts of the liturgy, and is frequently washed with water and sprinkled with milk. It consists of a number of slender rods, varying with the nature of the ceremony, but usually from five to thirty-three. These rods were formerly twigs cut from some particular trees, but now thin metal wires are generally used; and when not in the hand of the priest they are laid upon the crescent-shaped tops of two adjacent metal stands, each called a mâh-rû, 'moon-face,' and both together forming the baresôm-dân or 'twig-stand.' The baresôm is prepared for the sacred rites by the officiating priest while reciting certain prayers (see Haug's Essays, pp. 396-399), during which he washes the twigs with water, and ties them together with a kûstîk, or girdle, formed of six thread-like ribbons split out of a leaflet of the date-palm and twisted together. This girdle, being passed twice round the middle of the bundle of twigs, is secured with a right-handed and left-handed knot on one side of the bundle, and is then passed round a third time and secured with a similar double knot on the other side, exactly as the kûstîk or sacred thread-girdle is secured round the waist of a Parsi man or woman (see Chap. XXXIX, 1).

sees the fire *and* does not say 'tava âthrô[1],' it is proper. 6. And a lamp also has the same contingency (ham-brâh) as a fire; and by our teaching they do not consecrate a sacred cake *at* a lamp on which there is no burning of firewood, *but* they should cause a burning of firewood on that at which they consecrate a sacred cake, and they say 'tava âthrô[2].'

7. And *there is* a propitiatory dedication *for* each separate consecration of a sacred cake, and not again from the first to the last[3]; and the first is the nearest to the first day, Aûha*r*ma*z*d, just as Âtûr ('fire') *and* Â*v*ân ('waters') are other days in the series; and the last is the day Anîrân, because in the same series the day Anîrân is the latest[4]. 8. When the seven

---

[1] These Avesta words, meaning 'for thee, the fire,' are used when addressing the fire, or presenting anything to it, such as firewood and incense (see Yas. III, 52, VII, 3, XXII, 10, 22, &c.); they are not to be used, however, when the fire is so far off, or so feeble, that its light cannot be seen by the speaker (see Sls. X, 37).

[2] Meaning that in his opinion a lamp is no proper substitute for a sacred fire unless a little firewood is burnt in it.

[3] In the liturgy for the consecration of the sacred cakes, which consists chiefly of Yas. III, 1–VIII, 9 (see Haug's Essays, p. 408), the portion contained in Yas. III, IV, VI, VII is filled with propitiatory formulas, some of which are fixed, but others vary according to the hour, day, and month of the service. Some of the variable propitiatory dedications for the day and month are, however, identical with some of the fixed ones, such as those for fire, waters, &c. And in case of the day or month requiring the use of a variable dedication of this description, the object of the text is to prohibit the use of the corresponding fixed dedication, which would be an unnecessary repetition of the same words. This appears to be the meaning of the words va akha*r* min zak-î levînŏ va*l* akha*r* lâ translated in the text; but it would be hardly possible to express so simple a meaning in a more obscure fashion.

[4] The series of propitiatory dedications for the thirty days of the

archangels are in the propitiatory dedication it is proper to put the seven archangels first in their own order, then the period of the day[1], then the day, then the month of the consecration, and, afterwards, the other dedications in such order as they are written.

9. And *as to* the earlier which they should put later, one is when they shall put a dedication before the seven archangels, one is that when they shall put the day before the period of the day, one is when they shall put the month before the day, and one is that when a dedication, distinct from the seven archangels, the period of the day, the day, *and* the month, on account of *being* before the archangels, or before the period of the day, or before the day, or before the month, is accounted as improper a dedi-

month (which are also used for months of the same names) constitute the Sîrôzah, which is given in two forms, one in which the names and titles are in the genitive case, and the other in which they are in the accusative. From the first form of the Sîrôzah the proper dedications for the actual day and month are taken and substituted for Yas. III, 50, 51, IV, 40, 41, VII, 41, 42 (which passages, as they stand, are correct only for the first day, Aûha*r*ma*zd*, of the first month, Fravar*d*în); and from the second form of the Sîrôzah they are similarly taken and substituted for Yas. VI, 37, 38; somewhat in the same way as the Collect, Epistle, and Gospel for the day are taken from the complete series of such writings, and inserted in the Communion service of the Church of England. The first day is Aûha*r*ma*zd*, the ninth day and ninth month are Âtûr, the tenth day and eighth month are Â*v*ân, and the last day is Anîrân. Following these variable dedications for the day and month are the fixed dedications for Âtûr, 'fire,' and Â*v*ân, 'waters,' unless they have been already recited for the day or month.

[1] The dedication for the gâh or period of the day occupies the place of Yas. III, 21–37 (in which the formulas for all five gâhs are given); so that when the archangels are to be propitiated the dedications for them must precede Yas. III, 21.

cation as *that of* yesterday, *or* the day before, is for this day.

10. So that when *it is* the propitiatory dedication for the day Khûr of the month of consecration Â*v*ân[1], the day *and* month are such that their order and the Âtûr ('fire') and Â*v*ân ('waters') succeeding them are thereby set in reverse order to the *proper* sequence[2]. 11. Then, too, when in the same month[3] its propitiatory dedication for the day *and* month becomes *alike for* day and month[4], it is recited as regards *both* the month and the 'waters' (â*v*ân), because *they are* not connected together and *have* again become non-inclusive; *and* then *one* is to consider them as proper.

Chapter XLIV.

1. *As to* the forty-third question *and* reply, that which you ask is thus: *There is* a man who is superintending (a*v*ar-mândakakŏ) and skilful, in whom great skill as regards religion is provided, and the high-priest's duty and officiating priest's duty (magô-patîh) are performed by him; or they are not performed by him, but in him great skill as regards

---

[1] The eleventh day of the eighth month.

[2] The meaning is that in such a case the dedications for the day and month, and the fire and waters (Yas. III, 52, 53) which follow, will stand in the following order:—Khûr, Â*v*ân, Âtûr (the second Â*v*ân being omitted as directed by § 7), which is precisely the reverse order of those names among the days of the month.

[3] The eighth month, Â*v*ân.

[4] That is, on the tenth day of the eighth month, when both day and month are Â*v*ân, in which case there would be three Â*v*ân dedications, but only two are to be used as here directed.

religion is provided. 2. In a place of *that* district there is no one who rightly knows the commentary *and* 'the proper *and* improper[1],' so that he comes forth into a place of such decay (sapakhân); *and* the people of the district—who constantly order all the religious rites (dînô[2]) of many sacred ceremonies from any poor *man* of the various persons from other districts whose skill and superintending are not *like* his, but they constantly come *to* that district—shall constantly receive *from him* all the many religious rites and many sacred ceremonies. 3. *And* that man, who is revered and skilful, proceeds not undejectedly (lâ anaskandîhâ) and bashfully *to* his own superintending position, the position of the religion and position of the skill which are his; he does not demand any employment in the district or any award (dînâ) from the district, and does not know *how* to pro ide any other employment or award, in which there would be *any* fitness for him. 4. Are the people of the district—on account of the skill and activity which that man has exercised in religion, due to the performance of all the religious rites and sacred ceremonies which they constantly order—

[1] From this it would appear that a treatise called 'Shâyast Lâ-shâyast' existed a thousand years ago, which probably bore some resemblance to Sls., the work which now bears the same name.

[2] The words hamâk dînô, translated 'all the religious rites' both here and elsewhere, are a technical term which (as I am informed by Dastûr Peshotanji Behramji, the high-priest of the Parsis in Bombay) is applied to 'those obligatory religious rites and festivals that every Parsi is bound to observe by performing certain ceremonies, in his or her name, with the assistance of priests engaged for the purpose. These rites and festivals include the Rapithvan, the Gâhâmbârs, the Fravardîgân, the monthly festivals, &c.'

thereupon to prepare that man a stipend (bâhar)[1], and is it necessary for them to give a stipend to that man, or how is it necessary to act; and is it necessary for them to collect *it* for him, or not? 5. And of the much advantage of all the religious rites and work is it necessary to speak thus: 'Until the *time* that thou hadst come it was not possible for us to order except of him who is inferior to thee,' or how is *it* to be done? 6. Is it necessary to collect a stipend for him on account of the benefit and reasoning thought (vîrmatŏ) on other subjects, of which *he was* the means, or how is it necessary *for* the superintendent *of* our people to collect such stipend of skill, position, and religion?

7. The reply is this, that a man of such description as written *above*, and superintending the exercise of skill and provision of ability, is very worthy of a stipend and courtesy (khûpîh); also, through good management of all religious rites *and* the ceremony of the sacred beings, *he* is very confident in any uncertainty. 8. Therefore it is necessary to consider that he manages more openly and better than those whose skill and ability are not *like* his; and also as regards stipend and reasoning thought, owing to the worthiness of the ceremony of the sacred beings, his are more whose skill, ability, and activity in religion are greater. 9. And *as to* a man who is as written *above*—when all those religious rites and ceremonies are well-managed by him, and his repeated direction and right continuance of proper duties are an accumulation of his own reasoning

[1] Literally 'a share' of the produce of the district, analogous to tithes.

thought and great capability, and are ordered of him with great solicitude—*one* is also to consider him a stipendiary[1] thereby, and a thriving acquirement of ample reasoning thought. 10. And *as to* him, moreover, who is less skilled than he, *and* of inferior position, by as much as he is not *so* worthy, *his* custom is therefore to produce a want of himself again.

11. But he who *has* much skill should have[2] a great stipend, and he of medium ability should have[2] a medium *one*, he *having* less means of benefiting worthily, maturely, and necessarily. 12. And the value is as it is said in revelation thus: 'The stipend they should announce to him who is an upholder of religion is two shares, *and* to him who is mediocre *only* one, to him whose lot is inferior.'

13. That man is a master *and* high-priest[3] whose usage also (âîn-îkŏ) is wise, and in ability, goodness, and skill is the best of *those of* the religion of the Ma*zd*a-worshippers, which is the religion of wise upholders. 14. And the exercise of his religious disposition—originally possessing a religious stipend—which they shall order of him in *that* place, and that *of* the other worthy *ones and* applicants in the place and coming applying to the place, as much

---

[1] Literally 'a shareholder.'

[2] Assuming that the adverbial suffix -îhâ may be taken here (as it can be probably in all cases) as the Pâz. conditional form hâê of the verb 'to be,' equivalent to the more usual forms aê, âe, and the Huz. hômanâe (see Chap. XLVIII, 23).

[3] Or, ra*d* dastôbar may mean 'an awarding high-priest,' as he is called ra*d*, 'master, chief,' in virtue of his power of sentencing sinners and governing the religious body, and he is called dastôbar, 'upholder of customs,' in virtue of his control over rites and ceremonies.

as it is worth *and* happens *to be* their own want, *one* is to altogether thoroughly well consider for him. 15. Good destiny is not fulfilled by granting *to* those applying, *but* through forward ability, the forward, kind-hearted[1], *and* extreme skill provided, *and* grand position he is worthy of much stipend, *and* it is important to make *them* stipendiary in their own gradation of applying. 16. For the observance of moderation *and* the granting of applications are mutually destructive, *and* it is discriminatively said that the high-priest *G*âmâsp of the Hvôvas[2] considered, in that mode, the much skill of that good superintendent *being* without a stipend *as* not disproportionate, *but* most justly very moderate.

17. Moreover, to collect *for* all except for one skilful *man*, and to provide a stipend *for* any other applicants, is not right; and the limits should be[3] moderate, for each one really shares the moderate apportionments according to his own want, apart even from the sacred ceremony. 18. But to collect for such a man, who *has* kind-heartedly superintended by rule during reasoning thought, is a greater good work than to approve even him *who* is superintending much more authoritatively. 19. And he who *has* himself requested is to obtain everything last; for, except *in* that *case* when a virtuous doer *has* in any

---

[1] Literally 'good-hearted.'

[2] The Av. *G*âmâspa Hvôgva (or Hvôva) of Yas. XLV, 17, L, 18, Fravar*d*în Yt. 103. He was high-priest and prime minister of Kaî-Vi*s*tâsp; but probably the opinion of some much later *G*âmâsp is here erroneously attributed to him, much in the same way as the comparatively modern Book of Enoch is attributed to Enoch, 'the seventh from Adam,' in Jude, 14.

[3] Reading hâê instead of -îhâ, as in § 11.

mode begged a livelihood[1] *and* is not capable *of earning it*—so that something even of the righteous gifts[2] of clothing is begged by him—to live in idleness is not the way to be assisted; *but* he who *has* not himself requested, and is wise, is to beg a suit of clothes (rakht-hanâ).

20. They give to the good provider of gifts much praise, *and* for the preservation of the perfect giver are many religious friends[3], *and* the position of the upholders of religion[4]; so it is necessary to give, *and* to consider *it* as provided for the great female whom revelation greatly celebrates[5], that patron spirit (ahû) connected with religion, as it is said that *in* the opinion of Hûmân[6], the high-priest, the propitious religion is, as *it were*, the way of saving their souls[7].

---

[1] M14 has zîvisnŏ, and K35 has zîvandân.

[2] Charitable donations given to the priesthood and poor for the purpose of acquiring religious merit on certain solemn occasions; they often consist of clothing, and are then supposed to furnish the giver, or the person in whose name they are given, with garments in the other world after the resurrection (see Bd. XXX, 28).

[3] The angels who assist his soul after death, such as Srôsh, Mitrô, Rashnû, Âstâd, and the good Vâê (see Chaps. XIV, 3, 4, XXX, 2–4).

[4] That is, he will occupy the same grade in heaven as the priesthood.

[5] Referring to the maiden spirit supposed to meet the good soul after death and to conduct it over the *K*invad bridge to heaven (see Chaps. XXIV, 5, XXXVII, 117). She is described in Vend. XIX, 98–101, and more fully in Hn. II, 22–32 and the later Pahlavi works. Her beauty is said to be proportional to the religious merit of the soul, and she is here identified with the ahû or patron spirit.

[6] Probably some one nearly contemporary with the author, such as Âtûr-pâd son of Hêmîd (see Bd. XXXIII, 11), who is called hû-manô, 'well-meaning,' and styled 'the leader of the people of the good religion' in the Dînkard (III, ccccxiii).

[7] The maiden spirit, being developed by religious actions, is

21. About upholders of religion, and a more particular rule how the lawful computation should be for glorifying with moderation, a chief of the priests[1] *has* spoken thus: 'Shouldst thou be our father in wealthiness, I am thy protector in body, *and* thou becomest thy protector in soul[2].'

22. The same collection[3] is the way of the friends of religion for begging from the upholders of reli ion the preservation of the soul, *and* for well considering, extremely gracefully *and* fully reverently, the advantage *and* pleasure of the position[4] of the upholders of religion, so that they shall properly collect for the preservation of souls by the mode of going to collect thoroughly with great gain.

CHAPTER XLV.

1. The forty-fourth question is that which you ask thus: Of priesthood (aêrpatîh) or discipleship (hâvi*s*tîh) which is the priest's duty (aêrpatîh), *and* which the disciple'*s*; which is that which it is necessary to have in priesthood, *and* which in discipleship?

---

called the soul's 'own religion' in AV. IV, 23; it is, therefore, that spirit's assistance which is probably meant here, when speaking of religion saving the soul.

[1] A môbad of môbads.

[2] Meaning that the wealthy man can easily protect his own soul by a proper expenditure of his wealth on good works. The connection of this with the first part of the sentence is rather obscure.

[3] Mentioned in §§ 17, 18.

[4] In heaven (see § 20). To induce the laity to collect ample property for paying the priesthood they are promised a share of the priest's happiness in heaven.

2. The reply is this, that the priesthood and discipleship are connected together; the priests teach the scriptures[1], *and* the disciples learn the knowledge of the religion, that is, the Avesta and Zand[2]. 3. The priest have been disciples; through the teaching of his own priest they make the aroused existence[3] of even a disciple become a priest, *and* in one body with the learner are the priesthood and discipleship. 4. Through that which he has learned as a disciple from the priest *he* is wiser, and owing to the priesthood in his own person he teaches the disciple who is a learner; the desire which is his craving for learning is also owing to that in his own priest, when *he was* a disciple unto his own priest.

5. And the disciple *and* priest are even such as is said thus: 'The director (farmâ*d*âr) of the profession of priests (âsravŏân) of Pârs[4], *and* chieftain over the faithful and the officiating priests (magôpatân) of Pârs, is the leader of the religion; and *his* disciple (ashaka*rd*ŏ) is a disciple *in* a selected foremost position among the priests of the religion, set up (madam â*g*ast) over those acquainted with the commentary (zand-âkâsânŏ).' 6. The

[1] The word mâ*d*îgân means a treatise upon almost any subject, but it is specially applied to the Nasks or books of the complete ancient literature of the Maz*d*a-worshippers, which are now nearly all lost. It should be noted that 'teaching' and 'learning' are expressed by the same word in Pahlavi.

[2] The Avesta is the religious literature in its original language, erroneously called Zend by Europeans, and the Zand is the Pahlavi translation of the same literature, with the Pahlavi commentary (see Bd. Introd. p. x).

[3] Reading ham-vîkhtŏ yehevûnîh and taking ham-vîkhtŏ as equivalent to Pers. angîkht.

[4] This was the post held by the author himself (see Chap. XCIV, 13).

more infallible (a*s*aktar) of these is the powerful skill of the priest (aêrpatŏ) put forth through the ritual *and* Visparad[1], and *his* skill in the commentary (zand); the skill of disciples in the Avesta is, further, fully understood, *and* sin *recognised* as oppressive, through the formulas (nîrang) of the sacred ceremony, ablution and non-ablution, purity and pollution.

7. And both professions are the indispensable preservers of great decisions *as to* that which the priestly disposition *has* taught, done, and considered about the perpetual existence of every being, the complete goodness *and* final success of the non-existent evil *and* entire good of the sacred beings, the annihilation of the demons[2], *and* the complete understanding of the friends of the sacred beings.

Chapter XLVI.

1. The forty-fifth question is that which you ask thus: Is it allowable *that* those of the priesthood, when there is no daily livelihood for them from the life of the priesthood, should abandon the priesthood, and *that* other work *be* done, or not?

[1] The term ya*s*tô, 'ritual,' means any form of prayer with ceremony, and appears to include the Yasna or chief ceremonial ritual. The Visparad (here written Vispôrê*d*ŏ) is a particular form of ceremonial prayer, the various sections of which are interspersed among those of the Yasna and Vendidâd in the full liturgy of the Mazda-worshippers; it is called Visparad, 'all chiefs,' because it commences with an invocation of all the spiritual chiefs of the universe.

[2] K35 has kha*s*ânŏ, which might stand for khasânŏ, 'reptiles,' but is more probably a slight alteration of *s*êdânŏ, 'demons,' which would correspond to the more modern form, *s*êdââŏ, in M14.

2. The reply is this, that there is no loss of reputation to priests from priestly duties (aêrpatîh), which are themselves the acquired knowledge *that* is accumulated *by* the priestly disposition, care for the soul, *and* the requisite good works. 3. *And* there is this advantage, that, through acquaintance with the religion *of* the sacred beings, *and* certainty as to the reward of the spirit, they make *them* become more contented in adversity, more intelligent as regards stability of character in difficulty *and* restriction, and more through knowledge the abode of hope for those saved. 4. So that it is not fit they should abandon the priesthood, which is both harmless *and* an employment *with* advantages *that has* required much trouble to learn.

5. But, indeed, when they do not obtain[1] a daily livelihood from priestly duty, and the good do not give them chosen righteous gifts[2] for it, and they do not let *them* obtain *any* from next of kin *or* the wicked even by begging, a livelihood *may be* requested from the paid performance of ceremonies, management of all religious rites (dînô), *and* other priestly disciple's duty therein[3]. 6. When even by that they do not obtain *it*, *they* are to seek a livelihood by agriculture, sheep-rearing, penmanship, *or* other proper employment among priests; *and* when *it* is not possible for them to live even by these, *they are to seek it* by bearing arms, hunting, *or* other proper employment in the profession of a virtuous warrior. 7. And when even it is not

[1] K35 has 'beg,' both here and in § 6, the difference between the two words in Pahlavi being only a stroke.

[2] See Chap. XLIV, 19.

[3] That is, from the general funds of the priesthood.

possible for them to maintain their own bodies, which are in requisite control, by that which is cravingly digested, *they* are to beg a righteous gift[1] authorisedly (dastôbarîhâ) as an effectual remedy; by living idly, or not expending strength, their own bodies, which are in control, are without livelihood, but not authorisedly[2].

Chapter XLVII.

1. *As to* the forty-sixth question *and* reply, that which you ask is thus: At a sacred feast (myazd)[3] of those of the good religion, in which *there* are fifty or a hundred men, more or less, just as it happens, and seven men who are *engaged* in the performance of the religious rite (dînô) which is celebrated by them are feasting together with them, of those seven men there are *some* who are easily[4] able to pray five sections (vîdak)[5], and *some* six subdivisions (vakhshisnŏ), of the Avesta, *but* no chapter (fargar*d*ŏ)[6] of the commentary (zand) is

---

[1] That is, charity.

[2] That is, they are not authorised to beg charity for maintaining themselves in idleness.

[3] The sacred feast consists of the consecration of the sacred cakes (see Chap. XXX, 1), followed by that of wine and fruit with the recitation of the Âfrîngân or blessings (see Haug's Essays, p. 408), after which the consecrated food and drink are consumed by those present, both priests and laymen.

[4] That is, they know the prayers by heart, which is necessary in reciting the Avesta.

[5] Compare Pers. vaî, vîd, vîdâ, 'part, little,' *g*uz, 'a portion, a bundle of folios.' M14 has nask, 'book,' but this is clearly an unlucky guess.

[6] The chapters of the Vendidâ*d* are called fargar*d*s, as are also

easy to them; and all seven of them are disputing about the right (râs) to the foremost places. 2. And he to whom thirty chapters in[1] the commentary are easy speaks thus: 'The foremost place is mine, and it became my place owing to great retentiveness *of memory*, for I know the commentary well and "the proper *and* improper[2];" and my place must be good, for whenever I do not indicate this *as* the place of religion unto the people I am not in the security of religion; *but* you should not dispute about my place, for *it* is not becoming to dispute *it*, because this neglect and outlandishness (an-aîrîh), which *some one* brings constantly into the religion, is not *due* to me.' 3. Those seven men, moreover, speak constantly unto him thus: 'Our place is *more* important and must ever be *so*, for every man of us is able to pray several sections in his own officiating priestly duty (zôtîh), *and* it is ever necessary to consider who is more participating in sharing a reward.' 4. Then *as to* those whose Avesta is very easy, or him who knows the commentary *and* 'the proper *and* improper' well, and *their* goodness and greatness, as asked by us in this chapter, direct *some one* to make *them* clear unto us, for when he demonstrates the littleness and greatness in this

---

those of the Vistâsp Yast and many of the lost Nasks or books. The text here applies the term specially to the chapters of some scripture with commentary, and it may be noted that the thirty fargards, subsequently mentioned, are the exact number contained in the Vendidâd and Vistâsp Yast taken together, the learning of which by heart (as the word 'easy' implies) is a very serious task, comparable with learning the whole Greek text of the four Gospels.

[1] Perhaps 'with' is meant, but the word used is pavan.

[2] See Chap. XLIV, 2.

subject his great religion is then completely an advantage.

5. The reply is this, that, as to that which you ask *me* to write, so that they may decide *whether* thirty chapters in the commentary are easier, *or* really the other, be they five *or* be they six sections of the Avesta, are easier, *there* is no deciding, because which are the chapters and which the sections? 6. For, as regards more cleverness and less cleverness, it is not clear; there are *some* of the sections greater than many sections, and there are chapters *as* great *as* many chapters, but to understand severally the divisions (buris) and enumeration of him to whom five sections of the Avesta are easy, *and* also of him whose thirty chapters in the commentary are easy, it is necessary for making the calculation to consider every single division in the commentary as *equivalent to* seven *equal* divisions apart from the commentary[1]. 7. And it is thereby thus manifest who *has* skill *in the one* and who *has* skill *in the other*[2], and whoever *has* less, when there is nothing in it regarding which *he* is otherwise *than* when the superintending command *of* rulers (khû*d*â-yân) delivered over to him the place of duty—or on account of a new officiating priestly duty or directorship (ra*d*îh) of the season festivals[3], or the

[1] The reason for this difference is that it is only necessary to learn the words of the Avesta, without understanding them, whereas a knowledge of the Zand, or commentary, implies understanding both texts as well as knowing the Avesta by heart.

[2] M14 omits the repetition of the words mûn afzâr, but it seems necessary for the completion of the idiomatic phrase.

[3] The six Gâsânbârs or Gâhambârs are festivals, each held for five days, and severally ending on the 45th, 105th, 180th, 210th, 290th, and 365th days of the Parsi year. They were probably

foremost places *being* occupied, or like causes he becomes otherwise—is fit for all the great share *and* very good estimation of the place of *one* much more skilful, when their *being* fitting *and* skilful, or *their* excess *or* deficiency, is not specially manifest from their skill[1]. 8. And him to whom the commentary is very easy, *having* prayed much, it *has* seemed important to consider more thriving proportionable to *his* eating[2].

9. And great and ample respect for both their ways of worthiness is an advantage *and* fully necessary, skill in the commentary *and* that in the Avesta *being* together mutually assisting; for even the solemnizers of the Avesta *have* need for information from the commentary about the scattered (parvand) 'proper *and* improper' *usages* of the sacred ceremony. 10. The more efficient information from the commentary is advantageous when the ceremonial is proceeded with by them, and one of those two is one of the skilful, *and* a friend, provider, glorifier, and aggrandizer for the other; and the friends of religion are good friends and, therefore, also providers of fame for both of them.

---

intended originally to celebrate the periods of midspring, midsummer, the beginning of autumn, the beginning of winter, midwinter, and the beginning of spring (see Sls. XVIII, 3), when the Parsi year was fixed to begin at the vernal equinox. In later times they were supposed to commemorate the creations of the sky, water, earth, vegetation, animals, and man.

[1] The meaning seems to be that a priest once acknowledged as pre-eminent is not to lose his right of precedence merely because others become rather better qualified, so long as he himself does not retrograde, or is not superseded in his official duties. But if through any accidental circumstance he be excluded from the chief seat, he ought not to dispute the matter.

[2] Or, perhaps, 'through *being* moderate in *his* eating.'

11. When, too, they are publishing accusing statements, one about the other, from necessity, or from the violence which is owing to the adversary[1], *it* is important to become an excuser as regards them, and not a diminisher of their share, *nor* a bringer (âkhtâr) of unhealthiness to *their* united strength.

CHAPTER XLVIII.

1. The forty-seventh question is that which you ask thus: How is a liking for the desirableness, joy, and pleasure *arising* from the sacred ceremony (yazisn) friendly to Aûharmazd, the archangels[2], and the guardian spirits of the righteous[3]; in what manner is the perfection of him by whom the ceremony is ordered and the people of the country then exalted by them; and how *and* in what manner does it become the vexation, defeat, anguish, *and* discomfort of the evil spirit, the demons, *and* the fiends? 2. How is the purpose of the ceremony, what is the ceremony, where is the place[4] when they shall perform *it*, what is good when they shall

---

[1] The evil spirit.

[2] The archangels are usually reckoned as seven in number, because Aûharmazd, their creator, is considered as presiding over the six others, whose names are Vohûman, Ardavahist, Shatvairô, Spendarmad, Horvadad, and Amerôdad. These names are merely corruptions of Avesta phrases meaning 'good thought, perfect rectitude, desirable dominion, bountiful devotion, health, and immortality,' respectively, and the archangels, or 'immortal benefactors,' are personifications of these ideas. They are said to have been the first creatures created, after the guardian spirits or prototypes of creation, the light, and the sky (see Bd. I, 8, 23–26).

[3] See Chap. II, 5.

[4] Or gâs may mean 'time.'

perform *it*, *and* how *is it* good when they shall perform *it?*

3. The reply is this, that the great satisfaction of Aûharmazd and the archangels *arising* from the sacred ceremony is in the purity of its formulary (nîrang), *and* also in this, that *it* is completely fulfilling his own blessed commands; because he ordered that entire goodness for the complete procedure of those of the good religion (bûndakŏ hûdînakânakîh), *as* the recompense and full allotment of the sure upholder of religion *among* those who rightly recite *it*. 4. From the performance of the ceremonial of the sacred beings are the propitiation of the good spirits, the destruction (drûgisnŏ) of violence, the increase of digestiveness, the growth of plants, the prosperity of the world, *and* also the proper progress of living beings, even until the movement of the renovation *of the universe and* the immortality of the creatures arise therefrom. 5. It became *so*, it is expressly said, because the sacred beings are great; and unitedly opposing it the demons are particularly undesirous *of it*, and owing to it their defeat *and* vexation are severe; its *consecrated* cup (tâstîkŏ)[1] also becomes the express preservation of the ceremony.

6. And its purpose enquired about is this, that religion is transmitted clearly to the intelligent, that is, *it is* not the wisdom whose comprehension *exists* in worldly beings; and as, moreover, even that which is not understood by worldly wisdom is really the

---

[1] Referring probably to the cup of Hôm juice, the preparation, consecration, and use of which are essentially characteristic of the Yazisn or sacred ceremony, and are, therefore, supposed to be very repulsive to the demons.

creature of the spirits, that also which is the spiritual formulary (nîrang) is for making *it* intelligible to worldly beings through the body[1]. 7. That religion which is comprehensible by the world *and* authoritative (nikê*z*akŏ) is rightly connected with that which worldly beings are quite able to understand through worldly wisdom; and the understanding about its evidence as to that which is spiritual *and* powerful, apart from the worldly evidence of superiors (a*v*arîkânŏ), is the right way of the intelligent. 8. That proper (kânŏ) purpose—in which, moreover, the ceremonial, owing to timely memory for its own completion, is unique—is this unique exhibition of purity in the pure glorifying of the heavenly angels, as is commanded; just as the purpose of the ceremonial of a season-festival *being* before the season-festival, *and* of maintaining (dârân) the exposure of the body of a jackal (*s*akhâl)[2] *or* a man, is to make the body clean from the corrupting (nasû*s*îkŏ) pollution[3], *and* also from outward contamination.

9. That also which might be written, as to the much retribution appointed as regards washing the limbs outside with clean moisture from clean

[1] That is, the purpose of the ceremonial is to afford an outward symbol of the spiritual mysteries of the religion.

[2] This reading is uncertain, but the reference appears to be to the exposure of the dead. M14 has the sentence altered as follows:—'just as the ceremony of a season-festival is exhibited more royally (or more joyously) before the season-festival, and a man who is a judge is for the purpose of making the body clean from the corrupting pollution, and also from contamination which is even outside the body, as much as is proper.'

[3] That is, the pollution due to the Nasû*s*, or fiend of corruption, who is supposed to seize upon all corpses (see Chap. XVII, 7).

animals[1] *and* plants, and then completely washing the body with the purifying water streaming forth; as to the clean scents among those which they rightly perceive, and making the body *and* clothing[2] sweet-scented; *and* as to the putting on of the white and proper garment of Vohûman[3], and supposing the power[4] of avarice *to be* the sight of distress, is *all* superfluous. 10. *But it* is needful still as regards these *matters*, that is, while *engaged* in the ceremonial *it is* not to be hurried owing to any hunger *or* thirst, owing to liability of punishment for religious practices[5], *or* even owing to deficiency[6] of vacant space. 11. And before the ceremonial *one* is to eat at the appropriate time, and such food, too, as is preparable and *only* moderately troublesome (navâs); and any of that which *one has* to perform aloud in leaving the heavenly-minded, yet moderate, duty in the abode of fires[7]—which is perpetual light—is proper, pertaining to good works, and good for him, and thereby lodging in *him*. 12. And they, that is,

---

[1] Referring to ceremonial purification by washing with bull's urine.

[2] Or 'the clothing of the body.'

[3] The sacred shirt (see Chaps. XXXIX, 19, XL, 2).

[4] Reading va zôrîh, but it may be nizôrîh, 'weakening.'

[5] This seems to be the meaning of min pâ*d*afrâhîh-î dînôîkîh. At the time this was written the religion was often persecuted, and its ceremonies were liable to interruption; but even when such a misfortune was apprehended, they were not to be hurried over.

[6] The word is kamîh in the MSS., but it may possibly have been kâmîh originally, in which case the meaning would be: '*or* even owing to wishing for evacuation.'

[7] The fire temple, where the sacred fire is kept perpetually burning.

the gloomy ones[1], thereby see the service (yasâk) for them themselves is short; *and* good are *they*[2] who come into the world glorified by praise.

13. The position of the *ceremony*-holders[3] themselves, that is, the position of the officiating priest (zôtŏ) *and* his co-operators, is the Aûrvês[4] place; and, if *it be* the precinct (dargasîh) of prayers[5], *one* should wash *it* over (madam pasâyâ*d*) *with* the water of purification, to make *it* clean. 14. The apparatus of the ceremonial, *together* with its own man, who is a solemnizer, and the two creatures *which* are solid[6] out of these four: fire, metal, water, and plants, just as *one has* to bring *them* together in readiness, the stone Aûrvês, the stone *and* mortar Khân[7], *and* the Hôm-mortar[8] (hâvanîh), cups, *and* crescent-shaped (mâh-rûpŏ) stands[9] set upon *it*, are *all* ceremoniously washed (pâ*d*yâvînî*d*) with the water of purification. 15. The

[1] The demons. In M14 the sentence, already obscure, is altered so as to be unintelligible.

[2] The angels. The meaning is that, by the utterance of the proper formulas at the proper times, the demons are discouraged, and the angels are induced to come to the ceremony.

[3] Perhaps we should read sâkhtârân, 'preparers,' as in M14, or else ya*s*târân, 'solemnizers,' instead of dâ*s*târân, 'holders.'

[4] This is the name of the consecrated space within which the ceremony is performed. It is often written Arvîs, but is probably to be traced to the Av. urvaêsa, 'goal.'

[5] That is, when the place is about to be used for a ceremony.

[6] Literally 'material;' meaning the metallic and vegetable portions of the ceremonial apparatus.

[7] The slightly raised platform or table upon which all the apparatus, except the fire and unconsecrated water, is placed.

[8] In which the twigs of Hôm are pounded and mixed with water.

[9] For the Barcsôm or sacred twigs (see Chap. XLIII, 5).

bright fire on the clean fire-stand (âtîstŏ)[1] is increased by the dry firewood delivered *to it* purified, *and one* is to put upon *it at* appropriate times the wholesome perfumes of *various* kinds of plants; and the water of purification, which is ritualistically produced[2] by *reciting* the words of revelation, is in the clean metal cups. 16. The well-grown Hôm[3] through which the world is possessed of creatures[4], the Hôm through which the production of Zaratûst occurred[5], is a symbol of the white Gôkerânô[6] as

[1] A small stone platform on which the fire vase is placed, now usually called âdôst.

[2] Reading nîrangîkîhâ dâ*d* instead of the unintelligible nîrang ashâyâ*d* of K35, which is very similarly written in Pahlavi; M14 has 'which *one* is to keep pure by the ritual of words of revelation.'

[3] A plant said to grow among the mountains in southern Persia, which has not yet been botanically identified, but Anquetil Duperron was told that it resembled a vine without fruit. Twigs of this plant are brought to India 'by traders and are, therefore, considered impure until they have been purified, laid aside for a year, and again purified' (see Haug's Essays, p. 399). A few fragments of these twigs are pounded and mixed with water in the Hôm-mortar, and the juice is tasted by the priest who performs the ceremony. The Avesta Hôm and the Sanskrit Soma must have been originally the same plant, but both Parsis and Hindus now use plants which are no doubt mere substitutes for that original. In southern and western India the Soma plant now used by the Brahmans is the *Sarcostemma Brevistigma*, a leafless bush of green succulent branches, growing upwards, with flowers like those of an onion; when not in flower it can hardly be distinguished from the *Euphorbia Tirucalli*, or thornless milk-bush, commonly used for hedges in many parts of India.

[4] Reading dâm-hômand; or it may be sem-hômand, 'renowned.'

[5] Zaratûst is said to have been begotten in consequence of his parents drinking Hôm-juice and cow's milk infused, respectively, with his guardian spirit and glory (see Zs. XI, 10 n). K35 has hôman, and M14 has hômand, instead of hôm, in this clause.

[6] Av. gaokerena, sometimes called gôkar*d* in Pahlavi, the

regards the immortality of the renovation *of the universe* manifest therefrom, and the resting-places of its vengeance[1] are the various demons; and with it *one* is to put attentively (*s*invi*s*nŏ-dahak) in *its* appropriate place the pomegranate (hadanapag)[2] plant of the Aûrvarâm. 17. The vegetable[3] sacred twigs carefully girded with the vegetable belt (parvand) and girdle, *and* the metallic[4] crescent-shaped *stands*—which are in the position of those who are sovereigns *of* the worldly creatures who are interpreted *as* the sacred twigs[5] of the treatises—are prepared.

18. *When* arranged (stôr*d*ŏ) by the bringing together of clean worldly productions, so much the more purely as is possible, the arrival of the pure renders all the symbols reliable. 19. Those celebrators of whom the outside of their own bodies is defiled with their bodily refuse and in clean clothing, and *their* disposition—if[6] in the religion of

---

mythic white Hôm-tree which is said to grow in the wide-formed ocean, and from which the draught of immortality is prepared for mankind at the resurrection (see Vend. XX, 17, Bd. XVIII, 1-4, XXVII, 4, XXX, 25).

[1] Reading ayêngîh nisîm, but this is uncertain.

[2] Av. hadhânaêpata, to represent which the Parsis now use a twig of the pomegranate bush, but it must originally have been some sweet-scented plant (see Vend. VIII, 7). The Aûrvarâm (Av. acc. urvarãm) consists of this twig, a small fragment of which is pounded with the Hôm-twigs when preparing the Hôm-juice.

[3] From this it would appear that the practice of using metal wires, instead of twigs of trees, for the baresôm (see Chap. XLIII, 5) was not in use a thousand years ago.

[4] Literally 'Shatvaîrian;' the archangel Shatvaîrô (Av. khshathra vairya, 'desirable dominion') having special charge of all metals (see Bd. XXX, 19, Sls. XV, 14-19).

[5] Reading baresom; K35 has basom and M14 bîm-i*k*.

[6] M14 substitutes yôshdâsarînî*d*ŏ for denman hîgarînî*d*ŏ;

moderate eating in which is a thirst for lawfully drinking—is customarily sleep *and* lethargy through the tendency (rûnŏ) to falsehood of *their* wisdom, are to consider, even from *their* innermost hearts and minds, the retribution of the body of wrath, the falsehood, and bad thoughts in that disposition of infamy, *and* the recompense of their own renunciation *of it; they* are to atone for *their* sinfulness, *and* to seek great purification of mind. 20. And *having* acquired eyes speaking[1] forth, hands in *a state of* ablution, and every other member of the body—especially there where well-accomplishable—*free* from its bodily refuse and covered *with* the clean clothing, the tongue is preserved *and* guarded *from* falsehood *and* the hand from sin, the mind is established *by* little preparation with good consideration for knowledge of the sacred beings, and even the good are to recite by direction (radîhâ) the verbal renunciation *of sin*[2].

21. The officiating priest (zôtŏ), *having* directed *and* purified the place[3] of the fire with liturgical words[4], is to go *and* walk unto the place of the officiating priests[5] while glorifying the sacred beings,

---

and padmûkht for va khîm hat, so as to read 'the outside of their own bodies is purified and attired in clean clothing,' but this can hardly be reconciled with the context. The term hîgar or hîkhar (Av. hikhra), here translated 'bodily refuse,' is applied to any refuse or dirt from the living body, or any *liquid* exudation from a dead one.

[1] Reading gôvak, but it may be yûvâk, 'wishing,' or dûvâk, 'flowing.' M14 alters it to vênâk, 'looking,' which suits the eyes well enough, but hardly seems to express the author's idea.

[2] See Chap. XLI, 5.

[3] M14 has '*having* purified around the place.'

[4] The Âtas Nyâyis (see Haug's Essays, p. 403).

[5] This place is at the end of the ceremonial area farthest from

and to consider invokable the glory given to the luminaries *and* the guardian spirits of the good. 22. Of those[1] also who, co-operatively, conjointly, and interspersed (ham-rê*s*), *have* each separately remained in their own places *and* thought of the sacred beings, with propitiation of Aûha*r*ma*zd and* scornful notice (tar dahi*s*nŏ) of the evil spirit, the employment stands forth prominently at the ceremonial. 23. *As to* the position of others co-operating *with* him who is an officiating priest of good leadership, there are *some* who are for the Avesta[2], there is the solitude (khadûî*d*ârîh) by the fire, there are *some* who are bringers[3] forward of water, there are *some* who are for carriers away, there are *some* who are solitary ones, there are *some* who are gregarious ones, there are *some* who are directors of duties, and their own needful arrangement in the place is arranged in the ceremony.

24. In cleanliness, purity, *and* truth, as much as *there is* in *this* mingled existence[4], if *one has* to commence a ceremony glorifying the sacred beings,

---

the fire. Here the priest first invokes the spirits in whose honour the ceremony is about to be performed, by reciting their several propitiatory formulas (see Chap. XXIX, 1).

[1] Referring to any other priests who may be present.

[2] M14 has 'for carriers,' omitting the three clauses about the Avesta, fire, and bringing water.

[3] Or, perhaps, 'there is *he* who may be a bringer;' and similarly in the following clauses. The plural suffix -îhâ being identical in form with the Pâz. conditional form of the verb 'to be,' which seems to be the origin of the adverbial suffix corresponding to -ly in English when added to an adjective; occasionally it is added to a substantive, as is probably the case here, and can then be only translated by 'may, or would, be' (see Chap. XLIV, 11).

[4] This first clause may belong to the preceding section.

when the righteously-disposed temperament is purified *along* with the apparatus the abundant ritualism (nîrangakîh) of the spirit is a symbol *and* reminder of the will of the sacred beings, undesired by the fiend[1], *and* remains a blessing deservedly unto *those* come together. 25. Then is explained the text (avistâk) of that great scripture (naskô) which is called the Hâdôkht[2], *that* is itself the best of the chiefs of the scriptures, *and* of the sublime Dvâzdahhômâst[3] *that* is not recited by any voice with falsehood (âkadbâ)[4], *and* is called 'the origin of every truth[5].'

26. The pure glorification of the sacred beings is in the light, this is in the morning time (frâyar gâs)[6]; and even until night the ritualistic *and* true

---

[1] K35 has drôn, 'sacred cake,' instead of drûg.

[2] The twentieth Nask, which is said to have chiefly treated of religious ceremonies and texts (see Byt. III, 25). Two Avesta fragments, published by Westergaard as Yt. XXI and XXII, are traditionally ascribed to this Nask.

[3] Another name for the Dâmdâd Nask, from which the Bundahis appears to have originated (see Zs. IX, 1). The name is also applied to a particular series of ceremonies, continued for twelve successive days in honour of each of the twenty-two sacred beings whose names are given to the 1st–7th, 9th–14th, 16th–22nd, 24th, and 26th days of the month; these ceremonies last, therefore, for 264 days (see Byt. II, 59).

[4] It can hardly be akadbâ, as that would imply that it 'is not recited by any undeceitful voice.' The use of the prefix â- in the sense of 'with' is rare, but it occurs in âpûstanû, 'pregnant,' (whence Pers. âbistan), and is noticed by Dastûr Jâmâspji in his Pahlavi Dictionary, p. 2.

[5] Reading bun-î kolâ râstîh, apparently a forerunner of the modern name Bundahis.

[6] The frâyar period of the day corresponds to the Hâvan Gâh or morning (compare Farh. Okh. p. 42 with Bd. XXV, 9), at which time the Yasna ceremonial should be performed when not accom-

recitation of revelation (dînô) is unchangeably proceeding, undivided and faultless. 27. This, too, is in benediction of the angels; this, too, is producing restraint of the fiends; this, too, is in praise of the glorious ones, the mighty doers; this, too, is as an admonition for creatures subject to command; this is in the true words of the ancients who *have* passed *away;* this, too, is as a suitable servant for the righteous, these good doers; this, too, is to obtain a permanence (patîstân) of requisites; this, too, is suitable for the discreet *and is* merciful; this, too, is as another way *in* which the promoters of good (vêh-yâvkârân) are pardoned, as soon as the Hôm-juice (parâhôm) is digested, through not *having* eaten from dawn till night during the pure utterance of the pure glorification. 28. And, moreover, *one* performs no work[1], nor is even a word uttered; *one* does not go to sleep, nor should they allow any pollution to the body; the sequence (patîsârîh) of the religious formulas is, likewise, not changed from that ordered, nor is even a detached thought away from that truth *and* purity; *but* always *with* phrases rightly consecutive *and* properly worded (hû-sakhunagânŏîhâ) the Avesta is uttered; and even the manner of response of one's co-operators is *in* modes contributing to good (hû-pa*d*âyâkŏ), or they utter the scripture (nask).

29. Since the production of stench is needing *something* essentially purifying, many formulas in the ceremonial are tokens *and* signs which, while they

panied by the Vendidâ*d*; or, according to the text, it must be performed by daylight.

[1] During the ceremonial.

are strongly manifested, are terrifying *and* vexing to the demons, *and* inviting *and* rejoicing to the angels. 30. Such as, indeed, the pure Hôm, which is squeezed out by four applications of holy-water (zôrîh)[1] with religious formulas, is noted even *as* a similitude *of* the understanding[2] and birth of the four apostles bringing the good religion, who are *he who* was the blessed Zaratûst *and they who* are *to be* Hûshêdar, Hûshêdar-mâh, and Sôshâns[3]. 31. As also the metal mortar (hâvan) which is struck[4] during the squeezing of the Hôm, and its sound is evoked *along* with the words of the Avesta, which becomes a reminder of the thoughts, words, and deeds on the coming of those true apostles into the world. 32. As *also* the proper rite as regards the water, that they should perform three times[5], which is showing the world the glorious seizing of water[6] and formation

[1] In preparing the Hôm-juice fresh holy-water (zôr) is added four times to the Hôm-twigs which are each time pounded anew, while reciting the Ahunavar formula, and their liquor strained into a cup (see Haug's Essays, p. 402).

[2] There is no authority for translating sinvisnŏ by 'conception,' otherwise that meaning would suit this sentence better. M14 has yehevûnisnŏ, 'existence,' which differs by only one extra stroke of the pen in Pahlavi.

[3] See Chap. II, 10.

[4] The word sikâvî-aîtŏ really means 'is split.' During the pounding of the Hôm-twigs the pestle is struck several times against the sides of the mortar, so as to produce a ringing sound (see Haug's Essays, p. 401).

[5] Reading vidanâg, instead of gûn-aê, by transposing the first two Pahlavi characters. After the first series of poundings of the Hôm-twigs holy-water is added to them three times while reciting, each time, the Ashem-vohû formula (ibid.).

[6] The evaporation from the ocean, said to be effected by Tîstar for the production of rain (see Chap. XCIII, 2, 3).

of rain, *and* the healthfulness of the production of rain[1]. 33. *And* as the purification of the milk, by the glorious ritualistic *product* (nîrang)[2] taken from the purifying cattle, is divided in two, by means of which the token is that which is great, glorious, *and* good; one *being* for the daughter *of* Pâûrvâ*g*îryâ[3] the Maz*d*a-worshipper, *and* from her *was* Aôshnôr full of wisdom; and one *being* Farhank, *daughter* of Vidhirisâ[4], and from her came Kaî-Kavâ*d*[5].

34. And, as to the high-priests of the glorious religion, it is said many concomitants (pa*d*vandîhâ) are obtained; such as, much discrimination of scripture (nask), the holy-water which is indispensable as a remedy, the healthfulness which is given in that ceremonial to the sacred fire[6] which the world destroys, that pre-eminent strength which is given at the end of the world from the ox Hadhayã*s*[7] unto the good *people* scattered about (fravaftân)—it is

[1] The delightfulness of rain after an eight-months' drought cannot be adequately appreciated by a dweller in Europe.

[2] That is, bull's urine.

[3] The reading of this name, as well as that of Aôshnôr, is doubtful; but if these names occur at all in the extant Avesta, they may perhaps be found in the Aoshnara pouru-*g*îra of Fravar*d*în Yt. 131, Âf. Zarat. 2; the epithet pouru-*g*îra, when it occurs after the name, would naturally be considered a patronymic, whence a father or grandfather could be easily created, if he did not exist already in legendary history.

[4] This name is written in Pâzand, and is evidently meant for the same person as the Pâz. Vîdharg-âfrâ*s*taka of Bd. XXXI, 31, where Farhank is said to have been the mother of Kaî-Apîvêh and, therefore, the wife of Kaî-Kavâ*d*.

[5] M14 has 'from him she came unto Kaî-Kavâ*d*,' which would tally better with the statements in Bd. XXXI, 25, 31.

[6] Literally 'the fire of Varahrân (Bahrâm).'

[7] See Chap. XXXVII, 99.

mingled with the fire of men's bodies[1], and they, therefore, become perfect and immortal through it—and there are also other *things*. 35. There are *also* in the ceremonial many tokens *and* signs of spiritual mysteries, glorious matters, and habitual practices of which statements *would* be very tedious.

36. And if the wish (ayûpŏ) should be this, that they should be *engaged* in a single ceremony of the length of a day, a man who is righteous in purification, inside and outside the body, should stay away from all *his* relations and the worldly transaction of business, *from* malicious actions *and* covetous practices, separated from all lying *and* falsehood of relatives; *and his* words are to be all those which are serving the angels, glorifying, *and* begging favours. 37. Then, indeed, the way of the spirit and the harmoniousness[2] of the sacred beings are manifest therefrom; *and* those which are as much the means due to the primitive good creations as is more purely possible are strengthening as regards the utility (bûn) for offering, encouraging for purity, confounding for the confusers (gûmê*g*akân), terrifying for the fiends, and propitiating for the sacred beings.

38. The ceremonial which is good is when they shall perform *it* for a pure disposition and assured wisdom, a minder of the religion of the sacred beings of the spheres, and *with* pure thoughts, just thoughts[3], wise deeds, a purified body, a tongue worthy of good

[1] The vital heat or Vohu-fryãn fire (see Bd. XVII, 1, 2).

[2] Reading âhankânakîh, as in K35; M14 has khadûkânakîh, 'unity,' which is a much commoner word, nearly identical with the other in its Pahlavi form.

[3] So in the MSS., but it was probably 'true words' originally, so as to complete the triad of thought, word, and deed.

(vêh-sazâk), a scripture (nask) *made* easy[1], a true text (avistâk), ablutions performed, proper rites, undivided, and faultless. 39. Near which fashion, with like abilities, *and* innumerable times, it is very purely solemnized in the abode of the ever-growing fire, then in the abode of the other sacred fires[2], then in the abodes of Mazda-worshippers *and* other good *people*, *and* then *in* other places pronounced clean. 40. That of the three *days*[3] is in the abode of the fire-place which is nearest to that of the departed; the ceremony of the guardian spirits of the righteous[4] is solemnized in purity there where the dwelling is which is nearest that of the departed whose soul is honoured. 41. And that for victories in war is then *at* its times of battle, the husbandry of Sâm[5] and other offenders (vinâsagân) who *were* for keeping away husbandry, the household attendant's place for a warrior of another rank, the occasion of the outcry of those not possessing (adârîgân) a lodging, unto the rest of the same temperament (mûnôkŏ), expressly to produce *and* maintain a proportional resemblance[6].

---

[1] That is, learnt by heart.

[2] Literally 'fires of Varahrân.'

[3] The three days after a death, during which ceremonies are performed in honour of the angel Srôsh, who is supposed to protect the departed soul from the demons during that period, while it is still hovering about the body (see Chap. XXVIII, 6).

[4] On the fourth day after a death (see Chap. XXVIII, 7).

[5] That is, Keresâsp the Sâman (see Chap. XVII, 6); having been a famous warrior his husbandry is said to be battle, the destruction of all ordinary husbandry.

[6] That is, the ruin of people by war leads them to demand a share of the property of those more fortunate, so as to produce an equality. The whole section seems to be a bitter sarcasm upon the effects of war, representing the generals as cultivators of

CHAPTER XLIX.

1. *As to* the forty-eighth question and reply, that which you ask is thus: *As to them* who shall buy corn and keep *it* in store until it shall become dear, *and* shall then sell it at a high price (pavan girânŏîh), what is the nature of the decision?

2. The reply is this, that when there is nothing therein on account of which I *should* so deem[1] *it* otherwise than due to the eating of the requisite amount (a*v*âyi*s*n) of food for one's self, that which is his controlling impulse (sa*r*dârîh), and not the teachings of the worthy *and* good, is the internal instruction which a time of scarcity *has* taught by means of the occurrences during that time[2]; but clamorous worldly profit is want of diligence (akhapârakânîh), for they would buy to make people distressed, and in order that they may sell again dearer. 3. Moreover, the store *one* keeps, and keeps as closed even unto the good as unto the bad—*and* though it be necessary for a man of the good *and* worthy, and they beg for *some* of the food, they shall not sell at the price it is worth at that time, on account of *its* becoming dearer—*one* keeps in store unauthorisedly *and* grievously sinfully, *and* every calamity *of* those good people they shall suffer who would not sell it at the price they beg.

---

slaughter and rapine, with the soldiers as their domestic servants, driving the people into social democracy.

[1] K35 has a blank space for this word, but it is given in M14, and also occurs in a similar phrase in Chap. LIV, 6.

[2] That is, so long as one does not lay in a store more than sufficient for one's own requirements, it is only an act of prudence taught by former experience.

4. On account of that non-obtainment of corn, or that unlawfully heinous sin, and because of dearness of price it is not proper to give *it* for that non-distribution (an-af*s*ânŏîh) unto *him* himself, or those under *his* control, or the poor to whom it would be given by him[1]; and the distribution (rêshi*s*nŏ) *which* occurs is then retaliative upon him. 5. And if the corn be spoiled[2], through keeping too long a time in store, *he* is suffering assault from the hungry *man* (gûr*s*nŏ) who is injured even by that damaging (bô*d*yôzê*d*îh)[3] of the corn; if through that unlawful want of preservation (adâri*s*nŏîh) noxious creatures are associated with the corn, he is overwhelmed also by that heinous sin; *and*, through the profit of improper diligence *he* is unworthy.

6. But if it be necessary for their own people who are under their control, on account of the fear *of* a time of scarcity, they should buy at their own suitable time, and should afford protection. 7. Or, because of the teachings of the good *and* worthy, they should buy corn at a cheap price from a place where the corn is more than the requirements of the eaters, *and* they should bring *it* unto there where corn is scarce, provided (va hatŏ) the good *and* those requiring corn are sufficient (vasân). 8. So that, while their information of a scarcity of corn is even

[1] That is, corn is not to be sold to a man who keeps it in store for the purpose of raising the price, nor to his people, nor is it even to be given to the poor whom he relieves, so that he may be compelled to support them out of his own stores, as a penalty.

[2] Reading tapâhî-aît, as in M14.

[3] Literally 'destroying the consciousness,' or 'injuring the existence.' Bô*d*yôzê*d* is a technical name for sins whereby animals are ill-treated, or useful property injured (see Sls. II, 39).

from him himself to whom the price would become profit[1], or *is* the persistence of *these* same teachings of the good—so that it may become more abundant unto them than unto the bad, even in the time of scarcity *when* it is very much raised in price[2]—they should buy corn *at* a cheap price during an excess of corn, so that *one* may keep *it* until the time of a period of scarcity. 9. When *there* occurs a necessity for it *among* the good he sells *it* at *such* price as *one* buys it at that time, that is, the market price (ar*g*-î shat*r*ôîk)[3]; by that means, in a season of scarcity, much more is obtained in price, *and* it becomes more plentiful among the good; then a more invigorating (pa*d*îkhûînagtar) praise of him is commendable.

10. And, yet, as regards that which is suitable profit—and also apart from the eating of corn, *from* anything eatable for the maintenance of life, *from* medicine and remedies for the healthfulness of life, and *from* whatever is for the preservation of life—it is allowable *that* they shall buy *and* shall sell dear[4].

Chapter L.

1. The forty-ninth question is that you ask thus: *If* they should sell wine unto foreigners and infidels what is then the decision *about* it?

---

[1] And, therefore, likely to be correct, as it is given in opposition to his own interest.

[2] M14 has 'begged at a price,' by inserting a stroke.

[3] Without holding it back for an exorbitant rise in prices.

[4] That is, there is no harm in speculating upon prices, except in the case of necessaries of life.

2. The reply is this, that *there* is very vehement danger of grievous sin, and it would be an evil occupation. 3. But if through the operation of that wine-selling of theirs the wine is kept more away from those who become worse through immoderate drinking of wine, *and* comes to those who drink wine in moderation[1]—*whom* they cause to become better through drinking the wine—more than when they shall not practise that selling of the wine, then through that selling of theirs the power which is in the wealth[2], by their keeping away of which a man is confirmed (pa*d*ayînî*d*ŏ) in the good religion and diverted from going into infidelity, the progress of sin is impeded *and* good works are promoted, becomes the assistance of the good and protection of religion, the hindrance of sin and aid of good works, which, when they shall not practise that wine-selling, do not arise, *and* which are much more promoted than the various sins that might have arisen from the unlawfully drinking of wine. 4. Or, otherwise, the greater decision—and great are the good works which are assured therein—is thus: 'They who shall sell wine[3] to foreigners, infidels, and others from whom unlawful conduct arises through drunkenness, *act* very sinfully and not authorisedly.'

---

[1] That is, when the supply of wine is so limited that by selling it to moderate drinkers they keep it away from drunkards.

[2] The wealth they acquire by selling wine, which would have produced evil in the hands of the buyers, and ought to produce good in their own.

[3] K35 has vinâs, 'sin,' instead of âs, 'wine,' which is clearly wrong.

Chapter LI.

1. The fiftieth question is that which you ask thus: *As to one* of the good religion who drinks wine immoderately, and loss *and* injury happen to him owing to that immoderate drinking, what is then the decision about him? 2. And how is the measure of wine-drinking *which* when they drink is then authorised for them?

3. The reply is this, that whoever through the influence of opportunity drinks wine immoderately, *and* is adult and intelligent, through every loss *and* injury which thereupon come to him from that immoderate drinking, or *which* occasion anything unto any one, is then his causing such pollution to the creatures, in his own pleasurably[1] varied modes, that the shame owing to it is a help (dastakîh) out of that affliction. 4. And even *he* who gives wine authorisedly[2] unto any one, and he is thereby intoxicated by it, is equally guilty of every sin which that drunkard commits owing to that drunkenness.

5. And concerning that drunkenness, what is said is that that is to be eaten *through* which, when *one* eats *it*, *one* thinks better, speaks better, and acts

---

[1] K35 has a blank space here for a word, but no word seems really necessary. M14 fills up the blank by changing gvî*d*ŏ into gar*d*înî*d*ŏ, and reads 'converted unto his own pleasure, and the mode,' &c.

[2] M14 has 'unauthorisedly,' a very natural emendation of the text as it stands in K35, but it does not appear that the author intended to limit the responsibility of the person giving the wine merely to those cases in which his action would be quite unjustifiable.

better; and such even is the food *by* which, through *having* drunk wine, *one* becomes more virtuous, or does not become more vicious, in thought, word, and deed. 6. When an experiment as regards its *being* good is tried, so that *having* drunk it in that proportion *one* becomes better, or does not become worse, then it is allowable to drink *it*.

7. When an untried *person*, for the sake of *being* tried, *has* drunk a mingled portion, first of one drinking-cup[1], secondly of two drinking-cups, *and* thirdly of three drinking-cups, *and* through drinking *it* he becomes more virtuous, or does not become more vicious, in thought[2], word, *or* deed, *he* is to increase the drinking-cups, and the experiment is allowable unto those tested just so far as the proportion is *such* that he becomes better, or does not become worse. 8. To those tested *it* is authorisedly *given* to that amount through which the experimenting that is mentioned *has* extended; and to *him* who *it* is proved will become worse through the drinking of wine, that amount, through the drinking of which, *when* given[3] in the experiment, *it was* seen that he became worse, is not authorisedly given.

9. In a case of doubt *one* is to consider *him who is* orthodox (hû-dînô), who *has* chanted the *sacred* hymns, *and is* of good repute, whose drunkenness

---

[1] Reading âv *g*âmakŏ, 'water-cup;' but it is written like âv sîmakŏ in the MSS.

[2] K35 has mân, M14 mîni*s*nŏ.

[3] Reading yehabûntŏ instead of the unintelligible *g*ân bû*d*ŏ of K35, the alteration being merely lengthening the bottom stroke of the Pahl. b. M14 substitutes ba*r*â yehevûnê*d* for bû*d*ŏ *g*ân bû*d*ŏ, which gives the following meaning: 'through the drinking of which, in the experiment, *it is* seen that he becomes thoroughly worse.'

is not manifest, in this *way*, that he drinks as much wine as *was* tried by him when he became no worse *by* drinking *it*. 10. It is necessary to consider *him whose* religion is unseen, whose religion is wrong, and him who is a child furnished even with the realities of religion, in this *way*, that he becomes worse through *having* drunk wine. 11. When *apart* from the decision there is no assignable (ban*g*is*n*îk) reason as regards *it*, the share of wine which they gave not authorisedly who themselves drank wine, *one* considers as *some of* the wine on *its being* given more authorisedly [1].

CHAPTER LII.

1. *As to* the fifty-first question *and* reply, that *which* you ask is thus: *There is* a man who hands over a dirham [2] as regards five bushels (kafî*z*) of

[1] The meaning appears to be that, when there is no special reason to the contrary, the quantity of wine one may have already drunk elsewhere is to be considered as part of one's allowance.

[2] The dirham (δραχμή) is a weight, and also a silver coin of that weight, but its amount is rather uncertain. According to the Pers. MS. M5 (fol. 55), written A.D. 1723, the proper dowry for a 'privileged' wife is 2000 dirhams of white silver, or 2300 rûpîs, and 2 dirhams of red gold, or $2\frac{1}{4}$ tolas. The rûpîs formerly current in Gu*g*arât were less in value than the present Indian coinage, but the tola, which is the weight of the present rûpî, was probably much the same as it is now, or 180 grains; the statement in M5 is, therefore, equivalent to saying that the dirham contained 202 grains of pure silver. This is so much more than the amount deducible from other authorities that it might be supposed that the stîr (στατήρ) or tetradrachm was meant, if it were not confirmed, to some extent, by the Pers. Rivâyats, which state the dowry at 2000 dirhams of pure white silver and 2 dînârs of red gold of the Nîshâpûr currency; the dînâr being a gold coin containing a dirham weight of pure

wheat, thus: 'I give this to thee as an instalment (bôn-ae)[1] of five bushels of wheat at the end of a month;' and during the month, *and* at *its* end, those five bushels of wheat become five *times* the price; would they authorisedly seize the five bushels of wheat *when* winnowed (pêkhtŏ kar*d*ŏ) by him, through that instalment which he handed over, or not?

2. The reply is this, that when they who shall take his dirham *have* to intrust the five bushels of wheat, unsuspiciously *and* by their own will, *to him* to winnow, even so as *they* are advisedly *and* unsuspiciously winnowed by him they should take *them* just as winnowed; *this* is the decision authorisedly given. 3. But when *it* is winnowed by him on account of very grievous necessity for payment, *it* is more suitable for the soul to beg the giver of the money, who is the purchasing payer[2], for *some* of that excess of undivided (apâr) profit. 4. For *he has* to consider the profit of *his* successors as among the profit of money on the spot[3]—*when* more than

gold. It is safer, however, to rely upon the average weight of the Sasanian dirham coins, which, according to Dr. Mordtmann's statement in ZDMG. vol. xii, pp. 44, 45, is about 63 grains, or $5\frac{3}{5}$ annas' worth of silver; so that the stîr would be 252 grains or $22\frac{2}{5}$ annas. But the actual value of such coins of former times can be ascertained only from the quantity of corn, or other well-defined necessary of life, which they would purchase.

[1] K35 has vaban twice in this sentence, but bôn in § 4. M14 alters this word and others, so as to make the chapter unintelligible. The money is supposed to be given merely as a deposit, in acknowledgment of a bargain to be carried out after the corn is ready for delivery.

[2] Reading zednunand dûkhtâr, but, perhaps, this is a corruption of zednûnînî*d*âr, 'a causer of purchase, a broker.'

[3] That is, 'ready money.'

such instalment demanded—*and* not as a fresh carrying off of a gift[1].

Chapter LIII.

1. *As to* the fifty-second question *and* reply, that which you ask is thus: *If* people of the good religion, in *their* country *or* out of *their* country, shall buy *and* sell with those of a different religion as regards cattle, *or* shall lay hold of traders (vanîkgarân) and shall sell to them, what is then the decision about it? 2. When *those of* the good religion shall not buy, as they have not come *up to* the price, but *the orthodox dealers* shall sell to traders *and* those of a different religion, what is then the decision about it? 3. *And* about him, of whom the means of existence (zîvisnŏ mindavam) are such, what is then the decision?

4. The reply is this, that it would be very grievously sinful, and it would be an evil occupation to transact such business through the influence of opportunity, *and* to seek profit unauthorisedly in that manner. 5. But if *it be* the means of existence of those *of* the good religion *of* whom *you have* written, and *they* are not able to seek *it* in any other business *and* proper occupation which *would be* a less sinful means of existence, complete[2] purchasers who *have* acquired

---

[1] That is, having made a bargain, he is not to be aggrieved at any unexpected excess of profit made in good faith by the other parties to the bargain; a rather high standard of commercial morality.

[2] The word is pûr, but it may be suspected of being a blunder, as tôrâ, 'ox,' would be a more likely word.

the good religion shall sell unto those of the good religion[1]; because it is possible for him *to be* less sinful *to* whom *it* is allowable to beg the life of a comrade, for still the rule *of* a righteous man, with the righteous who are in his guardianship, is to live. 6. So it is possible, when they shall sell cattle for slaughter *and* foreign eating, many cattle—amounting even to a diminution of the maintenance of Irân—are more wretched than a righteous man forced to kill *them* through a living becoming unobtainable *and* the fear of death.

Chapter LIV.

1. *As to* the fifty-third question *and* reply, that which you ask is thus: A man whose wife, daughters, sisters, and relations are many, and *who* is the master of much wealth, becomes sick, *and* during the sickness *has* given this hoard of wealth unto one daughter. 2. And his other sisters and daughters are not contented therewith, *and* speak thus: 'This wealth ought *to have been* given during health and consciousness, not during sickness; and now it should not be allowable to give anything whatever unto any one during sickness, for if anything happens[2] the wealth all comes back for division amongst *us*.' 3. Would it be allowable to give anything whatever of that wealth to any one, during sickness, or not?

---

[1] Who would not be likely to kill the animal, and with whom they could come to an understanding as to its good treatment, so as to avoid the sin of bôdyôzêdîh (see Chap. XLIX, 5 n).

[2] M14 has 'if he gives anything.'

4. Is it necessary[1] *for* one of such wife, daughters, and sisters as *there* happen *to be* to appoint an adopted son for that man, because of that wealth, or not? 5. Are the wife, daughters, and sisters who shall take their share of the wealth responsible for[2] the religious rites of every kind, and is it necessary for them to order the annual ceremonies for that man at the daily and yearly *periods*, or not[3]?

6. The reply is this, that, when there is nothing therein on account of which I *should* so deem *him* otherwise than a man in sickness *and* nearly passing away, *it* is not allowable to give *it* up, except when *it is* for his debts, or his wife *and* children, or an aged *person* (zarmân) or father who is in *his* guardianship—whom it is indispensably necessary to maintain—*and* is such as, or as much as, is discreetly requisite for payment of the debt, or *for* the food, maintenance, *and* protection of those that I *have* written *about;* then, *however, it* is allowable to give it up away (bîrûnŏ) from those of whom *you have* written, as much as during his consciousness. 7. In other sickness, not while passing away, whatever is given up by him himself during consciousness is allowable; when *he is* not conscious *it* is not allowable. 8. And on that which he says during unconsciousness *one* is not reliant and *it* is not credible (vâ*v*ar); *but* that which *he says* during

[1] K35 has 'is it not necessary,' by using lâ, 'not,' instead of râî, 'for,' which latter reading is adopted in the text from M14, but it is doubtful which reading is the better one. The same variation occurs in § 5.

[2] Literally 'are the rites on their necks.'

[3] Ceremonies for the dead have to be performed on the first four days, the tenth day, and then at the end of a month and a year from the time of death (see Sls. XVII, 5).

consciousness, and that, too, which the same man gave unto a daughter when he was ill, if given by him consciously, are even then proceedings to be granted; if given by him during unconsciousness it is just as though he died without an opportunity of speaking (avâng-pîrû*z*)[1].

9. Of the property left by will[2], one share is needful for each separate daughter for whom a husband is not provided, *and* two shares for a wife *who* may be a privileged *one*[3]; *and* so long as the wife is living *she* exists as the house-mistress of the family; moreover, it is not needful to appoint an

---

[1] For this uncommon word M14 substitutes a*v*îk-andar*z*, 'intestate;' but the meaning is that the gift is as invalid as if he had been unable to make a declaration of his intentions.

[2] Levatman andar*z* in K35, but M14 has a*v*îk andar*z*, 'without a will,' which, at first sight, appears the more plausible reading (especially as a*v*îk, 'without,' is written very much like a*v*âk, 'with,' the Pâz. synonym of levatman). But on further consideration it seems equally probable that this section is intended to limit the power of a testator, so as to prevent him from dividing so much of his property as he leaves to his family in any unfair manner. The rule here laid down would, of course, also apply in cases of intestacy when the testator has no son; and is that given in the Persian Rivâyats.

[3] This does not imply that a man might have more wives than one, but that wives are of five classes, according to the circumstances of the marriage. A pâ*d*akhshah or 'privileged' wife is one who was a maiden married with the consent of her parents who have another child. A yûkan or 'only-child' wife differs from the last merely by being an only child, and having, therefore, to give up her first child to her parents. A satar or 'adopted' wife is one who was a maiden enabled to marry by receiving a dowry from the relatives of a man who has died unmarried, on condition that half of her children shall belong to the deceased. A *k*akar or 'serving' wife is a widow who marries again. A khû*d*-*s*arâî or 'self-disposing' wife is one who marries without her parents' consent (see Bd. XXXII, 6 n).

adopted son (satôr), for the adopted son's duty (satôrîh) remains with her, *and* she manages to claim guardianship for the family from some man out of the relatives most nearly allied. 10. Out of the portion of the property for food and maintenance the wife should provide the daughters with husbands; and to keep going the necessities in the guardianship, the nurture which the *deceased* man afforded, *and* the ceremonies *and* good works imposed upon the family, *and* thereby become indispensable, *she* herself is to take lapfuls and armfuls[1] out of the income (bar).

11. *As to* the sisters of that man, if they have been necessarily in his guardianship, even as to nourishment, and there is no property for them in *any* other way, their food and maintenance are also needful to be out of the income of the property, unless[2] that man *has otherwise* devised, or the appointment of a husband is not provided on account of the non-subjection (lôîtŏ aîrîh) *in which* they have been unto the guardianship of that man, or anything else opposed to it, so that nothing whatever of the property of that man is needful for them.

12. He who is a husband of *one of* the daughters is a leader in the management (dastôbarîh) of the family, *but with* the concurrence of the house-mistress of the family, and *even* so when the action *is one* which they should not do, and his son is not born, *or* becomes passing *away*[3].

---

[1] Literally 'the bosom size and arm size,' a Pahlavi idiom for 'plenty.'

[2] In the Pahlavi text this latter half of the section precedes the foregoing provisional clauses.

[3] The meaning seems to be that so long as he has no son (who

13. *As to* a daughter not provided with a husband, should the one whose husband is not provided be an only *child*[1], to keep *her* subject also to the house-mistress of the family it is needful *for* her *that there* should be an adopted son in it; *and* when they shall appoint *her* husband unto the adopted-sonship the property then comes over into his possession.

14. When the house-mistress of the family passes *away*, and the daughters are provided with husbands, the adopted-sonship is to be appointed.

Chapter LV.

1. *As to* the fifty-fourth question *and* reply, that *which* you ask is thus: What is the occupation and capacity (giriftârîh) of the person *that has* to preserve those who are in their three nights' *trials*[2], *and* who is he?

2. The reply is this, that it is said a husband (gab*r*â) is indispensable for preservation through the three nights' *trials* which shall be *for* a privileged wife, a father *for* those of a child, *and* a master *for* those of a servant.

---

would be a member of the family in direct descent through his mother) he can only assist and advise the widow, but on the birth of his son he can act more authoritatively, as the representative of the child.

[1] Written aêvôk-aê in Pâzand. She becomes a yûkan or 'only-child' wife (see § 9 n) until she has given up her first child to her mother, after which she is a 'privileged' wife.

[2] The three nights after death (see Chap. XXIV).

CHAPTER LVI.

1. *As to* the fifty-fifth question *and* reply, that which you ask is thus: What is this adopted-sonship *and* guardianship of the family, and what does it become; *in* what manner is it necessary to appoint *it*, whence is it necessary to provide food and clothing for it, and how is it necessary to be *for* it?

2. The reply is this, that the adopted-sonship is thus:—It is requisite whenever a man of the good religion is passing *away*, while *he is* a complete ruler of a numerous household[1], who has no wife and child that may be privileged[2] and acknowledged, *nor* associating brother, *nor* son by adoption, and his property is sixty stîrs[3] of income. 3. The controlling (khû*d*âyînag) of the property is to be publicly provided *out* of the kindred of the deceased, and is called the adopted-sonship; and he is to be appointed to it who is the nearest of the same lineage (min ham-nâfân), who *will* manage *and* keep the property united in its entirety.

---

[1] Reading vad marak khân shah bundakŏ, but the phrase can also be read vad malkâân shah bandakŏ, 'while *he is* a servant of the king of kings (that is, a subject of the Irânian sovereign),' which is evidently the reading adopted by M14 in Chap. LVII, 2, where it substitutes the Huz. synonym malkâ for shah, but here the word shah is uncertain. This ambiguous phrase can also be read vad mark-âhangihâ bundakŏ, 'while the agonies of death are complete.'

[2] See Chap. LIV, 9.

[3] About 84 rûpîs (see Chap. LII, 1 n); but the actual value of such an income depends upon the value of silver at that time, or, in other words, upon the prices of the necessaries of life.

4. The guardianship of a family is that when a guardian *has* to be appointed in that manner over the family of a man whose wife[1], or daughter, or infant son is not fit for their own guardianship, so it is necessary to appoint *some one*. 5. And it is necessary to appoint the adopted son *and* the family guardianship at *such* time as may be convenient to them; and when the man passes *away* as *I have* written it is necessary to appoint at such period as *I have* written, and to neglect *it* temporarily, even the length of a year, would not be authorised.

6. *Fit* for adoption is a grown-up sister who is not adopted in another family[2], then a brother's daughter, then a brother's son, *and* then the other nearest relatives. 7. *Fit* for the family guardianship is first the father of the serving *wife* (*k*agar)[3], then a brother, then a daughter, and then the other nearest relations; among brothers he who is the eldest (mas) among *them* is the fittest.

8. The food *and* clothing of a wife that may be privileged—who is the house-mistress of the family, and is one kind of adopted son—*of* a living infant son till he becomes grown up, *and of* a daughter of the family while she is in the guardianship of the family guardians[4], are out of the property of the family so long as it exists for the purpose.

9. *It has* become the custom *that* the lapfuls *and*

---

[1] Because she is not a privileged wife, but a serving one (see Chap. LIV, 9), as appears from § 7.

[2] A woman or child cannot be adopted by more than one family (see Chap. LVII, 3). The case under consideration is that mentioned in § 2, when the deceased leaves no wife, child, or brother.

[3] Referring to the case assumed in § 4.

[4] That is, till she is married.

armfuls[1] of the family guardian are every month four stîrs of, it may be, sixteen[2], which is the disbursement (andâzisnŏ), for food, clothing, medicine, *and* shelter, out of the income (bar), or out of the capital (bûn), of the property which remains in the family, by a perfect[3] wife when she is capable—such as the former house-mistress—so as want of nourishment (atafdâdŏ) may not come nakedly and unlawfully upon them.

Chapter LVII.

1. *As to* the fifty-sixth question *and* reply, that which you ask is thus: Who is suitable *for* adoption, *and* who is not suitable?

2. The reply is this, that a grown-up man of the good religion who is intelligent, a complete ruler of a numerous household[4], expecting offspring, *and* not *having sins* worthy of death is suitable for adoption; even when he has accepted either one adoption, or many adoptions, he is then still suitable for another adoption. 3. And a grown-up woman, *or* even a child, is suitable for one adoption, *but* when adopted in one family she is not suitable for another adoption.

[1] That is, an ample remuneration (see Chap. LIV, 10).

[2] So the sentence may be literally translated, but it is not quite certain that this is the meaning intended, as the language used is very involved. This would imply that the family guardian is entitled to one-fourth of the family expenditure.

[3] It is doubtful what noun is to be connected with the adjective pûr; perhaps we should read 'full disbursement' in the foregoing part of the sentence, and omit the word 'perfect' here.

[4] M14 has malkâânŏ malkâ bôndak, 'a servant of the king of kings;' but see Chap. LVI, 2.

4. A woman requiring a husband—though a complete worshipper—or a foreigner, or an infidel, or *one* having *sins* worthy of death, is unfit for adoption; so also those who are demon-worshippers, she who is a concubine (shûsar nêsman) *or* courtezan, *and* she who is menstruous are unfit.

CHAPTER LVIII.

1. The fifty-seventh question is that which you ask thus: How many kinds of family guardianship and adoption are *there?*

2. The reply is this, that it is said *there* are three kinds, which are the existent, the provided, and the appointed. 3. An adopted son who is existent is such as a wife who may be privileged, *or* an only daughter is a kind of adopted son owing to confidence in herself, such as happens when there is no wife, *and* a daughter for whom there is no husband, *and* none is provided, is the one *that* has remained.

4. An adopted son *who* is provided is such *as* a son that is acknowledged, who is accepted by one's self[1], and *free* from *being* appointed, or *from* necessity[2].

5. And an adopted son who is appointed is he who is to be appointed among the relations who are suitable for adoption—and are nearest to him who is to be appointed *as* adopted son—and the ministers (padân) of religion, *and* he performs the duty of

---

[1] That is, adopted during the man's lifetime.

[2] Reading ayûf nîyâzŏ, but it may be ayûfŏ êyâvŏ, 'or *from* discovery.'

family guardianship[1]; he who is the appointed *one* is he who is appointed by the men *who are* the nearest relations (nabânazdistânŏ) on account of proximity.

Chapter LIX.

1. *As to* the fifty-eighth question *and* reply, that which you ask is thus: For how much property is it then necessary to appoint an adopted son?

2. The reply is this, that when the property which *has* remained his for whom it is necessary to appoint an adopted son is as much as sixty stîrs[2] of income, *it* is then indispensable to appoint an adopted son for him. 3. Even when *it* is less they should recognise him whose adoption is needful, *and who* conducts an adopted son's duty; and, similarly, an adoption is to be appointed for him, though it may not come as a possession unto him who is fittest for adoption.

Chapter LX.

1. *As to* the fifty-ninth question *and* reply, that which you ask is thus: What is the sin owing to not appointing *an adopted son?*

2. The reply is this, that *for the man* himself *it* is allowable when he gives up all the property in

[1] M14 has 'an existent family guardianship is *in* the son of him appointed, and a provided *one* is that when he himself performs the duty in the guardianship;' but the phrase interpolated is hardly grammatical.

[2] About 84 rûpîs (see Chap. LVI, 2).

righteous gifts, *and* when he has no property they should not provide an adopted-sonship for him, *and* his relations are innocent as regards it. 3. But should they recognise him who has the adopted-sonship of the deceased, or has accepted the position of his adopted-sonship [1], *or* should they have seized the property for the adopted-sonship *in order* to appoint an acting adopted son (satôrgar), *and* he conducts the adopted-sonship, and throws away *both* the portion (bôn) provided for disbursement (vishôpŏ) and the entirety, and quite destroys the property, and thoroughly ruins the adopted sonship, though, on account of not restraining him, it is said *to be* a sin worthy of death for *every* single dirham, it is not said *they are* killed outright [2].

Chapter LXI.

1. *As to* the sixtieth question *and* reply, that which you ask is thus: What is the propriety *and* impropriety, the merit *and* demerit, of family guardianship?

2. The reply is this, that the merit is the appointment *and* recognition of him who accomplishes more worthily the greater benefit; the demerit is *as to*

---

[1] M14 has 'or any one who has accepted the adoption as an adoption.'

[2] The meaning appears to be that, though, owing to their misplaced confidence and neglect, they have been guilty of many mortal sins, they are not liable to capital punishment. It is evident that the writer had no apprehension that any property would lie neglected through want of administration, but that he had considerable doubts of the prudence and honesty of administrators.

him who is unworthy, or him whose worthiness is not appointed to avert a lesser benefit and the ruining of a worthy adoption. 3. Nearer details (khûr*d*akŏ) of the family guardianship which is proper *and* which is not proper for an adopted son's duty, of the child of good religion with whose business *it* is connected, *and* of the fathers for whom a family guardian is to be appointed, are *in* the recital of five chapters (fragar*d*ŏ) of the Hûspârûm *Nask*[1], and *in* the abstracts (giriftakŏîhâ) of the good ideas in various scriptures (naskô) in which many decisions are together.

Chapter LXII.

1. *As to* the sixty-first question *and* reply, that which you ask is thus: How stand the shares in the inheritance (mîrâtŏ) of property among those of the good religion, and how is it necessary for them to stand therein?

2. The reply is this, that in the possession of wealth the wealth reaches higher *or* lower, just like water when it goes in a stream on a declivity, but when the passage shall be closed at the bottom it goes back on the running water (pûy-â*v*ŏ), *and* then it does not go to its after-*course*[2].

---

[1] The seventeenth book of the complete Maz*d*a-worshipping literature, whose sixty-four sections are described in detail in the Dînka*r*d (see Sls. X, 21). The five chapters here mentioned were evidently in that one of the last fourteen sections which is said to have consisted of six chapters on the ownership of property and disputes about it, on one's own family, acquiring wife and children, adoption, &c.

[2] This metaphor seems to mean that property, like water, always

3. When there is nothing *otherwise* in the will and private[1], property *goes* to a wife *or* daughter[2] who is privileged; if *one* gives her anything by will then she does not obtain the share (dâ*s*) *pertaining* to her[3]. 4. Whenever[4] a share for a son is not provided by it, every one *has* so much and the wife who may be a privileged *one has* twice as much; and the share of that *one* of the sons[5], *or* even the wife of a son, who is blind in both eyes, or crippled[6] in both feet, or maimed in both his hands, is twice as much as that *of one* who is sound.

5. And *it* is needful *that* he who *was* in the father's guardianship *shall* remain in guardianship, as when a father or mother is decrepit and causing awe (*k*agarîn), or *of* a nurture different from that of the guardian[7]—or a child of his brother or sister, or a father, or *one*[8] without nurture apart from him, is

---

descends until it meets with an obstruction to its downward progress in the shape of the nearest descendants, but, when once in their possession, it can again ascend (like the dammed stream) for the support of the survivors of an older generation (see § 5).

[1] Or, it may be 'in the provisions (vûyagân) of the will;' or, by omitting two strokes, we have simply 'otherwise (hân) in the will.'

[2] That is, they have a share of the property when there are other next of kin. M14 adds, 'and they should provide a living son *as* father and husband unless privileged,' referring to the necessity of adoption when there is no son and the wife is not a privileged one.

[3] It being assumed that the will provides as much as is intended for any one whom it mentions.

[4] Reading amat, 'when,' instead of mûn, 'who,' which words are often confounded because their Pâz. equivalents are nearly identical.

[5] M14 has 'daughters.'

[6] Armê*s*t probably means literally 'most immovable.'

[7] M14 omits this last clause.

[8] M14 has 'mother.'

without a guardian—the ready guardianship of a capable man, and the shelter *and* nourishment *that have* become inadequate[1] are as indispensably forth*coming*[2] from the possessors of wealth, of those who *have* taken the property, as that *taking* was indispensable[3].

6. If *there* be no son of that *man*, but there be a daughter or wife of his, and if *some* of the *affairs*[4] of the man are such as render a woman not suitable for the guardianship, it is necessary to appoint a family guardian; if there be, moreover, no wife *or* daughter of his it is necessary to appoint an adopted son. 7. This—that is, when it is necessary to appoint a family guardian *and* who is the fittest, *and* when it is necessary to appoint an adopted son *and* which is the fittest—is written in the chapters *on* the question[5].

Chapter LXIII.

1. The sixty-second question is that which you ask thus: Would they authorisedly carry off any property whatever from foreigners and infidels, or not?

2. The reply is this, that wealth and property and anything that foreigners (an-aîrânŏ) possess and is carried off by them from the good with violence, *and which through* obstinacy they do not give back

[1] Literally 'not issuing.'

[2] M14 has 'are thus forth*coming*.'

[3] M14 has 'or *have* become indispensable to it.'

[4] Or, it may be '*dependents;*' the text is merely va hatŏ min zak-î gab*r*â.

[5] See Chaps. LVI–LIX.

when it is proper, it is well allowable in that case *that* they should seize from the foreigners. 3. So long as *it* is the lawful order of the procurator of its owners[1] *it* is allowable for a just decider to consider properly, and to demand authoritatively the sending of interest (sû*d*ŏ) thereon for himself. 4. But *if* they proceed in their obstinacy *he* is sent to come *up* with them in obstinacy, not to dissemble with them[2].

5. *It is* the custom to give an infidel (ak-dînô), who is not a foreigner, food, clothing, *and* medicine, when his renunciation (vâ*z*) has come, for keeping away matters (*k*is*â*nŏ) of death and sickness owing to hunger *and* thirst, cold and heat; but wealth, horses, accoutrements, wine, *and* land are not given authorisedly, it is said, unto foreigners *and* idolators[3].

CHAPTER LXIV.

1. *As to* the sixty-third question *and* reply, that which you ask is thus: Whence *was* the first creation of mankind, and how was the formation of the original race of men? 2. What issued from Gâyômar*d*[4], *and* what did it really become; *and* from what have Mashyâîh *and* Mashyâyôîh[5] arisen?

3. The reply is this, that Aûhar*m*az*d*, the all-

---

[1] Reading vad zak amata*s* khû*d*âyân ayâ*v*î-aîtâr farmân-î dâ*d*îk. The form of ayâ*v*î-aîtâr has not yet been met with elsewhere, but it seems to mean 'one who holds the obtainment,' though whether as agent or officer of justice is uncertain.

[2] M14 has merely 'but should they proceed in their obstinacy, to come with them is not to dissemble.'

[3] Literally 'demon-worshippers.'

[4] See Chap. II, 10.

[5] The same as the Marhayâ and Marhîyôih of Chap. XXXVII, 82.

ruling, produced from the endless light the shape of a fire-priest (âsrûkŏ) whose name *was* that of Aûhar-mazd, and *its* brilliance that of fire; *its* incombustibility was like *that* inside the light, *and its* expansion like the western (khûrbarag) land. 4. And in the shape of the fire-priest *was* created by him the material existence (stih) *that* is called man, *and for* three thousand years[1], when it did not progress and did not eat, it did not speak; likewise, it did not utter, but it thought of, the righteousness of the perfect *and* true religion, the desire for the pure glorification of the creator.

5. Afterwards, the contentious promise-breaker[2] injured the life of it, *and* produced a burdensome mortality; and the mortality is *clear* from the appellation, Gâyômard[3], of the nature produced. 6. The seed which *was* the essence of the life of the leader (mîrakŏ) of life, who *was* Gâyômard, flowed forth on *his* passing away, came on to the earth of the beneficent angel[4], *and* is preserved in the earth until, through the protection of the angels, a brother and

[1] This is the second of the four periods of three thousand years of which time is said to be composed (see Chap. XXXVII, 11 n). The 'shape of the fire-priest' is one of the spiritual creations of the first period, in which shape man was created during the second period, and this primeval man became Gâyômard (that is, 'a living mortal') through the persecution of the evil spirit (see § 5) at the commencement of the third period. The first two steps of this creation are not described in the text of the Bundahis known to Europeans.

[2] The evil spirit, who is said to be the origin of falsehood (see Chap. XXXVII, 11).

[3] Which means 'the living mortal,' or 'the mortal living one.'

[4] The female archangel Spendarmad, who has special charge of the earth. Or the phrase may be 'came on to the earth which the beneficent *spirit* produced.'

sister of mankind[1], connected together, have grown from it, *have* attained to movement *and* walking upon the earth, *and* have advanced even to intercourse and also procreation.

7. The ground where the life of Gâyômar*d* departed is gold, *and* from the other land, where the dissolution of *his* various members occurred, as many kinds of decorative metals flowed forth it is said[2].

Chapter LXV.

1. *As to* the sixty-fourth question *and* reply, that which you ask is thus: Where *and* from what did the origin of race, *which* they say *was* next-of-kin marriage (khvêtûdâ*d*ŏ)[3], arise; and from what place did it arise?

---

[1] The Mashyâîh and Mashyâyôîh, or man and woman, of § 2, who are said to have grown up, in the course of forty years, connected together in the shape of a plant; but, after a breathing soul had entered them, they became human beings, and fifty years later they began to be the progenitors of mankind (see Bd. XV, 1–30).

[2] Zs. X, 2 states that eight kinds of metal arose from the various members of the dead Gâyômar*d*, namely, gold, silver, iron, brass, tin, lead, quicksilver, and adamant.

[3] Usually written khvêtûk-das (Av. *hv*aêtvadatha, 'a giving of, or to, one's own'). It is a term applied to marriages between near relations, and is extolled as specially meritorious. For centuries past the Parsis have understood it to refer to marriages between first cousins, and all allusions to marriage between nearer relations they attribute to the practices of heretics (see Sls. XVIII, 4 n); though, like the professors of all other religions, they must admit the necessity of such a practice in the first family of mankind, as detailed in the text. Translations of other passages relating to the subject will be found in Appendix III, and it is also mentioned in Chaps. XXXVII, 82, LXXVII, 6, and LXXVIII, 19.

2. The reply is this, that the first consummation of next-of-kin marriage was owing to that *which* Mashyâîh *and* Mashyâyôîh[1] did, who were brother and sister together, and their consummation of intercourse produced a son[2] as a consummation of the first next-of-kin marriage. 3. So that they effected the first intercourse of man with woman, *and* the entire progress of the races of every kind of lineage of men arose from that, *and* all the men *of* the world are of that race.

4. It is truly said, that it was the joy of the lord *and* creator after the creation of the creatures, and, owing to that, its consummation, which *was* his complete accomplishment of the existence of the creatures (dâmânîh), was owing to him. 5. And its occurrence, too, is in evidence that the creator, who is so with unflinching (atôrâk) will, is as much *the cause of* the begetting and entire progress of his own perfect creatures[3], in whom begetting is by destiny, as Hôshâng[4] by whom two-thirds[5] of the demons *were* smitten, Tâkhmôrup[6] who overturned Aharman through the power of the angels, Yim by

---

[1] See Chap. LXIV, 2. The names are here written Mashyêîh and Mashyêyôîh.

[2] Twins, according to Bd. XV, 22, 24.

[3] That is, he is not only the original creator, but also the perpetual promoter of the increase and progress of the creation, as much as those who appear to be such promoters, though merely acting as his agents.

[4] Here written Hôshyâng. For the Av. names of these four primeval monarchs, see Chap. II, 10 n.

[5] K35 has 'three-thirds,' but see Âbân Yt. 22, Râm Yt. 8, Zamyâd Yt. 26.

[6] He is said to have subjugated the evil spirit, and to have used him as a steed for thirty years (see Chaps. II, 10, XXXVII, 35).

whom order *was* arranged and death *was* driven away (avakâl*d*ŏ)[1], Frê*d*ûn *who* fettered A*z*-î Dahâk[2] and stripped his blaspheming (nîrangâk) from the world, and the many princes (kayân) and high-priests of grave spirit *who* were, *and* are, *and will* be.

Chapter LXVI.

1. *As to* the sixty-fifth question *and* reply, that which you ask is thus: *There is* a man of wealth of the good religion who fully intends to order a *celebration of* all *the rites* of his religion; and a priest of it, to whom the five chapters (fragar*d*ŏ) of the Avesta ('text') of the correct law of the Nîrangistân ('religious-formula code')[3] are easy through the Zand ('commentary'), is ever progressing in priestly manhood (magôî-gab*r*âîh). 2. And he (the man) goes unto him, and he (the priest) speaks thus: 'All the religious rites are *performed* for 350 *dirhams*[4], as a gift always given beforehand by them *who* give the order unto me, so that I *may* come to *them*.'

3. A man of the disciples[5], to whom the five

---

[1] He is said to have kept away cold and heat, decay and death, and other evils from the earth (see Râm Yt. 16, Zamyâd Yt. 33).

[2] See Chap. XXXVII, 97.

[3] This was the name of one of the first thirty sections of the Hûspârûm Nask (see Chap. LXI, 3), and a portion of it, containing the Pahlavi commentary (or Zand) of three chapters, with many Avesta quotations, is still extant.

[4] The word *g*û*g*anŏ, 'dirham,' is here omitted, but occurs in §§ 16, 20. The sum of 350 dirhams would be about 122½ rûpîs (see Chap. LII, 1 n).

[5] That is, those who are still learning their priestly duties (see Chap. XLV).

sections (vîdag) of the Avesta are easy, and nothing whatever of its Zand is easy[1], then says unto him—unto that man who intends to order all the religious rites—thus: 'For this gift I will conduct all the religious rites for thee twice, with the appliances in the land of Pârs[2], shouldst thou give the order unto me. 4. For it is quite possible for me to pray so many sections through my own exertion (dastŏ), *but* for him[3] it is necessary to order again of an officiating priest (pavan zôtakŏ), who is himself not able to pray any section, *or* does not himself pray; and it is not necessary for him to go for the control (parvâr)[4] of all the religious rites when a stipend (bâhar) is the one consideration within him, *and* the matter is *that* he[5] *may* receive again. 5. *He* who *has* always himself prayed is better than he who shall accept readily *and* orders *the work* again, and is not able to pray it himself, when a fulfilment is tedious to him; when *it* is I who[6] receive, I always pray myself better than he who would accept readily *and* orders again, and it brings on my business to a *closing* point.'

6. The priestly man speaks thus: 'The considera-

---

[1] It being far easier to learn the Avesta by heart than to understand its meaning by aid of the Pahlavi commentary; a competent knowledge of the latter being sought only by advanced disciples, and rarely attained by any but the most learned priests.

[2] Reading pavan bûm-î Pârs, as in § 15; K35 has here pavan bûn-frâs, 'for opening the beginning,' which might be understood to refer to the preliminary ceremonies for preparing the ceremonial apparatus, if the phrase were not otherwise written elsewhere. In § 21 K35 has pavan bûn-î Pârs.

[3] K35 omits the last letter of valman.

[4] Or, it may be 'to the precincts.'

[5] Literally 'I.'

[6] Reading li mûn, instead of lanman, 'we.'

tion of stipend is more necessary to arise *with* me than[1] other men, owing to the position of religion, not the other portion (*s*ânŏ) of all religious rites; therefore, it is more authorisedly received *and* conducted by me when I accept readily and again intrust *the work;* but I direct so that they pray thoroughly, and it brings on much business to its *closing* point; moreover, *if* I seize upon it, even then I should be authorised, for this is the stipend of religion.'

7. Should they seize this that is authorisedly theirs, or not? *And* is *it* the custom of a man who is frequently ordering all the religious rites to reduce his gift for the ceremonial, or not?

8. Order *some one* to decide for us clearly, when they do not dispute the gift *for* the ceremonial, or *when* they do dispute *it*, how is then its great advantage; *and* the harmfulness that exists therein, in many ways *and* many modes, when they give an insufficient gift for the ceremonial. 9. Is the property which is given up as a gift for the ceremonial—so long as it thus becomes the remuneration which *one* gives to a receiver of remuneration (mozdô-bar)—that property which they can seize? 10. And is the work which is done, *or* deputed, and its great advantage, more than they would perform when, in the period of the evil millenniums[2], they diminish the gift for the ceremonial; *and* in how many modes

---

[1] Reading li min, instead of the imperfect word lanm.

[2] Of the twelve millenniums of time, mentioned in Chap. XXXVII, 11 n, the most evil one is said to have been that in which the author lived, the millennium of Hûshê*d*ar (about A.D. 600–1600 according to the chronology of Bund. and Byt.), for 'mankind become most perplexed in that perplexing time' (see Byt. II, 62, 63), a period of great tribulation for the religion of the Maz*d*a-worshippers.

does its harm then proceed therefrom? 11. Of whom are all the religious rites always more authorisedly ordered, of that priestly man, or of that disciple? 12. *For* what reason, also, is it proper to diminish the gift for all the religious rites of him who is a priestly man, or to give *it* in excess? 13. When they do not diminish the gift for the ceremonial, and *it* is given in excess, in what manner does its great advantage then arise therefrom; *and* why *and* through what source (bêkh) is it possible *for* advantage to arise therefrom? 14. When they diminish the gift what harm to it (the ceremonial) is then possible to arise therefrom, *and* how is *it* better when they give the gift for the ceremonial?

15. For when the family householders, with those of the good religion of Irân, are early (pê*s*) *with* every single *celebration of* all the religious rites with holy-water, in the land of Pârs, unless they are in distress, their gift is then 400 dirhams[1]; and we have given more than this, *even* 450 dirhams[2], for it. 16. And now should it be needful, when we diminish anything from the 400 dirhams, or from the 450[3] dirhams, of their gift, they would then not accept *it* from us, *and* they speak thus: 'For 400 dirhams, or *at* least for 350 dirhams[4]; nothing less do we

[1] About 140 rûpîs (see Chap. LII, 1 n). M14 has 300 dirhams.

[2] About 157½ rûpîs. M14 has 350 dirhams. The actual value of all these sums depends upon the cost of the necessaries of life in Pârs in the ninth century.

[3] M14 has '350.'

[4] About 122½ rûpîs. K35 has ângûn, 'so,' instead of *g*û*g*anŏ, 'dirham' (the two words being nearly alike in Pahl. letters); this would alter the phrase as follows:—'or less; as to 350, so paltry a thing we do not accept.'

accept.' 17. *But* there are needy *men*[1] who always come to us *and* speak thus: 'For 350 dirhams we will twice conduct all the religious rites with holy-water[2], as you have always ordered us before for 400 dirhams; order *it* only of us, *for* shouldst thou have *it* managed by priestly men, they always say that they should always perform a curtailment (kâstârîh) of the religious rites and ceremonies of the sacred beings, *and* that all the religious rites are not authorisedly ordered except of them.'

18. Although a priest (aêrpatŏ) who becomes a ruler of the ceremonial should be doubly a decider, yet order *some one* to explain to us clearly concerning these questions, as asked by us.

19. The reply is this, that the *man* of the good religion who intended to order all the religious rites is he whose desire is goodness, and he should be a decider of questions about it.

20. *As to* the priest who spoke thus:—'Thou shouldst order *it* of me for 350[3] dirhams, as you have always given before your business *was arranged; and* it becomes your own non-religious share of the duty, to be authorisedly given, because you have proceeded with the alleged demeanour of the country *and* for the purpose of intercession; and all the

[1] The disciples, who are represented as applicants for employment.

[2] That is, in the most solemn manner, and with all appliances. It appears from Chap. LXXXVIII, 9, that the religious rites without holy-water were then performed for 120 to 150 dirhams, or little more than one-third the fee demanded for those with holy-water; whereas the merit of some rites with holy-water is said to be a hundred times as great as that of the same rites without holy-water (see Sls. XVI, 6).

[3] M14 has '400' here, but see § 2.

religious rites with holy-water are such as they solemnize repeatedly (pavan dôr), among which there are many in which[1] I *act* and *am* very well performing'—the gift of 350 dirhams is then not excessive remuneration for him.

21. *As to* the disciple who spoke thus:—'For 350 dirhams I will *twice*[2] conduct all the religious rites in the land[3] of Pârs'—such of them as they then conduct repeatedly are not many in the aggregate (*k*înakŏ), and they certainly damage his (the man's) property, and all the religious rites of fire, through that deficiency. 22. And they would accept it on this account, that through a love of righteousness they might cause an advantage (khan*g*înakŏ) unto all those religious rites by their own inferior eminence[4]. 23. And he extends *and* impels the ceremonial of the sacred beings into much progress who promotes it through that eminence which is owing to his own wealth, *and* which is thus more possessed of a share (bôn) of the ceremonial of the sacred beings and of the good work of praise—except, indeed, a like good work of praise of his—when they shall cause that manifestation of eminence[5]. 24. So that the orderer of the good work understands that that which is diminished by him[6] is the eminence

[1] Reading mûn, 'which,' instead of amat, 'when' (see Chap. LXII, 4 n).

[2] The cipher '2' is omitted in the Pahl. text here, but see §§ 3, 17.

[3] K35 has bûn, instead of bûm (see § 3).

[4] Or, it may be 'by the eminence of their own wealth,' as aîr, 'inferior,' and khêl, 'wealth, property,' are alike in Pahlavi; but neither reading is quite satisfactory here.

[5] By a proper disbursement of wealth.

[6] When he diminishes his payment.

of the disciple, which his own wealth *has* to order for those who are not able to give wealth which is their own property for it; *and* he makes no curtailment (bangisnŏ) of those scanty remunerations.

25. And if that disciple should accept as remuneration less than is the custom *for* all the religious rites, *the orderer* is not undiminished in wealth[1], for the reason that the good effect owing to the advantage of holy-water is such as *when* they conduct *them* repeatedly, unless it be necessary to conduct *them* in a manner as *if* unpaid (pavan agazî*d*). 26. That curtailment of the good effect is not afterwards demandable (pasîn-sakhunîkŏ), if it *has* to be accepted by him; *and* if that acceptance of less remuneration by him be an opposing of him to the malice and ill-temper (vushâî) of the priests, this also is not *the way* that they should cause progress as regards their own *business*.

27. And the proximity (nazdîh) of a master of the house[2] *who* keeps away from all the religious rites requested *and* accepted—more particularly when the accepter accepts all the religious rites of the requester for that remuneration—is itself necessary; he may not be of a religious disposition, but it is yet requisite *for him* to be where this is requested

---

[1] M14 has '*it* is not eminence in wealth;' but the meaning is evidently that there is no real saving when the expenditure is reduced, because the good effect of the rites is also diminished when they are insufficiently paid for.

[2] Or, khânŏpânŏ may mean 'a keeper of the sacred table,' or low stone platform on which the ceremonial vessels are placed, which is often called khân. In either case the orderer of the ceremony is meant, and the author evidently contemplates the probability of the order being given as a mere formal matter of duty, without any really religious feeling.

and accepted for that scanty remuneration of his, owing to the extent and impetus of *his* share of the duty.

28. Moreover, it is perceived by us in Pârs *that* they who would accept the work for half the remuneration which was requisite as profit for it formerly would seize the remuneration. 29. And the reason of it is this :—The peasants relied upon the corn of the field (khânŏ) *which* has not come, *and they* said : 'We are hurried ; we never obtain *anything* even on a single one of various debts, and by this payment we *shall* save *our* lives for the time ; so we calculate that whatever we seize in the manner of a debt or two, when the corn arrives *and* we sell the corn, we *shall* make *as* profit on that business[1] ;'—and it seemed to me very desirable *for* such a man.

30. If, also, they should approve that scanty remuneration of that disciple, it is an injury of all the religious rites, of which the forgivers[2] *have* to cast the consideration of the unequally-shared advantage out of the body[3]. 31. All the religious rites ordered of him who is a better performer, owing to not diminishing the proper remuneration, *having* proceeded unaltered, the remuneration of righteousness *one* does not approve is important as regards such as they solemnize and conduct in the period[4].

[1] This parable justifies the taking of religious stipends by force, in cases of necessity, by a practical appeal to the sympathies of the enquirers ; but it really evades the question proposed in § 7, which refers to seizures not justified by necessity.

[2] Probably the priests who appoint atonements for sins confessed and renounced (see Sls. VIII, 1, 2, 5, 6).

[3] Of those who have obtained a disproportionate share of the profit of the good works by not paying properly for them.

[4] There are several doubtful points in the construction of this section.

32. Since, for the 350 dirhams, all the religious rites which they conduct once with holy-water are, it is affirmed, all the religious rites caused to be conducted twice with holy-water in that same place *and with* the same good effect, it is more important to order of *them* who shall allow all the religious rites twice; for, with as much wealth, as much efficiency, and as much good effect, more ceremonial is good.

33. The worthiness of the disciple, which is owing to himself, is the preparation; *and* the priest is worthy, of whose performance in the religion *you have* spoken[1]; therefore, supreme worthiness is unattainable by either of them; so it is more significant when the disciple is the preparer, *and* the priest, *as* director, becomes a demander of good effect; both strive for good progress, *and* through many kinds of participation they may be worthy. 34. And both of them, praising together—whereby the participation is brought *to* an end—may authorisedly seize[2]; but that worthiness of theirs is owing to the duty and the praise therein—this *one* in preparing, *and* this *one* in superintendence (a*v*ar-ma*d*îh) of the recital—*and* the after discourse and petitioning, *and* other good done.

[1] See § 1.

[2] Probably the remuneration, if it be withheld; provided always they do their duty thoroughly, as mentioned in the concluding clause.

CHAPTER LXVII.

1. *As to* the sixty-sixth question *and* reply, that which you ask is thus: What is this appearance[1] which is girded on the sky?

2. The reply is this, that *it is* a mingling of the brilliance of the sun with mist and cloud that is seen, of which *it* is *at* all times and seasons, moreover, a characteristic appearance, whereby *it has* become their sign above from spiritual to earthly beings. 3. That which is earthly is the water above to which its brilliance is acceptable; and the many brilliant colours (gunakân) which are formed from that much mingling[2] of brilliance and water, and are depicted (mânâkî-aîtŏ), are the one portion for appearing[3].

CHAPTER LXVIII.

1. *As to* the sixty-seventh question *and* reply, that which you ask is thus: What is this which, when the sun and moon *have* both come up, is something[4]

---

[1] Reading dî*d*anŏîh; but the word can also be read sa*d*-vanîh, which might stand for sa*d*-gûnîh, 'a hundred-coloured existence,' a possible term for the rainbow, but the Persian dictionaries give no nearer term than sadkas, or sadkês.

[2] M14 has 'that mingling of many portions and few portions.'

[3] Reading dî*d*anŏkŏ; but it can also be read sa*d*-vanakŏ, a similar alternative to that in § 1.

[4] The only probable reading for this word is mindavam, 'a thing;' it occurs three times in this question, but is a very vague term for the phases of the moon, probably referring to a supposed body covering the dark part of the moon's disc.

come, *and* comes on as *it were* anew when it (the moon) becomes new, *and* men want the thing to go down from the place *where it* is becoming apparent? 2. When it *has* been several times, what is then the thing *which* comes up *and* exists, and how is its motion by night and day?

3. The reply is this, that the sun and moon are always seen[1] there where they stand, and they exist for men and the creatures. 4. The sun is swifter-moving[2] than the moon, *and* every day becomes a little in advance; at the new moon the sun is shining, and the moon owing to diminution backwards, on account of the slenderness of the moon by much travelling[3], and on account of the brilliance of the sun, is not apparent. 5. As the sun goes down a light which is not very apparent is the moon, and not *having* gone down the moon is seen[4]; and each day the moon increases, comes up more behind the sun, *and* goes down more behind, *and* is, therefore, more seen. 6. When increased to the utmost, which is approaching a likeness of the sun, it comes spherical (aspiharakŏ), and is seen the whole night; to diminish anew it comes back to the companionship of the sun, and goes into the splendour of the sun.

[1] The MSS. have astî-hênd, 'have remained,' instead of khadîtunî-hênd, 'are seen;' but the difference between these words in Pahlavi letters is merely a medial stroke.

[2] Apparently so, as the moon rises and sets about 48 minutes later every day, on the average.

[3] A very anthropomorphic mode of accounting for the waning of the moon into a slender crescent.

[4] Most Orientals consider the day of the new moon to be that in the evening of which it is first possible to see the moon; this is usually the first, but sometimes the second, day after the actual change of the moon according to European ideas.

Chapter LXIX.

1. *As to* the sixty-eighth question *and* reply, that which you ask is thus: When *something* takes hold of the moon *or* sun what is then its residence (khânŏ), *and* whence does it always seize upon *it?*

2. The reply is this, that two dark progeny of the *primeval* ox[1] move and are made to revolve from far below the sun and moon, and whenever, during the revolution of the *celestial* sphere, they make *one* pass below the sun, or below the moon, it becomes a covering which is spun (ta*d*) over the sun, *and* it is so when the sun or moon is not seen. 3. Of each of those two progeny of the *primeval* ox—one of which is called 'the head,' and one 'the tail'—the motion is specified among astronomers[2]; but *in* remaining upon those luminaries, and producing that covering, they do not attain unto those luminaries

---

[1] Supposing the reading should be 2-ân gô*k*îhar-î târ here, and 2-ân gô*k*îharân in § 3. Gô*k*îhar is a supposed planetary (and, therefore, malevolent) body, connected with the sun and moon and having a head and tail, which falls on to the earth at the resurrection (see Bd. V, 1, XXVIII, 44, XXX, 18), and is here described as the cause of eclipses. Its name implies that it sprang from, or contained, the seed of the primeval ox, the supposed source of animal life (see Bd. XIV, 3), and in its Av. form, gao*k*ithra, it is a common epithet of the moon; in Pers. it has become gôzihr or gavaz*k*ihr. As the words stand in K35 they look more like 2 andô*g* dâlan-î târ, 'two dark store-lobbies,' or 2 andô*g* gâl-î târ, 'two clusters of dark spiders;' and in § 3 the word han*k*îrŏ is substituted for the nearly synonymous andô*g*. In M14 the words seem to be 2 ângûn *k*îharânŏ-î târ, 'two such dark faces.'

[2] M14 has 'in the calculations of astronomers.'

within that covering. 4. *There* occurs no difference whatever of the descending *rays*[1] from those luminaries into a place of purity and freedom from disturbance far below those luminaries, except this, that the light which they divert to the world, and their activity as regards the *celestial* spheres are not complete *for* so much time, *nor* the coming[2] of the light to the earth.

CHAPTER LXX.

1. *As to* the sixty-ninth question *and* reply, that which you ask is thus: What are these river-beds[3], and what is the cause of them; whence do they always arise, *and* why is *there* not a river-bed everywhere *and in* every place where *there* is no mountain?

2. The reply is this, that any place where a mountain is not discernible and a river-bed exists *it* is a fissure (a*s*kûpŏ); and it is declared as clear that, even before the growth of the mountains, when the earth was all a plain, *by* the shaking of the world the whole world became rent (zandakŏ)[4]. 3. Even

---

[1] Literally 'fallers.'

[2] Assuming that mâ*d*ârîh stands for ma*d*ârîh. The meaning is that an eclipse produces no harm beyond a short interruption of the descent of the sun's or moon's rays to the earth.

[3] There is some doubt as to whether the word should be read zôgakŏ (comp. Pers. zô*gh*, 'a river'), or zandakŏ (comp. Pers. zandah, 'fissured'), but the meaning is tolerably certain from the context.

[4] When the evil spirit rushed into the earth it is said to have shaken, and the mountains began to grow (see Bd. VIII, 1–5); and at the resurrection it is expected that the earth will recover its original perfect state of a level plain (see Bd. XXX, 33).

Frâsîyâv of Tûr[1] *was* specially mighty by causing the construction of channels (vidarg) there where *it* is mountainous, *and* also *in* low-lands[2], in which there is no mountain, and the shaking in its creation *was* the formation of great sunken[3] springs and river-beds. 4. And if it *has* been prepared *in*, *or* if *it be* in a ravine (sikaftŏ) of, the mountains, the cause, too, of the contraction, thundering, and tearing of a river, if *its* confinement *be* in the earth, is the resistance which it *meets* in seeking a passage; and as it is a spring of the waters of the earth, so also it is in the earth, whose contraction *and* panting are mighty *and* full of strength. 5. And when *it is* a time that they would make a constructed channel at the outside of its ravine, as regards the contraction which is within it, the resistance by which it is contracted at the outside of the ravine is the ground[4].

Chapter LXXI.

1. *As to* the seventieth question and reply, that which you ask is thus: Is anything which happens

[1] Frangrasyan, the Tûryan, in the Avesta; called Afrâsiyâb in the Shâhnâmah (see Bd. XXXI, 14). He is often mentioned as constructing canals (see Bd. XX, 17, 34, XXI, 6), but being a foreign conqueror he was considered as specially wicked by the Irânians.

[2] Assuming that sîtân is a miswriting of sîpŏân, occasioned by joining two of the letters, just as harvispŏ, 'all,' is often written harvist.

[3] Or, perhaps, 'hidden.'

[4] That is, a watercourse which is confined by its natural rocky channel in the mountains, when carried across the plain in a canal, is confined only by softer soil.

unto men through fate or through action, is exertion destiny *or* without destiny, *and* does anything devoid of destiny happen unto men, or what way is it? 2. *As to* that which they say, that, when a man turns unto sinfulness, they ordain anew a new death[1]; *as to* that which they say, *that* anything which happens unto men is a work of the moon[2], and every benefit is connected with the moon, and the moon bestows *it* upon worldly beings; and *as to* what way the moon *does* this, and bestows all benefits, order *some one* to decide the literal explanation of how and what way it is, by the will of the sacred beings.

3. The reply is this, that the high-priests[3] have said thus, that there are *some* things through destiny, and there are *some* through action; and *it* is thus fully decided by them, that life, wife, and child, authority and wealth are through destiny, and the righteousness and wickedness of priesthood, warfare, and husbandry are through action. 4. And this, too, is thus said by them, that that which is not

---

[1] This reference is to a phrase in the Pahl. commentary on Vend. V, 33, which commentary contains a good many of the statements made in this chapter, excepting those relating to the moon. The reading aôsh, 'death,' given by K35, is probably more correct than aûbas, 'for him,' given by our modern MSS. of the Vendidâd; but M14 has amended it, and states 'then many new *things* are ordained by it for him.'

[2] Assuming that vidanâg, 'time,' stands for bidanâg, the Huz. of mâh, which means both 'month' and 'moon.' In the following phrases the word mâh is used.

[3] It may be noted that most Pahlavi writers, when quoting the Pahlavi commentaries on the Vendidâd (as the author is doing here) or any other Nask, speak of them merely as the utterances of the high-priests, and reserve the term dînô, 'revelation,' for the Avesta itself; thus showing that belief in the inspiration of the Pahlavi translations of the Avesta is a very modern idea.

destined for a man in the world does not happen; *and* that which is destined, be it owing to exertion, will come forward, be it through sinfulness *or* slothfulness he is injured by it. 5. That which will come forward owing to exertion is such as *his* who goes to a meeting of happiness, or the sickness *of* a mortal who, owing to sickness, dies early[1]; *and* he who through sinfulness and slothfulness is thereby injured is such as *he* who would wed no wife, *and* is certain that no child of his is born, *or* such as *he* who gives *his* body unto slaughter, and life is injured by his living.

CHAPTER LXXII.

1. *As to* the seventy-first question *and* reply, that which you ask is thus: What are the heinous sins of committing unnatural intercourse, is it proper to order *or* perform the *sacred* ceremony for him who shall commit unnatural intercourse, *and* is it then proper to practise sitting together and eating together with him who shall commit *it*, and shall commit *it with* a longing for it, or not?

2. The reply is this, that of the evil Maz*d*a-worshippers[2]—who *were* the seven evil-doers of sin of a heinous kind[3], whose practice of Aharman's *will was* as much as an approximation to *that of*

[1] M14 has 'which comes forward owing to sickness.'

[2] M14 has 'of a like evil practice, in inclination for sins, *were* the very heinous in the religion of the Maz*d*a-worshippers.'

[3] Reading girâî van vinâs, and assuming that van is a miswriting of gûn.

Aharman *himself*—two are those whom you have mentioned, who are defiled with mutual sin. 3. For, of those seven evil-doers, one *was* Az-î Dahâk[1], by whom witchcraft *was* first glorified; he exercised the sovereignty of misgovernment, and desired a life of the unintellectual (ahangân khayâ) for the world. 4. One *was* Azî Sruvar[2], by whom infesting the highway *in* terrible modes, frightful watchfulness (vîmag-bî*d*ârîh)[3] of the road, and devouring of horse *and* man *were* perpetrated. 5. One *was* Va*d*ak[4] the mother of Dahâk, by whom adultery *was* first committed, and by it all lineage is disturbed, control is put an end to, and without the authority of the husband an intermingling of son with son[5] occurs. 6. One *was* the Vîptak[6] ('pathic')

[1] See Chap. XXXVII, 97.

[2] A personification of Av. azi srvara, a serpent or dragon thus described in the Hôm Yt. (Yas. IX, 34–39):—'(Keresâspa) who slew the serpent Srvara which devoured horses and men, which was poisonous and yellow, over which yellow poison flowed a hand's-breadth (spear's-length?) high. On which Keresâspa cooked a beverage in a caldron at the mid-day hour, and the serpent scorched, hissed, sprang forth, away from the caldron, and upset the boiling water; Keresâspa Naremana*u* fled aside frightened' (see Haug's Essays, pp. 178, 179). The same account is given in Zamyâd Yt. 40.

[3] M14 has bîmînî*d*ârîh, 'terrifying.'

[4] See Chap. LXXVIII, 2. There is possibly some connection between this name and the Av. epithet, Vadhaghana, which is thus mentioned by the evil spirit, speaking to Zaratû*s*t, in Vend. XIX, 23:—'Curse the good Maz*d*a-worshipping religion! *and* thou shalt obtain fortune such as the Vadhaghana sovereign obtained;' and Mkh. LVII, 25 calls him 'the Va*d*agân sovereign Dahâk.' The Pahlavi writers seem to have taken this epithet as a matronymic, owing to its form, but whether the mother's name be really traditional, or merely manufactured from the epithet, is doubtful.

[5] Reading levatman ba*r*man ba*r*man, instead of levatman bûm ba*r*man. M14 omits bûm.

[6] Av. viptô (p. p. of vip, 'to sow, to fecundate'), used in the

in the intercourse of males, the infecundity of which is the desire of men; and by him the intercourse of males *and* the way of destroying the seed *were* first shown unto males. 7. One *was* the Vîpînî*d*ak[1] ('pæderast'), the male by whom the use of females *was* first brought among the errors (khazdag) of the male, and *was* despised (dûkhtŏ) by him; he who is a cherisher of seed is delivering *it* to females, and that which is destroying the seed is the flowing of stenches into the prescribed vessels[2] for it, the delivering *it* to males by a demoniacal process, and carrying on a practice which effaces (âhan*g*ê*d*ŏ) *and* conceals the race[3] of the living. 8. One *was* Tûr-î Brâ*d*ar-vakhsh[4], the Karap *and* heterodox wizard, by whom the best of men *was* put to death. 9. And one *was* he by whom the religions of apostates[5] *were* preferred—through the deceitfulness of the perverted text and interpretation[6] which they themselves utter—to the law which the righteous

sense of 'a pathic' in Vend. VIII, 102. This name, as well as the next one, is used here more as representing a class than an individual.

[1] The p.p. of the causal form of vîptanŏ, 'to fecundate,' used as an equivalent of the Av. vaêpayô of Vend. VIII, 102.

[2] Assuming that pavan pavan mû*d*ragânŏ stands for pavan farmû*d* ragânŏ; but there is some doubt as to the correct reading of several words in this section.

[3] Or 'seed.'

[4] The eldest of five brothers who were wizards of the Karap race or caste, and deadly enemies of Zaratû*s*t (see Byt. II, 3). He is said to have slain Zaratû*s*t in the end.

[5] Aharmôkô, Av. ashemaogha, means literally 'disturbing the right,' and is a term applied to an ungodly man specially under the influence of the evil spirit, as an apostate is naturally supposed to be.

[6] The Avesta and Zand.

has praised, that existence *which* would have procured a complete remedy, *and* would have become the eternity of the records which bestow salvation, through the good righteousness which is owing to the pure religion, the best of knowledge.

10. And they who are defiled by a propensity to stench are thereby welcoming the demons *and* fiends[1], *and* are far from good thought[2] through vexing *it;* and a distance from them is *to be maintained* of necessity in sitting and eating with *them*, except so far as *it may be* opportune for the giving of incitement *by* words for withdrawing (pa*d*âli*s*nŏ) from *their* sinfulness, while converting *them* from that propensity. 11. *Should one* die, to order a ceremonial for him is indecorous, and to perform *it* would be unauthorised; but if *he were* to do *so* penitently *one* would then be authorised to perform his ceremonial after the three *nights*[3], for it is the remedy for atonement of sin. 12. And so long as *he* is living *he* is in the contingencies (vakhtagânŏ) owing to the sickness through which *he* is in that way an infamous *one* (akhamî*d*âr), and *there* are no preventives (bôndagânŏ) and medicinal powder for it; these are teachings also for the duty and good works of a ceremonial for the soul[4].

---

[1] Who are supposed to seize upon them and pervade them; hence the necessity of shunning such men, to avoid contamination from the demons who possess them.

[2] That is, from what is personified in the archangel Vohûman.

[3] During which the soul is supposed to remain on earth, hovering about the body, after death (see Chaps. XX, 2, XXIV, 2, XXV, 2).

[4] That is, they are warnings to him to repent.

CHAPTER LXXIII.

1. *As to* the seventy-second question *and* reply, that which you ask is thus: Does the stench of him, stinking withal, who commits unnatural intercourse proceed to the sky, or not; and to what place does the wind of that stench go *when* it goes *anywhere?*

2. The reply is this, that the material stench goes as far and in such proportion as there are filthiness and fetidness in the stinking existences, and the spiritual stench goes unto there where there are appliances (sâmânŏ) for acquiring stench, a miserable place; on account of the separation (gar*d*îh) of the sky, everywhere where it goes in the direction of the sky it does not reach to the undisturbed existences[1]. 3. Information about the stench is manifest in the omniscient creator, whose omniscience is among the luminaries, *but* that persistent creator *and* the primeval angels *and* archangels are *free* from its attack; and *his* information about the deception which is *practised* upon that labourer *for* hell and mind *allied* with the demons[2] is certain.

---

[1] The sky being divided into three parts, and the uppermost part being inaccessible to evil (see Chap. XXXVII, 24, 25).

[2] Reading a*v*â-*s*êdâ-mîni*s*nŏîh, but it is possible that a*v*â may have originally been kha*v*dak, for the Av. khavzô, 'male paramour,' of Vend. VIII, 99, 103 (trans. D.).

CHAPTER LXXIV.

1. *As to* the seventy-third question *and* reply, that which you ask is thus: Is *there any* discomfiture (vânî*d*ârîh) of the archangels from that stench, or not?

2. The reply is this, that the archangels are immortal and undistressed; their place, also, is in that best existence of light, all-glorious, all-delightful, *and* undisturbed; and the strength of the stench due to the demons[1] does not reach unto *anything* pertaining to the archangels. 3. The archangels are omniscient[2], friendly to the creatures, persistent, *and* procure forgiveness; they know that heinous practice which is the heinous practice[3] of that wretched dupe (frîftakŏ) who *has* become defiled in that most filthy manner (zî*s*ttûm ârang), which is like that which is provided *and* which is applied to him even in the terrible punishment[4] that *has* come upon him from the demons; and then, on account of *their* friendliness to the creatures, it *has*

---

[1] Reading az-*s*êdâîkŏ, but it may be âz-*s*êdâîkŏ, 'of the demon of greediness,' or it may stand for khav*d*ak-*s*êdâîkŏ, 'of a male paramour of the demons,' as mentioned in the last note.

[2] Omniscience with regard to what is taking place in the world being an indispensable characteristic of any being to whom prayers are addressed, or whose intercession is implored.

[3] These words are thus repeated in K35, and the repetition may be correct.

[4] Referring probably to the punishment of such a sinner, detailed in AV. XIX, 1–3, as follows:—'I saw the soul of a man, through the fundament of which soul, as it were, a snake, like a beam, went in, and came forth out of the mouth; and many other snakes ever seized all the limbs.'

seemed to them severe, and thereby arises their forgiveness which is according to whatever anguish is owing to the torment which galls him.

Chapter LXXV.

1. *As to* the seventy-fourth question *and* reply, that which you ask is thus: Do the angels have *his* dead *body* restored, or not?

2. The reply is this, that *there* was a high-priest who said that the angels do not have *his* dead *body* restored, because of the sin of the mutually-polluting, full of stench, and inglorious victims (khvâpî*d*ŏân)[1], the terrible kind of means for the exculpation of creatures[2], and that practice when males keep specially imperfect in *their* duty; it *being* then suitable for mankind to become *free* from him who—like A*z*-î Dahâk[3], who wanted many most powerful demons—resists *and* struggles, and is not possessing the perception to extract (patka*s*istanŏ) a pardon, owing to the course of many demoniacal causes. 3. But innumerable multitudes (amarakânîhâ), happily persevering[4] in diligence, have with united observation, unanimously, *and* with mutual assistance (ham-ban*g*i*s*nîhâ) insisted upon this, that they have the dead *bodies* of all men restored; for

---

[1] Victims of the deceptions practised by the demons (see Chaps. LXXIII, 3, LXXIV, 3); but the reading is uncertain.

[2] Probably the punishment of the wicked in hell.

[3] See Chap. XXXVII, 97.

[4] Reading farukhvŏ-tûshi*s*n, but it may be perkhûntŏ dahi*s*n, '*having* begged the boon;' and M14 has pôryô*d*keshânŏ, '*of* those of the primitive faith.'

the good creator, granting forgiveness *and* full of goodness, would not abandon any creature to the fiend[1]. 4. In revelation (dînô) it is said that every dead *body* is raised up, both of the righteous and of the wicked[2]; *there* is none whom they shall abandon to the fiend.

5. And this, also, is thus decided by them[3], that even *as to* him *who* is most grievously sinful, when he becomes mentally *seeking* pardon *and* repentant of the sin, *and*, *being* as much an atoner as *he* is well able, *has* delivered *up his* body *and* wealth for retribution *and* punishment, in reliance upon the atonement for sin of the good religion, then it is possible *for* his soul, also, to come to the place of the righteous[4].

Chapter LXXVI.

1. *As to* the seventy-fifth question *and* reply, that which you ask is thus: *As to* him who shall slay those who shall commit unnatural intercourse, how is then his account as to good works and crime?

2. The reply is this, that the high-priests, in *their* decision, *have* thus specially said, that all worthy of death are *so* by the decision of judges and the

[1] Except for temporary punishment in hell. All ideas of the vindictiveness of implacable justice are foreign to the Maz*d*a-worshipper's notion of the good creator.

[2] Compare Bd. XXX, 7.

[3] Probably by the 'multitudes' of § 3.

[4] By delivering up his body and wealth to the will of the high-priest, as an atonement, and mentally renouncing his sins, he is saved from hell, and the beneficial effect of any good works he may have performed returns to him (see Sls. VIII, 5).

command of kings, whose business is execution. 3. Whoever shall slay him who *has* heinous sins[1] after controversies three times with him, about the decision of those acquainted with the religion *and about* the command of kings, when he *has* thus remained in the sin in defiance of his own relations—and not inimically to the man *and* injuriously to the religion, but inimically to the sin *and* in order to keep away intercourse with demons—is to consider *it* as a great good work. 4. No command is given about the decision of *what one* is to do *in* the same matter, more heedfully and more authorisedly in *cases of* doubtful attention, for the good work exists undoubtedly more *and* more abundantly[2].

Chapter LXXVII.

1. *As to* the seventy-sixth question *and* reply, that which you ask is thus: Will you direct *some one* then to make the heinousness of this sin of unnatural intercourse clear to us?

2. The reply is this, that the first material creature *was* the righteous man, the smiter of the fiend, the righteous propitiator; so, also, in the world *he* is more recognising the sacred beings, more completely (hamâktar) for the production of creatures,

[1] Reading vinâsânŏ, as in M14, instead of the doubtful word vashkisn, which might perhaps be compared with Pers. buzhis, 'opposition.'

[2] The meaning is that no one is bound to put such sinners to death until they are condemned by the authorities, but should one do so upon his own responsibility, entirely for the good of the faith, and certain of the impenitence of the sinners, he is not only free from blame, but has done a meritorious deed.

and with more provision for the creatures[1]. 3. And with the manifestation of knowledge the best duty is that which *exists* in lawfully practising procreation, *and* the complete progression of righteous men arose therefrom.

4. In like manner he who is the omniscient creator formed mankind in the first pair, who were brother and sister, *and* became Mashyâîh and Mashyâyôîh[2], and all races of material life *exist* by means of acquiring sons and *his* omnisciently causing procreation. 5. The man and woman *were* also made to lust (gâmînî*d*ŏ) by him, and thereby *became* the father and mother of material men; and he naturalized among primitive man the qualities of a desire (âlû*d*anŏ) for acquiring sons together through glorifying. 6. And the law *and* religion authorised it as a proper wish, so long as *they proceed* from those who are their own *relations*, not from those who are not their own; and with those whom next-of-kin marriages[3], original duties, and desires for other sons have formed, complete progress in the world is connected, and even unto the time of the renovation *of the universe*[4], it is to arise therefrom. 7. And the birth of many glorious practisers of the religion, those confident in spirit, organizers of the realm, arrangers of the country, *and* even accom-

[1] Reading va*l*-dâm-nîvâri*s*nŏîhâtar; the syllables -âtar being written separately M14 has va*l* dâm-nîvâri*s*nîh aîyyâ*d*-tar, 'more remembering the provision for the creatures.' Promoting the increase of, and providing maintenance for, good creatures are considered to be important good works.

[2] Here written Mashyâ and Mashyâyâôîh, but see Chaps. XXXVII, 82, LXIV, 2.

[3] See Chap. LXV.

[4] See Chap. II, 8.

plishers of the renovation *of the universe*, which *arises* from *those* same *to* whom that practice shall be law—and when it occurs lawfully—is a miracle and benefit of the world, the will of the sacred beings and the utmost good work discernible, because the complete progress of the righteous arises therefrom, and the great female faculty (nekedîh) is manifested.

8. So when the opponent of the same, by whom the source *of* seed *and* procreation is spoiled, is intent upon a way for the death of progeny—and the intention is certain—*its* annihilation is owing to him[1]; and he is the devastating fiend[2], whose will is a desire of depopulation and ruin, and by the power of his Nîyâ*z* (*demon of* 'want')[3] he turns imperceptibly the esteem of the very indispensable production of men from the position of wishing for sons to a creature[4] who is opposed to it, through whom have arisen its ruin *and* corruption. 9. And the nature and power which are his cherishing of progeny are not suitable for receiving seed, and misrepresented (drôkînî*d*ŏ) by him is the accompanying evil intercourse, so that emitting the seed (shûdak), in delivering *it* at that time into that burning place, full of stench, is to produce *its* death, *and* no procreation occurs.

10. The dupes[5] turn the living seed from mingling with women *and* seeking for births, just as in the like vice of any demon, connected with a longing

---

[1] A free translation of a*g*a*s* lôîtŏ, which phrase is placed at the end of the section in the Pahl. original.

[2] The evil spirit.

[3] See Chap. XXXVII, 52.

[4] M14 has 'to a member.'

[5] Of the fiend.

for the dupes[1], they shall abandon that advantage of the world, the delights (vâyagânŏ) of a son[2]. 11. He who is wasting seed makes a practice of causing the death of progeny; when the custom is completely continuous, which produces an evil[3] stoppage of the progress of the race, the creatures *have* become annihilated; *and* certainly, that action, from which, when it is universally proceeding, the depopulation of the world must arise, *has* become and furthered (frârâstŏ) the greatest wish of Aharman[4]. 12. Such a practiser is the greatest wish of Aharman, through the demon's excretion[5] of doubt *in* the practice, owing to intercourse with the emitter, *which* is most filthy and most fetid, and the emitting member, which is causing death; and the demoniacal practice[6] is perceptible even from the same practice, and whatever is the heinousness *of* the sinfulness is clear to observers of the dead *body*.

CHAPTER LXXVIII.

1. *As to* the seventy-seventh question *and* reply, that which you ask is thus: *As to* the nature of the heinousness *and* sinfulness of committing adultery, *and* the worldly retribution specified *for it* in revela-

[1] Such men are said to become paramours of the demons (see Vend. VIII, 102–106), as further alluded to in § 12.

[2] M14 has 'seeking a son.'

[3] Reading dahê*d* va*d*, but M14 has yâîtyûntô, 'brought a,' and may be right.

[4] See Chap. XXXVII, 10.

[5] Reading rîkhîh, but M14 has râsîh, 'course.'

[6] In hell.

tion, *will* you then direct *some one* to point out to us the modes [1] of retribution for it?

2. The reply is this, that it is adultery, heinous *and* vicious, which first Dahâk *used* to commit, and *he* is known by the illicit intercourse which *was* his desire with Va*d*ak [2], who *was his* mother, in the lifetime of Aûrva*d*âsp [3], who *was* his father, without [4] the authority of Aûrva*d*âsp, who was the husband of Va*d*ak whose practising of sin, unauthorisedly *and* injudiciously, *was* itself heinous *and* very frequent. 3. And its modes *of* theft or spoliation are just as much more heinous than other theft *and* spoliation as a man *and* that which arises from his procreation of man are greater than the position of property.

4. One is this, that *it* is important to consider with steadfastness the courtezan life of the adulteress *and* the bad disposition assuredly *and* undoubtedly therein; she causes pillage unauthorisedly, and in *her* practice, also, intercourse during menstruation, owing to *its* resembling the burning of seed, is a frightful kind of handiwork (dastô).

---

[1] M14 has 'the various modes.'

[2] This is evidently the name written Udaî in Pâz. in Bd. XXXI, 6, who was, therefore, the *daughter* of Bayak; the fact of her being the mother of Dahâk is more clearly expressed in the Pahlavi text of Chap. LXXII, 5.

[3] This is the name written Khrûtâsp in Bd. XXXI, 6, which is a Pâz. reading, though confirmed by the Pahl. form in TD (as Udaî is, to some extent, by the Pahl. Aû*d* of TD). This Aûrva*d*âsp, whose name can also be read Khûrûtâsp, must be distinguished from his namesake, the father of Vi*s*tâsp, whose name became corrupted into Lôharâsp (see Bd. XXXI, 28, 29).

[4] K35 omits a*v*îk, 'without,' here, but has it in Chap. LXXII, 5. Without this particle the meaning would be 'who *was* the high-priest of his father, Aûrva*d*âsp.'

5. One is this, that it may be *that* she becomes pregnant by that intercourse, *and has* to commit on her child[1] the murdering of progeny.

6. One is this, that it may be in pregnancy, *by* her coming to intercourse *with* another man, *that* the living child which is in her womb has died through that intercourse.

7. One is this, that it may be that she becomes pregnant by that intercourse, *and* the pregnancy *having* given indications, through shame or fear she swallows a drug[2] [and seeks a remedy, and murders the child in *her* womb.

8. One is this, that it may] be that a woman who is foreign or infidel, and becomes pregnant by that intercourse, gives birth to a child, *and* it has grown up with the child which is known *to belong to* the husband of the woman, *and* remains in foreign habits (an-aîrîh) or infidelity. 9. The committer of the illicit intercourse is as unobservant and grievously sinful as *he* who shall lead his own child from *his* native habits (aîrîh) and the good religion into foreign habits and infidelity; as to the sin which that child may commit in childhood *he* is the sinner, and as to that which it may commit in manhood *he* is equally sinful with it. 10. Also, if that child be put to death in childhood, *and* be passed through water, rain, *or* fire, *or* be buried in the well-yielding earth[3], *he* is an equally vicious murderer, *and* is defiled thereby through *being* the invisible causer.

---

[1] M14 has '*and* with the assistance of another man *she has* so to commit on her child of that pregnancy.' The interpolation is clumsy, and does not make the sentence easier to translate.

[2] The passage which follows, in brackets, is from M14; there being evidently something omitted from K35 at this point.

[3] The contamination of water, rain, fire, or earth, by contact with

11. Likewise, if he who is a man of the good religion accustoms a woman to illicit intercourse, *and* through adultery a child is born and grows up, even then to practise undutifully that which undutifulness committed is to make a wretched *and* clandestine connection. 12. On account of the birth *having* occurred through illicit intercourse *it* is grievously sinful; through propriety *it* is praise*worthy*, and through falsity *it* is sinful[1], *and* it is said that a bastard is not appointed in superintendence over *any one*. 13. *If* it be done so that pregnancy does not occur, even then every single time—not to mention the text (avistâk) *as to* the matter regarding the destruction of his own living *seed*[2]—*it* is *a sin of* two Tanâpûhars, which are six hundred stîrs[3]; *and* regarding that emission *it* is inexpiable (atanâpûhar)[4].

---

a corpse, being considered a heinous sin (see Sls. II, 9, 50, 76, XIII, 19).

[1] That is, procuring the birth of a legitimate child is highly meritorious, but an illegitimate birth is sinful.

[2] Referring probably to Vend. VIII, 77–82, which states that the voluntary waste of seed is an inexpiable sin, as mentioned at the end of this section.

[3] A Tanâpûhar (Av. tanuperetha) sin was originally one that required the sinner to place his body at the disposal of the high-priest, in order to atone for it; but it was not necessarily a sin worthy of death, or mortal sin. At the time when the Vendidâd was written, such a sin was punished by two hundred lashes of a horse-whip or scourge (see Vend. IV, 72). Subsequently, when the Vendidâd scale of punishments was converted into a scale of weights, for estimating the amounts of sins and good works, a Tanâpûhar sin was estimated at three hundred stîrs (στατήρ) of four dirhams (δραχμή) each (see Sls. I, 1, 2). The weight of 600 stîrs was probably about that of 840 rûpîs, or $21\frac{3}{5}$ lbs. (see Chap. LII, 1 n).

[4] That is, a sin which cannot be atoned for even by giving up one's body for execution. Anâpûhar in Pahl. Vend. VIII, 82.

14. As much on account of the conversation as on account of the companionship *of* the man who goes unto various women, for the sake of a man's sin, and is unatoning, *should* his own body be also defiled with bodily refuse (hîgar-hômônd)[1], or *should* those kinds of harm be not *kept* away from another[2], even then every single time of the bodily refuse bringing harm to his own body is *a sin of* sixty stîrs[3], and through making his own body defiled with bodily refuse is each *time a sin of* sixty stîrs; and if he washes with water that defilement with his own bodily refuse, or that which is harmed *thereby*, every single time *it* is *a sin of* six hundred[4] stîrs.

15. And if it be a foreign or infidel woman, apart from the sinfulness *about* which *I have* written, *it* is a sin of sixty stîrs on account of not controlling the sins *and* vicious enjoyment of the foreign woman. 16. And, finally, the other various sins which are owing to *this* sin are very numerous, *and* grievous to thousands of connections, and *it* is thereby contaminating to them *in* a fearful manner.

17. The retribution is renunciation *of sin* in procuring pardon; and the renunciation in his turning from equally grievous disobedience[5], every single

---

[1] See Chap. XLVIII, 19.

[2] M14 has 'or he does not wash those harmful kinds of bodily refuse,' which is inconsistent with what follows.

[3] This is the estimated weight of a Khôr sin, originally the crime of inflicting a severe hurt, ranging from a bruise to a wound or broken bone not endangering life (see Sls. I, 1, 2). The weight was probably equal to that of 84 rûpîs.

[4] M14 has 'three hundred.'

[5] Reading asrûstîh as in M14, instead of the aîtrôîstŏîh of K35. Possibly the latter word might be read 3-trôîstŏîh, 'the

time that *he turns* from similar viciousness, and as an atonement for the sin, is to arrange, or order, four (arbâ) marriages of the next of kin to his own wife, lawfully, authorisedly, and most hopeful of offspring. 18. Through fear of the grievous sinfulness which *I have* recounted, *in case of* a child of those of the good religion who has no giver of shame[1], and to keep lawfully in subjection a child who is under control, he who is unnurtured is lawfully given nurture, *and* is nominated for lawfully bringing up. 19. And to turn a man *or* woman of bad disposition, by eulogy and entreaty, or[2] *by* distress (fangîm) and fear and other representations, from that bad disposition *and* vicious habit; to order next-of-kin marriage[3] and all the religious rites (hamâk dînô), the Dvâzdah-hômâst[4], the ceremony *in honour* of the waters[5], and the *presentation of* holy-water to the fires[6]; to remove the burden of offspring[7] which is distressing those of the good religion, and to force them from the infidelity acquired, which is a very atoning atonement for such sins, are extremely proper proceedings (a*v*îr-farhakhtîkîh).

passing away of the three *nights*,' referring to the Av. phrase thrity*a*u khshapô thrao*s*ta, 'on the passing away of the third night,' in Hn. II, 18; the three nights are those immediately after death, while the soul is supposed to remain hovering about the body, thinking over its sins, and dreading the approaching judgment of the angel Rashnu; but previous renunciation of sin would relieve it from much of this dread.

[1] That is, one not born in shame, but a legitimate child. M14 has shîr, 'milk,' substituted for sharm, 'shame.'

[2] M14 has 'woman of family with extending sins or bad disposition.'

[3] See Chap. LXV.

[4] See Chap. XLVIII, 25.

[5] Probably the Âbân Nyâyi*s*.

[6] Probably the Âta*s* Nyâyi*s*.

[7] By assisting in their support.

CHAPTER LXXIX.

1. *As to* the seventy-eighth question *and* reply, that which you ask is thus: What is the decision *about* water *with* the *word* Ithâ[1] and *him who* shall drink it? 2. When a man *has* performed his ritual *and* does not take the prayer (vâ*g*ŏ) *inwardly, but* drinks water with the *word* Ithâ, what is the decision *about* this efficacy[2] of which he takes up one half *and* abandons one half, how is it necessary, or not, to consider *it*, and what is the sin of it? 3. *As to him* who performs half, *or* less than half, of the efficacy, *and* drinks water with the *word* Ithâ, what is the retribution for this sin when he shall commit *it* occasionally, *and* what is good *in order* that this sin, when he shall commit *it*, may depart from *its* source?

---

[1] The first word of Yas. V, 1, 2 which forms the first portion (after the invocation) of the inward prayer, or grace, to be muttered before eating or drinking. This first portion may be translated as follows: 'Here then we praise Ahura-mazda, who gave (or created) both cattle and righteousness, he gave both water and good plants, he gave both the luminaries and the earth, and everything good.' This is followed by three Ashem-vohûs, each meaning as follows: 'Righteousness is the best good, a blessing it is; a blessing be to that which is righteousness to *the angel of* perfect rectitude.' After muttering these formulas, or 'taking' them inwardly as a protective spell, the mutterer can eat or drink, and after washing his mouth he 'speaks out' the spell or vâ*g* by reciting certain other formulas aloud. This chapter refers to those who mutilate the vâ*g* by muttering only its first word or words, which matter is also treated in Sls. V.

[2] Supposing that this word, which may be twice read mâânâê and four times mâênâê, represents the Ar. ma'hnî, but this is by no means certain.

4. *As to him* who *has* performed his Nâbar[1] ritual, *and* drinks water with the *word* Ithâ, not muttering (andâkŏ) the *inward* prayer (vâgŏ), and performs a ceremony (yastô), though he does not order a ceremony of Gêtô-kharîd[2] for himself, is the decision then *about* him anything better, or not; *and* does the good work of this ceremony of Gêtô-kharîd become just the same as *that* of the Nâbar ceremony, or not? 5. *As to him* who orders a ceremony of Gêtô-kharîd for[3] himself, what is then his good work, and what is the value[4] of his worthiness when he does not himself perform because he orders that they should perform for him? 6. And *as to* him who has not performed his ceremony, *and* is fifteen years *old*, what is then the decision *about* him?

7. The reply is this:—When a man *who has* chanted the Gâthas ('hymns')[5] drinks water with the *word* Ithâ, if, moreover, *being* preservable *from* suffering[6], he be not a righteous *one* overwhelmed by impotence, it is thus said that, when *in order* to consecrate the sacred cake (drônô)[7] it is not possible

[1] The initiatory ceremony of a young priest, written nâîbar or nâgbar in this chapter, and sometimes nônâbar (Pahl. navak nâîbar).

[2] This ceremony, which means 'the world-purchased,' and by which, according to the Sad-dar Bundahis, 'heaven is purchased in the world, and one's own place brought to hand in heaven,' lasts three days, and is performed by two priests; the first day's ceremonies are those of the Nônâbar, those of the second are of the angel Srôsh, and those of the third are of the Sîrôzah, or angels of the thirty days of the month (see Bd. XXX, 28 n).

[3] Reading râî instead of lâ, 'not.'

[4] Reading varkâ, instead of va neked, 'female,' which is much like it in Pahl. letters.

[5] And is, therefore, an initiated priest.

[6] M14 has 'from impotent suffering.'

[7] See Chap. XXX, 1.

to take the prayer *inwardly*, and *there* are no presentations of it for the tasting of the virtuous *with inward* prayer[1], or for the sake of relieving the sickness of a righteous person, which has come severely, when it is possible for him *to say* 'Ithâ' *and* one 'Ashem-vohû[2],' or it is possible for him to say 'Ashem,' *he* is to recite that which it is possible for him to speak, and *he* is to drink or eat[3] the water, or food, or medicine which is discreetly his, and may be the custom of his body and life[4].

8. But the sinfulness of *him* who *has* drunk water with the *word* Ithâ, not owing to suffering, is much the most sinful, except this efficacy of which *you have* written that, *having* taken up[5] one half, they shall abandon one half; for, when in eating the efficacy is possessed in that manner, *it* is then a chattering meal which is a very grievous sin[6]. 9. Every single drop (pashan)[7] which in that manner comes to the

[1] Reading vâ*g*ŏ atôfdâ*d*agân-î nadûgânŏ, which M14 has altered to mean 'and if in his state of hunger and thirst.'

[2] Merely the first words of the two formulas which constitute the inward prayer, or vâ*g* (see § 1 n).

[3] M14 has only '*he* is to eat.'

[4] M14 has 'and is authorisedly to preserve his own body.'

[5] Reading *frâg*, as in M14 and § 2, instead of pavan, 'in;' though the reading 'in taking up' is quite possible.

[6] The sin of drâyân-*g*ûyi*s*nîh, 'eagerness for chattering,' which arises from talking while eating, praying, or at any other time when a prayer (vâ*g*) has been taken inwardly and is not yet spoken out. The sin arises from breaking the spell of the inward prayer (see Sls. V).

[7] Comp. Av. parshuya and Pers. pashang, bashang. This word has been misread ya*z*i*s*n, 'ceremony,' in Sls. V, 3, 4, which ought to stand as follows:—'It is unseasonable chatter for every single drop; *for* him who has performed the ritual *it* is a Tanâpûhar *sin*; *for* him who has not performed the ritual *it* is less,

mouth *as* a new taste is *a sin of* three stîrs [1], and every single *thing* which is spoken like that word [2] is a sin of three stîrs, which is mentioned as the minimum.

10. The retribution is that way well perfected when, in renunciation of that sin which attacks, a proper efficacy is prepared *and* becomes a vestige (vûnakŏ) of the sin of the performer. 11. Whoever is not able to arrange it in this manner is to entreat the prayers of three men with a donation of wealth, and is to solemnize his Nônâbar *ceremony* [3], *or he* is to consecrate a sacred cake every day in the ceremonial place, to eat food lawfully, *and* to order the proper maintenance of the efficacy. 12. The assistance of performing the proper rituals through ordering the Nâbar *ceremony*, and the helping existence of discharging the burden of the trouble of a populous household seem to me suitable for the atonement of such-like sin, through the will of the sacred beings.

---

some *have* said three Srôshô-*k*aranâms. The measure of unseasonable chatter is a Tanâpûhar *sin;* this is where every single drop, or every single morsel, or every single taste is not completed.'

[1] The stîr is evidently taken here as equivalent to the Srôshô-*k*aránâm of Sls. V, 3 (see the last note). A sin of three Srôshô-*k*aranâms, 'lashes with a scourge,' is called a Farmân, and is usually the least degree of sin of which notice is taken; its amount is variously estimated (see Sls. IV, 14, X, 24, XI, 2, XVI, 1, 5), but the value given here, in the text, is very likely correct, and is equivalent to about 4⅕ rûpîs, either in weight or amount (see Chap. LII, 1 n).

[2] The word Ithâ. M14 has 'every single time it is spoken in tasting with an efficacy like that word,' but the meaning of this is not clear.

[3] See § 4.

Chapter LXXX.

1. *As to* the seventy-ninth question *and* reply, that which you ask is thus: Concerning him who does not order *ceremonies* what is then the decision?

2. The reply is this, that, excepting those among which is specially the selected religious rite (dînô) of him whose ceremony is not performed—who, even though *having* many good works, does not afterwards attain unto the supreme heaven, which is determined[1]—this, moreover, is thus said, that he who is not able to perform his ritual himself, when he orders a Gêtô-kharî*d*[2] *ceremony* and they shall perform *it*, can become *fit* for the supreme heaven (garô*d*mânîkŏ); this is greatly to be commended.

Chapter LXXXI.

1. *As to* the eightieth question and reply, that which you ask is thus: What is the purpose of this *ceremony for* the living soul[3], *and* why[4] is it necessary

---

[1] It is the general opinion that if the proper ceremonies are not performed during the three days after a death (see Chap. XXVIII) the deceased cannot attain to the highest grade of heaven; this is, however, denied by some of the commentators (see Sls. VI, 3–6).

[2] See Chap. LXXIX, 4 n.

[3] Dastûr Peshotanji Behramji, the high-priest of the Parsis in Bombay, informs me that every Parsi is bound to perform, or get performed, every year during his or her lifetime, ceremonies for three days in honour of his or her soul, analogous to those performed during the three days after a death. These Zindah-ravân, or Srôsh, ceremonies are generally ordered on the first three Fravardîgân holidays, extending from the twenty-sixth to the twenty-eighth day of the last month of the Parsi year.

[4] Reading maman râî, as in M14; K35 has lâ 'not,' instead of râî, 'for.'

to order *it?* 2. And, whenever *one* orders it, how is it necessary then to order it, how is it best when they celebrate *it*, and what is its great advantage *as* a good work?

3. The reply is this, that worship with the ceremonial *for* those newly passed *away*, *during* the three days which *they spend* in the account[1], is suitable for the discreet, just as the protection with nourishment of those newly born, in their infancy, is also much more suitable for the discreet. 4. He is a truly discreet man through whom *there* is ceremonial for the three *days*, on account of his own father, and privileged wife, and infant child, *and* well-behaved servant, on *their* passing away; and it is indispensable to order the triple ceremonial of the three days.

5. This, too, is said: where it is not possible to solemnize his three *days*, or they solemnize *them* afterwards, when information *of the death* arrives[2], three days are to be solemnized as a substitute *for* those three. 6. For the good work of the ceremonial which is ordered by him himself, or bequeathed by him, or is his *through* consenting to it by design[3], exists—even though it is thus possible that it will be conducted afterwards—whenever it comes into progress; therefore he is exalted for it at his account

[1] See Chaps. XXIV, XXV.

[2] M14 has 'or they do not solemnize *them*, after which the information arrives,' which is clearly inconsistent with the context. When a person dies away from home, and the ceremonies are not performed on the spot, they must be performed at his home immediately after information of his death arrives, and the three succeeding days are considered as representing the three days after the death (see Sls. XVII, 6).

[3] Comp. Chap. VIII, 5.

in the three *days*, and it comes on for his *being* exalted. 7. When that which is conducted afterwards comes on for aiding *his being* exalted in the three *days* of the account, that which *was* conducted by him himself beforehand is more hopeful *and* more certain of being exalted in that position.

8. On account of there being also a diminution (aîtŏ-*k* gahî*d*ârîh) of risk about their own souls, in the event of (min zak aîgh hat) their children not ordering the three *days' ceremonial*, or it not being possible to solemnize *it* at that time, it is desirable to order, in their own lifetime and *at* their own convenience, *the ceremony for* their own living souls, advisedly, without doubt, and *having* appointed the *mode of* life of the three *days*, and also to appoint by will him who is to conduct *it* in the end. 9. And when both are conducted, the increase of good works and exaltation, though the end is not possible, or is not proceeded *with*—and the previous good works are commendable, and, therefore, preservatory—*has* reached even unto the most lordly wishes.

10. *As to* the man *with* great *and* powerful children, to whom the ceremonial of the three *days* for himself *at* the final day, *and* also the progress of many good works *have* seemed certain, *but* on account of yet another way to freedom from doubt effectually (frârâstîhâ) existing, he *has* bequeathed the conduct of the three *days' ceremonial*, and also other good works, unto *his* children, in order that *the ceremony for* the living soul *may be* conducted *at* the final day, with him the angels are in triumph, the glory of the religion in the most lordly glory, *and* the solemnizers of ceremonial worship are many. 11. Then, moreover, owing to the contest of the

demons—so unjust that *on* the day of his passing *away it* is due to the uncleanness (apâdyâvîh) which *has* attained unto *its full* extent[1]—all the solemnizers *in* the country, of the acts of worship solemnized, *may have* become thoroughly doubtful of the worship, and until it goes on to the disciples, and the ceremony is prepared, it is not proper to perform the whole ceremonial; in that way is manifested the great advantage *and* commendableness which *arises* from that ceremony *for* his living soul.

12. The nature of *the ceremony* ordered *for* the living soul is a counterpart of the three *days*, so *it* is needful that *at* all times of the three days *and* nights, successively emancipative (avadîgînisnîk), a ceremonial *in honour* of Srôsh[2] *be* always conducted, and *that* it proceed; and a fire is lighted in the ceremonial, and the clean ligature of the limbs is to be tied. 13. As a rule it is so considered that[3] in the three days *there* are fifteen[4] ceremonies (yastanŏ) *in honour* of Srôsh, and three sacred cakes (drôn)[5] which are consecrated in each dawn (bâm-1) with various dedications; and the fourth day they solemnize the Visparad[6], the portion[7] of the righteous guardian spirits (ardâî fravardŏ). 14. And there

[1] The corpse being considered utterly unclean.

[2] See Chap. XIV, 4.

[3] The following clause, about the three days, is omitted in M14, which skips from 'that' to 'the fourth day.'

[4] The Pers. Rivâyats merely say that four priests are employed, two at a time, so as to relieve each other in the continuous series of ceremonies for three days and nights.

[5] See Chap. XXX, 1.

[6] Here written Visparêdŏ (see Chap. XLV, 6).

[7] Reading bôn, instead of nûb; M14 omits the word.

are fugitives of families of the period, *and* other still further diminishers[1] of good works, who *have* wished to produce the wealth which is necessary to perform advantageously, as a custom of the soul in those three days, one *celebration* of all the religious rites (hamâk dînô) *in honour* of Srôsh, *and* the consecration of three sacred cakes for Srôsh every day; and the third night, at dawn[2], the consecration of a sacred cake *dedicated in* three modes. 15. In accomplishing the *consecration of the* sacred cake specially for the righteous guardian spirits, *on* the fourth day, *one* is supposed to order a Dvâzdah-hômâst[3] *in honour* of the righteous guardian spirits, *and* the rest of the ceremonial.

16. And *he* who *has* intended much more laudably is declared *as* the more devout and more judicious of worshippers; and for the sake of the ceremonial he is cleansed by the Bareshnûm *ceremony*[4], *and* is to practise other descriptions of cleanliness as regards *his* body and clothing. 17. While in the performance of the ceremonial, bread *made* from corn which is ground *by* those of the good

[1] M14 has 'there are ghostly observers of the families of the period, *and* many other teachers.' But the original meaning was, no doubt as in K35, that there were many persons at that period who would have been glad to possess the means of ordering even a small portion of the proper rites for the dead.

[2] That is, at dawn on the fourth day. The rites here mentioned seem to have been considered as the minimum that could be approved.

[3] See Chap. XLVIII, 25.

[4] A tedious ceremony of purification, lasting nine nights and detailed in Vend. IX, 1–145 (see App. IV). Its name is the Av. word which commences the instructions for sprinkling the unclean person (Vend. IX, 48), and means 'the top' of the head.

religion, wine from that made *by* those of the good religion, *and* meat from the animal[1] which is slaughtered in the ceremonial are eaten; *and one* is to proceed into the abode of fires[2] and of the good, *and* to abstain from the rest of the other places which are dubious[3] *and* food which is dubious. 18. And with that thorough heedfulness *one* is to conduct and order that ceremonial in the abode of the ever-growing fire, or other fire of Varahrân[4]; whereby his numerous good works are effectual, *and* the path of good works[5] is very broad. 19. Concerning[6] the suffering of *him* whose capability in that which is his preserving efficacy[7] is less, it is thus revealed, that not he who is righteous is overwhelmed, as *it were* unwilling, by incapability[8].

CHAPTER LXXXII.

1. *As to* the eighty-first question *and* reply, that which you ask is thus: *As to* a man who shall order a ceremonial *and* shall give the money (diram), and the man who shall undertake his ceremonial

[1] A goat or sheep is meant by gôspend here.

[2] The fire temple, in, or near, which the priests ('the good') reside.

[3] Or, var-hômand may mean 'open to choice,' but it is generally used as the opposite of aêvar, 'certain.'

[4] Sacred fire (see Chap. XXXI, 7).

[5] Over the *K*invad bridge (see Chap. XXI, 5).

[6] Reading râî, instead of lâ, 'not,' here, and *vice versa* further on in the sentence, as in M14.

[7] That is, in good works. M14 omits the word 'less.'

[8] The construction of this quotation is suggestive of its being a literal translation from the Avesta.

and shall take his money, *but has* not performed the ceremonial, what is then the decision; and what is then the decision *about* the man who ordered the ceremonial?

2. The reply is this, that the merit of a ceremonial not performed is not set going, and does not come to the soul of the undertaker who shall take money for it, *nor* even *to* that of the orderer who gave money for it. 3. But, *as to* him who is the orderer, since his mental meritoriousness is so steadfast that he gave his money, the efficacy (tûbân) of the good work, mentally his own, *has* not stayed *away* from him, because he gave money authorisedly for the good work; the decision, then, *about* him is such as *about him* to whom harm occurs in performing a good work for the religion. 4. It is said that the angels so recompense him that he does not consider it as *any* other harm; and as much as the good money given[1] for the sacred feast[2] *and* ceremonial is then the pleasure *which* comes unto his soul, as much as would have been possible to arise in the world from that money.

5. And he who shall take his money, and did not perform his ceremonial, is just as though he had abstracted from the angels[3] and the righteous guardian spirits, *and* destroyed, as much propitiation as would have been possible from that ceremonial; and he is, therefore, overwhelmed by it[4], and expiates *it* in the soul.

---

[1] M14 has 'the money given by him,' which may be correct.

[2] See Chap. XLVII, 1.

[3] K35 has 'the good.'

[4] Or, we might perhaps read 'thereby it is his overwhelming (astarî*d*ŏ),' supposing astarî*d*ŏ to be a technical term implying a

CHAPTER LXXXIII.

1. *As to* the eighty-second question *and* reply, that which you ask is thus: Is it necessary for a priestly man[1] *that* he should undertake all the religious rites and other ceremonials, or in what way is it?

2. The reply is this, that a priestly man should necessarily undertake all the religious rites *and* other ceremonials, because the deciding and advising performers of the ceremonial, *these* same priestly men, well understand the merit *or* demerit, the propriety *or* impropriety, of the ceremonial. 3. When the undertaker *and* conductor of all the religious rites is a priestly man, *one* is more hopeful of *their* progress in merit.

4. *As to* the priestly man who shall undertake all the religious rites, if *he be* living comfortably (hû-zîvisnŏ) on a share of our house-rulership[2],

flogging, as appears probable from a passage in Farh. Okh. p. 34, ll. 1, 2, which, when restored to its form in the oldest MSS., runs as follows:—Astarîdanô âskârîh astaraspân snas pavan vinâs, which may be translated 'the manifestation of "overwhelming" is the blow of horsewhips for sin;' assuming that astarasp is equivalent to aspô astar, the usual translation of Av. aspahê astraya, 'with a horsewhip.'

[1] The term magavôg-gabrâ probably means strictly 'a man of a priestly family,' as distinguished from a priest appointed from the laity, an appointment that seems to have been occasionally made in former times (see Bd. Introd. p. xxxiii, note 1). According to the Nîrangistân any virtuous man or woman can perform certain priestly duties under certain circumstances (see Sls. X, 35), but would not, of course, be magavôg, 'priestly, or of priestly family.'

[2] Reading mânpatîh, instead of magôpatîh, 'priesthood,' which words are often confounded in Pahlavi, being written very nearly alike. And assuming that hatŏm, 'if my,' stands for hatŏmân, 'if our;' M14 has atûkhsh, 'without exertion,' but hatŏs, 'if his,' would be a more probable emendation, as it occurs in the next section.

village-rulership, tribe-rulership, and province-rulership, and his needful support of religion remain the consideration as to his living comfortably, and he have no need for the stipend of all the religious rites, then the rule for him is to distribute properly that recompense of the sacred feast[1], which is to be given *for* all the religious rites, among the solemnizers[2]. 5. If *it be* needful for him, the priestly man, as he is suitable, is not changed—whereby good management is not attained—and *if it be* needful even for his consideration of all those religious rites, his performance in the duty and ministration is then an approval of worthiness *and* management. 6. When they shall act so, all those religious rites are more meritoriously managed; and one day the solemnizers are brought from the fag-end (sar) into the rank of priestly manhood, which is the stipend for all the religious rites that they shall expressly take authorisedly, and are, therefore, worthy of it[3].

Chapter LXXXIV.

1. *As to* the eighty-third question and reply, that which you ask is thus: Is it desirable to give

---

[1] See Chap. XLVII, 1.

[2] That is, if the chief priest has already a sufficient income, he is not to appropriate the fees for such occasional ceremonies, but to distribute them among his assistants, who are the actual solemnizers.

[3] That is, when the chief priest requires the fees for his own support, the reward of his assistants must be the fact that they are rendering themselves competent to undertake the responsibility of the chief priest at some future time.

in excess the gift *for* the ceremonial *which* it is not desirable to diminish?

2. The reply is this, that *it* is proper not to diminish a gift where *it is* the gift[1] for a ceremonial, and the reasons for it are many. 3. One is this, that a gift is the money which in another good work suffices for the accomplishment of the good work, *and* the good work of a righteous gift[2] is a great good work, *and* not to diminish *it* is sure worthiness among the explainers. 4. When the sacred feast[3] *and* the gift for the ceremonial are supplied in excess, even that which is an excess of gift is an excess of liberality to the performers of the ceremonial, *and has* realized (frârâstŏ) an excess of good works that is commendable.

Chapter LXXXV.

1. *As to* the eighty-fourth question *and* reply, that which you ask is thus: *As to* a gift for the ceremonial *which* they do not reduce, and while they give *it* in excess, in what manner is then its great advantage, *and* how *and* in how many modes is it possible to occur?

2. The reply is this, that the advancement of the ceremonial of the sacred beings is by so much as the gift is more fully given; and the great advantage of the good work is more, and its reasons many, therefrom. 3. The desire of this wealth, which *has* come for the sake of the good work, is an experience

---

[1] M14 omits the repetition of the words aîgh dahisnŏ-î.

[2] See Chap. XLIV, 19.

[3] See Chap. XLVII, 1.

of the comfortable living of the angels, by whom the solemnizers are aggrandized, and is proper apart from *its* great judiciousness; to diminish *it* is improper.

4. When the gift *for* the ceremonial is abundantly given, the performers of the ceremonial, who, with much trouble annoying them, *have* solemnized the Avesta *and* chanted the hymns (Gâthas), and obtain the stipend of their solemnizing from the remuneration *of* the solemnization, are living comfortably, thriving, and blessed. 5. And also the undertakers of all the religious rites who, by means of the hope of rightful religion, render *one* certain as to the way *to* the distant awful place[1], and tempt the longers for righteousness into the religion[2], undertake all the religious rites *and* ceremonial *of* the sacred beings for the sake of the stipend of proper diligence.

6. And reasoning thought is cognizant as regards the advantageousness due to the undertakers and solemnizers of all the religious rites, and a great stipend is more obtained and observed *for them* than for *any* other profession. 7. The sons, too, of priests and disciples strive for the words prayed[3], and are more eager for their prayers; and many, likewise, shall engage for all the religious rites, and become more diffusive of the religion (dînô bâlis-nîktar); and, in like manner, the proper, more attainable, *and* more propitious path of the good for saving the soul becomes wider[4].

---

[1] The place of account (see Chap. XX, 3). Or, it may be, 'render one certain, in the course of time, regarding the awful place (hell).'

[2] M14 adds 'and acquire good works.'

[3] That is, they are more diligent in learning the prayers by heart.

[4] Referring to the *K*inva*d* bridge (see Chap. XXI, 5).

Chapter LXXXVI.

1. *As to* the eighty-fifth question *and* reply, that which you ask is thus: What is possible to become the harm of a gift *that* is reduced?

2. The reply is this, that since *those things* are to be properly given which are for the religious rites of the ceremonial[1], and are the consideration of the undertakers of all the religious rites, and are also the stipend of some solemnizers, both[2] are living comfortably *by* the ceremonial. 3. The sons of the disciples *who* wanted approval for the words prayed, become so much the more to be ordered *and* to be accepted; and the ceremonial of all the religious rites becomes more progressive.

4. So, moreover, when they go to undertake the well-operating activity of the ceremonial for a diminution of remuneration *and* gift, and owing to undertaking *and* ordering again[3], by way of routine (pavan dôr râs), they do not request so much stipend, *it is* as though they should buy my linen *and* should sell *it* again for their own payment (dâ*d*anŏ). 5. *As to* the performers of the ceremonial, likewise, who *have* to acquire approval with much trouble and words prayed, and obtain a remuneration which, for the soul even, is as little *for* the ceremonial as though *one were* annoyed—whereby

[1] M14 has merely 'since the proper donation for the ceremonial.'

[2] That is, both the undertakers and solemnizers, the chief priest and his assistants.

[3] Referring to a priest who undertakes ceremonies and then directs inferiors to perform them (see Chap. LXVI, 4, 6).

living is difficult—they become sorry for enduring the trouble, owing to lukewarmness (afsur*d*ŏminisnîh) *in* the same profession. 6. And even the sons of the disciples shall sell linen for wages, and they rejoice *that* it is possible to learn other callings *with* less pains; and thus they make *them* become lukewarm *and* meditating retreat (a*v*âz-âhang) from the words of fresh paragraphs continually prayed[1], from the approval requested of the learned (â*z*ân), *and* from all the religious rites they should undertake *for* the contented.

7. *As to* those, moreover, who, through fervent-minded undertaking of *what* is ordered, request less *for* all the religious rites, *and have* not obtained[2] even that which is due *to them*, it is not even as though they ordered *of them* for the fiends[3]. 8. And the disgrace, too, of the orderers of good works of lukewarmness is the exaltation of the profession of the disciples; and its deficient progress becomes the paralysation of the ceremonial of the sacred beings for saving the souls of the good from the deadly *one* (mar).

Chapter LXXXVII.

1. *As to* the eighty-sixth question and reply, that which you ask is thus: How is it good when they give a gift *for* the ceremonial?

---

[1] Literally 'prayed *and* prayed.'

[2] Reading ayâft, instead of the unintelligible ayâ*d*t, as *d* has, no doubt, been written for f.

[3] Meaning that the orderers would act more liberally if they wanted a ceremony even in honour of the fiends.

2. The reply is this, that as it is necessary, so that the ceremonial of the sacred beings *may* be more advanced, and such wealth *may* more come on to the good work, for the proper stipends of the undertakers *and* solemnizers—*that* they *may* become less lukewarm as regards the accompanying proprieties, and thereby diligent *in* performing *them*—and there is not in *it*[1] an express connection manifested with different work, and with that *which has* proceeded from so many previous good *people*, I deem the introduction *of it*[2] more expressly better.

Chapter LXXXVIII.

1. *As to* the eighty-seventh question *and* reply, that which you ask is thus: *As* family householders we of the good religion of Irân, before each *celebration of* all the religious rites with holy-water[3] which they have provided in the land[4] of Pârs, have then always given for it a gift of 400 dirhams, *or* 350 dirhams[5] *at* least. 2. And now if *we* should be needy, when we deduct something from the 400 dirhams, or from the 350 dirhams, of the gift for them, they would then not accept *it* from us, and speak thus: 'Less than 400, or than 350, dirhams we do not[6] accept.' 3. *But* there are needy *men*

---

[1] The ceremonial. [2] The gift. [3] See Chap. LXVI, 17.

[4] Reading bûm, as in M14, instead of the ba*r*manŏ, 'son,' of K35.

[5] About 140 or 122½ rûpîs (see Chap. LII, 1 note). As in Chap. LXVI, the actual value of these sums of money depended upon the price of the necessaries of life in the ninth century.

[6] K35 repeats the negative, but whether this is a blunder, or intended to intensify the negation, is uncertain.

who always come to us themselves and speak thus: 'For 350 dirhams we will always twice conduct all the religious rites *and* ceremonial with holy-water such as *those* which you have always ordered before for 400; only order us.' 4. Would a needy *one*, *apart* from the priestly men *who* always say that they are not, be authorised, or not?

5. The reply is this, that the priest *to whom your* predecessors *have* given a gift of 400 or 350 *dirhams*, for all the religious rites with holy-water, it is proper to consider particularly virtuous *and* faithful, when there is nothing else *about* him, on account of which he is otherwise. 6. A *celebration of* all the religious rites with holy-water, in which they shall use four pure animals[1]—*and* just according to the teaching of the high-priests they present *to* every single fire from one animal *and* one holy-water—and the offering of holy-water unto the fire whose holy-water *it is*, and bringing it on to another fire *apart* from that holy-water, and the *ceremonial* cleansing of the holy-water they maintain by agreement in thy name, the superiors solemnize with approval, faithfully, and attentively; *and* the remuneration of 350 dirhams would be a balancing of when they conduct the religious rite *at* the place of undertaking *it, and* when *it* is undertaken as regards a distant district[2].

7. In A*r*takhshatar-gadman[3], within my memory,

---

[1] Sheep or goats. [2] That is, it is a fair average charge.

[3] The Huz. form of Ar*d*ashîr-khurrah, the name given by Ar*d*ashîr son of Pâpak, the first Sasanian king, to the city and district of Gôr, subsequently called Pîrûzâbâd (see Nöldeke's Geschichte der Perser und Araber zur Zeit der Sasaniden, pp. 11, 19), about seventy miles south of Shîrâz.

they who would accept less than 300 dirhams[1] for it made a memorandum (farhâng), to keep in remembrance *that* 350 dirhams for all the religious rites performed *was* to be the rule declared by those of the religion *in* Artakhshatar-gadman. 8. Likewise, the glorified Âtûr-frôbag[2], *son* of Farâkhûzâd, who was the pre-eminent leader of those of the good religion, decided *in* the same manner.

9. And now, too, they always conduct those *rites* which are without holy-water for 150 dirhams, *or* even for 120 dirhams[3]; and the reason of it is the neediness of the disciples who, owing to that need, *and* in hope of obtaining more employment, always diminish *their demands, and* through deficient remuneration always become more needy, more importunate, and more moderate in desiring remuneration; and, in the course *of* the employment of resources and requesting *the charge of* all the religious rites, the labour and endurance of discipleship are exhausted.

10. And *as to* him who undertakes to conduct all the religious rites twice for 350 dirhams, if *he be* properly working *and* thoroughly reliable *for* the 350 dirhams *which* are always given him for the ceremonial of all the religious rites—just like those who would always undertake *them* once—and all the religious rites are conducted *and* secured twice, on

[1] About 105 rûpîs.

[2] The name of an early editor of the Dînkard, whose selections from various religious writings form the fourth and fifth books of that extensive work in its present form. He lived after the Muhammadan conquest of Persia, and probably in the eighth century of the Christian era.

[3] That is, 52½ or 42 rûpîs.

account of the merit due to the continuous ceremonial of the sacred beings it is more authorisedly ordered of those who solemnize all the religious rites twice[1]. 11. But *as* to *him* who would undertake all the religious rites twice for 350 dirhams, *but* is not able to conduct *them* unless he puts to it *some* of his own wealth, so that the progress *may be* acceptable to him as they conduct *them* through repetition, he should not undertake *them* owing to the reasons written in another chapter of ours[2], since *it tends* much more to neediness.

12. And more like unto the ancient sceptics (vimânakŏ) *have* become the disciples, among whom disagreement *and* enmity are produced, as is written in the same writing (khadû-gûn nâmakŏ)[3]; *and*, owing to admonishing words, these *become* enviousness and maliciousness unto the disciples, *and* trouble *and* disagreement less becoming among you and more contentious about you. 13. And at the time *in* which a great stipend existed, *they* contended with him through whose greatness *and* abundance of stipend their conflict was caused, one with the other, through envy; and now, too, they aways squabble *about* his deficient stipend, by which they will tempt them, on account of *its* inadequacy, for the sake of a way for preserving life, as was shown by my metaphor in the other chapter[4]. 14. When those who, through need of *employment in the rites of* religion, or the recitations[5]

---

[1] This is also stated in Chap. LXVI, 32.

[2] See Chap. LXVI, 24–26.

[3] Ibid.

[4] See Chap. LXVI, 28, 29.

[5] It is uncertain whether these are the correct technical meanings of kêsh and dôr.

which are its wisdom, would at once produce enmity, and the friends of religion, are for each *of* two sides, *it* is important to look to the procuring of forgiveness, kind regards, and the progress of the elect (pasandakânŏ) in the duty of the faithful.

Chapter LXXXIX.

1. *As to* the eighty-eighth question *and* reply, that which you ask is thus: When a man resolves within himself thus: '*In* the summer[1] time I *will* go into Pârs, and will give so much money for the high-priesthood, on account of the fires *and* other matters which are as greatly advantageous,' though he himself does not come into Pârs, *but* sends the money according to his intention, *or* in excess of it, unto the high-priests—so that he is like the great *who* send in excess of that unto the high-priests[2]—that, as the benefit is greater which is more maintained, they may provide for the fires of every kind *and* other matters, is then his proceeding of sending to Pârs, for that purpose, a sin, or not?

2. The reply is this, that if his coming be indispensable for the design he would undertake, then it is indispensable for him to accomplish his own mental undertaking; but in suffering which is excited *and* not avoidable, when *there* is really no possibility

---

[1] Assuming that hâmân stands for hâmînô.

[2] M14 omits this phrase.

of his travelling himself, any one whom he sends in his place, more particularly on *that* account, is not acceptable by the approval of the angels who *have* realized the affliction in *his* good thought, but the good work is to be eagerly well-considered. 3. Good gifts, and every office (gâs) about good works which it is possible to perform, are what are commendable *in* the well-housed *man* that is not able to work *himself*[1]; *they are* avoidable by him when not of good race, and are not indispensable for him whenever the good work is not announced. 4. When able to manage *it* himself *it* is better; and when otherwise, his appointment of a faithful *person* over *its* preparation, and *his* accomplishment of the work of selector are expedient.

Chapter XC.

1. *As to* the eighty-ninth question *and* reply, that which you ask is thus: Who, and how many are they who are without the religion (adînôîh) *but* are made immortal, and for what purpose is their immortality? 2. Where is the place they, each one, possess sovereignty, and *in* the place where they possess sovereignty are *there* people of the good religion of every kind, or how are they; are *there* sacred fires[2] and appointed worship, or how is

---

[1] M14 adds, 'he longs for good giving *and* good consideration; important *and* virtuous is he when able to do it;' but the sentence is hardly grammatical.

[2] Literally 'fires of Varahrân' (see Chap. XXXI, 7).

it; and for what purpose is each one of their sovereignties?

3. The reply is this, that the immortal rulers of the region of glory, Khvanîras[1], are said *to be* seven: one is Yôstô, son of Fryân[2]; the Avesta name of one is Yakhmâyûsad[3], son of the same Fryân; the name of one is Fradhakhstŏ, son of the Khumbîks[4]; the name of one is Ashavazang, son of Pôrûdakhstôîh[5]; one is the tree opposed to harm[6];

[1] The central one of the seven regions of the earth, which is supposed to contain all the countries best known to the Irânians, and to be as large as the other six regions put together (see Bd. XI, 2-6). The name is here corrupted into Khvanâîras.

[2] Av. Yôistô yô Fryananãm of Âbân Yt. 81, Fravardîn Yt. 120, who had to explain ninety-nine enigmas propounded to him by the evil Akhtya. In Pâz. this name is corrupted into Gôst-î Fryânô, whose explanation of thirty-three enigmas propounded by Akht the wizard, and proposal of three enigmas in his turn form the subject of a Pahlavi tale published with AV. He is not included among the immortals mentioned in Bd. XXIX, 5, 6, and Dk. (see § 8, note), but is one of those specified in Byt. II, 1.

[3] No doubt, the Av. Ashem-yahmâi-usta ('righteousness for which be blessing') who precedes Yôistô in Fravardîn Yt. 120. He is the Asâm-î Yamâhust of Bd. XXIX, 5, who is said to reside in the district of the river Nâîvtâk; but he is not mentioned in Dk. The names Yakhmâyûsad, Fradhakhstŏ, and Ashavazang are written in Pâzand, which accounts for their irregular spelling.

[4] Av. Fradhâkhsti Khunbya of Fravardîn Yt. 138. In Dk. he is said to be ruler on the Nâîvtâk waters, but in Bd. he is called Parsadgâ *Hv*embya residing in the plain of Pêsyânsaî.

[5] Av. Ashavazdang the Pourudhâkhstiyan of Âbân Yt. 72, Fravardîn Yt. 112. He is the Ashavazd son of Pourudhâkhst in Bd., and is said to rule in the plain of Pêsyânsaî in Dk.

[6] The many-seeded tree, said to grow in the wide-formed ocean, and also in Aîrân-vêg, on which the Saêna bird (simurgh) is supposed to sit and shake off the seeds, which are then conveyed by the bird *K*amrôs to the waters gathered by Tistar, who rains them down on the earth with the water; hence the growth of fresh vegetation when the rainy season commences (see Rashnu Yt. 17, Bd. XXVII, 2, XXIX, 5, Mkh. LXII, 37-42).

one is Gôpatshah[1]; *and* one is Peshyôtanû[2], who is called after the *K*îtravôkŏ-mîyânŏ[3].

4. The reign of Gôpatshah is over the land of Gôpatŏ[4], coterminous with Aîrân-vê*g*[5], on the bank (bâr) of the water of the Dâîtîh[6]; *and* he keeps watch over the ox Hadhayãs[7], through whom occurs the complete perfection of primitive man[8]. 5. The reign of Peshyôtanû is in Kangde*z*[9], *and* he resides in the illustrious Kangde*z* which the noble Sîyâvash[10] formed through his glory, *he* who is called the erratic youth[11] of the illustrious Kayânians. 6. And through his powerful spirit *arose* increase of cultivation and the ruler Kaî-Khûsrôî[12] among the highest of the mountains in the countries of

[1] Either a title or son of Aghrêra*d*, brother of Frâsîyâ*v* of Tûr (see Bd. XXIX, 5, XXXI, 20–22). He is a righteous minotaur according to Mkh. LXII, 31–36.

[2] Here written Patshâyôtanû, but he is the Peshyôtanû of Chap. XXXVII, 36.

[3] The *K*atru-mîyân river in Kangde*z* (see Bd. XX, 31).

[4] Which is a non-Aryan country according to Dk., but Bd. (XXIX, 5) calls it 'the land of the S*a*ukavastân,' and Mkh. (XLIV, 24–35, LXII, 31) places Gôpatshah in Aîrân-vê*g*.

[5] See Chap. XXI, 2.

[6] Av. Dâitya, a river which flows out of Aîrân-vê*g* (see Bd. XX, 13).

[7] See Chap. XXXVII, 99.

[8] Referring either to the complete peopling of the earth by emigration on the back of this ox in ancient times, or to the immortality produced at the resurrection by tasting an elixir, of which the fat of this ox is one of the ingredients.

[9] A settlement east of Persia formed, or fortified, by Sîyâvash (see Bd. XXIX, 10, Byt. III, 25).

[10] See Chap. XXXVII, 36.

[11] Or kang-î raftâr may mean 'jaunty youth;' but it is evidently an attempt to account for the name Kangde*z* as 'the fortress of the kang ("youth").'

[12] The son of Sîyâvash (see Chap. XXXVI, 3, Bd. XXXI, 25).

Irân *and* Tûrân; the purity of the sacred fire[1] of great glory *and* the recital of the liturgy exist there, *and* the practice of religious rites (dînô) is provided. 7. The custom, also, of him (Peshyôtanû) and *his* companions *and* coadjutors (ham-bâr), in the appointed millenniums, is the great advancement of religion and good works in other quarters likewise[2].

8. But, secondly, *as to* the whereabouts of the places which are theirs—just like his—of which *there* is no disquisition by me, this also is even owing to *my* not remembering[3].

---

[1] Literally 'fire of Varahrân.'

[2] He is expected to be summoned by the angels to restore the religious rites to the world, after the conflict of the nations in a future age (see Byt. III, 25–42).

[3] In the detailed account of the contents of the Sûdkar (or Stûdgar) Nask, given in the ninth book of the Dînkard, the latter part of its fifteenth fargard is said to have been 'on the seven immortal rulers who are produced in the region of Khvanîras, and also about the determination of their glory, and the goodness, too, of *their* assistants and living sovereignty in both worlds. The tree opposed to harm is on Aîrân-vêg in the place of most excavations (frêh-nigânân?). Gôk-patŏ is in the non-Aryan countries. Peshyôtanû son of Vistâsp is in Kangdez of the hundred-ribbed shape (sad-dandakŏ kerpîh?), in which a myriad of the exalted, who wear black marten *fur* (mûn sîyah samûr yakhsenund), are righteous listeners out of the retinue of Peshyôtanû son of Vistâsp. Frâdakhstŏ son of the mortal Khûmbîks, who is sovereign on the water of Nâîvtâk. Ashavazd son of Pôrûdakhstŏ, who is sovereign over the most manifest among uplands, the plain of Pêsinâs. Barâzd the causer of strife. And of the father-in-law's race (khast-tômagag?) of the famous Vistâsp is *he* who is called Kaî-Khûsrôî, who produces even an advance of thy religion of the Mazda-worshippers, *and* also understands about *it*; *and* who gives my good practices further blessings, so that the world maintains my doings with benedictions. Perfect is the excellence of righteousness.'

In this list of the immortal rulers of ancient times, the names of Barâzd and Kaî-Khûsrôî are substituted for those of Yôstô and

CHAPTER XCI.

1. *As to* the ninetieth question *and* reply, that which you ask is thus: From what is the sky made, *and* with what is it prepared?

2. The reply is this, that the sky is a dome (gar*d*ûn), wide *and* lofty; its inside and whole width and boundaries (âkhyakîhâ), besides its material existence, are the stone of light, of all stones the hardest[1] *and* most beautiful; and the grandeur of its spirit *and* even *its* internal bow[2] are like *those of* mighty warriors arrayed. 3. And that material of the sky reached unto the place *where* promise-breaking words exist[3], *and* was without need of preparation; *as* it is said *of* places such as those—where wisdom is a witness about *them*—that *that* which is not even itself a place, and its place does not yet exist, is without need of any preparing[4].

4. The light is for existing things, and they cherish a faculty (nîyûîh) of motion also of two

---

Yakhmâyû*s*a*d* in our text. Barâzd is the Ibairaz of Bd. XXIX, 6, and, possibly, the Av. Berezyar*s*ti of Fravar*d*în Yt. 101.

[1] The same notion as that indicated in Genesis by the word 'firmament.'

[2] The rainbow.

[3] Probably meaning that the sky extends downwards, below the horizon, as far as the second grade of hell, that for 'evil words,' Dû*s*-hûkht (see Sls. VI, 3, note).

[4] The word dîvâk, 'place' (zîvâk in the Sasanian inscription of Naq*s*-i Rustam, but traditionally pronounced *g*înâk), seems to be here taken in the etymological sense of zîvâk, that is, 'a living-place.' The text refers to the period, in the beginning, when the sky was indefinite space unprepared for the residence of creatures and merely a region of light (see Bd. I, 2), the light mentioned in § 4. Its preparation is referred to in §§ 8, 9.

kinds, *that* causing motion *and that* of movables[1]; as mobility is mentioned about thought[2] and immobility about material things. 5. Immovables are not moved, while movables are moved by their power of movement; and those movables, that way causing motion, are afterwards themselves a moving secret cause of motion, and then a cause of motion is not moving the movable, since *it* is not incapable of causing motion secretly by movement of itself. 6. Just as the force (kûnisnŏ) of a movement exists *and* does not become a force; only then it is declared by wisdom, that the causers of motion have been the causing of motion by force before movement, *and, being* unmoved, they are subsequently made to move by the force; later on, the causers of motion *have* to cause motion, by their power of causing motion, *in* the non-causers of motion, from which it is certain though the force of a movement exists it does not become a force; but, finally, that *which is* prepared with a source of activity[3], before force, becomes unmoved.

7. Natures without need of the trouble of a preparer are distinguished from such; where movement occurs through every force, the championship of a position (gâh) not made to move—except, indeed, *of that* whose force, when it is unmoved by other force, is its own—is unmoving and thirstless[4]. 8. *It*

---

[1] M14 has 'movables *and* immovables' instead of this clause.

[2] Perhaps we should read 'the spirits,' by inserting an additional medial stroke in the Pahlavi word.

[3] Reading tûkhshînîkîhâ, instead of the unintelligible tûkhshtîkîhâ. The author has so nearly lost sight of his argument in the mazes of his verbiage that there is some uncertainty about the translation of this paragraph.

[4] That is, the guardians of a place exposed to all attacks (as

was restored immovably when *there was* an approach to the sky of that actual contender for the place, the fiend, and the sky *was* shaken by him; for connected with the sky *were* arranged so many possessors of all resources, dignified (afrank*î*d) by their own all-powerful position and that well-operating, mighty, undrawn bow[1], righteous *and* well-discoursing (hû-fravakhsh), and many good spirits, gloriously co-operating for the preparation of the sky. 9. For that which *was* not even itself a place[2], when *it* is thus henceforth really a place, is *in* want of preparing; *and*, in the preparation *of* that visible[3] place, with the material of the sky is mingled that triumphing, powerful spirit who made its existence a seeking for principle *and* seeking for intention, drawing up from below *and* drawing down from above, so that through that seeking for principle it becomes a concord, the resting-place of united champions, and unadmonishable through that power of seeking for intention; such as this *it is* if, indeed, *it be* the will of him, the creator of all goodness.

10. And it is said summarily that the sky *was* shaken in the *period of* disturbance and restored *with* trouble; and, if the guardian spirits are in freedom from disturbance through the glory *of* the creator, when there is not even a place for it prepared by themselves[4], and *their* nature and own

---

the sky is supposed to be), unless it is a stronghold in itself, must be always on the alert.

[1] The rainbow; reading atang darûn.

[2] That is, 'a living-place' (see § 3 n).

[3] Reading dî*d*ŏ, 'seen;' but it may be stô for stî, 'material.'

[4] That is, while the sky was still indefinite space, the region of light, but no dwelling-place; although the guardian spirits had

strength are approving the trouble of preparation, it is not moved[1], except by the creatures of *his* will, a will which is subduing.

Chapter XCII.

1. *As to* the ninety-first question *and* reply, that which you ask is thus: Of waters and rivers, and whatever water is good, is Arekdvisûr[2] the greatest (mas), or *some* other water or good river; and, again, where is the place of Arekdvisûr?

2. The reply is this, that *it is* the water of Arekdvisûr; and *what has* gushed from Arekdvisûr is as large a mass as all the water in the world[3] except the Arvand[4]; within the wide-formed ocean[5] *it* is dominant over the thousand cascades (pashan) *and* thousand lakes[6] of the waters, and its place is most *renowned* throughout the spheres. 3. There flows the water of Arekdvisûr in a forest, the source of all seeds, whereby the species *which* plants possess are assimilated (aêdûnagîdŏ) by it, *and* healing existences of all kinds are mingled *with it* from medicinal plants. 4. The abundant power of the

---

been created as representatives of the creatures, both spiritual and material, which were to be afterwards produced (see Bd. I, 8).

[1] That is, when afterwards prepared as a dwelling-place the sky remains unmoved by evil beings.

[2] See Chap. XXXVII, 118.

[3] Compare Yas. LXIV, 12, Âbân Yt. 3.

[4] A name of the river Tigris (see Zs. VI, 20).

[5] As this ocean is supposed to encircle the world, the whole earth is within it.

[6] Compare Yas. LXIV, 17, Âbân Yt. 4, 101.

coming of healing to the purifying water is like the nature of the existences which it acquires, *and* then the nature which it thus acquires for its own the water draws up by the power which is drawing water to itself.

5. The water of Arekdvisûr is on Albûrz[1], and flows even to the summit of the star station during the coming of the healing of purification, even unto Hûkhîr the lofty[2], all-gorgeous *and* brilliant; thence *its* flowing is effected[3] into the lake of a summit to Albûrz, Mount Aûs,hin*d*ûm[4], which is in the middle of the wide-formed ocean. 6. And from that flowing of waters that destined river, the utter destruction of every night, comes on in the light of a dawn; by the sprinkling of spray (pash-pashanŏ) it extends through the seven regions *of the earth*, and from it arise the growth of their plants *and* the coming of the healing of purification; that which is called a drop (srî*s*k) of the primeval creatures *being* a particle (aham) of water of the bulk of a horse[5].

---

[1] The chain of mountains supposed to surround the world and reach to heaven (see Chap. XX, 3, Bd. XII, 1, 3); owing to its height any water from its summit must flow downwards to reach the lowermost grade of heaven, called the star station.

[2] Av. Hukairya berezô, the Hûgar of Bd. XII, 5, XXIV, 17, probably a western summit of the mythic Albûrz.

[3] M14 and J have nikûnî-aîtŏ, 'is precipitated,' instead of kûnî-aît.

[4] The Av. us Hindva*d*, 'up the Hindva,' of Tî*s*tar Yt. 32, a mountain summit where the clouds gather; it is the Aûsîndôm mountain of Bd. XII, 6, XIII, 5, said to be of the ruby material of the sky. In Bd. XIII, 4 the lake is said to be on the summit of Hûgar.

[5] Referring to the term aspô-keh*r*pa applied to waters in Hastân Yt. 13, Tî*s*tar Yt. 8, 46.

CHAPTER XCIII.

1. *As to* the ninety-second question *and* reply, that which you ask is thus: From what place should Tîstar[1] seize the water? How does it pass into a cloud, and how does he make the cloud move on? How does it rain upon the world? How can he carry on a struggle with demons, and with which demon can he carry *it* on? How does this always happen with the hail and snow, whenever hail and snow occur? And who can force away that hail and snow?

2. The reply is this, that the high-priests have thus said, that Tîstar seizes a place *which* is called 'abysmal' (vârûnak)[2], that is the last place of filtration in the ocean, *and* there are no removal of *any* kind and causing rain from any other place. 3. And the cause of its (the rain's) establishment is spiritually active, more particularly, however, through two kinds of material agency: one is that which is the rule (mang) in the atmosphere of the earth, whereby it is drawn up in atoms similarly to smoke, *and* in larger masses, well-soaring from the rivers; *and* one is that *which* blows with the power of the well-operating wind, and the blowing of the great united breath (ham-vâê) and strength of the com-

---

[1] The angel who is supposed to produce rain, being a personification of the star Tîstar or Sirius. His production of rain and conflict with the demons of drought and thunder are detailed in Bd. VII, 1–13.

[2] Assuming that the word is meant as a translation of Av. vairya, a term which is applied to the depths or depressed basins of the ocean in Yas. LXIV, 17, 18, Âbân Yt. 101, Zamyâd Yt. 51.

munity (*k*andîgânŏîh) of spirits[1], from the fully perfect distillation (pûr-hû-zûhîgîh) of the mighty ocean to the upper *regions*, and thereby the clouds are blown.

4. Afterwards, it (the rain) speeds in the cloud, through the great strength of the mighty wind, to where *there* is a necessity *for it*, to divert *it* from where *there* is no necessity; and so long as *there* is a necessity for *it* it (the cloud) discharges. 5. And when *there* is a necessity and it causes rain, and the necessity is *for* no *more* acquisitions of water, and the advantage is the effect of water upon the place, and it distributes *it* to the existing rivers for the use of the sea, and it causes rain *again*, it thereby produces even new water, new flowing, new coming of healing to plants, new growth, new golden colouring to lands, new purification to animals, new procreation, new proper breathings for other creatures, new dawn, and new *things of* that description. 6. The thriving of the world makes the advantage *and* perfection of the good creation increase; and, apart from a great craving for the effect of the glory of the spirits in the operations of cultivation and the performance of spiritual mysteries, *it* is said labours are aided even for *one* gloriously destined.

7. And Tîstar in seizing the water should seize upon the great strength of the wind of whirlwinds (gar*d*înâkân), which is figuratively (mînisnîk) the dragging *and* blowing that follow the whirling; *and* the purified water is expanded *and* carried up aloft to the higher *regions* of the atmosphere, just as that

---

[1] Altering mînisnŏ, 'thought,' into 'spirits' by inserting an extra medial stroke, as in M14 and J.

which is seen where it reaches up with the heaviness and weight of earth, and then is discerned in the plain[1] accompanied by the dragging of the whirling wind *which* would carry *it* afar to settle like *that* which is owing to dust; it (the atmosphere) is called Andarvâê ('the intermediate air'), and the wind is a whirlwind. 8. As the water is lighter, and owing to the more strongly dragging wind on the ocean than that which exists on the plain, so, also, the water from the ocean is much more in proportion, and transportable farther up than the dust[2] from the plain. 9. And as in the midst of a plain a medium whirlwind of wind is expanded into the wide plain by a medium dragging of the wind, and plenty of much buffeting is the violence of the dragging of winds, a whirlwind of wind which is seen very lofty and large is unknown; so, also, *one* is ignorant of what is spreading among the movements of the sea. 10. The water of that full and abundant flowing—which is through the power and glory of the heavenly angels and Tî*s*tar's control of the work—is blown up, both by the well-characterised water-drawing power, and also by the force of *various* kinds, the dragging, and upward blowing of the winds, into the atmosphere; and thence it rains the complete rain, as they *have* recounted from observation and much full evidence.

11. The demon who resists the *doings* of Tî*s*tar—and the glorious Tî*s*tar, meeting him, properly drives back such improper resistance of his—is

[1] Referring to the frequent small whirlwinds, sweeping up the dust, which accompany every complete change of wind in dry climates.

[2] K35 omits the first two letters of afrâ, 'dust,' by mistake.

a demon *of* the name of Apâôsh[1], which is interpreted *as* 'the destruction of water' (âp-aôsh). 12. He contends, moreover, with the uppermost *and* lowermost water; and desirous of *its* destruction that demon contends at three periods: first, for the non-existence of rain; secondly, for converting *it into* a cause of damage to a place; *and* thirdly, at the place of producing *it* with advantage; and the struggling is like a tree (vanô) which is set moving.

13. The seizers of the feminine[2] pure water are a benefit *for the existences* of the whole world; and the formation of rain, and the triumph and ascendancy of Tîstar over the demon, through that seizing (falânîh) of water, are due to the creator who strengthens him[3], the archangels who have him assisted[4], the religious who reverence him, *and* the worldly beings who glorify him. 14. Very properly do the archangels propitiate *him, and* mankind promote the strength and power, which are *engaged* about the business, by glorifying *and* invoking the good spirit who increases them in consequence of glorifying *and* worship, *and* through which

---

[1] Av. Apaosha, the demon of drought, who, in the form of a black horse, is said in the Tîstar Yast to fight with Tîstar in the ocean. Here his name is written Apâhôsh, but see Bd. VII, 8–12.

[2] Reading mâdagîk. According to Bd. XVI, 6 the sky, metal, wind, and fire are always male, while water, earth, plants, and fish are always female, and all other creations are of both sexes. Water and earth are also personified as female angels.

[3] In his first encounter with Apâôsh, Tîstar is vanquished, and attributes his defeat to his not being invoked by name in the ceremonies, whereupon Aûharmazd invokes him by name so as to give him enormous strength, when he returns to the conflict and conquers the demon (see Tîstar Yt. 20–28, Bd. VII, 8–10).

[4] Reading aîyyârînênd, as in M14 and J; in K35 it is written like âyênd rîvênd, 'they come *and* liberate.'

arises that advantageousness[1] of his—which owing to that benefit is the benefit of every one else—for this advantageous business.

15. And Tî*s*tar shall gradually (pa*d*manîkîhâ) seize upon the water to distribute *it* liberally, assiduously a similitude *of* that which a learned ruler said, in extolling a wise high-priest, that, 'just as the wind draws the up-flying water from rivers and springs *and* from seas, Tî*s*tar, through his own liberality, bestows the prepared apportionments of the whole production for the advantage of the creatures *by* the will of the sacred beings, and makes *it* rain. 16. And through that which he shall purposely seize to distribute suitably he distributes the water purified, he moistens the pleasant *existences* of animals *and* plants and spares[2] the polluted, he provides for the thirsty[3], he causes harm to the dye-like bloody *one*, and he makes the world thrive. 17. When that wide-*spread* liberality of his, the production of rain, is from the pure, healing water which he shall thus seize gradually and with just apportionment, *and* when through that acquiring of water-seizings the rivers, springs, *and* other existences (shavandagânŏ) are well-expanding, and even the diminution which is owing to the wasting (aîrîkhtagîh) of rivers and springs does not occur thereby, *it is* thus, too, the lordly, by a law (dâ*d*ŏ) moderate and varied—if the regulation (gûn) is to reach *away* from the region—are as much contributing, as

---

[1] Reading sû*d*akîh instead of î yû*d*akîh, 'which is unity.' M14 has nadûkîh, 'benefit.'

[2] Or 'forgives' (bakhshê*d*ŏ).

[3] M14 and J have 'he causes the thirsty to drink.'

Tîstar is by causing rain for the region and the good, to the aggrandizement of the many grades[1] and the replenishment of the region and creatures[2].'

Chapter XCIV.

1. And[3] those of the primitive faith, the ancients of those acquainted with the religion[4], thus considered, *that* in the *spirit of* life (ahvô)[5] there is

---

[1] Or 'to the great aggrandizement of the grades.'

[2] Reading dâm, as in M14 and J, instead of gadman, 'glory.' The chapter appears to break off here, without any reference to the queries about hail and snow; but it is uncertain if any portion of the work be here omitted (owing to loss of folios in some older MS.) because the author does not always reply to all clauses of the questions, as may be noticed in Chap. XXXVII. One reason, however, for supposing that some of the text is here lost is the allusion, in Chaps. XVII, 20, XVIII, 2, to a chapter no longer extant in Dd.

[3] The first eleven sections of this chapter are quoted from the beginning of the sixth book of the Dînka*rd*, which commences as follows:—'The propitiation of the creator Aûha*r*ma*z*d is even in the benedictions of the religion of Ma*zd*a-worship; this, too, *was* the settled decision of those of the primitive faith. The sixth *book* is on a compendium (vasang) which *was* prepared by those of the primitive faith to maintain about the sayings of the religion of Ma*zd*a-worship;' and then proceeds as in our text, with the variations and additional matter mentioned in the foot-notes. It is hardly probable that these quotations were intended as a conclusion to any reply, the beginning of which may be lost, as they refer to a variety of subjects; but they may have been selected by the author as authoritative opinions sufficiently comprehensive for his general peroration. At any rate they show that the Dînka*rd* must have been in existence in its present form before the Dâ*d*istân-î Dînîk was written. All the MSS. have this peroration written continuously with the preceding chapter, without stop or break of any kind to indicate a change of subject.

[4] Dk. has 'the ancients of the wise.' [5] Dk. adds 'of men.'

a thought and one appointed who[1] holds the position (gâs), *and* there is a fiend who stops[2] the way; and in the thought there is a word appointed which holds the position, *and* there is a fiend who stops the way[3]. 2. In the *spirit of* life[4] is a thought *and* Spendarmad[5] ('bountiful devotion') holds the position, *and* the fiend Tarômat[6] ('scornful thought') stops the way; in the thought is a word *and* Ard[7] ('the righteous') holds the position, and Varenô[8] ('lust') stops the way; in the word is a deed *and* Dînô[9] ('religion'), the good, holds the position, and self-conceit

[1] Dk. has 'which is appointed and,' &c.

[2] Literally 'holds.'

[3] It is evident from the context that something is omitted here, and Dk. supplies the following:—'and in the word there is a deed *for* the appointed position, *and* there is a fiend who stops the way. And in the *spirit of* life is a heart (vâlôm) *and* Vohûman ("good thought") holds the position, and Akômanô ("evil thought") stops the way; and in the heart is a will *and* Srôsh ("attention") holds the position, and Aeshm ("wrath") stops the way.' It seems probable that the author did not mean to quote the latter sentence of this passage.

[4] Dk. has 'and in the will.'

[5] The female archangel, who is a personification of Av. spenta ârmaiti, and has special charge of the earth and virtuous women (see Bd. I, 26, Sls. XV, 20–24).

[6] Here written Tarôkmatŏ (Av. tarômaiti); he is the arch-demon of disobedience, also called Nâûnghas (see Bd. XXVIII, 14, XXX, 29).

[7] Av. areta, a title of the female angel Arshisang or Ashisang (Av. ashis vanguhi, 'good rectitude'), whose name is given to the 25th day of the Parsi month (see Bd. XXII, 4, XXVII, 24, Sls. XXII, 25, XXIII, 4).

[8] Av. varena, 'desire,' personified as a demon (see Bd. XXVIII, 25).

[9] Av. daêna personified as an angel whose name is given to the tenth month and 24th day of the month of the Parsi year, and is also coupled with the names of other angels to form appellations

(khû*d*-dôshagîh) stops the way. 3. We men of all descriptions[1] have to become very[2] cautious that, while we do not desist from that way[3], we do not go on to the way of the demons *and* fiends[4]. 4. For the struggling of men[5] is *in* these three[6] ways and paths; *and* whoever is saved in these three[6] ways and paths is saved from every place, and whoever is misled there comes into the hands of the demons *and* fiends[7], and is thenceforth not master (*s*alîtâ) of himself, except when he shall do that which the fiends order him[8].

5. And this, too, *was* thus considered by them, that that nature only is good when it[9] shall not do unto another whatever is not good for its own self[10]; and that wisdom only is good when it thoroughly[11] understands *how* to utilize the advantage[12] of that happiness which has occurred, *and* shall[13] not suffer vexation *on account of* harm which has not occurred; and that intellect only is good which

---

for the 8th, 15th, and 23rd days (see Bd. XXV, 3, 11, 20, Sls. XXII, 8, 15, 23, 24, XXIII, 4). Dk. omits the epithet 'good.'

[1] Dk. omits the words 'of all descriptions;' it also places § 3 after § 4.

[2] Dk. omits 'very.'

[3] Dk. has 'from the way of the angels.'

[4] Dk. has 'go after the fiends.'

[5] Dk. has 'and the struggling of the fiend with men,' and places this section after § 2.

[6] Dk. has 'such' instead of 'three' in both places.

[7] Dk. has 'comes then to the hands of the fiends.'

[8] Dk. then proceeds with § 3, 'and we men have to become cautious,' &c.

[9] Dk. has 'which,' instead of 'when it,' both here and in the next clause.

[10] Dk. has 'for itself.'

[11] Dk. omits 'thoroughly.'

[12] Literally 'to eat the fruit.'

[13] Dk. has 'does.'

understands that it does not understand that which it does not understand.

6. And this, too, *was* thus considered by them, that *one* is to become[1] a friend of every one, and this is thy nature[2]; also, bring them on into[3] goodness, and this is thy wisdom; also, consider them as thine own, and this is thy religion; also, through them it shall produce[4] happiness, and this is thy soul[5].

7. And this, too, *was* thus considered by them, that, when[6] *one* shall do even that which he knows to be sin[7], that is disobedience, *and* disobedience is the nature of the adversary; when *one* shall not do even that which he knows to be a good work, that is cupidity (varenôîkîh), *and* cupidity is the wisdom of the adversary[8]; *and* when *one* shall do[9] even that which he does not know *to be* a good work or a sin, until it comes fully to[10] *his* knowledge,

---

[1] Dk. has 'it is the becoming.' [2] Dk. has 'wisdom.'

[3] Or 'through.' Dk. omits this clause, substituting 'and this, too, *was* thus considered by them.'

[4] Dk. has 'do thou produce.'

[5] Dk. continues as follows:—'And this, too, *was* thus considered by them, that nature is that which deceives no one, wisdom is that which does not deceive itself, and religion is that which is whatever knows where *one* should perform good works.'

[6] Reading amat, instead of mûn, 'which,' in all three clauses (see Chap. LXII, 4 n); Dk. omits the word altogether.

[7] Dk. has 'shall not do even that which he knows to be a good work,' as in the second clause which it omits.

[8] This clause is omitted by M14, J, BK, and the oldest MS. of Dk.; later MSS. of Dk. give it as follows: 'should they do even that they know to be a sin, that is lustful (varenôîk), and lustful is the wisdom of the adversary.'

[9] Dk. has 'does.'

[10] Dk. has 'before it comes unto.'

that is self-conceit, and self-conceit is the religion of the adversary[1].

8. And this, too, *was* thus considered by them, that Aharman[2] would do everything for the injury of Aûharmazd, *but* when it is done by him[3] *it* is then an injury of him himself, *and* an advantage of Aûharmazd; and Aûharmazd would do everything for his own advantage, *and* when it is done by him *it* is then, indeed[4], an advantage of him himself, *but* an injury of Aharman[5].

---

[1] In Dk. the following is here inserted:—'And this, too, *was* thus considered by them, that in *one's* nature there is no wisdom, *but* in wisdom *there* is nature, and in religion are both wisdom *and* nature. It is known *how* to manage the affairs of the spirit by the nature, they are preserved by wisdom, and the soul is preserved by a union of both. And this, too, *was* thus considered by them, that shame is that which should not allow *one* to commit sin, and disgrace is that it would not allow to cause. And this, too, *was* thus considered by them, that the essential thing of the primitive faith is freedom from sin. And this, too, *was* thus considered by them, that *one* becomes diligent about that *with* which *he* is conversant. And this, too, *was* thus considered by them, that the good thoughts that are in the records of the religion of every kind *one should* always put fully into practice, so far as he understands *them*. And this, too, *was* thus considered by them, that Aûharmazd, the lord, produced these creatures through *his* nature, maintains *them* through wisdom, and forces them back to himself through religion.'

[2] The evil spirit (see Chaps. II, 11, XIX, 1).

[3] Or 'when he has done it,' which would be expressed by the same words.

[4] Dk. omits 'indeed.'

[5] In Dk. the following is here inserted:—'And this, too, *was* thus considered by them, that people are to keep an eye most diligently on the world *for* these three things: that which is realisable *by* a sinner through sin, a follower made famous, *and* to beg the recompense of good works from the spirits: and keeping their eye on the world is said *to be* this, that *it is he* who observes himself, so that *a part* of whatever he really desires he should always perform. And this, too, *was* thus considered by them, that three

9. And this, too, *was* thus considered by them, that a person of whatever description is to be kept[1] in remembrance of the affairs of the spirit at every period and time, and *of* the happiness of heaven *and* misery of hell at that period when comfort, happiness, and pleasure have come to him.

10. And this, too, *was* thus considered by them[2], that happiness, indeed, would be there, in the heaven of light[3], when even here *it* is so happy, though, owing to many *things*[4], Aharman—with whom the happiness there is not connected—is even here so happy at the time when distress, vexation, *and* misery have come hereto; *and* this, too, *was* thus considered, that evils, indeed, would be there, in hell, when here is such misery, though even here much *of* the earthly happiness *of* Aûhar-

---

things which are very difficult to do are even such as these: one is not to render the sinfulness famous by the sin; one is not to exalt the opinions of the fiend, and the various sovereignties of the evil *one*, for the sake of wealth; and one is to beg the recompense of good works from the spirits, *and* not from the world.'

[1] Dk. has merely 'keeps.'

[2] Dk. has 'this, too, is to be considered,' as a continuation of the preceding section.

[3] Dk. omits 'of light.'

[4] The oldest MS. of Dk. has 'though *some* of the much happiness of Aûharmazd,' &c., as in the latter part of the section, omitting the passage referring to Aharman and hell; later MSS., however, insert a modified version of the omitted passage, and read as follows: 'When even here *it* is so happy at the period when it should be distressing *and* the mischievous vexation of much pain has come; this, too, is to be considered, that misery, indeed, is the calamity (âfatŏ) there, in hell, when even here *it* is so, though *some* of the much happiness of Aûharmazd,' &c., as before. This interpolation in Dk. is evidently modern (as the word âfatŏ is Arabic and not Pahlavi), and was probably composed by a copyist in India who was acquainted with the text of Dk.

ma*zd*—with whom the misery there is not connected—is here so evil.

11. And this, too, *was* thus considered by them, that that person is the more fortunate[1], in whom are soundness of body, happiness, and energy (râyînisnŏ)[2]; *who* has done those things *about* which the last wish of him who departs from the world is then thus: 'I *will* strive to do more;' *and who* shall have exercised much complete abstinence from those things *about* which his last wish, when he departs from the world, is then such as 'I *will* strive to do less, and it would have occurred more comfortably for my soul[3].'

12. Do you good people of those of the good religion of these countries of Irân keep in use the laws appointed *by* those of the primitive faith who *were* high-priests, so that your bodies *may* become more renowned, *and your* souls more perfect, in the radiant supreme heaven which[4] is the seat of Aûha*r*ma*zd* and the archangels, *of* the angels *and* all the guardian spirits of the righteous. 13. So these are so many answers of the questions provided, and are given explanatorily from the exposition of the religion *and* the statements of the high-priests *of*

---

[1] Dk. has 'that a person is most fortunate in that.'

[2] M14 and J have 'are the appearance of health of body and pleasure;' Dk. has 'is the appearance of perfection.'

[3] Dk. concludes as follows: '*who has* done those things which are done, *about* which *on his* last day—when the things of the world depart—his wish is then thus, that 'more endeavour should be made by me;' *and has exercised* much abstinence from those things *about* which his last day's wish is this, that the endeavour made should not be made.' The quotations from Dk. end at this point.

[4] Reading mûn, as in M14 and J, instead of amat, 'when,' (see Chap. LXII, 4 n.)

those of the primitive faith, and *are* the nature of the teachings *that* Mânûs*k*îhar, son of Yûdân-Yim[1], pontiff (ra*d*ŏ) of Pârs and Kirmân[2], and director (farmâ*d*âr)[3] of the profession of priests, ordered to write.

14. Steadfast in the propitiation and praise of the creator Aûha*r*ma*zd* is the righteousness of obtainments of prayers, perfect is Zaratû*s*t, *and* one *only* is the way[4] which righteousness obtains, the others are no ways; homage to the exalted pontiff *sent* from the creator Aûha*r*ma*zd*, the heavenly, most righteous Zaratû*s*t the Spîtamân.

15. Completed in peace and pleasure, joy *and* delight; happy for him who reads, *and* happier for him who keeps *it* in use and shall take his duty therefrom[5], if they exist unto time eternal.

---

[1] See p. 3, note 2.

[2] The two southern provinces of Persia, bordering on the Persian Gulf.

[3] This title seems to be always spelt in Pahlavi with â in the middle syllable, so that the form framadhâr in Nöldeke's Geschichte der Perser und Araber zur Zeit der Sasaniden, p. 9, must be looked upon as an Arabic corruption, and the idea that it means 'a preceder or one who has precedence' can hardly be maintained. It probably stands for farmâî*d*âr, 'a director or commander,' not in a military sense. It occurs also in Bd. XXXIII, 2, where the title 'great farmâ*d*âr' is evidently equivalent to 'prime minister, or grand vazîr,' but applied to a priest, as farmâ*d*âr is here and in Chap. XLV, 5.

[4] Reading râs, as in M14, instead of ra, which is merely an imperfect word. This clause of the sentence is a slight modification of a well-known quotation (said to be taken from the lost part of the Hâ*d*ôkht Nask) which is often used in perorations.

[5] Or 'who keeps to duty and shall do his duty thereby.'

EPISTLES

OF

MÂNÛS*K*ÎHAR.

I. TO THE GOOD PEOPLE OF SÎRKÂN.

II. TO HIS BROTHER, ZÂ*D*-SPARAM.

III. TO ALL OF THE GOOD RELIGION IN IRÂN.

A. D. 881.

OBSERVATIONS.

1. For all divisions into chapters and sections the translator is responsible, as the manuscripts are written continuously, with very few stops marked, and even those are often misplaced.

2–6. (The same as on page 2.)

7. The manuscripts mentioned are:—

BK, an old imperfect copy of K35 written in Kirmân, but now in Bombay.

J (about 60 years old), belonging to Dastûr Jâmâspji Minochiharji in Bombay.

K35 (probably written A.D. 1572), No. 35 in the University Library at Kopenhagen; upon the text of which this translation is based.

M10 (about 150 years old), a Persian Rivâyat, No. 10 of the Haug Collection in the State Library at Munich.

EPISTLES OF MÂNÛSKÎHAR.

EPISTLE I.

TO THE GOOD PEOPLE OF SÎRKÂN.

THROUGH the name and assistance of the creator Aûharmazd and the whole of the sacred beings, all the angels of the spiritual *and* the angels of the worldly *existences*.

A copy of the epistle of the priest Mânûskîhar[1], son of Yûdân-Yim, which *was* composed by him for the good *people* of Sîrkân[2], on the contents of the precepts (vigîr-kardŏ) which the priest Zâd-sparam[3], son of Yûdân-Yim, prepared.

CHAPTER I.

1. *In* the name of the sacred beings, who sent you a soul with long life, with provision for proper progress, *and* with the protection of increase of righteousness and wisdom, may such works and

---

[1] The high-priest of Pârs and Kirmân (see the heading to Dd., p. 3).

[2] Written Sîrkân once, Sîrkânŏ twice, and Sîrgânŏ four times, in these epistles. It was a town of considerable importance in former times (see Ouseley's Oriental Geography, pp. 138–145), about thirty parasangs south of Kirmân.

[3] He was high-priest of Sîrkân and brother of Mânûskîhar (as expressly stated in the heading to Ep. II), both being sons of the same father.

mysterious dignity, encompassed with[1] happiness, now possess increasing prosperity and a complete share of pre-eminent welfare and great exaltation in both worlds.

2. The epistle[2] which *was* wisely, properly, and with religious demeanour ordered by you, *and* sent by a courier (paîkŏ), *has* come, and *has* enveloped *and* assailed (*g*astŏ) me, indeed, with appalling intelligence on other subjects; and if even a portion[3] *of* the vast importance and great value, as regards your heavenly *concerns*, arrangements, and natural *and* unpremeditated (avarîk) prodigies[4], which are for my knowledge, for the sake of courteous (drû*d*îk) information, *be* owing to intelligence for which the courteousness *and* proper courageousness are among you, special pleasure is received *therewith*. 3. And praise is, thereupon, recited by me to the sacred beings, as regards the conflicting affairs even of this disordered (gûmê *z*is*n*îkŏ) existence; worldly possessions, as much as are suitable for the assistance of wisdom, are proper[5], and the gift of virtuous pleasure is the gain of the undeserving good work *or* prayer they (the sacred beings) shall accept; it causes aggrandizement *and* is as deserving as even that which the decision of

[1] Or, 'sent down in,' according as we read parvastŏ or frôstŏ.

[2] An epistle complaining of certain heretical teachings of their high-priest, Zâ*d*-sparam, which is no longer extant.

[3] Reading va hat vâhar-i*k*.

[4] The epistle which he had received from his brother, Zâ*d*-sparam, some time before, seems also to have mentioned certain omens (see Ep. II, i, 3).

[5] J omits shâye*d*ŏ, 'are proper,' because it follows the other shâye*d*, 'are suitable;' but it is not always safe to assume that the repetition of a word is a blunder.

the wise has said about *it*, that even from the management of disordered possessions which are impaired *there* is advantage through the power of wisdom; *and* they (the sacred beings) select and cleanse and uplift the good works *in* such manner as a precious stone (sag khêl) from the water, and gold brocade[1] from the dust.

4. My pleasure, also, is as much increased through the information due to the same courtesy, *and I have* a new *and* great desire for the arrival of information, continuously from henceforth, about the perfect courageousness, enduring humility, good works, worshipping, favouring position, and eagerness of soul of you who *have* recounted *your* great thoughtfulness for religion *and have* provided good works.

5. On account of the universal renown (aspôharakânîh) of the good *people* of Khvanîras[2], which is yours, owing to the favour that is your complete happiness, ardently *and* joyfully most desired, and constantly *so*, when *there* are opportunities of seeing you—though it is supposed *to be* the advantage of your own religion, joy of soul, courteousness, *and* proper constancy—since my will *resides* among you, you make known *and* command my actions, through the will of the sacred beings.

---

[1] Reading dîpakŏ-î zahabâ.

[2] The central region of the earth, containing all the lands best known to the Iranians (see Dd. XC, 3).

CHAPTER II.

1. Then comes that itself[1] which is dictated *in* the middle of your epistle, *and*, thereupon, it lays hold of me, and, owing to its hellish gloom, pallid appearance, *and* hellish effect, benediction is perplexedly dispensed by me in terror for *my* heart *and* mind; I *have*, also, grievously repented, as regards my own former arrangements in my warfare of violence—which *were* undeceptive in the balance pertaining to Rashnû[2]—of any real falsity of the co-existent *one*[3] I *may* have produced.

2. *Responsible* for the malice *and* annoyance of unjust kinds which are encountering *us* is the fiend of great strength, who is unobserving, seductive, astute in evil, eager for causing annihilation (gastŏ-kûn-varen), *and* full of deceit, so that *it* is possible for him to render doubtful, *when* so deceived, even him who is most a listener to essential righteousness, most desirous of steadfast truth, most performing proper religious customs, most acquainted with good ideas, most amazingly careful of *his* soul, most approved in the most wounding hell-brought conflict, *and* most at home (khânagîktûm) in truth of all kinds, *and* to show him a semblance of reality in unreality, *and* of unreality in reality. 3. Just as even that similitude which is mentioned in revelation thus: 'He intends righteousness *and* considers

[1] J has 'the writing.'

[2] See Dd. XIV, 4.

[3] The evil spirit who is supposed to be, for a time, co-existent with the beneficent spirit of Aûharmazd.

about it thus: "A good work is done by me," and he acquires fiendishness—that is, it becomes a source of sin for him—who shall bring forth water without holy-water to *one* contaminated by dead matter (nas-hômand), or who shall bring *it* forth without holy-water on a concealed *or* dark *place* in the night[1].'

4. And about this I *have* no doubt, that the wish of that spirit is not coincident with righteousness, for it is realised, understood, *and* known that, as regards his own *creatures*, *he* is not careful for the proper movement of body and for the long living of life; so that the furtherance *and* continuance of these, which are his original resources of body and activities (khapârânŏ) of life, become, for him who is among them (the fiend's creatures), an increase of the propitiation of the sacred beings, of the practice of religion, and of the advancement and benediction of the teachings of just high-priests[2]. 5. *It* is also manifest from the constantly-operating arrangement of manuscripts and synodical statements, about which Afarg[3] *wrote* without falsifying the religion *and* apart from controversies; because among them (the fiend's creatures) is *he* who *has* said they are like unto that which is now written

[1] Quoted from Pahl. Vend. VII, 194–196, with some slight variations from the existing text. The meaning is that it is quite possible to commit sin by doing a good action in an improper manner.

[2] That is, even the wicked, when they seek welfare, have to take to religious practices.

[3] A commentator whose opinions are frequently quoted in the Pahlavi translations of the Avesta (see Sls. I, 3). J has 'about which the splendour (afrand) of the religion is without falsehood.'

by him himself about it, and it has arranged much deliverance *from sin*[1].

6. Of this, too, I am aware, that, except there where a purifier is in no way reached, his great duty—which is just the purification *in* which there is a washer who is cleansed (masî*d*ŏ) in the religious mode for the profession of the priesthood—is then a means which the high-priests should allow[2]. 7. A washing which is not religiously ritualistic is ranked as an operation among the useless *ones; it is* vicious *and* grievously criminal, because the special means which, by preserving the soul[3], is the perfect happiness of men, is the puri-

[1] That is, any one who explains the scriptures in a new fashion to suit his own purposes, which he thereby represents as beneficial, is merely carrying out the wishes of the fiend. The author is here, referring to the heretical teachings of his brother, regarding purification, which are further described in the sequel.

[2] That is, whenever a properly-qualified purifier is procurable, the priests should require him to purify any one who happens to be defiled by contact with dead matter by means of the Bareshnûm ceremony (see App. IV). It appears from the sequel, and from Eps. II and III, that the heresy of Zâ*d*-sparam consisted chiefly of a misinterpretation of Vend. VIII, 278–299 (see App. V), which passage directs that a man in the fields, who has touched a corpse not yet eaten by dogs or birds, shall wash himself fifteen times with bull's urine, that he shall then run to some village, asking three different men on the way to cleanse him with the proper ceremony, and if they decline they each take upon themselves a share of the sin; when arrived at the village he shall ask a fourth time to be cleansed, and if no one will perform the ceremony he must wash himself with bull's urine and water in the ordinary manner, and shall be clean. The erroneous teaching of Zâ*d*-sparam was that the fifteen times' washing was sufficient, without the subsequent ceremonial cleansing; and the object of these epistles was to combat that view of the law.

[3] The ceremonial purification is supposed to cleanse the soul,

fication of men. 8. *It* is said[1]: 'The purification of men cleansingly is a something (aîtŏ) for the soul that should be after perfect birth; when they have been fully born the purification of others is the one thing which is good for the soul.'

9. And it is shown *in* another place that it is possible to obtain possession of purification also for the soul through purification of the body, even as it is said that a purifier is requested by him. 10. And it is necessary for him to speak thus: 'I have thus stood close by the body of him who is dead; I am no wisher *for it* by thought, I am no wisher *for it* by word, I am no wisher *for it* by deed; which is the reason—that is, on account of pollution—it is not possible to seek good works by thought, word, *or* deed, *and* it demands purification for me, that is, wash me thoroughly[2]!' 11. As it is thereby declared that when he whose body is not purified, until they thoroughly wash him, is not able to seek good works by thought, word, *or* deed, and is not able to purify his soul, it is then a matter for the truly wise *to seek* even for purification of the soul by the purification of the body, *for* whose religious purification are those *things* which are unsubdued (a*s*ikand) in the religious ritual.

12. When these are thus the statements of former upholders of the religion *and* high-priests of the religion, he who is more intelligent *and* more active

---

whereas ordinary washing cleanses the body only, and is spiritually useless.

[1] In Pahl. Vend. V, 65, X, 35, being a translation of a quotation from the Gâthas or sacred hymns (Yas. XLVII, 5, c).

[2] Quoted, with some variation, from Pahl. Vend. VIII, 283, 284 (see App. V).

in the religion of the Ma*zd*a-worshippers in every house, village, tribe, and province—*and*, very much more the man who is righteous, of fluent speech, speaking the truth, who *has* chanted the *sacred* hymns, acquainted with the ritual, trained for the work, of renowned disposition, and a friend of the soul—is *competent* for the purification which *it* is very important to prepare, to think of, *and* to promote.

13. When the period is so unworthy, the fiend so abundantly contentious, and the hasty preparer of holy-water of such base origin (dûs-vêkh)[1]—which *happens*, moreover, when the good are equally low-minded (ham-bâstŏ-mînisnŏ)—we strive for *what* encourages the preparation of that even which is a collectively virtuous profession. 14. Then, too, *there* remains such rising in strength of many new *things* from very many countries, which is particularly grievous distress and danger to us; they deliver tokens *of them* to us applaudingly, *and* the expansibility of the words of the delivering diffuser of these and also other religious customs, as the sacred beings' own persistency and complete glory, is a great *and* powerful capability.

Chapter III.

1. This, too, I am begging of you, that *you* may be desiring the truth, and *that* Vohûman[2], who,

[1] This seems to be an allusion to the unworthiness of some of the priests of the period (compare Ep. II, i, 13; v, 14).

[2] The archangel personifying 'good thought' (see Dd. III, 13).

when a ruler (shah) of yours, is an interpreter (pâkûkŏ) about the writing which[1] I write, *may* as regardfully *and* accommodatingly observe *and* direct as the variety of dispositions *permits*. 2. For you are of like opinion with me, to inform again the most initiated[2]; so that I am more steadfastly-determined (aûstîkânŏ-minisntar) thereon. 3. And if there be *anything* that seems to you otherwise, direct *some one* to point *it* out again, with the reason *for* maintaining *it* which occurs to you, just as a household companion is a responder *and* has spoken again for the sake of pointing out again; for there are many reasons, on account of which your kindly-regardful observation is needful, which are to be written about.

4. The first is this, that the penmanship of the spirits is not the profession of me and others[3]; *and as to* him by whom a theory (farhâng) not universally operating is disseminated, which is *distinct* from his more indispensable occupation, *there* is then no command for his teaching *and* apostleship therein. 5. On that account, too, the wise *and* the seekers for truth uphold the body of opinion about the statements of the writing of the spirits[4], and, therefore, direct less of the ingenuity of preparing again the penmanship of various tidings.

6. The second is this, that, in the distress (dahyakŏ) of this grievous time, he to whom

---

[1] Reading î instead of va, 'and.'

[2] That is, to severely admonish their high-priest, as he does in Ep. II.

[3] That is, he disclaims all pretensions to inspiration on the part of himself and his contemporaries.

[4] The inspired scriptures.

adherence *and* much indebtedness even as to his *fore*fathers *have* remained, is well-lamenting, owing to the proposals (dâ*d*anŏ) of the unfriendly, and much harm has occurred through the conflicting (âr*d*îkŏ) offer of remedies *and* lawful provision of means, full of trouble, except, indeed, to the upholder of religion who is more worldly-managing; and investigation by opponents is grievous danger, full of things inopportune *and* unnecessary for accomplishment[1].

7. The third is this, that a wise *man* who is a high-priest of the spirit-retaining[2] religion *and* acquainted with opinions, when also himself properly humble, fearless, and benedictive in the world, is then even, owing to his estimating[3] pardonings *and* long-*continued* dexterity (dêr zîva*k*akîh), united with the good creations in affliction *and* vexation. 8. And, on account of information about the worldly *and* spiritual misery of former evils of many kinds—always as much in the religion, *and* in the thoughts of others[4], as *one* delivers up his heart to ingenious verbiage and for the preparation of phrases—he speaks as in the question *in* revelation, thus[5]: '"Who in the bodily existence

---

[1] Referring to the risk of unfriendly and destructive criticism of the scriptures.

[2] J has 'spirit-observing,' by changing gîri*s*nŏ into nigîri*s*nŏ.

[3] Reading andasîh; the reference being to the sympathy acquired by a high-priest through performing his duty of appointing atonements for sins confessed to him.

[4] Assuming that aî*s*anŏ stands for aî*s*ânŏ.

[5] J has only 'as *one* speaks out his heart for ingenious verbiage and phrases, thus.' The question and reply here quoted seem to be no longer extant in the Avesta.

is more quickly fortunate?" *and* it is answered thus: "The youth who is observant *and* humble, O Zaratûst! who, as regards both that which has happened and that *which* happens, also sees that which is evil and good with gratitude, just like that also which *happens* unto another;"' because he knows this, that from this is a benefit, for he knows happiness and also misery[1]. 9. The glorified leader of those of the good religion, Hêr-Frôvag[2], son of Farukhûzâd, wrote: 'It is he understands the consequence of his own action; and *it* is his great household attendant, and the worldly desire provided at the *K*invad bridge[3] becomes less watchful.'

10. The fourth is this, that I *am* more universally hoping about the property of the profession *and* the much duty fit for the truly wise, *in* such manner as even that *in* which the glorified and greatly-learned leader of those of the good religion, Yûdân-Yim[4], son of Shahpûhar, always urged on a priestly man with many sons *and* equally clever[5] discourse.

---

[1] It is doubtful whether this last clause be a portion of the quotation, or not.

[2] This name is corrupted into Hê-Fôrvag in the MSS., but Âtûr-Frôbag is probably intended. He was the compiler of a great part of the Dînkard, and is also mentioned in Dd. LXXXVIII, 8. The names Âtûr and Hêr are synonymous, both meaning 'fire.' The passage quoted in the text has the same form (beginning with the word hômandŏ, 'it is') as nearly all the sections of the third book of the Dînkard, but it has not yet been discovered among them.

[3] Here written *K*is-vidarg (see Dd. XX, 3).

[4] So written in J, but K35 and BK have the syllable dân somewhat corrupted. The person meant, both here and in Chap. VII, 5, was probably the author's father, though Bd. XXXIII, 11 seems to make Yûdân-Yim the son of Vâhrâm-shâd.

[5] Reading ham-gôkŏ, but J has ham-dûdakŏ, 'of the same family;' it also omits several other words by mistake.

11. That *was* through my instigation, alone and with little assistance, in the beginning; and, on account of the deficiency of warriors [1], the abundance of opponents, the very rapid arrival of disturbance, *and* the fourfold supplication for keeping away the ruin *or* hasty unlawful maintenance of the fires *of* the Ma*zd*a-worshippers, my constant distress is such that most of my time speaks of the same subject [2]. 12. They may leave the abundance of despondency and thoughtfulness of the bodily existence to such remedial writing of his, unto whom the pleasantly comfortable thought of an evaded (vîrikhtô) seizure is requisite, but *there* is little worldly leisure for me for writing more *in* this direction (hanâ-runtar). 13. And specially in this passing *time*—when, alike limited by the coming of the period of giving daily *supplies* to the performers of worship, *and by* the ever-triumphant fire and *its* produce [3], it was necessary for me to go to Shirâ*z* [4] on account of some indispensable provision of means—the work was much *and* the leisure little.

---

[1] From this and Ep. II, v, 14 it would appear that the priests at that time maintained a body of troops for the protection of their followers.

[2] That is, regarding the proper maintenance of the priesthood, which had already engaged his anxious attention during the lifetime of his father.

[3] The word var may either mean 'ashes' (see Sls. II, 49), alluding to clearing out the fire, or it may mean 'ordeal' (see Sls. XIII, 17).

[4] See Dd. I, 17. This name is written Shirâzŏ once, Sîrâzŏ thrice, and Sirâzŏ four times in K35. Mânûs*k*îhar appears to have come to Shirâz on this occasion to hold a general assembly of the priests and leading members of the community, and he wrote this epistle from that city (see Ep. II, i, 11; v, 10).

14. The fifth is this, that the custom of providing for all the duties even of the *sacred* fire (âtû*r*) by me, and my own desire[1], trained hand[2], unhardened mind, and unhardened heart *for* managing many *things* should have become the joy of *my* mind. 15. Then, too, from *having* read such writing *and* such news the healer of distress would be thoroughly connected with my heart and mind, *owing* to which my intellect would have become quickly fatigued (mândakŏ) by a limited preparation of phrases.

16. The sixth is this, that even he who is a rescued[3] *and* better-operating (hû-dâgtar) man—when, owing to the writing of a learned *man* of the realm who is desiring the truth, *he* is so perplexed[4] on account of a doubt of increasing the after-tearing of the same perplexity—*has* no doubt of the falsity *and* little training existent in the worldly.

17. The seventh is this, that if none of these six *of* which I *have* written should exist, even then your approved cleverness (*s*îvagdârîh), extolled freedom from strife, hereafter-discerning and complete mind-

---

[1] Reading kâmakŏ, instead of the unintelligible kâmûn.

[2] The MSS. omit the last letter of yadman.

[3] That is, delivered from contamination or sin; vîrikhtô is probably to be traced to Av. vi+irikhta, rather than to vi+rikhta (Pers. gurêkht).

[4] K35 has a blank space here, and again a few words further on, but it is doubtful if any words be missing. The spaces are filled up in J and BK, apparently by guess, as follows: J has 'he sees so perplexing a chance, concerning which, owing to the increase of after-tearing of the same perplexity and the arrival of evil, *he* is doubtful, *has* no doubt,' &c. And BK has '*he* is so perplexed on account of no doubt of the falsity *and* little training *that* existed in the worldly for increasing the after-tearing of the same perplexity, *has* no doubt, &c.'

fulness, practised[1] attention to the good, and much affection[2] for the faithful—so kindly regarding, truly judging, *and* with a liking for praising (srî*d*anŏ), as regards whatever I write truly *and* with true conviction—are, I consider, to make provision, and *have* realised a preparation striven for.

Chapter IV.

1. I *have* also seen the spiritual life[3] in the writing which is in such statements of incompleteness[4], *and* owing to the same reason they should not cease from the operation[5] of washing you—whom may the angels protect!—with the Bareshnûm *ceremony*[6]. 2. Because the ancients have said that, when it shall be discarded from use, every water, fire, plant, righteous man, *and* animal, and all the creatures of Aûha*r*ma*z*d are afflicted, diminished, and made to leap *away*. 3. As it is said in revelation that, *as to* him *who* stands *by* a dead body upon which the Nasû*s*[7] *has* rushed[8], 'anusô zî, Spitama Zara-

---

[1] J has bûr*z*îdakŏ, 'extolled,' instead of var*z*îdakŏ, 'practised.'

[2] Reading dûkhsharmîh as in J; the other MSS. have m instead of û.

[3] Reading dî*d* ahvôîh; but it can also be read stihânŏîh, in which case the translation would be:—'And my worldly condition.'

[4] Meaning the incomplete kind of purification which their statements complained of, or his referred to.

[5] K35 and BK omit the *r* in ka*r*dakŏ.

[6] See App. IV.

[7] The fiend of corruption (see Dd. XVII, 7).

[8] The three Avesta passages here quoted, with their Zand (Pahlavi translation), are from Vend. IX, 161–163, and are freely translated (trans. D) thus:—'It grieves the sun, indeed, O Spitama

thu*s*tra! aêsha yâ[1] paiti-irista ava*d*[2] hvare â-tâpayêiti[3], anusô hâu m*a*u, anusô avê stârô[4] —discontentedly, moreover, O Zaratû*s*t the Spîtamân! does the sun shine upon him who *has been* by the dead, so discontentedly [does the moon][5], thus discontentedly do the stars—khshnâvayêiti zî, Spitama Zarathu*s*tra! aêshô nâ yô yao*z*dâthryô, ya*d* aêtem[6] paiti-iristem frâ-nasûm kerenaoiti—the man who is purifying propitiates *them*, O Zaratû*s*t the Spîtamân! when *he operates on* him *who has been* by the dead, *on* whom the Nasû*s* is put forth, *and* he has become *parted* from the sacred twigs[7]—he propitiates fire, he propitiates

---

Zarathu*s*tra! to shine upon a man defiled by the dead; it grieves the moon, it grieves the stars. That man delights them, O Spitama Zarathu*s*tra! who cleanses from the Nasu those whom she has defiled; he delights the fire, he delights the water, he delights the earth, he delights the cow, he delights the trees, he delights the faithful, both men and women.' The Avesta text is given according to the standard edition of Westergaard (IX, 41, 42), and all variants of any importance, in the three MSS. here used, are mentioned in the notes. These passages are also referred to in Ep. II, iii, 5.

[1] K35 and BK insert the last three words, anusô âvâ stârô, here.

[2] J inserts yâ here.

[3] J has â-tâpayaêta, but K35 and BK omit the word.

[4] K35 and BK have khshathrô-chinanghô, 'of a desire of authority' (which occurs in Fravar*d*în Yt. 112 as the name of a man) instead of avê stârô, which they have inserted earlier. They also leave a blank space for the words maman akhû*r*sandîhâ, 'moreover, discontentedly' (which begin the Pahlavi translation), as if they were descended from a damaged original.

[5] All three MSS. omit the words in brackets, which are necessary to complete the Pahlavi version.

[6] K35 and BK omit aêtem.

[7] J has 'who has become polluted,' which separation from the sacred twigs (see Dd. XLIII, 5), or other ceremonial apparatus, implies. The phrase is omitted in Pahl. Vend. IX, 162.

water, he propitiates animals *and* plants[1], he propitiates the righteous man[2], he propitiates the righteous woman, both *of them*,' as *in* the Avesta[3] of it:—khshnâvayêiti âtarem, &c.

4. When *there* is no purifier all the angels of the worldly *existence* become afflicted *and* dissatisfied; and religious purifiers who are intelligent are even now not to keep backward the work of purification, just as *it has* come to them by practice from those of the primitive faith, and are not to diminish it. 5. To change a good work properly appointed they shall not accept a law which is not right, a good work not properly appointed[4]; not to do the work thereof is accounted very sagacious *and* perfectly wise; and through your freedom from inferiority[5] the glorifying, commendation, praise, and blessing are your own. 6. For it is said that in all the work of forming and maintaining the law (dâdistânŏ) those of the primitive faith *were* very greatly particular about every single thing; and *as to* the whole operation of that proceeding into which they *have* entered, those of the primitive faith have become aware of the power which *resides* in true authority. 7. But, otherwise[6], the routine which is brought out

---

[1] J has 'he propitiates plants,' as in Pahl. Vend. IX, 163.

[2] Literally 'male.'

[3] The initial words of which here follow their Pahlavi translation, instead of preceding it.

[4] J omits these six words.

[5] Reading afrôtarîh, as in BK; K35 had originally a*v*artarîh, 'pre-eminence,' as in J, but the copyist wrote afrô (=aparva) over the a*v*arta, as a correction, leaving it doubtful whether he meant afrôtarîh or aparvarîh, 'want of education.'

[6] That is, unless confirmed by the decisions of the ancients.

from revelation[1] and the teaching of the high-priests is then not authorisedly changed by that priestly man whose decree of the fifteen[2] *washings* is written in *your* epistle[3]; because, on account of the whole and any perversion (gastakîh) of the same writing, not of similar utterance with revelation, before which the custom did not exist, I am without doubt as to that decree.

8. And in it[4], moreover, is written, declared, *and* contained (vangîdŏ) that once *washing* is mentioned[5], until a purifier comes who is acquainted with the ritual, who washes just as declared in revelation. 9. *To be* so washed I consider just as a thing for which he is even now as *it were* a purifier who is a good washer[6], that of which *it* is written below *and* clearly realised that it should not be decreed; *and* through the scanty deliverance written therein[7] *it* is manifest it would not be the statement above[8].

---

[1] J has 'which is brought out with knowledge of the *purifying* cup (tâstîk), with preservation of faith, *and* with manifestation from revelation.'

[2] All three MSS. have 'sixteen' in ciphers, but it is evident that Zâd-sparam and his erroneous teaching of the sufficiency of fifteen washings (see Ep. III, 1, 2) are here referred to.

[3] Reading semag, a Huz. hybrid for nâmak.

[4] The decree of Zâd-sparam, apparently.

[5] Referring probably to Vend. VIII, 299, which provides a washing for the polluted person by himself, if he can find no one willing to purify him (see App. V).

[6] That is, for such a purpose any ordinary washer would be sufficient.

[7] In Pahl. Vend. VIII, 299, which states that, although pure enough for ordinary purposes, he must still abstain from engaging in ceremonies for others (see App. V).

[8] That is, it is very different from the propitiation mentioned in § 3.

10. If learned knowledge, *relating* both to that about inferior matters (agîrtarîhâ) and that about superior matters, *be*[1] true authority praised *and* declared by the great primitive faith, former high-priests *and* those newly arisen (navakgandakânŏ) would be *and* would have been similarly forward; then, too, it would exist not so much with the priestly men *of* the time *as with* the learned officiating priests (magôpatân) of Aûharmazd *who* have been before. 11. And when, moreover, all the Avesta and Zand are easy *to* a priest[2], pre-eminently acquainted with the liturgy *and* a supreme Zaratûst, *he has* attained *unto*, *and* should remain with, Aûharmazd and[3] the officiating priestship of Aûharmazd, and the supreme, world-managing, religion-observing (hû-dîn-nikah) sovereignty as to *religious* treatises[4]. 12. To change then their practice in the law would be entirely an outcry apart from deliberation, and a like violation of the unanimity of the spirits who are the heads *and* guardians[5] of the religion, *and of* the unanimity of the source of opinion of the good themselves, for the sake of *what is* not acceptable.

13. But the statement above[6] is, was, *and will* be that which remains a good idea well considered by them with the centre of thought, as to *its* well-

[1] J has 'because if even for that about superior matters, acquaintance with religion, and learned knowledge *there be*,' &c.

[2] That is, when he knows all the scriptures and commentaries by heart.

[3] J omits 'Aûharmazd and.'

[4] That is, he has full authority to interpret the scriptures.

[5] Reading sarân sardârân, but in K35 the two words overlap, so that sar-sardârân, 'head guardians,' might be intended.

[6] Probably referring to the quotation from the Vendidâd in § 3.

operating characteristics, just contention, and complete powerfulness. 14. Also from the teaching of just high-priests, through the preservation of much evidence, and ascertained for the members of the assemblies of various provinces (shat*r*ô shat*r*ô), are shown the opinion *and* experience of most priestly men; and to make the various districts (kûstakŏ kûstakŏ) thrivingly steadfast, an unperverted *one* should be set up in all four quarters (pâ*d*kôs) of the same province.

15. And a semblance of it is apparent even from that which the glorified Nîshahpûhar, the supreme officiating priest[1], and also other officiating priests of Aûha*r*ma*zd have* said, *that one is* not to change any teaching of theirs thereon after *it is* provided, *and* not to render useless the statements of other authority thereon. 16. But that which they should accept *from* them as a certainty is to maintain the statements of other high-priests as pre-eminent; *and* not to change the operation of statements of another description *has* appeared lawful. 17. Even so it was as that *same* Nîshahpûhar, in the council of the glorified (anôshakŏ rûbânô) Khûsrô[2], king of

[1] This môbad of môbads is mentioned in Pahl. Vend. III, 151, V, 112, VI, 71, VIII, 64, XVI, 10, 17, AV. I, 35, and twenty-four times in the Nîrangistân (see Sls. I, 4 n). His name is spelt in various ways.

[2] King Khûsrô, son of Kavâ*d*, who is best known by his title Nôshirvân, or Anôshirvân, 'immortal-soulled,' reigned A.D. 531–579; and the statement that Nîshahpûhar was one of his councillors (made little more than three centuries after his death, and, therefore, probably correct) is of considerable importance for fixing a limit to the age of those Pahlavi books in which he is mentioned. These books are the Pahlavi Nîrangistân, a late recension of the Pahlavi Vendidâ*d*, and the Book of Ar*d*â-Vîrâf, in which last it is

kings *and* son of Kavâ*d*,—by preserving old things (ligânŏ)—showed that way on whose thoughts they are established, and wrote them unaltered, so that such thoughts thereon became as *it were* decided; and their thoughts thereon, after such decree of his, have so become unanimous. 18. Through the importance *of his* assured rank, and the rest which *was* said by him in the work of sustaining the faithful, he maintains as much as the other statements, one *by* one, from the deliberative teaching of those high-priests.

Chapter V.

1. That writing which comes amid the writing of your epistle is a correct fragment[1] as regards the nothing in which *one* is to change the operation properly maintainable, and it is becoming; because, if it be even for him, by whom it is written from the

---

stated that Vîrâf was called by the name of Nikhshâpûr by some. From the statements made in our text it seems probable that the council was employed in revising the Pahlavi Vendidâ*d*, in which they were careful not to erase the opinions of older commentators, and thus confirmed their statements by their own authority. It is possible that this council was that mentioned in Byt. I, 7, where the name Nishâpûr also occurs, but whether it refers to a man or a city is not quite certain. This council, which seems to have been summoned for condemning the heresy of Mazdak, was held probably two or three years before Khûsrô came to the throne (see Nöldeke: Geschichte der Perser und Araber zur Zeit der Sasaniden, p. 465).

[1] Reading bang*is*nîh, but it may be bû*gis*nîh, 'deliverance *from contamination*.' The reference is to the decree of Zâ*d*-sparam mentioned in Chap. IV, 7, the 'writing' alluded to in Ep. II, ii, 1; iii, 1.

statements of Mê*d*yôk-mâh, Afarg, and Sôshâns[1], the several statements *and* teachings of the same high-priests, yet then the elaboration *and* publication thereof are not such as that which is sent down by his further elaboration[2]. 2. And thereby it *has* seemed manifest *that it* is sent so that a wish for the spirit *may* proceed from the truth of *its* minister (pa*d*ŏ), or *from* his thought for the desired decision; or his understanding *may* be of that kind which is warped (vukû*s*tŏ), as though he believed it as other than the exposition of the religion *and* the teaching of the high-priests. 3. But until the unparalleled arrival of Sôshâns[3] any one not sharing in complete knowledge is not appointed unto a patron spirit (ahvô), *and* the fiend specially contends more experimentally with the thoughts of the high-priests of the religion for a religious decision.

4. And even the recompense of community[4] of property is that when *one* gladly observes pure thoughts; *and* the swift action of voluble (pûr) speakers and kind regard of religious characters for deliverance[5] *and* for the noticeable undeceitfulness of the same spirit[6]—which is itself the desire of settled observation that is in it for the sake of the

[1] The names of three of the commentators whose opinions are most frequently quoted in the Pahlavi Vendidâ*d* (see Sls. I, 3). Each of them appears to have written a complete 'teaching' or dissertation upon the ceremonial laws, from which the quotations are taken (see § 6).

[2] That is, in collecting the opinions of the ancients, he has twisted them so as to suit his own views.

[3] The last of the future apostles (see Dd. II, 10), not the commentator of the same name mentioned in § 1.

[4] Literally 'fraternity.'

[5] From pollution or sin.

[6] See § 2.

same kind of full religious diffusion—are the swift action of the patron spirit, which, for the sake of preparing him for a deliverance that is not falsifying revelation *and is* without disputants, is a kind regard for the deliverance itself of *him* whose spiritual life (hûkŏ) it is.

5. *As to* that which is thought by him [1] of those deliverances sent down, completed, *and* announced, I consider more particularly about the meaning of one thing, which is their solemnized observance. 6. The solemnized observance of Mê*d*yôk-mâh is in the teaching [2] of Mê*d*yôk-mâh, and those of Afarg and Sôshâns are each one meditated *and* indicated in a teaching; and the pointedly superior position of each one of them is mentioned by him in *his* statement of any teaching and *of* the decision set up. 7. Also with a kind regard for his own choice he *has* thought it (the former teaching) imperfect, and, on account of *what* was not attained by it—which *was* a re-explainer of the same good ideas provided—*its* dissimilarity to it is not unnoticed [3]. 8. *But* when *one* hears the re-explainers of a true reply he is well protected (hû-zinharî*d*ŏ) by complete mindfulness [4], *and* is himself confident that the teaching of Mê*d*yôk-mâh is not the whole statement of Mê*d*yôk-mâh, for there are many opinions of

---

[1] Za*d*-sparam the writer of the decree mentioned in § 1.

[2] The word *k*â*s*takŏ means usually a written course of teaching or exposition, a commentary, dissertation, or manual of instruction.

[3] Implying that Zâ*d*-sparam had been more inclined to enforce his own opinions than to examine those of the commentators.

[4] The Pahl. translation of Av. ârmaiti, 'devotion,' which is usually personified as a female archangel protecting the earth.

Mê*d*yôk-mâh[1] *which* have decided *in* another manner; not *that* whatever Mê*d*yôk-mâh said is not good, *but* in the teaching of Mê*d*yôk-mâh *it* is certain that even *what* is not proper is mentioned many *times* as a possibility[2].

CHAPTER VI.

1. *As to* that which is written in that epistle, that in the teaching of Sôshâns he thus states, that 'of both the purifiers necessary he is suitable by whom the ritual is performed[3],' they have been similarly very unanimous that when one is incapable (atû)[4] it is the other *that* is suitable, who is written *of* in connection with him; and that, moreover, because the statement of Afarg is in a teaching of his[5], and, on

---

[1] J inserts 'rules which are mentioned in the special teaching of Mê*d*yôk-mâh.' It appears probable that the author had access to much more complete commentaries than the fragments now extant in the Pahlavi version of the Vendidâ*d*.

[2] Meaning, probably, that Mê*d*yôk-mâh was disposed to relax the rigid enforcement of the law in cases of doubt or difficulty, as the Avesta itself does in several cases.

[3] Quoted from Pahl. Vend. IX, 132, *b*, where it may be read either as an opinion of Afarg (as mentioned in our text), or as a statement of the Pahlavi translator, who would, therefore, appear to have been Sôshâns. A complete translation of the Pahlavi version of Vend. IX, 1–145 and the commentaries relating to the Bareshnûm ceremony, which are frequently alluded to in these epistles, will be found in App. IV.

[4] Perhaps 'impotent,' as the Rivâyats (M10, fol. 103 a) provide that a purifier shall be neither aged nor youthful, not less than thirty years of age.

[5] See note 3, above; from this it appears that Afarg was the earlier commentator.

that account, that declaration of his seemed *to be* from him, which is as though *it were* decided by him. 2. Then, when *one* reaches the eulogistic (afrâsînâkŏ) reply of his re-explainer, owing to his just will it is itself well perceived that Afarg comes into account as one of the high-priests; and that which is the special teaching of Sôshâns *has* mentioned that they have been very unanimous that when there is one he would be suitable[1].

3. That evidence, too, which many high-priests, and especially one teaching, are alike diffusing, is stated also in the teaching of Mê*d*yôk-mâh, that when he who is washing[2] understands the profession, then one purifier is plenty for him. 4. When it is abundantly declared, in particular by two teachings, *that* when there is one he is suitable, *it* is then not to be rendered quite inoperative through the solitary statement of Afarg; for Afarg only said, as it appeared so to him himself, *that* 'two purifiers are requisite[3].' 5. The customs of another high-priest are not declared to exist with like evidence; and this is set aside (spê*g*î*d*ŏ) even by him himself, that another custom is not suitable to exist, because his own view is mentioned as it appeared to him.

6. Those of the primitive faith have been fully[4] of the custom that other *one* selected, as to this, where *it* is the performance of the Vîkaya ('exorcism')[5]; because its explanation is this, that an

---

[1] See Pahl. Vend. IX, 132, *b*, but the earlier part of the section refers to statements no longer extant.

[2] That is, the person undergoing the purification.

[3] See Pahl. Vend. IX, 132, *b*, Ep. II, ii, 7.

[4] J inserts 'of the same opinion.'

[5] That is, they have considered one purifier sufficient for reciting

opinion upon which the priests (magavôgânŏ) are without dispute is that which he says is the custom of a priest, *and* the business of the two priests, of whose other custom he speaks as much, is a performance by those two witnesses indicating the same as the priest.

7. This, too, is evident, that, by confession of Afarg, when there is *only* one purifier *he* is to be considered as being suitable[1]; *and* an attainment *to* more evidence is that which is written by you, that Mê*d*yôk-mâh *has* said that every customary *part* (pî*s*akŏ) is to be washed three times[2], and now the purifiers *do it* once. 8. That teaching remains *in* the same manner as written by him, but the threefold washing of Mê*d*yôk-mâh is not a washing to be striven for, but *one* to be well considered, *of* which he spoke; and this, too, is not said by him, that when *one* shall not wash three times it is not proper[3]. 9. Afarg said that when *one* shall[4] wash once it is proper, and about this once the opinion of Mê*d*yôk-mâh is the after statement, and the opinion of Afarg is the prior statement; *and* since in the life of man the first *thing* to be considered is about purity, not the indispensability of washing, and, further, the

---

the passages from the Avesta (see Vend. VIII, 49–62, IX, 118) which are supposed to drive away the fiend (comp. Ep. II, ii, 7).

[1] See Pahl. Vend. IX, 132, *b*.

[2] See Pahl. Vend. IX, 132, *j*, where, however, the statement as to three times washing is attributed to Afarg, who is the prior authority quoted (as mentioned in § 9), and that as to once washing is attributed to Mê*d*yôk-mâh, who is the after authority.

[3] Reading lâ khalelûnê*d*ŏ-ae lâ shâyedŏ instead of lâ khalelûnê*d*ŏ a-lâ shâye*d*ŏ.

[4] Reading aê instead of va a. This statement is attributed to Mê*d*yôk-mâh in Pahl. Vend. (see note 2, above).

pollution diminishes, about which it speaks in the religious cleansing, during so many times washing *as* is declared, then the consideration of it is a consideration about the one time which is the first computation[1]. 10. That which mentions more than once washing is a contradiction of the prior deponent, not a declaration; *and* the consideration of that operation, so long as *it is* declared, is about the statement of him who *has* mentioned once washing with the opinion of a prior deponent[2], owing to the same *reasons*. 11. But if it be even that much washing which is the merit of the operation, then the statement of Afarg about these times[3] is manifestly very preservative, *and* that of Mê*d*yôk-mâh is a necessity for declaration.

Chapter VII.

1. And *as to* that which is written[4], that 'in the teaching of Afarg *it* is thus declared, that "for every single person, at the least[5], one cup of water *and*

[1] In Vend. IX, 48–117 the washings of the several parts of the body are mentioned only once, which is 'the first computation' here mentioned.

[2] Reading pêsmâl, as equivalent to the pê*s*mâl or pê*s*îmal previously used; but the word can also be read pasîmal, 'after deponent,' which would be inconsistent with the context. The two terms are very liable to be confounded in writing Pahlavi, and in Ep. II, ii, 6 they are again written alike, though put in opposition to each other. The 'prior deponent' is Afarg.

[3] That is, 'about this one time,' as J has it.

[4] In the epistle to which he is replying.

[5] The words pavan kâmîstîh, both here and in §§ 5, 6, would be better translated 'as a desideratum, or desired quantity;' but in

one cup of bull's urine, which are well alike (vêh-mâl)[1], are requisite;" *and in* the same manner it is said in the teaching of Mê*d*yôk-mâh, that "the water and bull's urine, when it is possible, are all to be thoroughly consecrated; when not—and, at the lowest, one cup of water and one cup of bull's urine, which are well alike, for every single person—*they* are to be set down *in* that place and are afterwards to be mingled together[2]." 2. And since two teachings have so stated, are *we* to perform the operation more preservatively[3] and according to a more correct opinion than this?'

3. Also, 'a correct apportionment is not understood by us, and clear reasons *have* not come to *our* knowledge that a less measure of the thing is proper.' 4. But I well imagine (hû-minam) this is not the operation of the *purifying* cup (tâ*s*tîkŏ), where a less thing is not proper, because the information with which they have existed—owing to that information of theirs, of which a former high-priest and deliberator *was* the communicator—is that which *was* heard by me, that there are *some* who, for the sake of diminishing the measure *of* water *and* bull's urine, speak of this apportionment thus: 'Vî*k*ithr*ek*i*d*[4], in everything the operation

Pahl. Vend. IX, 132, *c* the phrase is pavan kamistîh, which can mean only 'at the minimum, or least.'

[1] In Pahl. Vend. IX, 132, *c*, where this statement occurs, the first letter of this word is omitted, which converts it into shumâr, 'alike.' Either word may be correct, but vêh-mâl occurs twice in this section.

[2] This statement of Mê*d*yôk-mâh seems no longer extant in the Pahlavi Vendidâ*d*.

[3] That is, in a way more delivering from pollution and sin.

[4] This word, which probably means 'in whatever is varied,' was

which accomplishes this, that is, when *there is* as much as is discernible from his body[1], is proper.' 5. And the saying is not perceived by me *as* a correct apportioning, because the judgment of the greatly-learned leader of those of the good religion, the glorified Yûdân-Yim[2], and of other deliberators, the opinion of good thinkers, was thus, that that saying is spoken about that of which the measure is not declared as the least by the high-priests' teaching of revelation. 6. Finally, when it is really of the same origin *and* suitable, then less than the least of that, of which the measure is declared as the least, is not proper, if, owing to much evidence in the teaching which has mentioned *it* as suitable, *it be* more of a blessing, and the operation performed thereby *be* more legitimate; because that teaching is for confessing that the statements of high-priests are most evidence of the practice.

7. This is that which is equally perpetual: it is very important *for* the purifiers to keep the intellect of life in operation, *and for* the good to become mentally a powerful giver of aid to them; and now, too, a purifier is ordered to keep in use his own most universal equal measure. 8. That which is perceived by me, and *has* come to my knowledge, more particularly when washed by myself, is the keeping in use an equal measure[3]. 9. And even if there be a purifier who does not completely keep in use the

evidently the beginning of an Avesta phrase whose Pahlavi translation concludes the sentence. The phrase does not appear to be extant elsewhere.

[1] That is, just sufficient to wet the body.

[2] His father (see Chap. III, 10).

[3] That is, the two liquids should be provided in equal quantities,

consecrated water and bull's urine, still then *it* is not worse than when it does not really arise *from* the same origin[1], and its religious rite also does not take place.

10. Also the words of both the solemnization of the Vendidâ*d* and the recitation of the Avesta are likewise to be uttered by him; because[2] 'Zaratûst enquired of Aûharmazd *about* it thus: "How *shall* I purify[3] where he does not attain unto the Airyemâ[4]—there are *some* who say *where* everything is anusô ('discontented')[5]? 11. How as to the fire, how as to the water, how as to the earth, how as to animals, how as to plants, how as to the righteous man, how as to the righteous woman, how as to the stars, how as to the moon, how as to the sun, how as to the endless light, how as to the independent light[6], how as to all the prosperity, created by

---

which differs from the present practice, as stated in the Persian Rivâyats; thus, M10, fol. 104 a, mentions $3\frac{1}{4}$ mans of water and $1\frac{1}{4}$ man of bull's urine as suitable quantities to be provided. This section is omitted in J, probably by mistake.

[1] Apparently deprecating the use of mingled liquids derived from various sources.

[2] The passage quoted here is from Pahl. Vend. XI, 1–5, with a few variations.

[3] Pahl. Vend. inserts 'as to the abode.'

[4] The Airyemâ (written Airyêmê in the MSS.) is Yas. LIII, which commences with the words 'â airyemâ ishyô,' and is the last of the Gâtha spells mentioned, in Vend. X, 22, as having to be recited four times in order to exorcise the fiend. The meaning of the question in the text, therefore, is: how is the purification to be effected when all the spells are not recited?

[5] Referring to Vend. IX, 161–163 (see Chap. IV, 3).

[6] This clause is omitted in Pahl. Vend., being merely a repetition of the preceding one, the Av. anaghra raokau being first translated by asarag rôshanŏîh, and then partially transliterated by

Aûharmazd[1], which is a manifestation of righteousness?" 12. And Aûharmazd spoke to him thus: "Thou shalt chant the purification *liturgy*, O Zaratûst!—that is, fully solemnize a Vendidâd *service*—then he becomes purified, *&c.*,"' as mentioned by me *above*[2]. 13. Where they do not make *them* solemnize a Vendidâd so that they keep in operation that which is written of it as a rite, this does not drive *pollution* from any *one;* and then, too, they should abandon the commands of a decree of leaders who are not over *them*[3].

14. Keep the Bareshnûm *ceremony*[4] in operation, so that the consecrated water and bull's urine are in the proportion *which* is taught by the high-priests of the religion, unless a scarcity occurs as regards these. 15. Then *together* with it, also, this is *to be observed*, that what is mentioned in two teachings is certainly more correct; afterwards, too, where a possibility for it is not obtained by them, *there* is *what* is mentioned as suitable by one teaching, and I do not decide *that it* is not an expediency.

16. And *as to* that, also, *which* is written concerning the three hundred pebbles[5] that, sprinkled

---

anagrag rôshanŏ. As sar means 'head, end' in Pahlavi (hardly ever 'beginning'), the only meaning common to the two terms asarag and anagrag seems to be 'without a head or superior, independent,' that is, in this case, independent of the light of other luminaries.

[1] K35 has 'righteousness, created by Aûharmazd,' but this is evidently a mistake, as 'righteousness' does not translate the original Av. vohû.

[2] That is, as to the fire, &c. mentioned in § 11.

[3] Referring to the heretical decree about which he is writing.

[4] See App. IV.

[5] See also Ep. II, iii, 12. The word generally used in these

in *ceremonial* ablution (pâ*d*yâ*v*ŏ), are cast into (va*l*) the bull's urine and water, that is taught even *in* the same manner; the *inward* prayer (vâ*g*ŏ)[1], even for when *one* does not cast *them*, is in the existing teaching, which is proper. 17. Then, too, on account of the cheapness[2] and harmlessness of the pebbles the purifiers are less curtailing as to them, *and* to drink the thing so is well-curative in performance. 18. In the existing teaching of imperfect purifiers it should be very advantageous to maintain it as easy; moreover, it is not said of it *that it* is not suitable, and in the teaching of Afarg it is said that it is proper.

Chapter VIII.

1. *As to* that which is written[3], that it is declared in the Sakâ*d*ûm *Nask*[4], that the consecrated bull's

---

epistles is sang, 'stone,' but Chap. IX, 6 has sagî*k*akŏ, and Pahl. Vend. IX, 132, *c* mentions sag*k*ak, 'a pebble,' as being cast into (dên) the consecrated water and bull's urine, without specifying any number. The practice appears not to be mentioned in the Persian Rivâyats, and seems now obsolete; the addition of a small quantity of the ashes of the sacred fire to the bull's urine, which is tasted at the beginning of the rite, is, however, mentioned in the Rivâyats.

[1] See Dd. LXXIX, 2. The prayer or grace has to be taken inwardly, that is, murmured, before the drinking mentioned in § 17. According to this text provision seems to have been made for not using the pebbles, by means of a special prayer.

[2] Or 'value,' as ar*g*ânîh means both.

[3] In the epistle to which he is replying.

[4] This was the eighteenth of the lost books of the Ma*zd*a-worshippers (see Sls. X, 25, note). It was one of the seven law books, and treated of many legal matters. Among the contents of its first thirty sections the following items are mentioned by the Dînka*rd*,

urine, when it becomes fetid, is to be stirred up (ba*r*â agâr*d*ŏînis*n*ŏ), *and* they should not carry *it* forth so to the fire, so that the stench extends to the fire; because, if that stench extends to the fire, on account of the moisture *and* through carrying bodily refuse (hîgar)[1] on and forth to the fire, it overwhelms it; that is taught *in* like manner lest, and owing to what is said, it then seemed to one that the bodily refuse and pollution of fetid bull's urine is on account of the stench. 2. But it is proper to observe it more fully mindfully, perfectly completely, *and* with better understanding, because that which is said by it, that the carrying of bodily refuse forth to the fire overwhelms *it*, is not on account of the pollution of the bull's urine, but the proportion of the sin through this; so that it becomes the origin of as much sin for him as that pollution of the bull's urine; but the stench, on account of moisture, is like *him* even who shall bring clean *and* purified water into the fire, *and* thereby becomes sinful[2].

---

and one of these passages probably contained the statement quoted in our text:—'On carrying forth the holy-water and also the pot (dîgŏ-*k*) to the fire, that is, *with* purified *and* thoroughly-washed hands; *and* the sin of carrying *them* forth with unpurified *and* imperfectly-washed hands. On preserving the pot and the other *things*, whose use is with the fire, from defilement with bodily refuse; when, through want of care, defilement occurs, *and* any one shall carry *it* unawares to the fire, he who is careless overwhelms *it* thereby. . . . On lawfully warming the bull's urine on the fire, *and* the sin when *it* is not *done* lawfully.'

[1] See Dd. XLVIII, 19, note.

[2] The argument is that the urine being a consecrated liquid, its corruption is not contaminating (provided it be not occasioned by foreign matter, as alluded to in § 7); but if the stench be sufficient to extinguish or injure the fire, it is as sinful to expose the fire to its influence as it would be to injure the fire with holy-water.

3. This, too, is a saying, that the proportion of the sin is mentioned not on account of the pollution of the bull's urine; it is said *to be* a counterpart even of that *which* is declared of the care of the *flesh of the* ass and pig, so that when they shall now carry unto the fire more than the proportion which is ordered, it overwhelms *it* through carrying bodily refuse forth to the fire, and even then that flesh, investigated as to purity, is mentioned as a supply for the season-festival[1].

4. The fetid bull's urine is itself likewise prepared, so that on this account it is ordered that *it* is to be stirred up, that so long as *it* is stirred up they *may* thereupon order the use of it; if then *it* is to be rendered quite useless, *there* is afterwards no necessity for stirring it. 5. The stirring is declared a purification as regards polluted *things*, where bodily refuse is only such that *it* is not endless, and so pure that it purifies even that of another.

6. When *it* is written of it itself, that *it* is thus declared in the Sakâ*d*ûm *Nask*, that consecrated bull's urine which is fetid is to be stirred up for the fire, *it* is afterwards declared that *it* is not speaking *only of* the bull's urine *which* is provided those three days[2]; but that, too, which is old *and* consecrated,

---

[1] So the damage to the fire is not occasioned by any impurity of the flesh of the ass or pig (which could be used for a sacred feast), but by the excessive quantity brought to it. The pig was formerly domesticated by the Parsis (see Sls. II, 58), but they have long since adopted the prejudices of the Hindus and Muhammadans as regards its uncleanness.

[2] Referring probably to the times of the three washings, subsequent to the chief ceremony, which take place after the third, sixth, and ninth nights, respectively, (see Vend. IX, 136, 140, 144.)

become fetid *and* is stirred again, when they keep it in use, is proper. 7. And that which the Sakâ*d*ûm *has* declared is, specially, that one of the high-priests *has* individually said: 'That stench is mentioned with reference to the *occasion* when a stench reaches it of a different kind *from that* which exists naturally in it.'

CHAPTER IX.

1. And *as to* that which is written[1], that '*the teachings of* Mê*d*yôk-mâh, Afarg, and Sôshâns[2] have all three come *and* remained, and, on that account, whoever *has* washed just as they always wash therein is certain that he is worthy.' 2. Also, 'should it have been as *it were* proper to them, would Mê*d*yôk-mâh have said that "not even the purifier is single?"' 3. *And* the rest as written on that subject, which, on account of its acute observation, *has* seemed *to be* from their statements; they, however, *have* not decided it so by the teaching which is in their names, as *was* indicated by me before[3].

4. But I do not so understand that 'if those should have been all the particulars of the peculiarity of all three teachings, would *the teachings* of Mê*d*yôk-mâh and Sôshâns have said, concerning any one who should have so washed that the purifier was single, that it is suitable, because the high-priests have been thus very unanimous that when

---

[1] In the epistle to which he is replying.

[2] See Chap. V, 1.

[3] See Chap. VI, 2-4.

there is one he is unsuitable[1]? 5. And when it should be to them as *it were* proper that, apart from the hands, the other[2] customary *parts* (pîsakŏ) *should be* washed once by them, would Afarg have said it is proper[3], because washing them three times is not mentioned in the Avesta? 6. And when it would have been as *it were* proper that the three hundred pebbles (sang) *should* not *be* cast *into* the water and bull's urine, *would* Afarg's *teaching have* said that it is proper[4], because there is not a single use for a pebble (sagî*k*akŏ)? 7. And when it would be as *it were* proper that *he who* is washed at the ablution seats (mak) at which any one *has been* washed *during* the length of a year, is not injured thereby—only they shall take them away *and they* are again deposited[5]—would Mê*d*yôk-mâh's *teaching* have said that it is proper, because, when the stones (sagŏ) are again deposited by one, *it* is to effect the cleansing (vistarisnŏ) of some one,

[1] The writer says he does not understand this argument of his correspondents, because it differs from the view he takes in Chap. VI, 2, but it must be confessed that the meaning of the passage in dispute (Pahl. Vend. IX, 132, *b*) is not very clear, as the word ashâye*d*, 'he is unsuitable,' can also be read ae shâye*d*, 'he would be suitable,' both there and in our text.

[2] K35 has one line blank here, but this was probably owing to the state of the paper, or some inadvertence of the copyist; as it is evident that none of the text is omitted.

[3] Compare Chap. VI, 9–11.

[4] Compare Chap. VII, 16–18.

[5] This shows that the places for ablution during the Bareshnûm ceremony were, a thousand years ago, the same as now, namely, stones deposited on the ground, not holes dug in the ground, as directed in Vend. IX, 13, 14, 16. They are, in fact, the stones or hard material directed to be deposited at the holes in Vend. IX, 29, 30, but they go by the old name for the holes (magh).

and when a *shower of* rain occurs thereon so *that* the whole place shall be thoroughly wetted, inside *and* outside, it is proper? 8. And if some one says that this is the case of a rite by a teaching of authority, and the rule is by a teaching of private authority, is not the whole rite by any teaching proper, that *consists* in this washing which is thoroughly preserved as they keep *it* in practice[1]?'

9. The reply is even this, that every rite (nîrông) is to be performed *in* such manner as *that* which is said *to be* most preservative, and most connected with the declaration of revelation *and* the testimony of the high-priests *concerning* it. 10. And not for the reason that Mê*d*yôk-mâh's *teaching* is more preservative[2] as to one rite, and after that something of Afarg is more preservative, is the operation to be performed by the statement of Mê*d*yôk-mâh; *but* whatever is the more preservative of Mê*d*yôk-mâh'*s* is collected from Mê*d*yôk-mâh, all the more preservative of Afarg from Afarg, *and* that which is the more preservative of *any* other high-priest from that which *has* the most preservative approval of the high-priest. 11. That which those high-priests *have* said, which they decide by just authority, is the commandment of the learned of the realm, which has lawfully arisen over the provinces (shôhârânŏ); but even that statement opposing it *which* is much testified *and* manifestly more of a deliverance, or which is declared *as* an exposition

[1] This string of arguments appears to be quoted from the epistle to which the writer is replying, but as they are separated from their context it is difficult to understand the exact line of argument, or to be sure that they are translated correctly.

[2] From pollution or sin.

of the teaching of high-priests of the religion in a dissimilar case, they shall then [1] wholly accept, and *they* are to perform the operation authorisedly *and* preservatively thereby.

12. This, too, I so consider, *that* even if each separate teaching should be as *it were* proper, it would then not be determined by them as to the impropriety of the *purifying* cup, for Mê*d*yôk-mâh *has* stated, only as *it was* apparent to him, that every single customary *part* is to be washed for three times [2], *and has* not specifically determined that when all shall be *so* once it is not proper. 13. By the special teaching of Mê*d*yôk-mâh and the washing which is in the law that says—concerning those interpreting revelation—that whoever becomes quite polluted shall thoroughly wash by that law, so that his *being* washed is to be considered as *being* washed, it (the rite) is not performed by me if, also, that other high-priest *has* said, that every one who becomes quite polluted, *and* washes not by the law of the primitive faith, is not to be considered as washed. 14. Then, too, in the special teaching of Mê*d*yôk-mâh *it* is not said, *of* that washing which is washed by the law of those of a portion of the religion (pârak-dînôân), that it is not proper.

15. He who washes by the law of those of the primitive faith, which many high-priests maintain as excellent, because it is suitable, *and* imagines that regarding the threefold washing it should be said that it is not proper, even he—when he also

[1] That is, when the dissimilar case arises, or when it is manifestly more efficient.

[2] See Chap. VI, 7.

has become of the same opinion as to this, that the statements of the high-priests are on an equality, and the most evidence of the high-priests is the *right* course—would have attained to confidence about this, that in a doubtful matter *there* should be a high-priest[1], and also that *of* which Afarg and Sôshâns *have* alike understood a similar thing is proper.

CHAPTER X.

1. And *as to* the many other *matters to* which an explicit reply is not written by me—be it the determinableness of it, be it the flow of *inward* prayer[2], be it the pouring of the water, and likewise the rest which is written *to* me—the statements, when deliberation and conjecture about such arrangements become needful, are not *to be made* unto the multitude, but *unto* the priestly at once[3]. 2. And this much, also, which is written by me is on this account[4], *that* when a writing has come to you which is the purport of my re-explanation, *and it has* seemed that it is written after *well*-weighed (sakhtakŏ) observations[5], even so they *would* cause *some* of those of good desires to understand, who are thoughtful friends of the soul *and* observers of

[1] To consult about the matters in doubt.

[2] Reading vâg-rêgisnŏîh; but J omits the first letter, and thereby converts the word into apardazisnîh, 'want of leisure.'

[3] J has merely 'the statements are when deliberation and conjecture become at once needful.'

[4] Reading hanâ râî, as in J; the other MSS. have hanâ lâ.

[5] Or, perhaps, 'strict observations' here, and 'strict observers' further on.

well-weighed *ideas*, in whose heart and mind, owing to that *other* writing[1], the existence of doubtfulness may fully remain; and, owing to that, this much re-explanation *has*, indeed, seemed to me good.

3. And then the desire[2] to sprinkle[3] in many modes is also an incorrect presentation[4], on which same subject there is this in consideration, that afterwards, peradventure, the same priestly man[5] by whom it is written *may* come—whose assured wisdom[6] may the angels make steadfast! *and* whom my approaching causing a purifier to travel for *various* quarters *has* occasioned to write it—so that while they are, therefore, awed by him, and shall provide more completely for use the full measure of water *and* bull's urine, the complete words of the Avesta, *and* other proper rites, they shall proceed more approvably. 4. And if *it be* even not auxiliary for the same purpose (âhanŏ) *that it was* written by him—except, indeed, through consideration of its details—no reason for a writing of that kind is to be assigned.

5. But if for the reason *it was* written by him *it be* manifest as an existence which is very little threatening, then I consider his opinion, which is in his decree, not so perplexing; and, till[7] now, the perplexing consideration *was* more particularly as

---

[1] To which he is replying.

[2] Reading adîn gâm, but this is doubtful.

[3] The Huz. verb zerîkûntanŏ, 'to sprinkle,' is not found in the glossaries, but is readily traceable to Chald. זְרַק.

[4] Reading arashnîkŏ-*k*ŏ-dahi*s*nîh.

[5] Meaning his brother, Zâ*d*-sparam.

[6] The usual Pahlavi phrase for the Av. âsnô khratu*s* or instinctive wisdom (see Dd. XL, 3).

[7] Assuming that val stands for va*l*.

to that, when, owing to the great learning thereof to be seen by me, this was not doubtful, that *as to* the great opinion of the world *about* the existing law of the profession of the priesthood, *and* the practice of all those of the good religion of the realm, they should make a decree only by the deliberation of me and other priestly men *and* religious observers[1]. 6. For if even he retorts a further statement[2] as to the appointed observance, *its* origin is then also a propagation from the diverse teachings of those great high-priests of those of the primitive faith, *who* were they *who* have been formerly great.

7. On account of the depth and much intricacy of the religion they mention many opinions *and* well-considered decrees *which were* likewise formed devoid of uniformity, *and* the utterance *of* the different opinions of the priests is with the reciters of the Nasks; but even among themselves the most supremely just high-priests were of a different opinion, different judgment, different teaching, different interpretation, and different practice only in the peace, mutual friendship, and affection which they had together. 8. Just as that even which *was* prominent about these chief priests (magôpatânŏ magôpatŏ), whose names *were* Âtûrŏ-Frôbag-vindâ*d* and Âtûrŏ-bûgê*d*, who have been, each separately, the high-priest of the realm of the true religion and the scholar of the age.

[1] Implying that the more learning there is manifest in an erroneous teaching, the more necessary it is to submit it to careful examination.

[2] Reading f*r*â*g*ŏ va*k* patŏ-yekavîmûnê*d*, and assuming that the last word stands for patŏ-îstê*d*.

9. To many, when an opinion is afterwards so obtained, *pertaining* to the high-priests *in* the spiritual *existence*[1], *it* is as is said about Zaratûst the Spîtamân, that 'the first time when the archangels are seen by him, the Spîtamân, *it* is then supposed by him that they are Aîndar, Sârû, Nâkisîyyâ, Tâûîrêv, *and* Zâîrîk[2], who are most mighty[3].' 10. From such as those the decree and its original perversity (bûn-gâstîkŏîh) and scanty preservativeness are so written *and* prepared, and afterwards, also, your opinion is that way irritated by the habit of good thinking—of which there is so much manifest[4] from those of the primitive faith and the high-priests—because even its words and those written with *it*, *and* the completeness of will *and* religion which is written, inclined the mind *away* from the teaching of the high-priests.

11. But as the same decree, *or* that which is resembling the same decree[5], is appointed (vakhtŏ)

---

[1] That is, such as have passed away.

[2] These are the last five of the arch-demons who are the special opponents of the archangels, being corruptions of the Avesta names Indra, Sauru, Naunghaithya, Tauru, and Zairika (see Bd. I, 27). The name of the first arch-demon, Akôman, is omitted here, probably by the mistake of some copyist, as six names are wanted to make up the number of the archangels exclusive of Aûharmazd himself.

[3] J continues as follows:—'"of the demons." 10. Written with the wretchedness (vakhârîh) and savageness of such as those, the oppressiveness and disaster of a decree of that description, and its original perversity,' &c. (as in the text).

[4] In the decree, which was so written as to appear to be directly derived from the teachings of the commentators, but, at the same time, so warped their statements as to lead astray. Hence, it might be compared to the conversion of an archangel into an archfiend through a mental hallucination, as mentioned in § 9.

[5] J omits these last eight words.

and specially decided, and is not to be accepted *from* him, and the operation is not to be performed thereby, its position is then to be considered, *by* those steadfast *in* the practice of the pre-eminent religion, with the most advanced understanding and discernment, which are the thought of its true station in the religion of the Mazda-worshippers. 12. And other religious decrees, intelligently preservative of the soul, which are made known *and* declared from the teaching of truthful high-priests of the religion of the Mazda-worshippers, are to be suitably accepted *and* fulfilled. 13. And since this opinion (dâstakŏ) of mine is, moreover, from the writing of Afarg, even about the preservation of different interpretations and different teachings, not specially owing to unobtainable statements of this shattered[1] religion of the Mazda-worshippers, nor even *to* distress through simultaneous strife, but owing to the desire of true opinions which *has* existed, there is safety abundantly, but temporarily, from the scribbling of the opposing, partial, and injurious writing of that priestly man[2].

Chapter XI.

1. For completion little is observed by me; and a man of my own, *in* a position of authority (sông gâh), comes with a second epistle[3] for that priestly man, opposing, disputing, showing the harm, making

[1] Reading hanâ giring, but it can also be read ân adarog, 'that undeceitful.'

[2] Zâd-sparam.

[3] Not Ep. II, but one which preceded it (see § 5, note).

aware of the deliverance[1], and applying for arrangement. 2. And the man who comes as a co-operator is announced by me, *and* the rite which is accomplished by him is *so* till further *notice*, which is for my further epistle[2]; because a double elucidation about that which it is necessary to arrange from afar is a custom more suitable for the discreet.

3. If *that* same priestly *man*[3] should have been in the vicinity, then interviews *with* me, with a few words, *would have been* more preservative than *trying* to convert that wretchedness (vakhâr) into that which is customary (pîsakŏ) even by further writing and much information. 4. And even now my prospect is a well-considering demand for explanation, so that, if the duties which are suitable for the discreet *be* really disposable for it, it is proper so to arrange what it is possible for me to complete *for* three months; *and* I *may* go myself into the presence of *that* same priestly *man* for the arrangement of the indispensable duties, and *may* diffuse this arrangement properly[4]. 5. *But* there are many reasons for private reflection (nâhî*d*ŏ) on account of which a descent from position is an evil resource; and *this* once a temporary epistle is written by me to him, and comes with this epistle[5]. 6. And Ya*zd*ân-

[1] From pollution, by means of the Bareshnûm ceremony.

[2] Probably referring to Ep. II, till the arrival of which (or that of Ep. III) they were to act as directed by the priest he sends with this epistle.

[3] His brother Zâ*d*-sparam.

[4] This intended visit to Sîrkân is also mentioned in Ep. II, v, 5; vi, 4, 6; vii, 3.

[5] Being apprehensive that personal interference might lead to altercations derogatory to his dignity, he prefers trying the effect of writing in the first place. The temporary epistle, here referred to,

pânak[1], a man who is instructed[2], shall come to him, *who* is friendly to custom (âînag-îyâr), *and* of like rank with his own man who is faithful; *and* I *will* write further *and* more controversially to him, and give the information advisedly with which I *shall* acquaint him, so that *it may be* more explanatory to him.

7. But if through this which is written by me, or *through* myself[3], he *should* come immediately (di-*g*andyî*s*) unto Pârs, I *shall* then be seeking an opportunity even for the retirement of him himself; I do not abominate *it* (madam lâ man*s*ôm) when it is necessary for them *and* private, as is better.

8. As to these other diffusions of arrangements which are pre-eminently the resources of that priestly *man*, and the acquaintance with revelation which is sought by him, for the sake of the advantage of the religion *they* should not be molested before[4].

9. May the arrangement and restoration and benediction of the revelation (dînô) of the Maz*d*a-worshipping religion reach a climax! *and* may the

---

could not have been Ep. II, as that was written after Ep. III, and was the further epistle promised in § 6.

[1] Or, perhaps, Yaz*d*ân-pahnak. This was a common Parsi name in former times, as it is found in two of the Pahlavi inscriptions in the Kanheri caves, dated A.D. 1009 (see Indian Antiquary, vol. ix, pp. 266, 267), and the very similar name, Yazd-panâh, occurs as the name of a Parsi convert to Christianity who was put to death about A.D. 541 (see Hoffmann's Auszüge aus syrischen Akten persischer Märtyrer, p. 87).

[2] Assuming that dinhâr*d*ŏ stands for zinhârî*d*ŏ.

[3] If I should come personally.

[4] Referring probably to further matters of complaint, which he did not think it advisable to notice seriously until the present controversy was settled.

eminence of you listeners[1] to the primeval religion consist in long-continued, supreme prosperity, through all happiness! then, through such thoughtful friends, the acquaintance *with* its difficult teaching and mighty words, which is to increase that gratitude of yours to me for my decisions, is made a blessing to you, if you observe therein a good idea which seems to you important, when it reaches your sight.

10. The correct writer *and* scribe is ordered that he do not alter *any* of[2] the words (mârîk), while he writes a fair copy of this epistle of mine, which is written by me to you, and he orders *some one* to give *it* to *that* same man, Yazdân-pânak, *along* with that epistle, so that it *may* come to him[3], for there are *times* when I seem aware that *it* is better *so*. 11. And may the angels increase *and* enlarge your many new *things* with full measure and complete exaltation! the pleasure, peace[4], righteousness, prosperity, commendation, *and* happiness *of* the powerful[5] who are all-controlling *and* happy-ending.

12. Mânûs*k*îhar, son of Yûdân-Yim, *has* written *it in* the day *and* month *of* Senda*r*ma*d*[6], in the

[1] Reading nyôkhshî*d*ârânŏ, as in J, instead of avakhshî*d*ârânŏ.

[2] Reading min, instead of mûn, 'who.'

[3] To Zâ*d*-sparam. This copy was that mentioned in Ep. II, vii, 1.

[4] Reading s*l*am, as in J; the other MSS. have shnuman, 'propitiation,' the two words being nearly alike in Pahlavi letters.

[5] Reading patûgânŏ; J has pa*d*vandânŏ, 'connections,' by inserting a stroke.

[6] The fifth day of the twelfth month of the Parsi year; and, as Ep. III (which was evidently written after further consideration) is dated in the third month of A.Y. 250, this must have been written in A.Y. 249. The date of this epistle, therefore, corresponds to the 15th March, 881.

enjoyment of righteousness, the glorification of the religion, trustfulness to the angels, and gratitude unto the creator Aûharmazd, the archangels, *and* all the angels of the spiritual *and* the angels of the worldly *existences*. 13. Praise to the month (mâh) of like kind which is exalted in its name with this.

EPISTLE II.

TO HIS BROTHER, ZÂ*D*-SPARAM.

Copy of an epistle of the priest Mânû*sk*îhar, son of Yûdân-Yim, which *was* prepared by him for the priest, *his* brother, Zâ*d*-sparam[1].

CHAPTER I.

1. *In* the name of the sacred beings who shall keep exalted the pre-eminent success of *your* priestly lordship, accomplishing *your* wishes in both worlds, I am longing for the children—formerly promoting health of body—and *for* activity, and fully desirous, and in every mode a thanksgiver unto the sacred beings, for the well-abiding *eye*sight, peace, *and* understanding of *your* priestly lordship.

2. The epistle that came *from* you in the month Â*v*ân[2], which Nîvshahpûhar[3] *was* ordered to write,

---

[1] See the heading to Ep. I.

[2] The eighth month of the Parsi year, which must have been A.Y. 249 (see Ep. I, xi, 12, note). This month corresponded to the interval between the 11th November and the 10th December, 880; but it is evident from Chaps. VII, 2, VIII, 1 that this reply was written about the same time as Ep. III, that is, in the interval between the 14th June and 13th July, 881.

[3] This appears to have been the original form of the name Nikhshahpûhar or Nîshahpûhar, applied both to a man (see Ep. I, iv, 15, 17) and to a city in Khurâsân, and in this place it is not quite

and . . . . by me from[1] . . . . and . . . . , would have been quite desirable to increase *my* gratitude unto the sacred beings *for* the health and salutation of *your* priestly lordship, though it had been *merely* to write intelligence of your own condition; for your writing of the epistle is not such as *that of* the distant who write in duplicate, but like *that of* neighbours who think that everything new should always be really mutual information. 3. *As to* that, too, which you ordered to write about omens *and* such occurrences—for which my form of words is not as is twice specified within the epistle, and from henceforth *one* should order to write intelligence more clearly—moreover, on account of want of leisure on many subjects, my heart is not disengaged even for the understanding of omens.

4. I apprize *your* priestly lordship that in this

certain whether a man or a city is alluded to. The text, as it stands in the MSS., is as follows:—'Nâmakŏ zîtanŏ dên bidanâ Â*v*ânŏ mûn Nîvshahpûhar nipi*s*tanŏ farmû*d*ŏ va ma*d*ŏ.' This can be translated as in our text, if the word va be omitted; but, if this word be retained and mûn be changed into min, the translation would be as follows:—'The epistle which *some one was* ordered by you to write in the month Â*v*ân from Nîvshahpûhar, and *which* came.' Now it is evident from Ep. I that Zâ*d*-sparam must have been in Sîrkân for some time previous to the date of that epistle, 15th March 881, and, therefore, probably in the previous November; but, at the same time, it must be noticed that there are allusions in this second epistle (see Chaps. I, 12, V, 3) to his having been formerly at Sarakhs and among the Tughazghuz, that is, in the extreme east of Khurâsân; it is, therefore, just possible that he may have been at Nîvshahpûhar, on his way to Sîrkân in the south, in November.

[1] J and BK attempt to fill up the blank with the words kêshvar ar*g*, 'the value of the realm;' but the original text probably stood thus:—'and *was received* by me from *so and so*,' the names having been torn off in some intermediate MS.

interval (tâhîkŏ)[1] a written *statement has* come unto me that the good *people* of Sîrkân are, indeed, so enveloped by you *in* distress, despondency, and trouble that its counterpart *was* when *there was* a liberation of *our* glorified fathers from the state of material existence. 5. For such as the insufficiency of the whole life of such *was* then to me, so even is the wounding and damage which comes *now* to *my* understanding and intellect. 6. The whole life of such is on the confines of the pure existence, a contest *with* the complete incorrectness that remains contaminating the liturgy by which the greatest intelligence of the religion of the Ma*zd*a-worshippers is aided; a little also, finally, of sagacity and observance of the apportionment of the more grievous impostures and more frightful delusions.

7. And, first of all, as to when your completely vile idea first destroyed your own enlightenment, and quite subdued your seconding of me, is inopportune (avidanâ) for me; and that ordinance[2], which though it be also right, is then even grandeur, because *it* is a law of the realm and an opinion of the world. 8. When even in the mansion of various thoughts, the residence of the assembly of Pârs, *and* many other conventions to deliberate, and the united opinions of a thousand priestly *men* (magavôg) of the good religion thereon, it could remain unaltered, then, also, the various good thoughts *and* opposing considerations that, *along* with me, the

[1] Since he heard from his correspondent. The word cannot be tîsgakŏ, 'nine *days*,' as that would not tally with the dates of Eps. I and III.

[2] Referring probably to the Bareshnûm ceremony which Zâ*d*-sparam wished to dispense with in many cases.

minds of other heads of the religion *have* promoted, *and* shaped *or* altered decisions thereon, *and* settled and issued orders thereon, could not have seen a grievance (seg) *therein*. 9. And this, too, should be observed among your requirements [1], that when the fattiness [2] of the body is in wrinkles (kîn), so that four perfect *ones* of the period are provided, even then the opinion of a high-priest of the religion is greater than every opinion, *but* the law of the realm of *various* kinds [3] is only through the deliberation of the same perfect *ones*; to make him decide then is not proper [4].

10. And it would be desirable for you to take account of that which is said thus: 'Thou shouldst not practise that, O Zaratûst! when thou and three or four companions, in the village of a thanksgiver of the assembly, shall say this: "Such is an evil notion."' 11. These words of his are then not taken into account by you; and *it* is firmly and *with* acute observation determined by you, and thought preservative for yourself, that even the sin be not privately (andarg) declared by me unto the assembly which *has* deliberated at Shirâz [5]. 12. You order this, and

[1] J omits this phrase.

[2] Reading mêsakh or miskhâ; but it may be masagîh, 'squeezing.'

[3] J has merely the words, 'even then the opinion of the high-priest *for* the realm,' which gives a reverse meaning to the text.

[4] It appears from this, that when a supreme high-priest became very old, his worldly duties were put in commission, by being intrusted to a committee of four of the most learned priests; but the opinion of the superannuated high-priest was still supreme in spiritual matters, though not to be trusted in worldly affairs.

[5] Whither Mânûskîhar had specially gone to hold this assembly before writing Ep. I (see Ep. I, iii, 13).

it is known that if it were a statement of yours in the assembly of the Tughazghuz[1], *you* would have been still less a speaker in private.

13. I consider that you are as much under-*hand* (aîr) about this, as regards yourself, as Zaratûst[2] the club-footed (apafrôbd) when he arranged his garments (vakhshakîhâ), and his club-foot is itself overspread thereby even to himself, so that *he was* then approved *as* good[3] by *some* of those of Kirmân[4] when they heard *of it*, and those of Râî[5] (Râzîkânŏ) wrote a reply that, if *he* should be appointed by you also at a distance, *he* would then be approved by them likewise *as* good. 14. This idea of yours is more heinous than that act of his, the reply from *various* sides is more mischievous, the disgrace among the people is more unslumberable, the load upon the soul is more consumingly heavy, and the

[1] The MSS. have Tughzghuz in Pâzand. Mas'âudî states (A.D. 943) that the *T*aghazghaz were a powerful Turkish tribe who dwelt between Khurâsân and China, in and around the town of Kû*s*ân, and not very far from the supposed sources of the Ganges. They had become Manicheans, having been converted from idolatry to the heretical form of Ma*zd*a-worship taught by Mazdak (see Mas'âudî, ed. Barbier de Meynard, vol. i, pp. 214, 288, 299, quoted at length in a note to Sls. VI, 7). It would seem from the allusion in our text that Zâ*d*-sparam had recently been among these *T*aghazghaz, and might have imbibed some of their heretical opinions, so as to lead to this controversy with his brother and the orthodox people of Sîrkân. That he had recently been in the extreme north-east of Khurâsân is further shown by the allusion to Sarakhs in Chap. V, 3.

[2] Evidently some recent pretender to the supreme high-priesthood, who had endeavoured to conceal the deformity that disqualified him for that office.

[3] That is, fit for the dignity he aspired to.

[4] Here written Gîrmân (see Dd. XCIV, 13).

[5] Near Teherân.

severance *from, and* contest *with*, Aûharmazd and Zaratûst become more incalculably perplexing. 15. And this, too, is my summing up (khapîr)[1]—when your own acquaintance with the religion and salvation of soul are *in* such force—by the parable (ângunî-aîtakŏ) of that physician of the body who, when they asked about destroying the toothache, thereupon gave his reply thus: 'Dig *it* out!' and they rejoined thus: 'He is always wanted *as* our physician, so that he may cure even a tooth which is diseased;' I *would* extract its teeth[2] more plentifully and *with* more suspicion than he.

16. And if, also, those of the good religion in the country of Irân be, therefore, always in want of the learning and acquaintance with religion of *his* priestly lordship, so that he disperses the profession and the preparation *and* management of the remedy[3] of many diseases, then he throws it away as a profession, *and* there is not much of a necessity for the wisdom *and* learning of *his* priestly lordship. 17. For *there* are *some* of the *present* time would never vouchsafe approval of a presiding fire[4], which is in many modes an advance of foreign habits; *and* of many *things* which are in writing, *of* a nature easier and more comfortable in a worldly *sense*, they offer and

[1] J converts the phrase into 'very heinous to me,' by reading avîr and adding girân.

[2] That is, he would drive the morbid ideas from his brother's mind.

[3] Meaning the practice of the Bareshnûm ceremony, for which the priests were specially required.

[4] Probably because they saw no necessity for the presence of the fire at the sacred ceremonies. He is warning his brother that his heretical teachings would soon make the people imagine that they could dispense with the priesthood altogether.

always give more than he who is a priest; and, *at* last, no one ever accepts *any* except him who is astute in evil *and* wicked[1].

Chapter II.

1. I *have* also examined that writing[2] in detail, and *it* is very unprepared for the remarks of the learned and those acquainted with the religion, for the sentences concocted *have* to be divided, and the slender demonstration is disconnected (aparvandî*d*ŏ); so I consider that *it* is not sent to be seen, as regards which such a course *would*, indeed, *be* a cause of terror to purifiers. 2. *It* is so written that, while on account of *that* same terror they are very much alarmed, and are thorough in maintaining the duty of the continuance of care for water and bull's urine[3], and *of* the formula of the operation, they shall more fully perform *it* as a duty provided for high-priests; even from that I am more fully of opinion that your like judgment and own concession *have* produced this explanation.

3. When I saw in the decree, such as that which you have written, that each time *one* comes unto a purifier who washes *in* such manner as is declared

---

[1] That is, some priest who teaches such heresies. These terms are those applied to the demons themselves in Pahl. Vend. XIX, 140, 141, 147.

[2] The decree of Zâ*d*-sparam, a copy of which had been sent to him by the people of Sîrkân (see Ep. I, iv, 7).

[3] The two liquids used in the purifying ceremony of the Bareshnûm (see App. IV).

in revelation—which is evident, indeed, from *his* existence when *he* is a religious purifier, *and* also from *your* priestly lordship's knowledge of the rite; indeed, there is no use of *that* same decree unless the scripture of revelation, likewise, be so—*he* is to do *it with* very strict observation, *now*, since, owing to the reception of terror by the purifiers, that preparation is evidently to produce, as regards their own disposition and movements, much harm *and* irregularity, *and* perplexed thoughts *among* the people, the discredit of the decreer is generated therefrom, and it would have been more reasonable to consider the terror and doubt of the purifiers in another way.

4. That which is so explained by you as though it would remain accomplished *and* would be in notice —and this is written by you like as it were from a teaching of *some* description—is not proper; because, thus, every rite in the performance of the desired operation, even by one *single* teaching, is suitable, *which*, like the preparation for the statements of lying litigants, is very like, *but* not correct. 5. For when there are *some* who *have* furthered Mê*d*yôk-mâh[1] better than the teaching of Afarg[1], *it* is well when every single rite in the teaching is right; and *as to* his rite *it* is not very clear that deliverance[2] is promoted by maintaining *it*. 6. Even on that *occasion* when Mê*d*yôk-mâh *has* mentioned threefold washing, *and* Afarg once washing[3], Mê*d*yôk-mâh is the after deponent and Afarg the prior

[1] See Ep. I, v, 1.

[2] From pollution.

[3] In Pahl. Vend. IX, 132, *j* (see App. IV), where the threefold washing is connected with the name of Afarg, and the once washing with that of Mê*d*yôk-mâh; but Ep. I, vi, 7–9 agrees with the statement here.

deponent[1]; and, on that account, the statement is to be made as long as Mê*d*yôk-mâh is preserved, *but* as regards the opinion of the words of Afarg *it* is to be maintained in a state of preservation.

7. *As to* that which Afarg *has* said[2], that 'two purifiers are requisite,' Mê*d*yôk-mâh *has* also said that one is plenty; *and*, since the teaching of Sôshâns[3] is similar evidence to his, as to that which is said by him, they have thus been more unanimous that when there is one it would be proper; *and* as several high-priests have announced just the same evidence, *and* Afarg himself *and* other priests have been of the same opinion where *it* is the performance of the beginning of the Vîkaya ('exorcism')[4], Mê*d*yôk-mâh is preserved. 8. Not on this account, that Afarg is more preservative[5] through once washing, is the operation to be performed according to the teaching of Afarg, but the once washing from Afarg who is the prior deponent, *and* the one purifier from Mê*d*yôk-mâh who is the most corroborated are to be accepted and to be conducted.

9. And even the computers of the stars would make the position of the stars which exists when that of the sun *and* moon is from the direction (min zîk) of *S*atvâharân[6], that of Saturn from the direc-

---

[1] The words pasîmal, 'after deponent,' and pêsmâl, 'prior deponent,' are here written alike (see Ep. I, vi, 10, note).

[2] In Pahl. Vend. IX, 132, *b* (see App. IV and compare Ep. I, vi, 1–4).

[3] See Ep. I, v, 1.

[4] See Ep. I, vi, 6.

[5] From pollution (see § 6).

[6] The high-priest of the Parsis in Bombay is of opinion that the names of the three 'directions' mentioned in this section are the Pahlavi forms of the names of three of the lunar mansions, whose

tion of Avênak, and that of Mars from the direction of Pa*d*ramgô*s*, a position *which* sends much good, *and* is said *to be* capable of undoubtedly (anârangak) bringing on maturity of strength. 10. That this is to be seen as an occurrence (*g*astŏ) is a conjunction (nazdakŏ) which is not possible[1], because, if the conjunction of *S*atvâharân *be* exact, yet, since Saturn *and* Mars are not at *their* conjunctions (min nazdak), its effect is not a good configuration (khûp tanû); if the conjunction of Avênak *be* exact, yet, since the sun, moon[2], *and* Mars are not at their conjunctions, its effect is not good; *and* if the conjunction of Pa*d*-ramgô*s* *be* exact, yet, since the sun, moon, and Saturn are not[3] at their conjunctions, the effect is

Pâzand appellations are given in Bd. II, 3; and he identifies *S*atvâharân with Kahtsar, Avênak with Avdem, and Pa*d*ramgô*s* with Padêvar. The reading of all these names is, however, very uncertain. *S*atvâharân is written *S*atâharân three times out of the five occurrences of the name, and the first syllable might easily be read Gaht=Kaht, so as to correspond with the Pâzand; on the other hand, the reading *S*at corresponds with *S*ata-bhisha*g* or *S*ata-târakâ, the Sanskrit name of the 25th lunar mansion, Kahtsar. As Pâz. Avdem seems to be merely Pahl. afdûm, 'last,' I prefer identifying Avênak (which can also be read Avê*r*ak) with the ninth lunar mansion, Avra (Avrak in Bd. VII, 1, A*v*rak in Zs. VI, 1), the Sans. Â*s*leshâ. Pa*d*ramgô*s* is also written Pa*d*ramgôs twice out of the three occurrences of the name; its identification with Padêvar makes it the first lunar mansion, the Sans. A*s*vinî. The aspect of the heavens, therefore, which is here mentioned as very auspicious, has the sun and new moon in the latter part of Aquarius, Saturn in the first part of Aries, and Mars in the latter part of Cancer, that is, twice as far from Saturn as the latter is from the sun and moon.

[1] That is, it very rarely happens; as rarely as the exact agreement of three different commentators, whom these three conjunctions are intended to represent.

[2] Reading mit*r*ô mâh, instead of Mê*dy*ôk-mâh.

[3] The MSS. omit lâ, 'not,' by mistake.

not good; on account of[1] which, in any conjunction which is not exact, they believe *it* possible *for* a firm mind also to accomplish this auspicious labour (sukh-var*z*i*s*nŏ), but they say the just and wise should make the decision[2]. 11. So that this one is a very good position, because that which is truly issuing (râst-ta*g*) through the conjunction of *S*atvâharân is from that mighty *S*atvâharân[3], *and* that of *S*atvâharân *being* better through the conjunction of Pa*d*ramgô*s*, that is done[4].

12. You *should* understand that of the same kind is the similitude of the three teachings, of which you *have* written, with this similitude which I *have* portrayed[5] *and* ordered to form *and* scheme, so that you *may* look at it more clearly, from a proper regard for your own deliverance[6], *for* the sharp

---

[1] Reading râî, as in J, instead of the lâ, 'not,' of K35 and BK.

[2] That is, the circumstances are too unpropitious for any one to come to a decision without consulting those who are better qualified to judge, as is also the case when commentators disagree.

[3] Reading min zak rabâ *S*atvâharân, but this is doubtful, because K35 has min rabâ âharân with zak *S*at written above min rabâ; BK has min zak *S*atŏ (or dâ*d*ŏ) rabâ âharân (or khârân), which is merely reading the same characters in a different order; while J omits most of the doubtful phrase, having merely min zak-î, which, with the alteration of râst-ta*g* into râsttar, changes the meaning into the following:—'because that which is through the conjunction of *S*atvâharân is more correct than that of *S*atvâharân, *and* that which is through the conjunction of Pa*d*-ramgo*s*, that is done.'

[4] Or 'that remains the effect.'

[5] Reading nî*s*ânînî*d*ŏ; K35 and BK omit the first letter so as to convert the word into dîhânînî*d*ŏ, which might mean 'presented.'

[6] From pollution. There is some temptation to use the word 'salvation' for bû*g*i*s*n, but this would introduce ideas that were, no doubt, foreign to the author's mind.

intellectuality of the re-explainers of *what is* not well-considered *in connection* with *its* purpose (âhankŏ), *and for* the accumulation *of opinions* that is steadfast in the law of the ancients *and* orders *you* to heed *it*. 13. For, owing to the miraculousness and pre-eminence of that[1], he who thinks to restore the good ideas of the ancients does not himself understand the knowledge in that wisdom of the ancients, *and* does not keep his own presumption (mînîh) lowly and teachable; much, too, which is through his own learning is declared *to be* out of it (the law), *and* how he orders *us* to understand *it* is *by* his own opinion[2].

Chapter III.

1. *It* is disquieting about this, too, which is declared in your writing[3], as regards *your* vehement desire and embarrassment (rûzdîh) for a new law, and *your* wish and longing for the establishment of the law of the apostles[4]; as also that which you *have* done about the gathering of the details of statements from the three teachings[5], *and* about

---

[1] The ancient law, as contained in the difficult language of the Avesta.

[2] That is, commentators are apt to attribute to the scriptures many opinions which really originate in themselves.

[3] The decree mentioned in Chap. II, 1.

[4] That is, the new law which the future apostles, Hûshê*d*ar, Hûshê*d*ar-mâh, and Sôshâns (see Dd. II, 10) are expected to bring, so as to restore the religion in preparation for the resurrection.

[5] Those of Mê*d*yôk-mâh, Afarg, and Sôshâns (see Ep. I, v, 1, 6).

causing the rapid bringing of the new law. 2. And on account of your embarrassment and wrong-*doing* (va*d*ag) they would give up the Frasnât*e*ê ('washing upwards[1]') and Upasnât*e*ê ('washing downwards'), to bring the fifteen *times* which are without ordinance (ba*r*â âînakŏ), that are after it[2], back to the fifteen which are a portion of the ordinance (âînakŏ vâî).

3. *As to* the three times, each of which times *one* runs a mile (hâsar) even until he obtains a purifier[3], since peradventure thy mile (parasang), too, *might* become more, all the good work is written purposely (a*g*-karîhâ) of three miles and more[4]. 4. And that, too, which the high-priests have so appointed, when *he has* striven in that manner for three persons[5], or that sin and retribution of his is apportioned unto them *and* brought to the balance (san*g*ag-âînî*d*ŏ), is because that commission and retribution of sin *might* now, peradventure, be

[1] These terms are quoted from Vend. VIII, 276, 279 (see App. V), and are thus explained in Pahlavi in Chap. IV, 2.

[2] Referring, apparently, to the second mention of the fifteen washings, in Pahl. Vend. VIII, 281, which does not occur in the Avesta text ('the ordinance'), but refers to its previous occurrence in § 279 of the Avesta. But, perhaps, the author means that they would confound the final washing appointed in Vend. VIII, 299 with the preliminary washing appointed in the previous § 279.

[3] See Vend. VIII, 280, 287, 291 (compare App. V and Ep. I, ii, 6, note).

[4] After the polluted person has thrice run a mile, he is to run further (see Vend. VIII, 294) to some inhabited spot; from which directions the author concludes that any excess of distance is immaterial. K35 and BK have 'four miles and more,' but this seems to be a copyist's blunder.

[5] To purify him, and, if they refuse, they each take a share of his sin (see Vend. VIII, 280–293).

allotted unto the priest[1]; for if *he were* impure (palistŏ) there *would* be no one whatever who would properly perform the purification as it is necessary.

5. Then it *has* become indispensable *for* you to perform the purification, for that operation—so suitable for the discreet where 'he who *has been* by the dead[2],' so that he has become polluted, and even 'the stars and moon and sun shine upon his life discontentedly'—is just as fit for the exalted when there is great 'propitiation of fire, water, earth, cattle, righteous males, and righteous women' thereby. 6. So great is *its* value *that* where there is no purification *of* the body *it* is not possible to purify the life *and* soul; *and* when there is a man in a realm who is able to perform it, that man is not justifiable except when he shall perform *it*.

7. Finally, when that pre-eminent operation is *being* accomplished, over which *there* is in revelation and the perfect information due to revelation that supreme[3] control which you are so disputing in the religion—which even through your trifling (khûr-*d*akŏ) in the name of authority is becoming a struggle (patkâr-yehevûn)—then, though it may not be possible for you to perform *it* yourself, it should thereupon be the duty of some one of your *disciples* to perform it in your sight, so that you *may* be aware of the rite, even apart from the great resources in *that* most learned (â*z*tûm) acquaintance

---

[1] Who is to purify him finally with the Bareshnûm ceremony.

[2] Referring to Vend. IX, 161–163, quoted at length in Ep. I, iv, 3.

[3] Reading mahîstô, but it can also be read Ma*zd*ayastô, 'Ma*zd*a-worshipping.'

with revelation which is associated with you[1]. 8. Also from that which is repeatedly written by you with understanding of the rite, as regards all three teachings[2], *it* is manifest those rites are mentioned even *as* those *which* are more maintained, *and* are not those which are unnecessary to perform. 9. You are a something therein that *tends* to preserve[3] a little *of* what it is not possible for thee to attain fully in any mode; when thou shalt obtain the operations of the voice[4], and the water and bull's urine, as well as the three men[5], or thou shalt give a man[6] to wash therein, the intellect of those controlling is then, indeed, not preservative therein.

10. It is proper also for you to consecrate the water *and* bull's urine by that ritual which is in all three teachings, to prepare your own ritualistic liquid *and* other *things* which are approved among you with mutual assistance, *and* to appoint a purifier who *has* performed fully acceptably *and* been wanted. 11. Then, to give *out* properly to the country that the purification is according to my order, I always

[1] That is, even when not performing the ceremony himself, his presence would be desirable, for the sake of securing due attention to all the details, with which his superior knowledge must make him better acquainted than his subordinates.

[2] See § 1.

[3] Reading bûkhtanŏ; the MSS. divide the word, so as to convert it into ba*r*â tanû, 'without a body.' The meaning is that by his presence he is, at all events, able to secure some efficiency in the ceremony, when he is compelled to intrust its performance to subordinates who are not fully competent.

[4] In the prayers and exorcisms.

[5] See § 4.

[6] That is, one thoroughly qualified (the priest mentioned in § 4) who requires no special supervision.

perform *it* more acceptably than that of other purifiers. 12. For the water *and* bull's urine are all consecrated by me, and the three hundred pebbles (sang[1]) are cast into them (aûbas) by me, just as it is directed; the operation is also directed by me in the three days[2] when it is performed, and all the customary *parts* are washed three times by me[3]; the ablution seats (makŏ) are also arranged by me anew for every single person, and the use of washed seats is not ordered by me therein[4]; every rite of the washing by the purifier is also so performed by me as all three teachings have mentioned as perfection. 13. You become the best of the district, as regards the minutiae (bârîkîdŏân) of the purification that is within your duty, so long as they excite the sight[5], *but* which are curtailed (kazd) by you in the way of washing disclosed to me[6], while, when it should be performed by you in this manner, your performance would be equally constantly extolled *and* your writing praised.

14. When, then, you write of it that they should always perform it just as now, the falsity therein is

---

[1] See Ep. I, vii, 16.

[2] The 'three washings' mentioned in Pahl. Vend. IX, 132, *o* (see App. IV); referring probably to those after the third, sixth, and ninth nights (see Vend. IX, 136, 140, 144), that is, on the fourth, seventh, and tenth days of the Bareshnûm ceremony. Most of this clause is omitted in J.

[3] As said to have been directed by Mê*d*yôk-mâh (see Chap. II, 6, Ep. I, vi, 7), though the extant Pahlavi Vendidâ*d* (IX, 132, *j*) attributes the order to Afarg.

[4] Compare Ep. I, ix, 7, Pahl. Vend. IX, 132, *q*, *s*.

[5] J has 'so long as they advance the purification as much as possible by a resemblance so approved.'

[6] In the heretical decree under consideration.

grievous (yagar), and I know none worse; for this washing and professional purification which *one* is to keep in operation—as is declared by revelation, the teaching of high-priests, and those of the primitive faith who are esteemable[1]—you withdraw (madam dârê*d*ŏ) from the midst *of us*. 15. That *which* you understand yourself is that unto Aûha*r*ma*zd* the confederate good creatures are as *it were* defiled, *and* in the eyes of the good *and* wise *they are* as *it were* propitiatory towards the mischievous Vâê[2]. 16. And your words about it are just as they say concerning a beggar[3], where a garment is given to him, thus: 'Wash the dirt (âlûg) on him thoroughly clean;' *and* that garment they shall take is put upon the fire *and* burnt; and he spoke thus: 'My dirt *was* a comfort.'

CHAPTER IV.

1. *It*[4] is both explained again *and* summarized *thus:*—If the decree be from a law of Zaratû*s*t, is it so decreed as he spoke it? and if they should never perform by that, do not bring the Avesta *and its* exposition into the midst *of it*. 2. For the fifteen times *of* which you *have* written, if from the revelation of Zaratû*s*t, are his mode of *washing* fifteen times upwards and fifteen times downwards[5], a rule

---

[1] That is, by the Avesta and Zand.

[2] Reading anâkŏ Vâê; he is the demon that carries off the soul (see Dd. XXX, 4). Even the best creatures are imperfect in the eyes of Aûha*r*ma*zd* and the righteous.

[3] Reading niyâ*z*kar, instead of the niyâ*z*ar of the MSS.

[4] His own line of argument.

[5] See Chap. III, 2.

which is fulfilled. 3. *It* is said, if *one's defilement be* owing to depositing any bodily refuse (higar-1), then nothing of this is ever necessary for him, for one reckoning (mar-1)[1] will smite that which he takes hold of with a finger and *it* is clean, or it will smite a golden yellow clean, or whatever[2] it shall smite is clean; but nothing *merely* clean is purified, unless a demon be clean[3].

4. And this, too, is very amazing to me, that when this is not taken into account by you, that when there should be, *and one* should obtain, no purifier[4] it would then be necessary for him to operate himself[5], how then is this knowledge obtained by you, on which information (âgahîh) *has* reached you, that the purifying of all the purifiers of the country of Irân is just as they should always perform *it*. 5. When, as I consider, there is then no complete acquaintance *with* the management of a house in you, its own master, in what manner then is your account of the gossip[6], *and your* information, about all the purifiers of the country of Irân

---

[1] That is, a single washing, which is sufficient for ordinary defilements unconnected with the dead.

[2] This is doubtful; the word seems to be *k*îkê in Pâzand, but, as the Av. î and û are much alike in Iranian MSS., it may be read *k*ûk-ê, and the phrase would then be 'or it will smite a penis clean.'

[3] That is, cleanliness can no more be considered purification than a demon, who is supposed to be an embodiment of impurity, can be considered clean.

[4] J has 'when there should be no purifier it would be necessary to beg the help of a chief of the religion, and when *one* should not obtain *that*.'

[5] As directed in Vend. VIII, 299 (see App. V).

[6] Reading va*k* sakhûn, but this is uncertain.

obtained? 6. If your *people* should abandon that *which is* most indispensable, and your account of the gossip, as regards that which the whole realm *has* done, *be* not according to the commands of religion and to sound wisdom; *and* if it has not come completely to your knowledge as the washing of the purifiers of the country of Irân—because, when you do not fix the number even of their footsteps[1], *it* is certain that *your* understanding of their disposition *and* virtuous practice is even less—then it was necessary for you to determine the reason that all the purifiers in the country of Irân always wash that way that is declared as improper, with whatever certainty *it be* uttered *or* written.

CHAPTER V.

1. If this which is said by you be a knowledge that is replete (a*v*kâr) with advantage, why was it then necessary for you to keep *it* as *it were* concealed[2] from me, when I thus consider that, if a knowledge should be rightly obtained by you, it should then have been needful for you to report unto me on the first rumour[3] from every *one* who is well-enlightened (hû-bâm)? 2. If this decree

---

[1] Referring probably either to the distance of the Bareshnûm place from pure objects, or to the distances between the holes or ablution seats, and from them to the furrows, mentioned in Vend. IX, 12, 14, 18, 22 (see App. IV).

[2] Reading nîhânŏ, as in J, but K35 and BK omit the first letter.

[3] Assuming that mayâg is a pseudo-Huzvâri*s* equivalent of â*v*âg (Pers. âvâ*j*; mayâ being the true Huzvâri*s* of â*v*, 'water.'

seemed so to you before, between when you have been in Pârs and this *time* when in Sîrkân, *it was* not well considered with those acquainted with the religion, the wise *and* the high-priests, *and* not even reported. 3. If not conceived by you before, then what learned acquaintance with the religion *was* acquired by you in Sarakhs[1] *and* Shirâz, about which you are enlightened? 4. And before it was to be well considered amid observation *and* meditation[2] what high-priest *was* obtained by you in Shirâz, who, when it was well considered with him, in completely securing himself, kept you *away* from deliberation to be decided with me *and* other priestly *men* and high-priests?

5. If not decided by you in Pârs on account of breaking *away* from me, that is *as* though you yourself understand that I *am* to keep, *in* my own person, not even in the rank of discipleship unto you, but in that which is like servitude; and my coming[3], which is on your account, is even an accumulation of harm *and* distrust (tars) which you *have* amassed for yourself by *having* written *and* acted, *and* has made *me* suffer sorrow (vî*d*varînî*d*ŏ) in my own person. 6. If it had been shown to me by you *that* it would be the preservation of the religion, it would then have incited me to accept *it* steadfastly. 7. If,

---

[1] A town in the extreme north-east of Khurâsân, between Nîshahpûhar and Marv, but nearer the latter city. When in this town Zâ*d*-sparam probably came in contact with the Tughazghuz mentioned in Chap. I, 12.

[2] J inserts the words 'by you, and through your good consideration *it was* more properly undeceiving, if done, then.'

[3] Referring to his intended visit to Sîrkân, mentioned in Chaps. VI, 4, 6, VII, 3, Ep. I, xi, 4.

for the sake of co-operation with me, a lawful decree had been even more privately propagated by you, and if the religious demonstration about it *were* conservative *and* correct, it would then have been less vexatious for you to explain *it* to me than to others who *have* less acquaintance with the decrees *and* declaration of revelation; *and* if a difference had arisen thereon, a correct reply would then have come to you more fully from me. 8. And if you conceive that it is not necessary to demonstrate *it* to me through the declaration in revelation, that deliverance which it is not necessary to announce is not to be so decreed, even in another place. 9. And, just as even in Pârs, if *it were* not decreed by you in Sîrkân on that account, when your conception *was* that they would not accept *it* from you, it was necessary for you to know that, because it *was* not possible for you to provide much interval for demonstration.

10. If *its* purport *be* now considered by you, when you are moving as to the writing from Shirâz[1]—which writes fully *of* your acquirement and interpretation of it, and *of* a mutilated deliverance[2]—the arrangements for iniquity on this subject are many. 11. And one of them is the erroneous writing[3] which is with me, for you conceive that they would accept from me your *view*, as *it were* swearing (sôkandîkŏ) that it does not go to the filth accumulated for[4]

[1] Referring probably to Ep. I, which appears to have been written from Shirâz after holding a general assembly (see Chap. I, 11, Ep. I, iii, 13); but this epistle, judging from the remark in the text, was probably written after Mânûs*k*îhar had left Shirâz, as was also Ep. III (see Chap. VIII, 1).

[2] From pollution. [3] See Chap. II, 1.

[4] Assuming that the Pâz. p*g*sâhu stands for paz sâkh-î; but,

Zaratûst, and does not contend with him; *and that* the opposition (hamêmalîh) does not strive *for* a new law, *and* does not increase the evil of the spirit *and* the world, since it labours *for* the hoard of the soul.

12. And, persistently concealed, that *was* done by thee, owing to which is the anguish of my life; for *it* is annoying when a wound of the soul is not actually realised by means of the decree; but if, too, it should be really avoidable, *it* is then even said *that* ignorance itself would be regenerative (navazû-*d*ârîhâ), since *it* is not dubious to me, unless a matured knowledge of creation and some of that even *of* the angels should be in sight[1]. 13. Also through their much talking, which is like Vîsaris[2], and much affliction, which is like the eradication of life, *there* is a perpetual demonstration then *in* every place of the country of Irân, where this information *about* its religion shall arrive, *that* they then consider thee as an apostate and an enemy of the religion.

14. And through this eager procedure of yours many troops in the provinces, who *have* to horse (aspînî*d*anŏ) themselves, *have* joined Âtûrŏ-pâ*d*[3];

as Av. *g* and *d* are much alike, it may be p*d*sâhu, which, when written in Pahlavi letters, can also be read pa*d* gêhân, 'protector of the world;' or p*d*sâhu may be merely a corruption of pa*d*-shâh=pâ*d*akhshah, 'sovereign.'

[1] Meaning that he should have preferred being ignorant of such a decree, unless it exhibited far more knowledge of the truth than it actually did.

[2] So written here in Pâzand; but, no doubt, the demon Vîzaresha (the Vîzarâsh of Dd. XXXII, 4, XXXVII, 44), who carries off the souls of the wicked, is meant.

[3] The name, apparently, of some rival of his in authority, who is also mentioned in Chap. IX, 11.

for, inasmuch as those most mounted on horses[1] are the washers[2] *of* Sîrkân, who would have always thought about their abundance which is due to the archangels, they have spoken with opponents about this interpretation of the section *of scripture* (vîdak)[3], *and* so become similarly testifying[4], thus: 'We do not conceive it is necessary to demand thy reason *for* this most grievous disaster[5], a thing which is more complete through your elucidation of doubt and the power of the enemy, owing to this way which is appointed by thee.' 15. And on that account, too, *it* is more disquieting unto me, when I am aware both of the origin *of* this perplexity *and* the surpassing contamination which is possible to arise from it.

16. And you always so observe as not to leap (lâ aîyyûkhtanŏ) without looking before; but temporary observation is nothing really of that *which*, by a well-stinging similitude, is what *one* observes, with the eyesight looking well forward, *when* dust of many kinds is domesticated with the sight of the

[1] Reading asp-vârakântûm, and this meaning tallies well with the previous mention of troops horsing themselves; but J, by prefixing a stroke, changes the word into vâspôharakântûm, 'those most *renowned* among the spheres.'

[2] The ceremonial washers or priests.

[3] The term vîdak is applied to sections or chapters of the Avesta in Dd. XLVII, 1, 5, 6, LXVI, 4; and here it must be applied to the Avesta of Vend. VIII or IX, to which the misinterpretations of Zâ*d*-sparam specially referred.

[4] J has '*and* so given similar testimony, which is written by them of a priest of your fame, and written by them to me.'

[5] The diminution of their means of livelihood by the decrease of ceremonial washing, more than their apprehension of the sinfulness of such decrease.

eye; and if his intellect be not judicious he is wonderfully deceived by it; and *should* it be even when he mentions the existence of two moons, *has it* become more proved thereby? 17. *It is* a custom of the most provoking in itself, and presented disquietingly when I, who believe with a fervent mind, *would have* delivered the life even of *my* body over to the perplexing bridge[1] for your happiness *and* enjoyment. 18. Also, on account of my want of leisure, even the information which is presented, asking peace, is information I believe with a generous mind; and *being* aware regarding my want of leisure is both an advantage and harmful, and the heart to write of them[2] is, therefore, miraculous. 19. Then it is always necessary for me, who *am* in want of leisure, to write unto you so much writing of the harassing of annoyers *and* against disputes, of whose end there is no conception in my heart.

CHAPTER VI.

1. When at *any* time I write more pleasantly, this directs *you* to understand that still with the steadfast are my affection and natural lowly-mindedness; afterwards, too, that which *happens* when you have kept me wide away from the way of brotherhood, and higher even than a father, master, leader, ruler, *or* high-priest, is due to the fame and happiness of

[1] The *K*invad bridge, or passage to heaven (see Dd. XX, 3); meaning that he would have been ready to lose his life for the sake of his brother.

[2] The heart to write of the 'happiness and enjoyment' of § 17.

my body *and* life, not *to* affection of character, but the position of religion *and* the command of the sacred beings. 2. On that account, when you have seen the pure religiousness, the learned knowledge, *and* the repose-promoting truth of the invisible (avênâpîh) *of* which my[1] heart is leaping with evidence, so that you are steadfast even unto the nôi*d* asta-*k*a ('not though the body') *of* which Zaratû*s*t the Spîtamân spoke[2]—and, because, turned by me to the religion which is thy passport (parvânakŏ) to the best existence, you have understood *that* it is the organizer of the greatest protection, *even* that is supposed by me—I undergo all the terror of the period in hope of the supreme recompense.

3. And the position that that religion *has* given, which on that account is mine, you have that way considered as supremacy[3]; and if, sent from you or another person, the opposition of *one of* the same religion is seen *to be* the dispersion and disruption of the appointed profession, I act against the continuance of the opposition, and as steadfastly as the series (zarah) of submissiveness and gratification of *your* priestly lordship *has* done to me. 4. And this *will* be undoubtedly realised by you, that if you do not turn away from this decree which is not preservative, but, *being* appointed, I reach out from

[1] The MS. J ends at this point, but the continuation of the text, as far as the word 'important' in Chap. IX, 7, is interpolated in Dd. XXXVII, 33 in the same MS.

[2] In Vend. XIX, 26, 'not though the body, not though the life, not though the consciousness should part asunder,' would he curse the good, Ma*zd*a-worshipping religion.

[3] He now proceeds from persuasion to an assertion of his authority, accompanied by threats.

the country of Irân[1], then I *shall* become its greatest attacker of you. 5. And so I consider that from my opposition it is possible *for* more harm to happen unto you than from many accusers who are like the leader of those of the good religion, the many who are as *it were* of like fame with me.

6. And also from my departure, and the non-existence *of one* that is a friend of yours, who, like me, is less able to be for your harm than he who is *one* of the many accusers of whom it is I who am the restrainer, you know this, that my coming is on account of the affection of some and the reverence of others. 7. From the exercise of religion I do not at all fall *away*, and for the sake of the position of the religion I am maintaining opposition[2] to any one; even when he is a friend *who* is loved by me, I am then his antagonist. 8. Fate (zîkŏ)[3] is the great truth of the vacant, the form (andâm)[4] which *has* procured the light of life.

Chapter VII.

1. A well-reflecting *person*, moreover, is able to understand that which is written by me, in private, in writing unto the good *people* of Sîrkân, as perhaps a legitimate copy[5] of a writing of that kind from

[1] Referring to his intended visit to Sîrkân (see Chaps. V, 5, VII, 3, Ep. I, xi, 4).

[2] J has 'I am an opposition.'

[3] Or 'living.'

[4] Or 'the time (hangâm).'

[5] The MSS. have pînŏ, instead of pa*k*înŏ. This copy of Ep. I is mentioned in Ep. I, xi, 10.

me *may be* near you; and it was like the production of some one for the tearing and rending of his own limbs, and for the purpose of bringing on that remedy—the burning, torturing medicine that is religious[1]—whose purpose is to remain *away* from the steadfast while *abiding* by the commands of religion. 2. This *same* epistle[2], which *was* one of very great incompleteness, and one as *it were* thinking very severely, *was* similar to the decision (azad[3]) *to* which I *have* come on the same subject, *which is* written *of* below and again; and accompanying this epistle *was* a man of my own with a further epistle[4]. 3. I am discharging (vi*g*ârakŏ) my own *duty* as regards it[5], where I so arrange affairs of every kind which *it* is possible for me to complete *for* a *period* of three months[6], *and* come myself to *where* you are, and that mastery (*k*îrîh) which is prepared is again arranged when it is wanted by them[7].

4. You *have* already become a reserver (khamosî*d*âr) and rapid preparer of the adaptation of words in which cogency *exists*, and *have* clearly explained

---

[1] Probably meaning 'remorse.' [2] Ep. I.

[3] Chald. אזּד, referring to his general mandate (Ep. III) mentioned again in Chap. VIII, 1.

[4] The temporary epistle to Zâ*d*-sparam (mentioned in Ep. I, xi, 1, 5), of which no copy has been preserved.

[5] J begins as follows:—'And I *will* come later on and more combatively, when it is requisite *for* the sacred beings (or for them); I am also myself in possession of an opportunity as regards it.'

[6] This period for his visit to Sîrkân is also mentioned in Ep. I, xi, 4.

[7] Or '*by* the sacred beings;' the words yaz*d*ân and *s*ân being written alike.

as much as is in sight about the reason of altering that decree, concerning which your opinion is written with great judiciousness. 5. But *as to* the understanding which prompted you to write properly, and not to alter the rites *and* purifications of the Avesta, and about the duty of purifying the purifiers [1], such as *has* entered into the practice of the good, the propriety is declared in the teaching of the high-priests; *and* to do *it* better, so far as is possible, is to strive forwards in goodness.

6. Also, as regards changing the law of the fifteen times *washing* [2], just as *it is* for Irân *in* which purifiers are to be found, it is ordered for *places* to be found without purifiers; *and it is* in the countries of Irân that the order is given regarding purifiers not thus appointed for the work.

Chapter VIII.

1. To arrange again for approval the other *matters*, *of* which a portion is written *about* by you, an epistle [3] is again prepared in advance for Sîrkân, Shirâz, *and* other *places*, so as thus to make your decree a writing of bygone offence. 2. Because, if your despatch (firîst) prepared this new proceeding, and you do not turn away *from* it, *and* do not recede through opposition *and* accumulation of vexation, *and* these others, too, like thee, shall

[1] J has 'and not to alter the purification *in* the rites of the Avesta.'

[2] See Chaps. III, 2, IX, 2, Ep. I, ii, 6, note.

[3] Ep. III, also mentioned as a 'decision' in Chap. VII, 2.

not now abandon routine of that kind, then *your* children, your own precious *ones* who are beloved—*of* whom I know that you make them love *you*, and do not, moreover, diminish in *your* protection *of them*—shall be your accusers; *and* they shall abandon confidence *in* me as refuge and guardian, *and* in the sacred beings, through want of advice *and* want of guardianship. 3. The fires of the sacred fires whose manager is a guard *and* protection such as I, lest they *should* not obtain such an officiating priest (zôtŏ), *will have* in defence and guardianship of themselves to make back to *their* Shirâ*z* abode. 4. And *I* myself *shall have* to retire (agvira*z*î*d*anŏ) from the countries of Irân, *and* to wander forth to far distant realms where I *shall* not hear a rumour about your evil deeds. 5. In *my* occupation, moreover, my fortune (*s*ukûn) *may be* to wander forth by water even to China, or by land even to Arûm[1]; but *to be* carried off by Vâê[2], that uplifter, is much more my desire than when I am there where, owing to you, I hear that, as regards the glorifying of the sacred beings, which, because of my reply obtained above, *would* then *be* as much as death to me; *it would* also be the ending of that internal strife, *so* distasteful (aparvârakŏ) to me, which is like *his* who *has* to struggle with his own life.

---

[1] The eastern empire of the Romans, that is, Asia Minor and the neighbouring regions.

[2] The bad Vâê, who carries off the soul (see Dd. XXX, 4).

CHAPTER IX.

1. This, too, this aged *one* (aûzvâr*d*ŏ[1]) orders, that, *as to* the polluted of the countries of Irân, when they do not obtain another washer, their way is then through thoroughly washing *themselves*[2]. 2. For you who are understanding the rite and capable of washing, *and* are the most forward and intelligent of the religious, so long as your previous washing is a way of no assistance, *there* is *this* tediously-worded epistle; moreover, all their sin you assign for your own affliction[3], whose after-course is thus for their Pa*nk*adasa ('fifteen*fold*') washing[4], *at* the time they shall abandon, *as* distasteful, that sin which is a new development by way of Upasnât*e*ê ('washing downwards')[4]; and the sinfulness is his who established that law for them.

3. And yours are truly creatures of a fetid pool (gand-â*v*ŏ), who, as regards my motive, always speak about it just as they spoke thus to a priest[5]: 'Why *has* the savoury meat-offering not become forgotten by thee, *while* the firewood and incense, because it is not possible to eat *them* up, are quite

---

[1] From this it appears clearly that Mânûs*k*îhar was an aged man when these epistles were written, though not too old to travel. The previous allusion to old age, however, in Chap. I, 9, may not have referred to himself.

[2] As provided in Vend. VIII, 299 (see App. V).

[3] J omits alag, 'affliction;' and in K35 it is doubtful whether it be struck out, or not.

[4] See Chap. III, 2 for both these terms.

[5] Implying that the laity were inclined to attribute his own strict enforcement of ceremonies, requiring the employment of the priesthood, to interested motives.

forgotten?' 4. Also, *as* a similitude of your affairs, they are saying that *it is* as though the stipend of guardianship *were* always to be demanded just *in accordance* with omissions *of duty* (avâg mânî-*d*îhâ)[1]. 5. So that even while the trifle of trifles which exists *as* an interval from the title of leadership unto *that of* high-priestship—in which, except a title that is no joy of the strictly religious, there is nothing whatever—is, that way, to prepare a source of dispute as to the work which you do for the guardianship, it should, therefore, be a sufficiency (khvâr-bâr), where your own supreme work is purification itself; and to do either *what* is taught, or is advantageous, would be withdrawing from the country a demand which *has* caused disturbance (balûbâkînî*d*ŏ); to subdue *it* thou shouldst always so decide the daily allowances[2].

6. And, to-day, I *have*, on that account, written everything sternly, because that which another person arranges and speaks so opposed *to me* in evil appearance—which is little fit *to be* prepared—when I write seasonably, and with friendly and brotherly exaltation, you direct and persevere more expressly in preparing, so that portion upon portion is thus brought forth. 7. In good old age[3] the great law of after-restoration is a harsh remedy, and, on that

[1] That is, the laity attributed his brother's laxity, on the other hand, to sheer neglect of duty, and had, therefore, begun to consider his supervision hardly worth paying for.

[2] Meaning that by adherence to long-established custom, as regards both priestly work and priestly allowances, the laity would be better satisfied and more easily managed.

[3] Reading hû-kahôbanîh; J has merely kahôbanîh, 'old age, antiquity.' He appears to be referring rather to the antiquity of the Avesta law, than to his own old age.

supposition, where *a rule* is shown to descend from their three teachings[1], *and* is itself regarded as true, *and* the wisdom of the period *as* impotent (anôzô-harîkŏ), you yourself fully imagine (hû-minê*d*ŏ)[2] that *further restoration* is not an important[3] and foremost thing. 8. Those of different faiths of various kinds *have* many usages and perplexing kinds of doubt, even about the accomplishment *and* explanation of the statements of the high-priests[4], for *on* this subject, about old age (gûnânîh), *and* even about sprinkling and about yourself accomplishing the religious *rites*, you are wisely *for* a preservation of the equally wise experience of the profession; *and as to* the heterodox, that writing which realised that even now memory is opposing you is itself evil-wishing[5], and you know *it* is your own arrangement.

9. This, too, they[6] say that, if *it be* on that account that the purifiers shall not always so perform the purification by all three teachings, or every rite which is proper according to one teaching, it will be necessary *that* the purifiers shall abandon purification. 10. Then about old age, the performance of the ceremonial[7], *and* the many times of this which

---

[1] See Chap. III, 1, Ep. I, v, 1, 6.

[2] J has khavîtûnê*d*, 'you know.' He deprecates all further investigation into the meaning of the scriptures, which had already been explained by three old commentators, as he doubted the religious wisdom of the age in which he lived.

[3] The continuation of the text in J ends at this point.

[4] The commentators.

[5] That is, the decree of Zâ*d*-sparam, though itself objectionable, was opposed to the heterodox who wished for further innovations.

[6] The heterodox.

[7] Referring perhaps to the performance of the Vendidâ*d* service

are mentioned as *though* this *were* proper, *it* is stated as regards how it is proper that, when on account of those of the good religion they always proceed just as is mentioned in the Zand teaching of the Avesta[1], it will then be necessary *that* they shall abandon the religion. 11. And many other sayings of things like unto these are scattered about (zerkhûnî-aîtŏ), and are named near Âtûrŏ-pâd[2] *as* hints from you; for this reason they are reckoned (khaprag-aîtŏ) in the thoughts of men.

12. And this much is written by me in distressing haste; I consider *it* complete, and *may* peace and every happiness perpetually become hospitably attainable *and* accomplishable for you thereby, through the severe anguish *and* discomfort, *and* the eternal distress and despondency *of* the healer of affliction, Mânûskîhar, son of Yûdân-Yim, director of the profession of priests of Pârs and Kirmân[3].

13. Written in propitiation, praise, and benediction of the creator Aûharmazd and the archangels, all the angels of the spiritual and the angels of the worldly *existences*, *and* every guardian spirit of the righteous. 14. Homage to the exalted pontiff (radŏ) *sent* from the creator Aûharmazd, the most heavenly of the heavenly, Zaratûst the Spîtamân. 15. The

---

(which includes the Yasna ceremonial) as directed in Pahl. Vend. IX, 132, *b*, *o* (see App. IV).

[1] It is possible also to read 'in the teaching of the Avesta *and* Zand;' but this would ignore the fact that the 'teaching' is the Zand itself.

[2] The same rival as is mentioned in Chap. V, 14.

[3] According to Dd. XLV, 5 the farmâdâr or 'director' of the profession of priests of Pârs was the pêsûpâî or 'leader' of the religion.

most prayerful *and* gainful of things is righteousness; great and good and perfect is Zaratûst; *and* one *only* is the way of righteousness, all the others are no ways[1].

[1] Compare Dd. XCIV, 14, Ep. III, 23.

EPISTLE III.

TO ALL OF THE GOOD RELIGION IN IRÂN.

In the name of the sacred beings.

A copy of the notification (vishâ*d*akŏ) of *his* priestly lordship Mânû*sk*îhar, son of Yûdân-Yim, regarding the grievous sinfulness of *assuming* the propriety of washing for fifteen times.

In the name of the sacred beings.

1. It *has* come unto the ears (va*s*ammûni*s*nŏ) of me, Mânû*sk*îhar, son of Yûdân-Yim, pontiff (ra*d*) of Pârs *and* Kirmân[1], that, in some quarters of the country of Irân, they whose chance happens *to be* so much[2] pollution, such as is decreed unto so much washing of the customary *parts* (pî*s*akŏ), always wash *themselves* fifteen times with bull's urine and once with water, consider themselves as clean[3], and go to water, fire, and *ceremonial* ablution, the ablution

---

[1] See Dd. XCIV, 13.

[2] Reading hâvan; but it may be 'pollution of the spiritual life (ahvô),' though this is hardly possible in the next phrase, where the same word occurs.

[3] By confounding the preliminary washing appointed in Vend. VIII, 279 with the final washing appointed in Vend. VIII, 299 (see App. V, and compare Ep. II, iii, 2, ix, 2).

of the sacred twigs. 2. Such—although[1] they say that Zâ*d*-sparam[2], son of Yûdân-Yim, *has* ordered, *and* the high-priests *have* appointed, washing of this kind—*has* appeared to my well-reflecting (hû-min) opinion, apprehension, and appreciation very marvellous *and* grave, and *merely* a rumour. 3. And *it* is needful for me to keep those of the good religion in *all* quarters of the country of Irân informed concerning the placing reliance upon their washing with the Bareshnûm *ceremony*[3], *and* to make my own opinion clear also as regards the writings collected.

4. And, first of all, about the indispensability of the Bareshnûm *ceremony* I write several such copies of a well-matured writing of mine[4] as may even be new light to the intelligent. 5. That my opinion of the information provided by revelation, the decisions *of* high-priests, *and* the teachings *of* those of the primitive faith is thus, that washing by the polluted with water is pollution for the life and spiritual life (ahvô)[5]; they render the material *body* clean thereby, *but* that which is known as the handiwork[6] of the immortals, and is also professionally called the Bareshnûm, when *there is* the protection of a ritual of *various* kinds, shall make the body clean from endless worldly attacks.

6. It is in the nine ablution seats (magakŏ)[7] and the furrow[8], even with prayer, bull's urine, water,

[1] Reading amat, instead of the very similar word hamâî, 'ever.'

[2] See the headings to Eps. I, II. [3] See App. IV.

[4] Meaning this epistle.

[5] Because it pollutes pure water, which is considered a sin.

[6] Reading yadman; but it may be gadman, 'glory,' which is written in precisely the same manner.

[7] See Ep. I, ix, 7.

[8] See Vend. IX, 21–28 (App. IV)

and other appliances, and the ritual which is such as is declared in the teaching of revelation; and even now the purifiers, who are just as written *about* below, keep *it* in use. 7. When there is a washing they wash just as in the well-teaching statements which are known as *those* of Mê*d*yôk-mâh, of Afarg, and of Sôshâns[1], or *in* the statement of one of those three teachings, or in the statement of one of the high-priests *by* whom those three teachings are declared as propriety, or has come unto me as the practice of those same three teachings *by* those of the primitive faith.

8. I deem *this* deliverance[2] one wholly approvable, and the washer *in* a washing of that kind, with the Bareshnûm *ceremony*—which is lawfully *of* that description—I consider as a purifier who is approvable. 9. And the polluted of every description, as *above* written, who *have* obtained, for any indispensable reason whatever, a purifier, as *above* written, whom even now various districts *and* various places have appointed *and* approved, are able to wash with the Bareshnûm ceremony as *above* written. 10. Then their washing fifteen times is no deliverance in any way, and to wash them quickly with the Bareshnûm *ceremony* as *above* written is indispensable.

11. Owing to a washing of the same kind through the Bareshnûm *ceremony*, as is intended, water, fire, and other *things*, not to provide care for which is un[3] . . . . authorisedly is grievously sinful.

---

[1] See Ep. I, v, 1.

[2] From pollution.

[3] At this point there is a blank page in K35, and also in the MS. belonging to Mr. Tehmuras Dinshawji, which is supposed to be older; and one line is left blank in BK. It is not, however,

12. When, on account of a cleansing through another washing, distinct from the Bareshnûm ceremony,

---

quite certain that any text is really missing, as this section can be read continuously and translated as follows, without much difficulty:—'*Apart* from a washing of the same kind through the Bareshnûm *ceremony*, as is intended, *there* would be a grievous sin *against* water, fire, and other *things*, not to provide care for which would be unauthorised.'

If some folios of text are missing, as seems quite possible from the terms applied to this epistle in § 4, the question arises whether a portion of the missing text may be contained in the following fragment on the subject of the Bareshnûm, which is appended to the passage (Ep. II, vi, 2–ix, 7) interpolated in Dd. XXXVII, 33 in the MS. J:—

'As it is declared in revelation that, if a man who *has* chanted comes upon a corpse, *whether* a dog, or a fox, or a wolf, or a male, or a female, or any *creature* on whose corpse it is possible *that* he *may* come, that good man becomes so that a man *may* become defiled by him, *and* it is necessary to wash the polluted *one*, so that it *may* not make him a sinner. In order that they *may* act *so* to the polluted *one* it is necessary to wash *him*, it is necessary to perform that Bareshnûm *ceremony* of the nine nights. If the man that is spoken of *has* worked about carrying the dead and contact with dead matter (nôsâ hamâlîh), so that they know about his defilement to whom he comes, then he *who has* done this work *in* contact with dead matter becomes afterwards disabled *for* that worship of the sacred beings which they perform. So, also, *some one* says (compare Vend. VIII, 271–299), where in a wilderness (vyâvân) are several priests (âsrûvô) *and* a man lies *on* the road, there he *who* carries the dead *body* of the man who passes away—as those others remain *and* stand away helpless, without offerings of *inward* prayer (vâgŏ vakhtagân) over that person (kerpô) according to the religious way—*having* washed his body, comes into the town and performs the nine nights' Bareshnûm *ceremony* twice; afterwards, his Gêtô-kharî*d* *ceremonies* (see Dd. LXXIX, 4) are performed, *and* he has acted well according to the religious way; then he comes into the ceremonial of the sacred beings. "How are those men purified, O righteous *one!* who shall stand up by a corpse *which is* very dry *and* dead a year?" (See Pahl. Vend. VIII, 107, 108.) The reply is this, that "those men are purified;

they consider themselves as clean *it* is more grievously sinful; just as when they do not wash with the Bareshnûm, as *above* written, *but* consider themselves as clean through *washing* fifteen times, as *above* written, or on account of any washing whatever distinct from the Bareshnûm, *it* is more grievously sinful; because, when they do not wash with a Bareshnûm, as *above* written, *but* wash for fifteen times, as *above* written, or any washing whatever distinct from the Bareshnûm, as *above* written, they do not become clean, through the professional washing which is decreed, from that pollution which remains[1].

13. When without similar trouble *and* great judiciousness they go unto water *and* fire, the sin is grievous; and when they go to the bowl (pa*d*mânŏ) for ablution of the sacred twigs[2] *it* is non-ablution advisedly, *and* to perform the ceremonial therewith would not be authorised. 14. And, *in* like manner, the washing of polluted Hôm *twigs*[3], for any indispensable purpose, with the Bareshnûm *ceremony*, as *above* written, is not possible.

15. Therefore, so that we *may* obtain as *it were* a remedy for it, I wash with the Bareshnûm *ceremony*, as *above* written; to keep the mind steadfast *and* to attain to a remedy I wash with the Bareshnûm, as *above* written; *and* to bestow the indispensable, comprehensive Bareshnûm, as *above* written, is indeed a good work suitable for the discreet *and* liberated

for *it is* not *to* the dry from that dryness—that is, it would not act from this polluted *thing*—*that* the existence *of* dry diffusion *has* arisen."'

[1] Even after the best ordinary washing.

[2] See Dd. XLIII, 5.

[3] See Dd. XLVIII, 16.

from bonds, and the purification of body *and* soul is connected with it.

16. These *things* those of the primitive faith, who provided for the moderns, *have* communicated, whose position *was* above us moderns who are now the law (gûn) of others, and are teachers and rulers; our station as regards them is the position (gâsîh) of disciples *to spiritual* masters, *that of* listeners *and* servitors to form *and* hold the opinion, about the same and other *things*, which those of the primitive faith formed; *and* the teaching of even one of those high-priests is greater *and* higher than our sayings and decisions.

17. And *as to* every custom there may be in the country of Irân, about casting away the Bareshnûm *ceremony*, as written by me, and about all the polluted, as *above* written—whom *it* is possible to wash, for any indispensable reason whatever, with the Bareshnûm as written by me, *and* one does not wash with the Bareshnûm as *written* by me, *but* is ordered to wash for fifteen times, as written by me, *and* to pronounce as clean—and *which* is established as a rule *one* is urged to practise, if Zâ*d*-sparam or any one else *has* ordered, said, or decided in the name of authority *that one* is to do *so, or has* established *it* as a rule, *or* set *it* going, this is to give authoritatively my opinion, decision, and enactment upon it likewise. 18. That *those* same sayings are short-sighted (aê-vênakŏ), *that* same order is unlawfully *given*, *that* same decision is false teaching, *that* same rule is vicious, *that* same setting going is grievously sinful, and *that* same authority is not to be accepted; *it* is a practice, therefore, not to be performed, *and* whoever *has* performed it, is to

engage quickly *in* renunciation of it. 19. And he who *has* decreed in the country of Irân, in the name of authority, washing of *other* kinds *as* all-remedial for the polluted, as *above* written, *and has* established a rule of that description is to be considered as a heretic (aharmôkô) deserving death.

20. So, when through his wilfulness that kind of injury without enlightenment (bâm) is decreed, *and* a rule of that description is established, as *above* written, *and one* rendered polluted is washed fifteen times with bull's urine *and* once with water, or *in* whatever other mode that is distinct from the Bareshnûm *ceremony* as written by me, *though* it is possible to wash him, for any indispensable reason whatever, with the Bareshnûm as *above* written, then, his renunciation *of sin being* accomplished, *he* is to be washed again at the nine ablution seats (magh)[1] with the Bareshnûm as written by me; *and* until washed again, as written by me, *he* is not to go to water and fire *and* the bowl for ablution.

21. And this epistle is written by me, in my own *hand*-writing, for the sake of *all* members whatever of the good religion of the country of Irân becoming aware of the opinion, apprehension, *and* appreciation of the commands of religion *entertained by* me, Mânûs*k*îhar, son of Yûdân-Yim; *and* several copies are finished *in* the month of the triumphant Ho*r*vada*d* of the year 250 of Ya*zd*aka*rd*[2].

22. In trustfulness and gratitude to the sacred beings, *and* homage to the exalted pontiff *sent* from[3]

---

[1] See § 6.

[2] The third month of the Parsi year 250, which corresponded to the interval between the 14th June and 13th July, 881.

[3] Reading min, as in Ep. II, ix, 14, instead of mûn, 'who.'

the creator Aûharmazd, the heavenly, most righteous, *and* glorified Zaratûst the Spîtamân. 23. For the sake of obtainments of prayers the one thing is the righteousness of the Spîtamân; great, good, *and* perfect is Zaratûst; one *only* is the way of perfect righteousness, which is the way of those of the primitive faith; all the others, appointed afresh, are no ways[1].

[1] Compare Dd. XCIV, 14, Ep. II, ix, 15. This epistle is followed, in K35, by the Selections of Zâd-sparam, of which the first portion is translated in the fifth volume of the Sacred Books of the East.

APPENDIX.

I. LEGENDS RELATING TO KERESÂSP.

II. THE NÎRANG-I KUSTÎ.

III. THE MEANING OF KHVÊTÛK-DAS.

IV. THE BARESHNÛM CEREMONY.

V. FINDING A CORPSE IN THE WILDERNESS.

OBSERVATIONS.

1. For all divisions of the translations into sentences or sections the translator is responsible, as such divisions are rarely made in the manuscripts.

2–6. (The same as on page 2.)

7. The manuscripts mentioned are:—

B29 (written A.D. 1679), a Persian Rivâyat, No. 29 in the University Library at Bombay.

BK, J, K35, M10 (as described on page 278).

L4 (written about A.D. 1324), a Vendidâ*d* with Pahlavi, in the India Office Library in London.

M7 (written A.D. 1809), miscellaneous Parsi-Persian writings, No. 7 of the Haug Collection in the State Library at Munich.

APPENDIX.

I. Legends relating to Keresâsp.

The Avesta informs us that Keresâspa was a son of Thrita the Sâman, and the brother of Urvâkhshaya[1]. From the name of his father's family he is sometimes called Sâma Keresâspa[2], but his more usual title is Nareman*a*u or Nairiman*a*u, 'the manly-minded[3].' He is described as 'a youthful hero, wearing side-locks and carrying a club[4],' to whom the witch Knãthaiti[5] attached herself; she whom Zaratû*s*t promised to destroy by means of the apostle Saoshyãs, who is to be born hereafter[6]. And his body is watched over by 99,999 guardian spirits[7].

---

[1] See Yas. IX, 30, 31.

[2] See Fravar*d*în Yt. 61, 136. Hence he is often called Sâm in Pahlavi works (see Bd. XXIX, 7, 9, Byt. III, 60, 61); and, in a passage interpolated in some manuscripts of the Shâhnâmah, we are informed that Gar*s*âsp was son of Atrat, son of *S*am, which is evidently a reminiscence of Keresâsp being a son of Thrita the Sâman (see also Bd. XXXI, 26, 27).

[3] See Âbân Yt. 37, Râm Yt. 27, Zamyâ*d* Yt. 38, 40, 44. Hence we have Sâm, son of Narîmân, as the grandfather of Rustam in the Shâhnâmah.

[4] See Yas. IX, 33. M. de Harlez converts the side-locks into some weapon called gaêsu*s*, but this word still survives in Pers. gês or gêsû, 'ringlet, side-lock.'

[5] See Vend. I, 36. Or it may be 'the witch whom one destroys, or to whom one prays,' if we translate the name.

[6] See Vend. XIX, 18.

[7] See Fravar*d*în Yt. 61. For the reason of this watchfulness, see Dd. XVII, 6 n.

Of his exploits we are told that he 'slew the serpent Srvara, which devoured horses and men, which was poisonous and yellow, over which yellow poison flowed a hand's-breadth high. On which Keresâspa cooked a beverage in a caldron at the midday hour, and the serpent being scorched, hissed, sprang forth, away from the caldron, and upset the boiling water; Keresâsp, the manly-minded, fled aside frightened[1].' We are further told that he slew the golden-heeled Ga*n*darewa[2]; that he smote Hitâspa in revenge for the murder of his brother, Urvâkhshaya[3]; that he smote the Hunus who are the nine highwaymen, and those descended from Nivika and Dâ*s*tayâni[4]; also Vareshava the Dânayan, Pitaona with the many witches, Arezô-shamana, and Snâvidhaka[5]; and that he withstood many smiters or murderers[6].

The details of these exploits, still extant in the Avesta, are very scanty; but some of them appear to have been more fully described in a legend about the soul of Keresâspa which formerly constituted the fourteenth farga*rd* of the Sû*d*kar Nask, the contents of which are thus summarized in the ninth book of the Dînka*rd*:—

'The fourteenth farga*rd*, A*d*-fravakhshî[7], is about

[1] See Yas. IX, 34–39, Zamyâ*d* Yt. 40 (translated in Haug's Essays, pp. 178, 179).

[2] See Âbân Yt. 38, Zamyâ*d* Yt. 41. A monster in the wide-shored ocean, who is also mentioned in Râm Yt. 28.

[3] See Râm Yt. 28, Zamyâ*d* Yt. 41.

[4] See Zamyâ*d* Yt. 41. For 'Hunus' some read 'sons.'

[5] See Zamyâ*d* Yt. 41–44.

[6] See Fravar*d*în Yt. 136.

[7] The name of Yas. XLIV, being the first two words, a*d* fravakhshyâ, of that chapter of the Gâthas. In the detailed account of the contents of each farga*rd* of the first three Nasks, given in the ninth book of the Dînka*rd*, each farga*rd* is distinguished

Aûha*r*ma*zd*'s showing the terrible state of the soul of Keresâsp[1] to Zaratû*s*t; the dismay of Zaratû*s*t owing to that terrible state; the sorrowful speaking of Keresâsp as regards the slaying of multitudes, for which mankind extol him, whereby abstentions from sin *occurred;* and the recognition of him by the creator, Aûha*r*ma*zd*, as extinguishing his fire. The supplication of Keresâsp *for* the best existence from Aûha*r*ma*zd* for those exploits when the serpent (gaz) Srôbar[2] *was* slain by him, and the violence of that adversary; when Gandarep[3] with the golden heels *was* smitten by him, *and* the marvellousness of that fiend; when the Hunus *of* Ve*s*kŏ[4], who are

by the name of some section of the Gâthas. The names thus employed are composed of the first one, two, or three words of the Yathâ-ahû-vairyô, the Ashem-vohû, the Yênhê-hâtãm, Yas. XXVIII–XXXIV, the Yasna haptanghâiti, Yas. XLII–L, LII, LIII, which supply the twenty-two names required. When the Nask contains twenty-three farga*rd*s, as in the case of the Var*s*tmânsar, the first farga*rd* remains unnamed. Whether these words were used merely as names, or whether their insertion implies that the farga*rd*s of these Nasks used to be recited (somewhat like those of the Vendidâ*d*) alternately with the sections of the Gâthas, can hardly be determined from our present information. It may be noted that the three Nasks (Sû*d*kar, Var*s*tmânsar, and Bakô), whose contents are thus detailed in the Dînka*rd*, all belong to the so-called gâsânîk or Gâtha class of Nasks; but whether that term implies that they were metrical, or merely that they were connected in some way with the Gâthas, is also uncertain.

[1] Written Kerê*s*âspô, or Gerê*s*âspô, throughout the Pahlavi text of this paragraph.

[2] The Srvara of Yas. IX, 34, Zamyâ*d* Yt. 40.

[3] The Ga*n*darewa of Âbân Yt. 38, Râm Yt. 28, Zamyâ*d* Yt. 41.

[4] Reading Hunû Ve*s*kŏ, but it is also possible to read khûnŏdâkŏ, 'blood-producing,' which is fully applicable to these highway-robbers. The 'Hunus in Vaêska' are mentioned in Âbân Yt. 54, 57 as opponents of the warrior Tusa, but the Hunus in Zamyâ*d* Yt. 41 have no country assigned to them.

descendants of Nîvîk *and* Dâstânîk[1], *were slain* by him, *and* the grievous harm and disaster owing to them; *and* when the mighty wind[2] *was* appeased by him, and brought back from damaging the world to benefiting the creatures; *and* for that which *happens* when, owing to confinement[3], Dahâk becomes eager, rushes on for the destruction of the world, *and* attempts the annihilation of the creatures; *and* his being roused to smite him and to tame that powerful fiend for the creatures of the world. The opposition of fire to Keresâsp, through *his* causing distress to it *and* keeping away *from it*, which *were* owing to his seeking hell; *the supplication of* Zaratûst to the fire to have compassion upon *him*, which was owing to his sin; the compliance of the fire *with* that request; and the departure of the soul of Keresâsp to the ever-stationary existence[4]. Perfect is the excellence of righteousness[5].'

Although the Sû*d*kar Nask has long been lost, the legend contained in this fourteenth farga*rd* still survives in its Pahlavi form, though probably somewhat abridged, and a Persian paraphrase of this Pahlavi version is also to be found in the Persian

---

[1] The Nivika and Dâstayâni of Zamyâ*d* Yt. 41.

[2] The wind (vâ*d*ŏ), though an angel when moderate and useful, is supposed to become a demon in a gale or hurricane; and is mentioned as such in Vend. X, 24.

[3] In the volcano, Mount Dimâvand (see Bd. XII, 31, XXIX, 9, Byt. III, 55–61). This exploit is expected to be performed hereafter.

[4] The hamîstîkŏ ahvânŏ, intermediate between heaven and hell (see Dd. XX, 3).

[5] The Pahlavi equivalent of the Av. ashem vohû, here translated, follows each summary of the contents of a farga*rd* or Nask in the Dînka*rd*, in the same way as ashem vohû follows each farga*rd* of the Vendidâ*d* and each section of the Gâthas in the Vendidâ*d* sâdah or liturgy.

Rivâyats[1]. The Pahlavi legend is included among a series of quotations, regarding the importance of fire, contained in a Pahlavi Rivâyat preceding the Dâ*d*istân-î Dînîk in some manuscripts[2]; and its close correspondence with the above summary of the fourteenth fargar*d* of the Sû*d*kar Nask will be seen from the following translation of it:—

. . . . 'And *it* is declared that fire is so precious that Aûha*r*ma*zd* spoke unto Zaratû*s*t thus: "Of whose soul is it *that* the actions[3], position, consciousness, and guardian spirit seem best when thou shalt behold *it*?"

'And Zaratû*s*t spoke thus: "Of him who is Keresâsp."

'Aûha*r*ma*zd* summoned the soul of Keresâsp, and the soul of Keresâsp saw[4] Zaratû*s*t and, on account of the misery which it had seen in hell, it spoke unto *him* thus: "I have been a priest of Kâpûl[5], which should be a power in support of me; and for the sake of begging life I have ever travelled through the world, and the world would have become hideous in my eyes, the world which should have feared my splendour[6]."

---

[1] In B29, fols. 167–169, where it is quoted from a work called the Sad-darband-i Hûsh.

[2] In BK and J; but in K35 this portion of the Rivâyat has been lost, with the first 71 folios of that MS.; it also appears to have been similarly lost from the older MS. belonging to Mr. Tehmuras Dinshawji Anklesaria.

[3] J omits this word.

[4] J omits the seeing.

[5] Kâbul. One of the three most sacred fires, the Frôbak fire, is said to have been removed by Vi*s*tâsp from Khvâri*z*em to Kâvulistân (see Bd. XVII, 6). The Persian version has 'would to God (kâ*s*kê) I were a priest!' and alters the rest of the sentence to correspond.

[6] Reading rê-î li; J has 100 var, 'a hundred lakes (or ordeals or results).'

'And Aûha*r*ma*z*d spoke thus: "Stand off, *thou* soul of Keresâsp! for thou shouldst be hideous in my eyes, because the fire, which is my son[1], *was* extinguished by thee, and no care *of it was* provided by thee."

'And the soul of Keresâsp spoke thus: "Forgive me, O Aûha*r*ma*z*d! and grant me the best existence! grant me the supreme heaven! The serpent (a*z*ŏ) Srôvbar[2] is slain outright, which *was* swallowing horses *and* swallowing men, and its teeth were as long as my arm, its ear was as large as fourteen blankets (nama*d*ŏ), its eye was as large as a wheel, and its horn was as much as Dahâk[3] in height. And I was running as much as half a day on *its* back, till *its* head *was* smitten by me at the neck *with* a club made for *my* hand, and *it was* slain outright by me[4]. And if that serpent had not been slain by me, all thy creatures would have *been* completely annihilated by it, and thou wouldst never have known a remedy *for* Aharman."

'Aûha*r*ma*z*d spoke thus: "Stand off! for the fire, which is my son, *was* extinguished by thee."

'Keresâsp spoke thus: "Grant me, O Aûha*r*ma*z*d! that best existence, the supreme heaven! for by me Gandarep[5] *was* slain outright, by whom twelve

[1] Fire is often called 'the son of Ahura-mazda' in the Avesta, as in Yas. II, 18, Vend. V, 9, &c.

[2] The Srvara of Yas. IX, 34, Zamyâ*d* Yt. 40. The Persian version has merely azdahâ, 'a dragon.'

[3] Or it may be shâk, 'a bough.' The Persian version has 'eighty cubits.'

[4] The Persian version adds 'and as I looked into its mouth, men were still hanging about its teeth;' which was evidently suggested by what is stated in the account of the next exploit.

[5] See p. 371, note 3.

districts *were* devoured at once. When I looked among the teeth of Gandarep, dead men[1] were sticking among his teeth; and my beard *was* seized by him, and I dragged him out of the sea[2]; nine days and nights the conflict *was* maintained by us in the sea, and then I became more powerful than Gandarep. The sole of Gandarep's foot *was* also seized by me, and the skin *was* flayed off up to *his* head, and with it the hands and feet of Gandarep *were* bound; *he was* also dragged by me out to the shore of the sea, and *was* delivered by me over *to* Âkhrûrag[3]; and he slaughtered *and* ate my fifteen horses. I also fell down in a dense thicket (aîsakŏ), and Gandarep carried off *my* friend Âkhrûrag, and she who was my wife *was* carried off by him[4], and my father *and* nurse (dâyakŏ) *were* carried off by him. And I took under *my* protection (dinhârîgînî*d*ŏ) and raised all the people *of* our pleasant *place*, and every single step I sprang forward a thousand steps, and fire fell into everything which *was* struck by my foot *as* it sprang forward[5]; I went out to the sea, and they were brought back by me,

---

[1] The Persian version says 'horses and asses.'

[2] For this clause the Persian version substitutes 'the sea was up to his knee, and his head up to the sun.'

[3] This is merely a guess. The word can also be read khârvarag, 'thorny, or a thorny brake;' but it seems to be the name of some person, being followed by the word dôstŏ, 'friend,' in the next sentence. Âkhrûra, son of Haosravangh, is mentioned in Fravar*d*în Yt. 137, next after Sâma Keresâspa, as 'withstanding Hashi-dava (or daêva), the wicked and covetous one destroying the world.' The Persian version omits from the dragging out of the sea in this sentence to the slaying in the next (p. 376, line 1).

[4] BK has 'by me,' which must be a blunder.

[5] J omits these last seven words.

and Gandarep *was* taken and slain by me[1]. And if he had not been slain by me, Aharman would have become predominant over thy creatures."

'Aûhar*ma*z*d* spoke thus: "Stand off! for *thou art* hideous in my eyes, because the fire, which is my son, *was* extinguished by thee."

'Keresâsp spoke thus: "Grant *me*, O Aûhar*ma*z*d*! heaven *or* the supreme heaven! for I have slain the highwaymen[2] who were so big in body that, when they were walking, people considered in this *way*, that 'below them are the stars and moon, and below them moves the sun *at* dawn, and the water of the sea reaches up to their knees.' And I reached up to their legs, and they were smitten on the legs by me; they fell, and the hills on the earth *were* shattered by them[3]. And if those fallen[4] highwaymen *had* not been slain by me, Aharman would have become predominant over thy creatures."

'Aûhar*ma*z*d* spoke thus: "Stand off! for thou shouldst be hideous in my eyes, because the fire, which is my son, *was* extinguished by thee."

'Keresâsp spoke thus: "Grant me, O Aûhar*ma*z*d*! heaven *or* the supreme heaven! When the wind *was* weakened (rakhtŏ) and paralysed by me, the

[1] The Persian version says, 'I slew him, and as he fell down many villages and places became desolate.'

[2] The 'nine highwaymen' of Zamyâ*d* Yt. 41. The Persian version says 'seven.' BK has 'walked,' instead of 'slain.'

[3] Instead of this sentence the Persian version has 'through fear of them people could not go on any journey, and every one whom they might see, on the road that he went, they would instantly eat up; and in three years they reckoned three hundred thousand men they had slain and destroyed. And I fought with them and slew all the seven.'

[4] J omits the word 'fallen.'

demons deceived the wind, and they spoke unto the wind thus: '*He* is more resisting thee than all the creatures and creation, and thou shouldst think of him thus, that "there is no one walks upon this earth more resistant of me *than* Keresâsp;" he despises demons *and* men, and thee, too, who shouldst be the wind, *even* thee he despises.' And the wind, when those words *were* heard by it, came on so strongly that every tree and shrub which was in its path *was* uprooted, and the whole earth which was in its path *was* reduced to powder (payan*g*ânŏî-aîtŏ ka*r**d*ŏ), and darkness arose. And when it came to me, who am Keresâsp, it was not possible for it to lift my foot from the ground; and I arose and sallied forth (ba*r*â yehabûn*d*) upon the earth, and I stood *upon* it, with both feet on an equality (mirîh), until a rampart (pû*s*tŏ) of it *was* completed, so that I *might* go again below the earth; that which Aûha*r*ma*zd* ordered thus: 'Should I appoint a keeper of the earth and sky, they would not forsake me[1].' And if that thing had not been done by me, Aharman would have become predominant over thy creatures."

'Aûha*r*ma*zd* spoke thus: "Stand off! for thou shouldst be hideous in my eyes, because the fire, which is my son, *was* smitten by thee."

'Keresâsp spoke thus: "Grant *me*, O Aûha*r*-ma*zd*! heaven *or* the supreme heaven! for *it* is thus

[1] The Persian version has 'and as it arrived near me, it was not able to bear my foot from the spot; and I seized the spirit of the wind, and overthrew him with my own strength, until he made a promise thus: "I *will* go again below the earth." And I did not keep back my hand *from* that work less than Aûha*r*ma*zd* and the archangels ordered me.'

declared by revelation, that, when Dahâk has escaped from confinement[1], no one is able to seek *any* other remedy *against* him but me; on that account grant me heaven *or* the supreme heaven! And if it be not possible to grant me heaven *or* the supreme heaven, give me again the strength and success which were mine during life! for when thou shalt give me again so much strength and success *as* were mine when I was produced alive, I will slay Aharman with the demons, I *will* eradicate darkness from hell, I will complete the beautiful light, and within its sole existence (tanû-aê)[2] you *shall* sit and move[3]."

'Aûharmazd spoke thus: "This I *will* not give thee, *thou* soul of Keresâsp! because men shall commit sin; and until men commit no more sin, it is not possible to make thee alive again, and thou wouldst also not be able to make other men alive again, for they produce the resurrection thus, when all men become quite innocent. When men shall die, and their souls are wicked, all comfort shall forsake them, and all the misery and discomfort occasioned by them *shall* remain."

'When Keresâsp *and* his exploits were spoken of in this manner, the angels of the spiritual *and* the angels of the worldly *existences* wept aloud, and

---

[1] See Byt. III, 55-61. The Persian version substitutes a legend about the gigantic bird Kamak (also mentioned in Mkh. XXVII, 50) which overshadowed the earth, and kept off the rain till the rivers dried up; it also ate up men and animals as if they were grains of corn, until Keresâsp killed it by shooting it with arrows continuously for seven days and nights.

[2] That is, when there is only light, and no darkness.

[3] J has 'I *will* sit and move alone within it;' and the Persian version has 'I will sit alone in that place.'

Zaratûst the Spîtamân wept aloud[1] *and* spoke thus: "Though *there* should be no deceiver, I would be the deceiver in *thy* eyes[2], O Aûharmazd! as regards the soul of Keresâsp; for when Keresâsp should not have existed as a bodily and living *existence*, *there* would have been no remnant of anything whatever, or of creature of thine, in the world[3]."

'When Zaratûst had become silent therewith, the *angel of* fire[4] stood upon *his* feet[5], and the sinfulness of Keresâsp unto himself *was* fully mentioned by him, and he spoke thus: "I shall not let him into heaven."

'And the *angel of* fire, *having* spoken thus many

[1] The Persian version does not mention the angels and the weeping.

[2] This can also be translated thus: 'Though thou shouldst be no deceiver, thou wouldst be a deceiver in *my* eyes;' the words hômanâyê, 'would be,' and hômanês, 'thou wouldst be,' being written alike.

[3] The Persian version of this speech is, 'O good creator! I know that hatred and anger are not in thy path, and when any one indulges in hatred of another, there is no acquiescence of thine therein, yet now I see this matter as though some one maintained hatred against another.'

[4] The Persian version says 'the archangel Ardîbahist,' who is the protector of fire (see Sls. XV, 5, 12, 13).

[5] The Persian version proceeds, and concludes the sentence, as follows: 'and Keresâsp groaned unto Zaratûst the Spîtamân, and Ardîbahist, the archangel, said: "O Zaratust! thou dost not know what Keresâsp has done unto me; that in the world, formerly, my custom and habit would have been so, that, as they would place firewood under a caldron, I would send the fire, until that caldron should be boiled, and their work should be completed, *and* then it would have come back to its own place. As that serpent that he speaks of *was* slain he became hungry, and because the fire fell one moment later upon the firewood which he had placed below the caldron, he smote the fire *with* a club and scattered the fire, *and* now I *will* not pass the soul of Keresâsp to heaven."'

words, desisted; and the angel Gôs-aûrvan[1] stood upon *her* feet, and spoke thus: "I shall not let *him* into hell, for the benefit produced by him for me *was* manifold."

'Gôs-aûrvan, *having* spoken thus many words, desisted[2]; *and* Zaratûst stood upon *his* feet, and homage *was* offered by him unto the fire, and he spoke thus: "I shall provide care for thee, and shall speak of thy exploits in the world, and I shall speak to Vistâsp[3] and Gâmâsp[4] thus: 'Observe fully that a place is made *for* the fire as *it were* at once!' when Keresâsp *has* engaged in renunciation *of sin*, and you shall forgive him[5]."'

The Pahlavi legend breaks off at this point, leaving

---

[1] Av. geus urva, 'the soul of the ox,' that is, of the primeval ox, from which all the lower animals are supposed to have been developed. This angel, who is usually called Gôs, is said to be a female, and is the protectress of cattle (see Bd. IV, 2–5); in this capacity she is supposed to be friendly to Keresâsp, whose exploits had chiefly consisted in slaying the destroyers of animal life.

[2] The Persian version omits these words, and the preceding paragraph, proceeding in continuation of note 5, p. 379, as follows: 'And as Ardîbahist, the archangel, spoke these words, the soul of Keresâsp wept and said: "Ardîbahist, the archangel, speaks truly; I committed sin and I repent." And he touched the skirt of Zaratûst *with his* hand, and said: "Of mankind no one has obtained the eminence, rank, and dignity that thou obtainedst; now, through this grandeur and glory which is thine, do thou entreat and make intercession of Ardîbahist, the archangel, for me! so that it may be that I obtain liberation from this distress and torment."'

[3] See Dd. XXXVII, 36.

[4] See Dd. XLIV, 16.

[5] The Persian version continues as follows: 'And as Zaratûst the Spîtamân made intercession, Ardîbahist, the archangel, said: "Thy reputation is immense, and thy will is great." And after that he made no opposition to the soul of Keresâsp, but pardoned *it* for Zaratûst the Spîtamân; and the soul of Keresâsp obtained liberation from that discomfort.' This version then concludes with an admonition as to the necessity of treating fire with proper respect.

the reader to infer that Zaratûst's request was granted. It is succeeded, however, by the following further remarks about Keresâsp, which are evidently connected with the same legend :—

'Zaratûst enquired of Aûharmazd thus : "Whose is the first dead *body* thou shalt unite (varâzês) ?"

'And Aûharmazd spoke thus[1]: "*His* who is Keresâsp[2]."

'And it seemed grievous *to* Zaratûst, and he spoke unto Aûharmazd thus : "When the business of Keresâsp was the slaughter of men, why is his the first dead *body* thou wilt prepare ?"

'Aûharmazd spoke thus : "Let it not seem grievous to thee, O Zaratûst! for if Keresâsp had not existed, and thus much work had not been done by him, which *has* been stated, *there* would have been no remains of thee, nor of any creature of mine."'

Besides the Persian paraphrase of this legend, in prose, the Persian Rivâyats contain another version in metre, which consists of 173 couplets[3]. The exploits of Keresâsp are also mentioned in the Mainyô-i Khard (XXVII, 49-53) as follows :—

'And from Sâm the advantage was this, that by him the serpent Sruvar, the wolf Kapôd which they also call Pehan[4], the water-demon Gandarfi, the bird Kamak[5], and the bewildering[6] demon *were* slain.

[1] J omits the following words as far as the next 'thus.'

[2] Referring to the revival of Keresâsp from his trance, in order to destroy Dahâk, which is expected to take place before the general resurrection (see Bd. XXIX, 8, Byt. III, 59-61).

[3] In B29, fols. 169-171, it is quoted from 'the book of Bahirâm Fîrûz.'

[4] Written Pêhînŏ, or Pasînŏ, in the Pahlavi text.

[5] See p. 378, note 1.

[6] Or 'seducing,' or 'desolating.'

And also many other great actions, that *were* more valuable, he performed; and he kept back much disturbance from the world, of which, if one of those special disturbances had remained behind, it would not have been possible to effect the resurrection and the future existence.'

II. The Nîrang-i Kustî.

The Nîrang-i Kustî, or girdle formula, is a religious rite which a Parsi man or woman ought to perform every time the hands have been washed, whether for the sake of cleanliness, or in preparation for prayer; but it is not always strictly performed in all its details.

The Kustî, or sacred thread-girdle, is a string about the size of a stay-lace, and long enough to pass three times very loosely round the waist, to be tied twice in a double knot, and to leave the short ends hanging behind. It is composed of seventy-two very fine, white, woollen threads, as described in Dd. XXXIX, 1, note, and is tied in the manner there mentioned, but with the actions and ritual detailed below[1].

The ceremonial ablution having been performed, and the Kustî taken off, the person stands facing the sun by day, or a lamp or the moon at night; when there is no light he should face the south, as he should also at midday, even when the sun is northerly[2]. The Kustî is then doubled, and the loop thus formed is held in the right hand, with the thumb in the loop; while the left hand holds the two parts of the string together, some twenty inches horizontally from the other hand; and the ends hang loosely from the left hand.

[1] For most of the details which follow I am indebted to Dastûr Jâmâspji Minochiharji Jâmâsp-Âsâ-nâ.

[2] As it is, in Bombay, for about two months in the summer.

Holding the Kustî in this fashion, the person recites the following prayer in Pâzand, bowing and raising to his forehead the horizontal portion of the string at the name of Aûha*r*ma*zd*, dashing the string loosely and sharply downwards towards the left when mentioning Aharman, and repeating this downward jerk to the left, less violently, as each of the other evil beings is named:—'May Aûha*r*ma*zd* be lord! *and* Aharman unprevailing, keeping far away, smitten, *and* defeated! May Aharman, the demons, the fiends, the wizards, the wicked, the Kîks, the Karaps[1], the tyrants, the sinners, the apostates, the impious, the enemies, *and* the witches be smitten *and* defeated! May evil sovereigns be unprevailing! May the enemies be confounded! May the enemies be unprevailing!'

Bending forwards and holding the doubled Kustî up, horizontally, as before, he continues: 'Aûha*r*ma*zd* *is* the lord; of all sin I am *in* renunciation and penitent, of all kinds of evil thoughts, evil words, *and* evil deeds, whatever *was* thought by me, and spoken by me, and done by me, and happened through me, and has originated through me in the world.'

Then, holding the Kustî single with both hands near the middle of the string, but as far apart as before, while the loose ends of the string are short-

[1] These two Pahlavi names are merely transliterations of the Av. Kavi and Karapan, the names of certain classes of evil-doers, traceable back to the earliest times, and, probably, to the Vedic kavi and kalpa, which would naturally be used in a bad sense in the Avesta (see Haug's Essays, p. 289). The Pahlavi translators of the Yasna explain these names by the words kûr, 'blind,' and kar, 'deaf,' which are merely guesses.

ened (to prevent their touching the ground) by being partially gathered up in a large loop hanging under each hand, like a pair of spectacles, he proceeds: 'For those sins of thought, word, *and* deed, of body *and* soul, worldly *and* spiritual, do thou pardon this one[1]! I am penitent *and* in renunciation through the three words[2].'

He then continues to recite the following Avesta phrases: 'Satisfaction for Ahura-mazda!' bowing and raising the Kustî to the forehead; 'scorn for Angra-mainyu!' jerking the Kustî to the left, without altering the mode of holding it; 'which is the most forward of actual exertions through the will. Righteousness is the best good, a blessing it is; a blessing *be* to that which *is* righteousness to perfect rectitude[3].' Applying the middle of the Kustî to the front of the waist at the first word, 'righteousness,' of the last sentence, it is passed twice round the waist during the remainder of the sentence, by the hands meeting behind, exchanging ends, and bringing them round again to the front.

The following Avesta formula is then recited: 'As a *patron* spirit is to be chosen, so is an *earthly* master, for the sake of righteousness, *to be* a giver of good thought of the actions of life towards Mazda; and the dominion is for the lord whom he has given

---

[1] The Pâzand word is ukhê or aokhê, which the Gugarâti Khurdah Avesta translates by khudâtâelâ, 'most high God;' but it seems more probably a misreading of Pahl. hanâ-1, 'this one.' These phrases are a portion of the Patit or renunciation of sin.

[2] That is, in thought, word, and deed. So far the phrases are recited in Pâzand, but the following recitations are in the Avesta language.

[3] This last sentence is the Ashem-vohû formula (see Bd. XX, 2).

as a protector for the poor[1].' At the first word the long ends of the Kustî, hanging in front, are loosely twisted round each other at the waist, with a right-handed turn (that is, with the sun), and the reciter, holding his hands together, should think that Aûhar*mazd* is the sole creator of the good creation, until he comes to the word 'actions,' after which the twist is drawn closer to the waist during the remainder of the recitation.

The same Avesta formula is then repeated. At the first word the second half of the knot is formed, by twisting the long ends of the Kustî loosely round each other with a left-handed turn (that is, against the sun), so as to complete a loose reef-knot, and the reciter, holding his hands together, should think that Mazda-worship is the true faith, until he comes to the word 'actions,' after which the complete double knot is drawn close during the remainder of the recitation.

Then, passing the long ends of the Kustî round the waist for the third time, from front to back, the previous Avesta formula, 'Righteousness is the best good,' &c., is recited. At the first word the ends of the Kustî are loosely twisted round each other behind the waist, with a right-handed turn as before, and the reciter should think that Zaratû*s*t was the true apostle, until he comes to the first occurrence of the word 'blessing,' when the twist is drawn close. During the remainder of the formula the second half of the knot is formed, with a left-handed twist as before, while the reciter thinks that he must practise

[1] This is the Ahunavar, or Yathâ-ahû-vairyô formula (see Bd. I, 21, Zs. I, 12–19).

good thoughts, good words, and good deeds, and avoid all evil thoughts, evil words, and evil deeds; the double knot being completed behind as the last word of the formula is uttered.

Afterwards, bending forward and holding the front knot of the Kustî with both hands, the person recites the following Avesta formula: 'Come for my protection, O Mazda[1]! A Mazda-worshipper am I, a Zarathustrian Mazda-worshipper will I profess *myself*, both praising and preferring *it*. I praise a well-considered thought, I praise a well-spoken word, I praise a well-performed deed. I praise the Mazda-worshipping religion, expelling controversy[2] *and* putting down attack, *and* the righteous union of kinsfolk[3], which is the greatest and best and most excellent of things that exist and will exist, which is Ahurian *and* Zarathustrian. I ascribe all good to Ahura-mazda. Let this be the eulogy of the Mazda-worshipping religion.' And the reciter then repeats the formula, 'Righteousness is the best good,' &c., as before, bowing reverently, which completes the rite.

---

[1] What follows is from Yas. XIII, 25–29, and is the conclusion of the Mazda-worshipper's creed.

[2] The meaning of the original term fraspâyaokhedhrãm is rather uncertain, and the Pahlavi version is not easy to understand clearly; it translates this sentence, as far as the next epithet, as follows: 'I praise the good religion of the Mazda-worshippers, from which the disunion cast forth *and* the assault put down are manifest (this is manifest from it, that it is not desirable to go to others without controversy, and with that which arises without controversy it is quite requisite to occasion controversy).'

[3] This is one of the earliest references to *hv*aêtvadatha, or marriage among next-of-kin; the passage being written in the later Gâtha dialect.

During the rite the person performing it must remain standing on the same spot, without stepping either backwards or forwards, and must speak to no one. Should anything compel him to speak, he must re-commence the rite after the interruption.

III. The Meaning of Khvêtûk-das or Khvêtûdâd.

That the term Khvêtûk-das is applied to marriages between kinsfolk is admitted by the Parsis, but they consider that such marriages were never contracted by their ancestors within the first degree of relationship, because they are not so permitted among themselves at the present day. Any statements of Greek, or other foreign, writers, regarding the marriage of Persians with their mothers, sisters, or daughters, they believe to be simply calumnies due to ignorance, which it is discreditable to Europeans to quote [1]. Such statements, they consider, may have referred to the practices of certain heretical sects, but never to those of the orthodox faith.

The Parsis are, no doubt, fully justified in receiving the statements of foreign writers, regarding the customs of their ancestors, with proper caution; a caution which is quite as necessary when the statements are agreeable as when they are disagreeable to present notions. The Greeks, especially, had such a thorough contempt for all foreign customs that differed from their own, that they must have found it quite as difficult to obtain correct information, or to form an impartial opinion about oriental habits as the average European finds it at the present time. On the other hand, the Parsis have to consider that the ancient Greek writers, whose statements they repudiate, were neither priests nor zealots, whose accounts of religious cus-

[1] See Dastûr Peshotanji's translation of the Dînkard, p. 96, note.

toms might be distorted by religious prejudices, but historians accustomed to describe facts as impartially as their information and nationality would permit. It is quite possible that these writers may have assumed that such marriages were common among the Persians, merely because they had sometimes occurred among the Persian rulers; but such an assumption would be as erroneous as supposing that the marriage practices of the Israelites were similar to those of their most famous kings, David and Solomon, forgetting that an oriental sovereign is usually considered to be above the law and not subject to it.

Rejecting all statements of foreigners, as liable to suspicion, unless confirmed by better evidence, it seems desirable to ascertain what information can be obtained, on this subject, from the religious books of the Parsis themselves. This matter has hitherto been too much neglected by those best acquainted with the original texts, and must be considered as only partially exhausted in the following pages.

The term Khvêtûk-das[1] is a Pahlavi transcription of the Avesta word *hv*aêtvadatha, 'a giving of, to, or by, one's own,' and is sometimes partially translated into the form Khvêtûk-dâ*d*, or Khvêtû-dâ*d*, in which the syllable dâ*d*, 'what is given, a gift,' is merely a translation of the syllable das (Av. datha).

The Avesta word *hv*aêtvadatha is not found in any of the Gâthas, or sacred hymns, that are still extant and are usually considered the oldest portion

[1] Occasionally written Khvêtûk-dat, as in Pahl. Vend. VIII, 36 (see p. 392).

of the Avesta. But its former component, *hv*aêtu, occurs several times therein, with the meaning 'one's own, or kinsman,' as distinguished from 'friends' and 'slaves.'

The earliest occurrence of the complete word is probably in Yas. XIII, 28[1], where it is mentioned as follows:—'I praise .... the righteous *Hv*aêtvadatha, which is the greatest and best and most excellent of things that exist and will exist, which is Ahurian *and* Zarathu*s*trian.' This merely implies that *Hv*aêtvadatha was a good work of much importance, which is also shown by Visp. III, 18, Gâh IV, 8, and Vi*s*tâsp Yt. 17, where the *Hv*aêtvadatha (meaning the man who has accomplished that good work) is associated with youths who are specially righteous for other reasons. But there is nothing in any of these passages to indicate the nature of the good work.

In Vend. VIII, 35, 36 we are told that those who carry the dead must afterwards wash their hair and bodies with the urine 'of cattle or draught oxen, not of men or women, except the two who are *Hv*aêtvadatha and *Hv*aêtvadathi,' that is, male and female performers of *Hv*aêtvadatha. This passage, therefore, proves that the good work might be accomplished by both men and women, but it does not absolutely imply that it had any connection with marriage.

Turning to the Pahlavi translations of these passages we find the transcription Khvêtûk-das, Khvêtûk-dat, or Khvêtûk-dasîh, with explanations which add very little to our knowledge of the nature of

[1] See p. 387, note 3.

the good work. Thus, Pahl. Yas. XIII, 28 merely states that it is 'declared about it that it is requisite to do *it;*' Pahl. Vi*s*tâsp Yt. 17[1] asserts that 'the duty of Khvêtûk-das is said *to be* the greatest good work in the religion, that, owing to it, Aharman, the demon of demons, is becoming hopeless, so that the dissolution of Khvêtûk-das is worthy of death;' and Pahl. Vend. VIII, 36 speaks of 'the two who are a Khvêtûk-dat man *and* woman[2], that is, it is done by them.'

Another reference to Khvêtûk-das in the Pahlavi translations of the Avesta occurs in Pahl. Yas. XLIV, 4, as follows:—'Thus I proclaim in the world that [which he who is Aûha*r*ma*zd* made his own] best [Khvêtûk-das][3]. By aid of righteousness Aûha*r*ma*zd* is aware, who created this *one*[4] [to perform

[1] The age of this Pahlavi version of the Vi*s*tâsp Ya*s*t is doubtful, and it is even possible that it may have been composed in India. The only MS. of it that I have seen belongs to Dastûr Jâmâspji Minochiharji, who kindly gave me a copy of it, but seemed doubtful about the age of the translation. He was aware that his MS. was written some forty years ago, but he did not know from what MS. it was copied. This version is, however, mentioned in the list of Pahlavi works given in the introduction to Dastûr Peshotanji's Pahlavi Grammar, pp. 18, 31, so that another MS. of the Pahlavi text probably exists in the library of the high-priest of the Parsis in Bombay.

[2] Or, perhaps, 'man *and* wife;' as gab*r*â, 'man,' is occasionally used for 'husband,' though shûî is the usual word, and nê*s*man means both 'woman' and 'wife.'

[3] Written Khvêtvadas or Khvêtûdas in the very old MS. of Dastûr Jâmâspji Minochiharji, the text of which is followed in this translation. The phrases in brackets have no equivalents in the original Avesta text, and, therefore, merely represent the opinions of the Pahlavi translators.

[4] Spenda*r*ma*d* apparently, as indicated by the sequel.

Khvêtûk-das]. And through fatherhood Vohûman[1] *was* cultivated by him, [that is, for the sake of the proper nurture of the creatures Khvêtûk-das *was* performed by him.] So she who is *his* daughter is acting well, [who is the fully-mindful] Spenda*r*ma*d*[2], [that is, she did not shrink from the act of Khvêtûk-das.] *She*[3] *was* not deceived, [that is, *she* did not shrink from the act of Khvêtûk-das, because *she* is] an observer of everything [as regards that which is] Aûha*r*ma*zd*'s, [that is, through the religion of Aûha*r*ma*zd* *she* attains to all duty and law.]' The allusions to Khvêtûk-das in this passage are mere interpolations introduced by the Pahlavi translators, for the sake of recommending the practice; they have no existence in the Avesta text, but they show that the Pahlavi translators understood Khvêtûk-das to

[1] The Pahlavi translator seems here to understand Vohûman not as the archangel (see Dd. III, 13), but as a title ('good-minded') of the primeval man, Gâyômar*d*, who is supposed to have been produced by Aûha*r*ma*zd* out of the earth (compare Gen. ii. 7), represented by the female archangel Spenda*r*ma*d*. The term vohu-manô is used in Vend. XIX, 69, 76–84 for both a well-intentioned man and his clothing.

[2] The female archangel, a personification of the Avesta phrase spe*n*ta ârmaiti, 'bountiful devotion;' she has special charge of the earth and virtuous women (see Bd. I, 26, Sls. XV, 20–24). She is called the daughter of Aûha*r*ma*zd*, even as the fire and Vohûman are called his sons, because devotion (representing the earth), fire, and good thought are considered to be his most important creations. And, as the earth is also, metaphorically, the mother of man, and the creator Aûha*r*ma*zd* is figuratively his father, this unfortunate combination of anthropomorphisms has induced later superstition to take these statements literally, and to quote them as a justification of marriage between father and daughter.

[3] This seems the most probable nominative to the verbs in this sentence, but it is by no means certain.

refer to such relationship as that of father and daughter, as will appear more clearly from further allusions to the same circumstances in passages to be quoted hereafter[1]. Regarding the age of the Pahlavi translation of the Yasna we only know for certain that it existed in its present form a thousand years ago, because a passage is quoted from it by Zâ*d*-sparam, brother of the author of the Dâ*d*istân-î Dînîk and Epistles of Mânû*sk*îhar, in his Selections[2], and we know that he was living in A. D. 881[3]. But it was probably revised for the last time as early as the reign of Khûsrô Nôshirvân (A. D. 531–579), when the Pahlavi Vendidâ*d* was also finally revised[4].

The Pahlavi versions of the lost Nasks must have been nearly of the same age as those of the extant Avesta, but of the contents of these versions we possess only certain statements of later writers. According to some of the modern Persian statements the Dûbâsrû*ged* Nask contained many details about Khvêtûk-das, but this is contradicted by the long account of its contents given in the eighth book of the Dînka*rd*, which was written more than a thousand years ago[5], and in which Khvêtûk-das is not once noticed. The practice is, however, mentioned several times in the Dînka*rd*, as an important good work noticed in the Nasks, but no details are given, except in the following passages from the ninth book:—

First, regarding the latter part of the eighteenth farga*rd* of the Vara*st*mânsar Nask:—'And this, too,

---

[1] See pp. 396, 401, 416.

[2] See Zs. V, 4.

[3] See Ep. III, 2, 17, 21.

[4] See Ep. I, iv, 17, note.

[5] This is proved by the long quotation from Dk. VI contained in Dd. XCIV, 1–11.

that thereupon they shall excite a brother *and* sister with mutual desire, so that they shall perform Khvêtûk-das with unanimity, and before midday are generated a radiance which is sublime, centred in the face, and peeping glances (vênîkŏ âlûs); and they make the radiance, *which* is openly manifest, grow up in altitude the height of three spears of a length of three reeds *each*[1]; and after midday they have learned expulsion (rânakîh[2]), *and* shall renounce the fiend who is before the destroyer.' This is clearly an allusion to the Khvêtûk-das of brother and sister, as it can hardly be considered as merely referring to the arrangement of marriages between their children.

Second, regarding the earlier part of the fourteenth fargar*d* of the Bakô Nask:—'And this, too, that the performance of whatever would be a causer of procreation for the doers of actions is extolled *as* the perfect custom of the first Khvêtûk-das; because causing the procreation of the doers of actions is the fatherhood of mankind, the proper fatherhood of mankind is through the proper production of progeny, the proper production of progeny is the cultivation of progeny in one's own with the inclinations (khîmîhâ) of a first wish[3], and the cultivation of progeny in one's own is Khvêtûk-das. And he who extols the fatherhood of mankind, when *it is* a causer of the procreation of the doers of actions, has also extolled Khvêtûk-das. And this, too, that the proper nurture for the creatures, by him whose wish is for

[1] A height of about 42 English feet (see Dd. XLIII, 5).

[2] That is, the capability of expelling the fiends that try to take possession of man.

[3] Reading gâm (—kâm), but it may be dâm, 'creature.'

virtue, has taught *him* to perform Khvêtûk-das. Virtue is its virtue even for this reason, because, for the sake of maintaining a creature with propriety, he reckons upon the proper disposition of the multitude, that which is generated in the race by innumerable Khvêtûk-dases[1]. And this, too, that Spenda*r*ma*d* is taught *as being* in daughterhood to Aûha*r*ma*zd* by him whose wisdom *consists* in complete mindfulness. Even on this account, because wisdom *and* complete mindfulness[2] are within the limits of Aûha*r*ma*zd* and Spenda*r*ma*d*; wisdom is that which is Aûha*r*ma*zd*'s, complete mindfulness is that which is Spenda*r*ma*d*'s, and complete mindfulness is the progeny of wisdom, just as Spenda*r*ma*d* is *of* Aûha*r*ma*zd*. And from this is expressly the announcement that, by him who *has* connected complete mindfulness with wisdom, Spenda*r*ma*d* is taught *as being* in daughterhood to Aûha*r*ma*zd*. And this, too, the existence of the formation of that daughterhood, is taught by him whose righteousness *consists* in complete mindfulness.' This quotation merely shows that Khvêtûk-das referred to connections between near relations, but whether the subsequent allusions to the daughterhood of Spenda*r*ma*d* had reference to the Khvêtûk-das of father and daughter is less certain than in the case of Pahl. Yas. XLIV, 4, previously quoted[3].

Third, regarding the middle of the twenty-first

---

[1] That is, the useful peculiarities of a particular breed of domestic animals are maintained and intensified by keeping up the purity of the race.

[2] 'Complete mindfulness' is the usual Pahlavi explanation of Av. ârmaiti, 'devotion,' the latter component of the name Spenda*r*ma*d*.

[3] See pp. 392, 393.

fargar*d* of the Bakô Nask:—'And this, too, that a daughter is given in marriage (nê*s*manîh) to a father, even so as a woman to another man, by him who teaches the daughter and the other woman the reverence *due* unto father and husband.' The reference here to the marriage of father and daughter is too clear to admit of mistake, though the term Khvêtûk-das is not mentioned.

Next in age to the Pahlavi versions of the Avesta we ought perhaps to place the Book of Ar*d*â-Vîrâf, because we are told (AV. I, 35), regarding Vîrâf, that 'there are *some* who call *him by* the name of Nikhshahpûr,' and this may have been the celebrated commentator of that name, who was a councillor of king Khûsrô Nôshirvân[1], so that we cannot safely assume that this book was written earlier than the end of the sixth century. It gives an account of heaven and hell, which Ar*d*â-Vîrâf is supposed to have visited during the period of a week, while he seemed to be in a trance. In the second grade of heaven, counting upwards, he found the souls of those who had 'performed no ceremonies, chanted no sacred hymns, and practised no Khvêtûk-das,' but had come there 'through other good works;' and it may be noted that the two upper grades of heaven appear to have been reserved for good sovereigns, chieftains, high-priests, and others specially famous. In hell, also, he saw the soul of a woman suffering grievous punishment because she had 'violated Khvêtûk-das;' but this passage occurs in one MS. only. We are also told (AV. II, 1–3, 7–10) that 'Vîrâf had seven sisters, and all[2] those seven sisters

[1] See Ep. I, iv, 17.

[2] The word translated 'all' is the ordinary Huz. ko*l*â, equivalent

were as wives of Vîrâf; revelation, also, *was* easy to them, and the ritual had *been* performed . . . . they stood up and bowed, and spoke thus: "Do not this thing, ye Mazda-worshippers! for we are seven sisters, and he is an only brother, and we are, all seven sisters, as wives[1] of that brother."' This passage, supposing that it really refers to marriage, seems to attribute an exaggerated form of the Khvêtûk-das of brother and sister to Vîrâf, as a proof of his extraordinary sanctity; but it can hardly be considered as a literal statement of facts, any more than the supposed case of a woman having married seven brothers successively, mentioned in Mark xii. 20–22, Luke xx. 29–32.

In another Pahlavi book of about the same age, which is best known by its Pâzand name, Mainyô-i Khard[2], we find Khvêtûk-das placed second among

to Pers. har, but a Parsi critic has suggested that it ought to be read kanîk, 'virgin,' so as to get rid of the idea that the sisters were married to Vîrâf. This suggestion is ingenious, because the difference between ko*l*â and kanîk is very slight, when written in Pahlavi characters; but it is not very ingenuous, because the substitution of kanîk for ko*l*â, both here and in the similar phrase at the end of the passage quoted in our text, would render the sentences quite ungrammatical, as would be easily seen by any well-educated Parsi who would translate the phrases literally into modern Persian words, which would give him the following text: ân har haft '*h*vâharân Vîrâf *k*ûn zan bûd and for the first phrase, and har haft '*h*vâhar ân birâdar zanî êm for the second. To substitute any Persian word for 'virgin' in place of the pronoun har, in these two phrases, would evidently produce nonsense. The really doubtful point in these phrases is whether zan and zanî are to be understood as 'wife' and 'wifehood,' or merely as 'woman' and 'womankind;' but it would be unusual to use such terms for the unmarried female members of a family.

[1] Or 'the womankind.'

[2] From a facsimile of the only known MS. of the original Pahlavi

seven classes of good works (Mkh. IV, 4), and ninth among thirty-three classes of the same (Mkh. XXXVII, 12); and the dissolution of Khvêtûk-das is mentioned as the fourth in point of heinousness among thirty classes of sin (Mkh. XXXVI, 7).

In the Bahman Yast, which may have existed in its original Pahlavi form before the Muhammadan conquest of Persia[1], it is stated that, even in the perplexing time of foreign conquest, the righteous man 'continues the religious practice of Khvêtûk-das in his family[2].'

The third book of the Dînkar*d*, which appears to have been compiled by the last editor[3] of that work, contains a long defence of the practice of Khvêtûk-das, forming its eighty-second[4] chapter, which may be translated as follows:—

'On a grave attack (hû-girâyisnŏ) of a Jew upon

text of this work, recently published by Dr. Andreas, it appears that its Pahlavi name was Dînâ-î Mînavad-î Khar*d* (or Maînôg-î Khir*d*), 'the opinions of the spirit of wisdom.'

[1] See Sacred Books of the East, vol. v, pp. liii–lvi.

[2] See Byt. II, 57, 61.

[3] The name of this editor was Âtû*r*-pâ*d*, son of Hêmî*d*, as appears from the last chapter (chap. 413) of the same book. He was a contemporary of the author of the Dâ*d*istân-î Dînîk (see Bd. XXXIII, 11).

[4] Chap. 80 in the recent edition of Dastûr Peshotanji Behramji, because his numbers do not commence at the beginning of the book. His translation of this chapter (see pp. 90–102 of the English translation of his edition) differs considerably from that given in our text. This difference may be partly owing to its being translated from the Gugarâti translation, and not direct from the original Pahlavi; but it is chiefly due to the inevitable result of attempting a free translation of difficult Pahlavi, without preparing a literal version in the first place. The translation here given is as literal as possible, but the Pahlavi text is too obscure to be yet understood with absolute certainty in some places.

a priest, which *was* owing to asking the reason of the custom (âhankŏ) as to Khvêtûk-das; and the reply of the priest to him from the exposition of the Maz*d*a-worshipping religion.

'That is, as *one* complaining about wounds, damage, *and* distress comes on, *it* is lawful to dispute with him in defence begirt with legal opinion (dâ*d*istânŏ parvand), and the consummation of the accusation of an innocent man is averted; *so* of the creatures, the invisible connection of their own power to fellow-creations *and* their own *race*, through the propitiousness of the protection *and* preserving *influence* of the sacred beings, is a girdle, *and* the consummation of the mutual assistance of men is Khvêtûk-das. The name is Khvêtûk-das, which is *used* when *it is* "a giving of *one's* own" (khvê*s*-dahi*s*nîh), and its office (gâs) is a strong connection with one's own *race and* fellow-creations, through the protection *and* preserving *influence* of the sacred beings, which is, according to the treatises, the union of males *and* females of mankind of one's own *race* in preparation for, and connection with, the renovation *of the universe*. That union, for the sake of proceeding incalculably more correctly, is, among the innumerable similar races of mankind, that with near kinsfolk (nabânazdi*s*tânŏ), *and*, among near kinsfolk, that with those next of kin (nazd-pa*d*vandânŏ); *and* the mutual connection of the three kinds of nearest of kin (nazd-pa*d*-vandtar)—which are father and daughter, son and she who bore *him*[1], and brother and sister—is the most complete (a*v*îrtar) that I have considered.

[1] Literally 'bearer' (bûr*d*âr), which is not the usual word for 'mother,' but equivalent to the Av. baretar that is used in that sense.

'On the same subject the exposition of the obscure statements of the good religion, by a wise high-priest of the religion, is this:—"I assert that God (yêdatô) is the being, as regards the creatures, who created *any* of the creatures there are which are male, and *any* there are which are female; and that which is male is a son, and, similarly, a daughter is that which is female. The daughter of himself, the father of all, *was* Spendar*m*ad[1], the earth, a female being of the creation; and from her he created the male Gâyômar*d*[2], which is explained *as* the name for him who *was* specially the first man, since it is Gâyômar*d* living who is speaking *and* mortal, a limitation which *was* specially his, because of these three words—which are 'living, speaking, *and* mortal'—two of the limitations, which are 'living and speaking,' *were* through the provision of *his* father, the creator, and one, which is 'mortal,' *was* proceeding from the destroyer; the same limitation is upon all mankind, who are connected with that man's lineage, until the renovation *of the universe.* And now I say, if the aid of the father *has* produced a male from the daughter, it is named a Khvêtûk-das of father *and* daughter[3]."

'This, too, is from the exposition of the religion, that the semen of Gâyômar*d*—which is called seed—when he passed away, fell *to* Spendar*m*ad[4], the earth, which *was* his own mother; and, from its being united

---

[1] See p. 393, note 2.

[2] See Dd. II, 10, XXXVII, 82, LXIV, 5.

[3] It is uncertain whether the high-priest's statement continues beyond this point, or not.

[4] See Bd. XV, 1, 2, Dd. LXIV, 6.

*there*with, Mashya *and* Mashîyôî[1] *were* the son and daughter of Gâyômar*d* and Spenda*r*ma*d*, *and* it is named the Khvêtûk-das of son and mother. And Mashya and Mashîyôî, as male and female, practised the quest of offspring, one with the other, and it is named the Khvêtûk-das of brother and sister. And many couples *were* begotten by them, *and* the couples became continually[2] wife and husband[3]; and all men, who *have* been, are, and *will* be, are from origin the seed of Khvêtûk-das. And this is the reason which is essential for *its* fulfilment by law, *that* where *its* contemplation (andâ*g*i*s*nŏ) exists *it* is manifest from the increase of the people of all regions.

'And I assert that the demons are enemies of man, and a non-existence of desire for them consists *in* striving for it when Khvêtûk-das is practised; it then becomes their[4] reminder *of* that original practice of contemplation which is the complete gratitude of men, and *has* become his[5] who is inimical to them. Grievous fear, distress, and anguish also come upon them, *their* power diminishes, and they less understand the purpose of causing the disturbance *and* ruin of men. And *it* is certain that making the demons distressed, suffering, frightened, *and* weakened is thus a good work, and this way of having reward and *of* recompense is the property of the practisers of such good works.

'And I assert that the goodness of appearance and growth of body, the display of wisdom, temper,

[1] See Dd. XXXVII, 82, LXIV, 2, LXV, 2, LXXVII, 4, where these names are spelt differently.

[2] Literally 'have become *and* have become.'

[3] See Bd. XV, 22, 24–26.

[4] The demons'.

[5] Aûha*r*ma*zd*'s.

and modesty, the excellence of skill *and* strength, and also the other qualities of children are so much *the more* as they are nearer to the original race of the begetter, and they shall receive *them* more perfectly *and* more gladly. An example is seen *in* those who *spring* from a religious *woman* who is gentle, believing the spiritual *existence*, acting modestly, of scanty strength, who is a forgiver and reverential, *and from* a mail-*clad* (gapar) warrior of worldly religion, who is large-bodied *and* possessing strength which is stimulating (âgâr) *his* stout heart while he begets. They[1] are not completely for war—which is a continuance of lamentation (nâ*s*-ravandîh)—and not for carefulness and affection for the soul; as *from* the dog *and* wolf—and not the ruin (se*g*) *of* the sheep—arises the fox, like the wolf, *but* not *with* the strength of the wolf like the dog, and it does not even possess *its* perfect shape, nor that of the dog. And *they are* like those which are born from a swift Arab horse and a native *dam*, and are not galloping like the Arab, and not kicking (pa*d*âyak) like the native. And *they have* not even the same perfect characteristics[2], just as the mule that *springs* from the horse and the ass, which is not like unto either of them, and even *its* seed is cut off thereby, *and its* lineage is not propagated forwards.

'And this is the advantage from the pure preservation of race. I assert that *there* are three[3] species

[1] The offspring of such a match, which the apologist evidently considers an ill-assorted one, as tending to deteriorate the warlike qualities of the warrior's descendants, although he himself is no advocate for war.

[2] As their parents.

[3] Dastûr Peshotanji has 'four,' because the Pahlavi text seems

(vâg) *and* kinds of affection of sister *and* brother for that which shall be born of them :—one is this, where *it is* the offspring of brother and brother; one is this, where the offspring is that of[1] brothers[2] and their sister; and one is this, where *it is* the offspring of sisters[3]. And *as to* the one *of* these where the offspring is that of[4] a brother, and for the same reason *as applies to all* three[5] species of them, the love, desire, and effort, which arise for the nurture of offspring of the three species, are *in* hope of benefit. And equally adapted are the offspring to the procreators; and this is the way of the increasing love of children, through the good nurture which is very hopeful.

'And so, also, are those who are born of father and daughter, *or* son *and* mother. Light flashed *forth* (*g*astŏ) *or* unflashed (aparvâkhtŏ) is always seen at the time when *it is* much exposed, and pleased is *he* who has a child of *his* child, even when it is from some one of a different race and different

---

to speak of four species in the next sentence; here it seems to have 'six' in ciphers, but the first cipher can also be read aê, the conditional suffix to the verb which immediately precedes the ciphers in the Pahlavi text, and the second cipher is merely 'three,' which corresponds to the three possible kinds of first cousins that are about to be detailed in the text.

[1] Reading zak-î instead of zî*s* (which might be read zakîh if there were such a word).

[2] Literally 'brother.'

[3] Literally 'sister.'

[4] Reading zak-î instead of zî*s*, as before. This is Dastûr Peshotanji's fourth species of cousinship, which he understands as meaning second cousins.

[5] Reading î 3, by dividing the Pahlavi cipher for 'four' into two parts, both here and near the end of the sentence. This paragraph can hardly be understood otherwise than referring to the present form of Khvêtûk-das, the marriage of first cousins.

country. That, too, *has* then become much delight (vâyag) *which* is expedient, that pleasure, sweetness, and joy which are owing to a son that a man begets from a daughter of his own, who is also a brother *of that* same mother; and he who is born of a son and mother is also a brother *of that* same father; this is a way of much pleasure, which is a blessing of the joy, *and* no harm is therein ordained that is more than the advantage, and no vice that is more than the well-doing (khûp gâr). And if it be said that it is of evil appearance, it should be observed that when[1] a wound occurs in the sexual part of a mother, or sister, or daughter, and she flees (fravê*d*) from a medical man, and there is no opportunity for him to apply a seton (palîtŏ), and her father, or son, or brother is instructed in similar surgery, which is more evil *in* appearance, when they touch the part with the hand, and apply a seton, or *when* a strange man *does so?*

'And, when *it* is desirable to effect their union, which is the less remarkable (kam hû-zanâkhîktar) in evil appearance, when they are united (hamdvâ*d*î-hênd) by them in secret, such as when the hearing of their written *contract* (nipis*t*ŏ) of wifehood and husbandhood[2] is accomplished in the back*ground* (dar pûs*t*ŏ), or when the sound of drums and trumpets acquaints the whole district, where

[1] Reading amat instead of mûn, 'who,' (see Dd. LXII, 4 n.)

[2] Showing that the practice advocated was understood to be a regular marriage (performed in private probably on account of the authorities being of a foreign faith) and not any kind of irregular intercourse. It is here approvingly contrasted with the noisy celebration of a marriage with a person of foreign faith, in accordance with foreign customs.

these people are renowned, that such an Arûman[1] intends to effect such a purpose with the daughter, sister, or mother of such a Pârsî man?

'On this account of less evil appearance is even the good appearance which is to be mutually practised; and after the mode is seen, even the advantageousness in the accomplishment of the daily duty of concealing disgrace, the mutual desire, the mutual advantage and harm, and the contentment *which arise* as to whatever has happened are also mutual assistance. Some, with a husband and faint-heartedness, *have* a disposition (*s*ânŏ) of incapability, and the diligence which is in their reverence of the husband, who is ruler of the family (bûnag shah), is *due* even *to* the supremacy which he would set over them through the severity of a husband. Very many others, too, who are strange women, are not content with a custom (va*g*) of this description; for they demand even ornaments to cover *and* clothe the bold *and* active *ones*, and slaves, dyes, perfumes, extensive preparations, and many other things of house-mistresses which are according to their desire, though *it* is not possible they should receive *them*. And, if *it* be not possible, they would not accept retrenchment; and, if they should not accept retrenchment, it hurries *on* brawling, abuse, and ugly words about this, and even uninterrupted falsehood (avisistak-i*k* zûr) is diffused as regards it; of the secrets, moreover, *which* they conceal they preserve night and day a bad representation, and unobservantly. They shall take the bad *wife* to

[1] A native of Asia Minor, or any other part of the eastern empire of the Romans.

the house of *her* father and mother, the husband is dragged to the judges, *and* they shall form a district assembly (shatrô angêzŏ) about it. And lest he *should* speak thus: "I will release *her* from wifehood *with* me[1]," vice and fraud of many kinds *and* the misery of deformity are the faults which are also secretly attributed to him.

'A wife of those three classes[2] is to be provided, since they would not do even one of *these* things[3]; on which account, even through advantageousness, virtuous living, precious abundance, dignity, and innocence, mutual labour is manifestly mighty *and* strong.

'And if it be said that, "with all this which you explain, there is also, afterwards, a depravity (darvakh) which is hideous," it should be understood in the mind that hideousness and beauteousness are specially those *things* which *do* not *exist* in themselves, but through some one's habit of taking *up* an opinion and belief. The hideous children of many are in the ideas of procreation exceedingly handsome, and the handsome forms of many are in the ideas of a housekeeper (khânŏpânŏ) exceedingly ugly. We consider him also as *one* of our enemies when any one walks naked in the country, *which* you consider hideous; *but* the naked skins of

---

[1] That is, lest he should pronounce her divorce.

[2] The three nearest degrees of relationship must be meant, as the sequel admits the possibility of the union being considered objectionable; otherwise, the three kinds of first cousins might be understood.

[3] As a special pleader for marriage between near relations the apologist feels himself bound to argue that all bad wives must have been strangers to the family before marriage.

the country call *him* handsome whose garments, which seem to them hideous, have fallen *off*. And we are *they* in whose ideas a nose level with the face is ugly, *but they* who account a prominent nose ugly, and say it is a walling *that* reaches between the two eyes, remain selecting a handsome *one*[1]. And concerning handsomeness and ugliness in themselves, which are only through *having* taken *up* an opinion and belief, *there* is a change even through time and place; for *any* one of the ancients whose head *was* shaved *was* as *it were* ugly, and it was so settled by law that *it was* a sin worthy of death for them[2]; then its habits (*s*ânŏ) did not direct the customs of the country to shave the head of a man, *but* now there is a sage who has considered *it* as handsome *and* even a good work. Whoever is not clear that *it* is hideous is to think, about something threatening (girâî), that *it* is even so not in itself, but through *what is* taken into themselves they consider that *it* is hideous.

'Then for us the good work of that thing[3], *of* which *it* is cognizable that it is so ordained by the creator, has *its* recompense; it is the protector of the race, *and* the family is more perfect; *its* nature

---

[1] That is, those who admire flat noses select their beauties accordingly. Beauty being merely a matter of taste, which varies with the whim of the individual and the fashion of the period.

[2] This law was evidently becoming obsolete at the time the apologist was writing, and is now wholly forgotten. All Parsi laymen have their heads shaved at the present time, although the priests merely have their hair closely cut. This change of custom, in a matter settled by religious law, should warn the Parsis not to deny the possibility of other complete alterations having taken place in their religious customs.

[3] Khvêtûk-das.

is without vexation (apîzâr) and gathering affection, an advantage to the child—the lineage *being* exalted—gathering (avarkûn) hope, offspring, and pleasure *it* is sweetness *to* the procreator, and the joy is most complete; less is the harm *and* more the advantage, little the pretence and much the skill of the graceful blandishments (nâzânŏ) which are apparent, aiding and procuring assistance (bangîsnŏ), averting disaster, and conducting affairs; less is the fear, through itself is itself illustrious, and the steadfast shall abandon crime (kam). And all our fathers and grandfathers, by whom the same practice *was* lawfully cherished, maintained *it* handsomely in *their* homes; and to think of mankind only as regards some assistance is the enlightenment of the steadfast, a reason which is exhibiting the evidence of wisdom, that no practice of it[1] is not expedient.

'And if it be said that the law[2] *has* afterwards commanded as regards that *custom* thus: "Ye shall not practise *it!*" every one who is cognizant of that command is to consider *it* current; *but* we are not cognizant of that command, and *by* an intelligent *person* (khapârvârakŏ) this should also be seen minutely, through correct observation, that all the knowledge of men has arisen from Khvêtûk-das. For knowledge is generated by the union of instinctive wisdom and acquired wisdom[3]; instinctive wisdom is the female, *and* acquired wisdom the male; and on this account, since both are an achievement by the creator, they are sister and brother. And

[1] Khvêtûk-das.
[2] Perhaps the law of the foreign conquerors is meant.
[3] See Dd. XXXVII, 35, XL, 3.

also of everything worldly the existence, maturing, *and* arrangement are due to union in proportion; water, which is female, and fire, which is male[1], are accounted sister *and* brother in combination, and they seem as *though one* restrains *them* from Khvêtûk-das, unless, through being dissipated themselves[2], seed—which is progeny—arises therefrom; *and* owing to a mutual proportionableness of water and fire is the power in the brain, for if the water be more it rots *it* away, *and* if the fire be more it burns *it* away.'

This elaborate defence of Khvêtûk-das shows clearly that, at the time it was written (about a thousand years ago), that custom was understood to include actual marriages between the nearest relatives, although those between first cousins appear to be also referred to.

In the 195th[3] chapter of the third book of the Dînka*r*d we are told that the eighth of the ten admonitions, delivered to mankind by Zaratû*s*t, was this:—'For the sake of much terrifying of the demons, and much lodgment of the blessing of the holy[4] in one's body, Khvêtûk-das is to be practised.' And the following chapter informs us, that 'opposed to that admonition of the righteous Zaratû*s*t, of practising Khvêtûk-das for the sake of much terrifying

[1] See Dd. XCIII, 13 n.

[2] Into the forms of moisture and warmth in the body. Water and fire in their ordinary state being incapable of combination.

[3] This will be the 193rd chapter in Dastûr Peshotanji's edition, because his numbers do not commence at the beginning of the book. A similar difference will be found in the numbering of all other chapters of the third book of the Dînka*r*d.

[4] The technical name of Yas. LIX.

of the demons from the body of man, and the lodgment of the blessing of the holy in the body, the wicked wizard Akhtŏ[1], the enemy of the good *man* on account of the perplexing living which *would arise* from his practising Khvêtûk-das, preferred not practising Khvêtûk-das.'

The practice is also mentioned in the 287th chapter of the same book, in the following passage:—'The welfare of the aggregate of one's own limb-formations—those which *exist* through no labour of one's own, *and* have not come to the aid of those not possessing *them* (anafsmanân) owing to their own want of gratitude—even *one* of a previous formation *has* to eulogize suitably; *and* this which *has* come, completely establishing (spôr-nih) the Avesta, *one* calls equally splendid, by the most modestly comprehensive appellation *of* Khvêtûk-das.'

In the sixth book of the Dînka*rd*, which professes to be a summary of the opinions of those of the primitive faith[2], we are told that, 'when the good work of Khvêtûk-das shall diminish, darkness will increase and light will diminish.'

In the seventh book of the Dînka*rd*, which relates the marvels of the Ma*zd*a-worshipping religion, we are informed that it was 'recounted how—Gâyômar*d*[3] *having* passed *away—it was* declared secondly, as regards worldly *beings*, to Masyê and Masyâôê[4], the first progeny of Gâyômar*d*, by the word of Aûha*r*ma*zd*—that is, he spoke to them when they

[1] Av. Akhtya of Âbân Yt. 82, who propounded ninety-nine enigmas to Yôis*t*ô of the Fryâns (see Dd. XC, 3).

[2] See Dd. XCIV, 1 n.

[3] The sole-created man (see Dd. II, 10, XXXVII, 82).

[4] See p. 402, note 1.

were produced by him—thus: "You are the men I produce, you are the parents of all bodily life, and so you men shall not worship the demons, for the possession of complete mindfulness[1] *has been* perfectly supplied to you by me, so that you *may* quite full-mindfully observe duty and decrees." And the creativeness of Aûha*r*ma*zd* *was* extolled by them, and they advanced in diligence; they also performed the will of the creator, *they* carved (parkâvînî*d*ŏ) advantage *out of* the many duties of the world, *and* practised Khvêtûk-das through procreation *and* the union and complete progress of the creations in the world, which are the best good works of mankind.'

The following passage also occurs in the same book:—'Then Zaratû*s*t, on becoming exalted, called out unto the material world of righteousness to extol righteousness and downcast are the demons; and, "homage *being* the Ma*zd*a-worship of Zaratû*s*t, the ceremonial and praise of the archangels are the best for you, I assert; and, *as to* deprecation (aya*z*i*s*nîh) of the demons, Khvêtûk-das is even the best intimation, so that, from the information which is given *as to* the trustworthiness of a good work, the greatest is the most intimate of them, *those of* father *and* daughter, son *and* she who bore *him*[2], and brother *and* sister." *It is* declared that, upon those words, innumerable demon-worshipping Kîks and Karaps[3] disputed (sâri*s*î*d*ŏ) with Zaratû*s*t and strove for his death, just like this which revelation states:—"It is then the multitude clamoured (mar ba*r*â vîrâ*d*) who are in the vicinity of the seat of Tûr, the well-

---

[1] See p. 396, note 2.
[2] See p. 400, note 1.
[3] See p. 384, note 1.

afflicting[1] holder of decision; and the shame of the brother of Tûr arose, like *that of* a man whose shame *was* that they spoke of his Khvêtûk-das so that he might perform it. This Tûr *was* Tûr-î Aûrvâîtâ-sang[2], the little-giving, *who* was like a great sovereign of that quarter; and he maintained many troops and *much* power. And the multitude told him they would seize the great *one* from him who is little[3]. *But* Tûr-î Aûrvâîtâ-sang, the little-giving *and* well-afflicting, *spoke* thus:—'*Should* I thereupon smite him, this great *one* who mingles together those propitious words for us—where we are thus without doubt *as to* one thing therein, such as Khvêtûk-das, that it is not necessary to perform *it*—it would make us ever doubtful that it *might* be necessary to perform it.' . . . . And Zaratûst spoke to him thus: 'I am not always that reserved speaker, by whom that I *have* mentioned is the most propitious *thing* to be obtained; and inward speaking and managing the temper are a Khvêtûk-das[4], and the high-priest *who has* performed *it* is to perform the ceremonial.'"' This passage attributes to Zaratûst himself the enforcement of next-of-kin marriage, but it is hardly necessary to point out that the Dînkard only records a tradition to that effect; which

[1] The word hû-nôsakŏ is the Pahlavi equivalent of Av. hunustâ (Yas. L, 10, b), but the meaning of both words is uncertain. This Tûr seems to have been more friendly to Zaratûst than the Tûrânians were in general, but he appears not to be mentioned in the extant Avesta.

[2] As this epithet has not been found in the extant Avesta, the reading is uncertain.

[3] Meaning that they demanded possession of Zaratûst in an insolent manner.

[4] In a figurative sense.

record may be quoted as evidence of the former existence of such a tradition, but not as testimony for its truth. It is also worthy of notice that this tradition clearly shows that such marriages were distasteful to the people in general; but this might naturally be inferred from the efforts made by religious writers to assert the extraordinary merit of Khvêtûk-das, because customs which are popular and universal require no such special recommendation from the priesthood.

In the Dâ*d*istân-î Dînîk (XXXVII, 82, LXIV, 6, LXV, 2, LXXVII, 4, 5) allusions are made to the Khvêtûdâ*d*[1] of brother and sister, formed by the progenitors of mankind. We are also told that Khvêtûdâ*d* is to be practised till the end of the world, and that to occasion it among others is an effectual atonement for heinous sin[2] (Dd. LXXVII, 6, 7, LXXVIII, 19); but it is not certain that the term is applied in these latter passages to marriages between the *nearest* relatives.

For later particulars about Khvêtûk-das we have to descend to the darkest ages of Ma*zd*a-worship, those in which the Rivâyats, or records of religious legends, customs, and decisions, began to be compiled. Of the earlier Rivâyats, such as the Shâyast Lâ-shâyast and Vi*g*irka*rd*-î Dînîk, which were written in Pahlavi, few remain extant; but the later ones, written in Persian, are more numerous and very voluminous.

A Pahlavi Rivâyat, which precedes the Dâ*d*istân-î Dînîk in many MSS. of that work, devotes several

[1] Another form of the word Khvêtûk-das (see p. 390).
[2] This is also stated in Sls. VIII, 18.

pages to the subject of Khvêtûdâ*d*, which fully confirm the statements of the defender of the practice, quoted above from the Dînka*rd* (III, lxxxii). The age of this Pahlavi Rivâyat is quite uncertain; it is found in MSS. written in the sixteenth century, but, as it does not mention the marriage of first cousins, it was probably compiled at a much earlier period, more especially as it is written in fairly grammatical Pahlavi. The following extracts will be sufficient to show how far it confirms the statements of the Dînka*rd*:—

'Of the good works of an infidel this is the greatest, when he comes out from the habit of infidelity into the good religion; and of *one* of the good religion, remaining backward (akha*r*-mân) *at* the *time* when his ritual is performed, this is a great good work, when he performs a Khvêtûdâ*d*; for through that Khvêtûdâ*d*, which is so valuable a token of Ma*zd*a-worship, is the destruction of demons. And of Aûha*r*ma*zd it* is declared, as regards the performance of Khvêtûdâ*d*, that, when Zaratû*s*t sat before Aûha*r*ma*zd*[1], and Vohûman, A*rd*avahi*s*t, Shatvaî*r*ô, Ho*r*vada*d*, Ame*r*ôda*d*, and Spenda*r*ma*d*[2] sat around Aûha*r*ma*zd*, and Spenda*r*ma*d* sat by his side, she had also laid a hand on his neck, *and* Zaratû*s*t asked Aûha*r*ma*zd* about it thus: "Who is this *that* sits beside thee, and thou wouldst be such a friend to her, and she also would be such a friend to thee? Thou, who art Aûha*r*ma*zd*, turnest not *thy* eyes away from her, and she turns not away

[1] As he is said to have done in heaven, when receiving instruction in the religion.

[2] The archangels (see Dd. XLVIII, 1 n), of whom Spenda*r*ma*d* is said to be a female (see p. 393, note 2).

from thee; thou, who art Aûharmazd, dost not release her from *thy* hand, and she does not release thee from *her* hand[1]." And Aûharmazd said: "This is Spendarmad, who is my daughter, the house-mistress of my heaven, and mother of the creatures[2]." Zaratûst spoke thus: "When they say, in the world, this is a very perplexing thing, how is it proclaimed by thee—thee who art Aûharmazd—for thee *thyself?*" Aûharmazd spoke thus: "O Zaratûst! this should have become the best-enjoyed thing of mankind. When, since my original creation, Mâharîyâ *and* Mâharîyâôîh[3] had performed it, you, also, should have performed it; because although mankind *have* turned away *from* that thing[4], yet they should not have turned away. Just as Mâharîyâ *and* Mâharîyâôîh had performed Khvêtûdâd, mankind should have performed it, *and* all mankind would have known their own lineage and race, *and* a brother would never be deserted by the affection of his brother, *nor* a sister *by that* of her sister. For all nothingness, emptiness[5], and drought *have* come unto mankind from the deadly *one* (mar), when men have come to them from a different country, from a different town, *or* from a different district, and *have* married their women; and when they shall have carried away their women, and they have

[1] This legend is an instance of the close proximity of superstition to profanity, among uneducated and imaginative people.

[2] She being a representative of the earth.

[3] See p. 402, note 1.

[4] That is, from marriage of the nearest relations, which is admitted, throughout these extracts, to be distasteful to the people; hence the vehemence with which it is advocated.

[5] Literally 'air-stuffing' (vâê-âkînîh).

wailed together about this, thus: 'They will always carry our daughters into perversion[1].'"

'This, too, *is said*, that Khvêtûdâ*d* is so miraculous that *it* is the preservation of the most grievous sin—such as witchcraft and *that* worthy of death—from hell. And the want of protection (a*v*îpâharîh) from hell *of one* unprotected from Aharman and the demons arises at that time when, owing to what *occurs* when *he* is begged by *some* one to exercise witchcraft, *he* is made worthy of death. And when they shall perform Khvêtûdâ*d*, when the Khvêtûdâ*d* is owing to him[2], the unprotected *one* is preserved from the prison of hell, *from* Aharman *and* the demons; so miraculous is Khvêtûdâ*d*.

'*In* a passage *it* is declared, that Aûha*r*ma*zd* spoke unto Zaratû*s*t thus: "These are the best four things: the ceremonial worship of Aûha*r*ma*zd*, the lord; presenting firewood, incense, and holy-water *to* the fire; propitiating a righteous man[3]; and *one* who performs Khvêtûdâ*d* with her who bore *him*, or a daughter, or with a sister. And of all those he is the greatest, best, and most perfect who shall perform Khvêtûdâ*d*. . . . When Sôshâns comes[4] all mankind *will* perform Khvêtûdâ*d*, and every fiend will perish through the miracle and power of Khvêtûdâ*d*.'

It is then explained why the several merits of the

[1] This fear of perversion to another faith was, no doubt, the real cause of the vehement advocacy of family marriages by the priesthood.

[2] That is, when he has arranged the next-of-kin marriage of others, before his death.

[3] That is, a priest.

[4] Shortly before the resurrection (see Dd. II, 10).

three classes of Khvêtûdâ*d* are considered to stand in the same order as that in which the classes are mentioned in the preceding paragraph; also that the third class includes the case of half brothers and sisters, and the second that of an illegitimate daughter. After this we find the following legend:—

'And Khvêtûdâ*d* is so miraculous, that *it* is declared, regarding Yim[1], that, when the glory *of* his sovereignty had departed from him, he went out to the precincts (var) of the ocean with Yimak, his sister, *in order* to flee from the people, demons, and witches of the assembly of Dahâk[2]. And *they were* sought by them in hell and not seen; and others sought them among mankind, water, earth, and cattle, among trees, in the mountains, and in the towns, *but they were* not seen by them. Then Aharman shouted thus: "I think thus, that Yim is travelling in the precincts of the ocean." And a demon and a witch, *who* stood among *them*, *spoke* thus: "We *will* go and seek Yim." And they rushed *off and* went; and when they came unto those precincts where Yim was—the precincts *where* the water of Tîr[3] was—Yim spoke thus: "Who are

---

[1] The third sovereign of the world, after Gâyômar*d* (see Dd. II, 10). This legend is also mentioned in Bd. XXIII, 1, as explaining the origin of the ape and bear.

[2] The foreign king, or dynasty, that conquered Yim (see Dd. XXXVII, 97 n).

[3] Evidently intended for Tî*s*tar, a personification of the star Sirius, who is supposed to bring the rain from the ocean (see Dd. XCIII, 1–17). Strictly speaking Tîr is the planet Mercury, the opponent of Tî*s*tar, whose name is given to the fourth month, and thirteenth day of the month, in the Parsi year (see Bd. V, 1, VII, 2, XXVII, 24); but the confusion between the two names is not uncommon in the later books (comp. Sls. XXII, 13 with XXIII, 2).

you?" And they spoke thus: "We are those who are just like thee, who had to flee from the hands of the demons; we, too, have fled away from the demons, and we are alone. Do thou give this sister in marriage to me, while I also give this *one* unto thee!" And Yim, therefore, when the demons were not recognised by him from mankind, made the witch his own wife, and gave his sister unto the demon *as* wife. From Yim and that witch were born the bear, the ape, Gandarep[1], *and* Gôsûbar[2]; *and* from Yimak and that demon were born the tortoise (gasaf), the cat, the hawk (gaving), the frog, the weevil (dîvakŏ), and also as many more noxious creatures, until Yimak saw that that demon was evil, and it was necessary to demand a divorce (zan-ta*k*â) *from* him. And one day, when Yim *and* that demon had become drunk with wine, she exchanged her own position and clothing with those of the witch; and when Yim came he was drunk, *and* unwittingly lay with Yimak, who was his sister, and they came to a decision *as to* the good work of Khvêtûdâ*d*; many demons were quite crushed *and* died, and they rushed away at once, and fell back to hell.'

The fact, that the zealous writer felt that he had to force his opinions upon an unwilling people, is betrayed by the exaggerated language he uses in the following statements:—

'This, too, is declared by the Avesta, that Zaratû*s*t enquired of Aûha*r*ma*z*d thus: "Many thoughts, many words, *and* many deeds are mentioned by

[1] See p. 371, note 3.

[2] Not identified, and the reading is, therefore, uncertain.

thee—thee who art Aûha*r*ma*zd*—that it is necessary to think, speak, and do; of all *such* thoughts, words, *and* deeds which is the best, when *one* shall think, speak, *or* do *it*?" Aûha*r*ma*zd* spoke thus: "Many thoughts, *many* words, *and* many deeds should be proclaimed by me, O Zaratû*s*t! *but*, of those thoughts, words, *and* deeds *which* it is necessary to think, speak, *and* do, that which is best and most perfect *one* performs by Khvêtûdâ*d*. For *it* is declared that, the first time when he goes near to it, a thousand demons will die, and two thousand wizards *and* witches; when he goes near *to* it twice, two thousand demons will die, *and* four thousand wizards *and* witches; when he goes near to *it* three times, three thousand demons will die, *and* six thousand wizards *and* witches; *and* when he goes near to it four times *it* is known *that* the man and woman become righteous [1]."

'. . . . Owing to the performance of Khvêtûdâ*d* *there* arises a destruction of demons equivalent *to* a stoppage of creation; and though, afterwards, *some* of those men *and* women shall become wizards, *or* unlawfully slaughter a thousand sheep and beasts *of burden* at one time, *or* shall present holy-water to the demons, *yet*, on account of that destruction *and* vexation of the demons, which has occurred to them owing to the Khvêtûdâ*d*, it does not become comfortable to them while completed; and *it* is not believed by them that "the souls of those *people* will come to us."

'Whoever keeps one year in a marriage of Khvê-

[1] Or, as stated in the Appendix to the Shâyast Lâ-shâyast (Sls. XVIII, 4), they '*will* not become parted from the possession of Aûha*r*ma*zd* and the archangels.'

tûdâ*d* becomes just as though one-third of all this world, with the water, with the trees, and with the corn, had been given by him, as a righteous gift, unto a righteous man. When he keeps two years in the marriage *it* is as though two-thirds of this world, with the water, trees, *and* corn, had been given by him unto a righteous man. When he keeps three years in the marriage *it* is as though all this world, with the water, with the trees, *and* with everything, had been given *by him*, as a righteous gift, unto a righteous man. *And* when he keeps four years in his marriage, and his ritual[1] is performed, *it* is known *that his* soul thereby goes unto the supreme heaven (garô*d*mân); *and* when *the ritual is* not *performed*, it goes thereby to *the ordinary* heaven (vahis*t*ô).

'Zaratû*s*t enquired of Aûha*r*ma*z*d thus: "*As to* the man who *practises* Khvêtûdâ*d*, and his ritual is performed, *and* he also offers a ceremonial (ya*z*is*n*ŏ-aê), is the good work of it such as *if one* without Khvêtûdâ*d had* offered *it*, *or* which way is it?" Aûha*r*ma*z*d said: "*It* is just as though a hundred men without Khvêtûdâ*d* had offered it."

'Zaratû*s*t enquired this, also, of Aûha*r*ma*z*d, that is: "How is the benediction (âf*r*înô) which a man who *practises* Khvêtûdâ*d* shall offer?" Aûha*r*ma*z*d spoke thus: "As though a hundred men without Khvêtûdâ*d should* offer the benediction."

'And this, too, *was* asked by him, that is: "*As to* them who render assistance, *and one* meditates and attains to Khvêtûdâ*d through* them, *and one*

[1] The proper ceremonies after his death, or for his living soul during his lifetime (see Dd. XXVIII, LXXXI).

performs Khvêtûdâ*d* on account of their statements, how is *their* good work?" Aûha*r*ma*zd* spoke thus: "Like *his* who keeps in food and clothing, *for* one winter, a hundred priests—each of which priests has a hundred disciples—*such* is his good work."

'Zaratûs*t* enquired this, also, of Aûha*r*ma*zd*, that is: "*As to* them who keep a man back *from* performing Khvêtûdâ*d*, *and* owing to their statements he shall not perform Khvêtûdâ*d*, what is their sin?" *Aûharmaz*d *spoke*[1] thus: "*Their* place is hell."

'*In* a passage *it* is declared that, wiser than the wise, *and* more virtuous than the virtuous is *he* in whose thoughts, words, *and* deeds the demons are less predominant; *and* Aharman *and* the demons are less predominant in the body of him who *practises* Khvêtûdâ*d*, and his ritual[2] is performed.

'*It* is declared by revelation that *at* the *time* when Zaratûs*t* came out from the presence of Aûha*r*ma*zd*, the lord, into a worldly place where he travelled, he spoke this, that is: "Extol the religion! *and* you should perform Khvêtûdâ*d*. I speak of the good and those existing *in* the religion; *as to* the negligent, the vile, and those in perplexity, this is said, that a thing so wondrous *and* important *as that* which is in our law *of* Khvêtûdâ*d* could not be for performance. This is a sublime (*k*îrag) custom, *and*, as the best of all things, *one* asserts that it is necessary to perform it. *To* me, also, this is manifest when, through all faith *in* the law *of* those existing *in* the religion[3], that which is called by

[1] The Pahlavi text is imperfect. [2] See p. 421, note 1.

[3] That is, the general law of Ma*zd*a-worship, as distinguished from what he is advocating as a peculiarly religious law sanctioned

them a very heinous sin, through faith *in* this law *of* the good, is that which is called the most perfect *and* best good work of Ma*zd*a-worship."

'This, too, is declared by revelation, that Aûha*r*ma*zd* spoke unto Zaratû*s*t thus: "You should cause the performance of duties *and* good works." And Zaratû*s*t spoke thus: "Which duty *and* good work *shall* I do first?" Aûha*r*ma*zd* spoke thus: "Khvêtûdâ*d*; because that duty *and* good work is to be performed in the foremost place of all, for, in the end, it happens through Khvêtûdâ*d*, when all who are in the world attain unto the religion [1]."

'This, too, is declared by revelation, that Zaratû*s*t spoke unto Aûha*r*ma*zd* thus: "In my eyes *it* is an evil (va*d*ŏ) which is performed, and *it is* perplexing that I *should* make Khvêtûdâ*d* as *it were* fully current among mankind." Aûha*r*ma*zd* spoke thus: "In my eyes, also, *it* is just as *in* thine; but for this reason—when out of everything perfect *there* is *some* miserable evil [2] for thee—it should not seem *so*. Do thou be diligent in performing Khvêtûdâ*d*, and others, also, will perform *it* diligently."'

The unpopularity of the practice advocated could hardly be more fully admitted than in this last paragraph, nor the objection more irrationally and dogmatically disposed of. As for the numerous quotations, which the compiler of this Pahlavi Rivâyat

---

by the priests ('the good'). This is evidently an admission that the practice advocated was contrary to the ordinary laws of Ma*zd*a-worship itself.

[1] As Pahlavi writers expect them to do before the resurrection.

[2] Reading va*d*ŏ-î vêsht; but it may be '*something* is difficult and hard' (tang va sakht).

professes to take from the Parsi scriptures, it is hardly necessary to remark that their authenticity must be accepted with great reserve.

Persian Rivâyats, copied in the seventeenth century, advocate the marriage of first cousins, and allude vaguely to those between nearer relatives as long extinct, though most of their remarks merely recommend the performance of Khêdyôdath[1], without explaining the meaning of the term. Thus, we are informed that a person worthy of death can perform Khêdyôdath as a good work, but it is better if followed by the Bareshnûm ceremony[2]. An unclean person can do the same, but the Bareshnûm should precede the performance, so as to avoid sins arising from the uncleanness. The performance also destroys demons, wizards, and witches; and if arranged by any one, at his own expense, for another person, it is as meritorious as if performed by himself. But the following quotations are more descriptive of the practice[3]:—

'Again, whereas the great wisdom of the king and of the assembly of priests fully understands that the ceremony of all the religious rites[4] is a great good work, besides that which is called Khêdyôdath, yet, in these days, both have fallen out of *their* hands; but they will make an endeavour, so that they may form connection with their own, and on account of

[1] The Persian form of the word Khvêtûk-das. It is also written Khetyôdath in some passages, and Khêtvadat in others.

[2] The great ceremony of purification (see App. IV).

[3] The Persian Rivâyat from which all this information has been extracted is M10 (fol. 50 a).

[4] See Dd. XLIV, 2 n.

the Musulmâns the connection is a medium *one*[1], better than that of an infidel. And Ormazd has said that *by* as much as the connection is nearer *it is* more of a good work; and they display *their* endeavour and effort, and give the son of a brother and daughter of a brother *to* each other. And just as this *is said:* "I establish the *performer of* Khêdyôdath, I establish the patrol of the country[2]," even on this account they certainly display an endeavour.

'Query:—"How are the connections that relations form?" Reply:—"A brother's children with a brother's children and a sister's children, and relations with one another form connections, *and* it is proper for them."

'Khêdyôdath is *that* which is a great good work, and has fallen out of their hands, owing to the reason that there is no king of the good religion; and if it be so they will make an endeavour, and will form connections with their own, and will give the son of a brother and daughter of a brother to each other, and if not it is not proper; and every such connection as is nearer is more of a good work. And the mode they will act who are at first without a king will be an infidel *one*, and to form connections among themselves will be very difficult now he (the king) is a Musulmân, *but* that which is nearer is better and more of a good work.'

---

[1] This seems to be an allusion to some interference of the Muhammadan government with marriages of those next of kin. A similar allusion occurs in the next paragraph but one, which, with most of this paragraph, is also found in M7, fols. 229b, 230a.

[2] This Avesta quotation, from Visp. III, 18, 19, is as follows:—'*hv*aêtvadathem âstâya, daɴhâurvaêsem âstâya;' and the meaning of the last term is uncertain.

These quotations indicate that a great change had crept over the meaning of Khvêtûk-das since the dark ages of the Pahlavi Rivâyat, previously quoted, although a tradition of the old meaning still lingered in the minds of the writers. The modern meaning is, however, most completely explained in a passage, appended to a Persian version of Aêshm's complaint to Aharman, regarding the difficulty of destroying the effect of the season-festivals, the sacred feast, and Khvêtûk-das (Sls. XVIII). After Aharman has confessed his inability to suggest a means of destroying the merit of the last, the Persian writer adds the following particulars:—

'Therefore it is necessary to understand, that the chief Khêtvadat is that of a sister's daughter and brother's son; a medium Khêtvadat is that of a brother's son and a younger brother's daughter, or of a sister's son and a younger sister's daughter; and inferior to a medium Khêtvadat is that of a sister's son and a younger brother's daughter. It is necessary to know that any person who performs Khêtvadat, if *his* soul be *fit* for hell, will arrive among the ever-stationary[1]; if it be *one* of the ever-stationary it will arrive at heaven. Another particular is to be added: if any one, in departing, settles and strives for the connection of Khêtvadat of a next brother it is a good work of a thousand Tanâpûhars[2]; if any one strives to break off the connection of Khêtvadat he is worthy of death.'

---

[1] See Dd. XX, 3.

[2] See Dd. LXXVIII, 13. Geldner in his Studien zum Avesta, I, pp. 3–12, suggests that the original meaning of Av. tanupere-tha and peshôtanu was 'outcast;' but, although these words are translated by Pahl. tanâpûhar, it is doubtful whether this last

With this quotation, which occurs in a MS.[1] written A.D. 1723, we may conclude our examination of all passages in the Parsi scriptures referring to Khvêtûk-das, the result of which may be summarized as follows:—

First, the term does not occur at all in the oldest part of the Avesta, and when it is mentioned in the later portion it is noticed merely as a good work which is highly meritorious, without any allusion to its nature; only one passage (Vend. VIII, 36) indicating that both men and women can participate in it. So far, therefore, as can be ascertained from the extant fragments of the Avesta—the only internal authority regarding the ancient practices of Ma*zd*a-worship—the Parsis are perfectly justified in believing that their religion did not originally sanction marriages between those who are next of kin, provided they choose to ignore the statements of foreigners, as based upon imperfect information.

Second, when we descend to the Pahlavi translations and writings of the better class, which, in their present form, probably range from the sixth to the ninth century, we find many allusions to Khvêtûk-das between those next of kin, and only one obscure reference to the marriage of first cousins[2]. Marriages between the nearest relations are defended chiefly by reference to mythical and metaphorical

word be a mere transcript of tanuperetha (which ought to have been tanûpûhar), or whether it expresses the different idea of tan-apûhar, 'a person without a bridge *to heaven*,' which might have been that adopted by the Pahlavi translators of the Vendidâ*d*; an outcast in this world being very liable to be considered as an outcast from the next.

[1] M5, fols. 54, 55.

[2] In Dk. III, lxxxii (see p. 404).

statements regarding the creation, and to the practice of the progenitors of mankind; they are also advocated with all the warmth and vehemence that usually indicate much difficulty in convincing the laity, and this zealous vehemence increases as we descend to the dark ages of the Pahlavi Rivâyat[1], the compilation of which may perhaps be attributed to some writer of the thirteenth or fourteenth century. Unless, therefore, the Parsis determine to reject the evidence of such Pahlavi works as the Pahlavi Yasna, the book of Ar*d*â-Vîrâf, the Dînka*rd*, and the Dâ*d*istân-î Dînîk, or to attribute those books to heretical writers, they must admit that their priests, in the later years of the Sasanian dynasty, and for some centuries subsequently, strongly advocated such next-of-kin marriages, though, probably, with little success. That a practice now reprobated by all Parsis should have been formerly advocated by their priests, as a religious duty, need not excite the surprise of those who consider how slavery has been advocated by many Christians, on scriptural grounds, within the present generation, and how the execution of supposed witches was similarly advocated a few generations ago.

Third, as we come to the modern writings of the Persian Rivâyats, which may have commenced about the fifteenth century, we find the present form of Khvêtûk-das, the marriage of first cousins (which was only slightly mentioned in the Dînka*rd* of the ninth century), the only form in use; though obscure allusions are made to the other forms as being long extinct.

[1] See pp. 415–423.

At whatever period the practice of next-of-kin marriage may have originated there were evidently two reasons for its establishment and continuance; one was the indispensable necessity of offspring[1], unfettered by duties towards any other family, for the purpose of maintaining the necessary periodical ceremonies for the souls of those passed away; the other was the wish of preventing any risk of religious perversion consequent upon marrying into a family of strangers or infidels. Both of these reasons must have become intensified as the Ma*zd*a-worshippers diminished in numbers, hence the increasing vehemence of priestly advocacy, until the foreign conquerors probably interfered, and put a stop to the practice.

That such marriages were not unusual among other races, in ancient times, we learn from many tales in Greek and Roman mythology, from the usual practice of the Greek dynasty of the Ptolemies in Egypt, and even from the laws prohibiting such connections in Lev. xviii. 6–16, which, as laws are not made to prohibit practices that do not exist, would hardly have been written unless the children of Israel had at one time adopted the custom to some slight extent. That Parsis now deny the existence of such marriages among their ancestors proves that they no longer approve the custom, but does not affect the historical evidence of its former

[1] The oriental feeling of such a necessity, for the mere purpose of perpetuating the family, is abundantly manifested in the story of Lot's daughters (Gen. xix. 30–38), which is related without reproval by its writer. Also by the exceptional law requiring a man to marry his brother's wife, when the brother has died childless (Deut. xxv. 5–10).

existence. Christians no longer approve the persecution and execution of women for the imaginary crime of witchcraft, but it would be both childish and useless for them to deny that their ancestors committed hundreds of such judicial murders less than two centuries ago.

IV. The Bareshnûm Ceremony.

The great ceremony of purification for any Parsi man or woman who has become unclean by contact with the dead, or through any other serious defilement, lasts for nine nights, and is called the Bareshnûm, which is the Avesta name for the 'top' of the head, the first part of the body appointed to be washed in the ceremony, after the hands. The description of this ceremony, given in Pahl. Vend. IX, 1–145, which does not differ very materially from the rite still in use, is as follows[1] :—

Pahl. Vend. IX, 1. Zaratûst enquired of Aûhar*mazd* thus : 'O Aûhar*mazd*, propitious spirit! creator of the material world! who art the righteous *one* [of righteousness!' that is, Aûhar*mazd* is the righteous creator through invocation, *and* the rest through praise]. 2. 'How, when in the material existence they see a [clean] man together with [that which is polluted], (3) how shall they purify him clean who

[1] Observing that the passages in brackets do not occur in the Avesta text, but are added by the Pahlavi translators; and that the sections are numbered to correspond with the alternating Avesta and Pahlavi sections in the MSS., which is the division adopted in Spiegel's edition of the texts. The readings adopted are those of L4, wherever they are not defective; this MS. was written about A.D. 1324, and differs occasionally from Spiegel's printed text; it begins the ninth fargar*d* with the following heading :—'May it be fortunate! may it destroy the corruption (nasû*s*) which rushes on from a dead dog and men on to the living! May the pure, good religion of the Maz*d*a-worshippers be triumphant!'

is with *that* fraught with corruption [together with pollution] owing to that dead body? [that is, how should they make *him* thoroughly clean?]'

4. And Aûharmazd spoke thus: 'A righteous man, O Zaratûst the Spîtamân! [a purifier], (5) who is a speaker [that is, it is possible for him to speak], a true-speaker [that is, falsehood is little spoken by him], an enquirer of the liturgy [that is, the ritual is performed by him], *and* righteous, (6) he who specially understands the purification of the religion of the Mazda-worshippers [that is, he knows the rite], (7) such a one shall cut up the plants on the fruitful earth, (8) *for* a length of nine separate reeds[1] in every one of the four directions, (9) *at a place* on this earth which is most devoid of water, most devoid of trees, land most purified [from bodily refuse][2], *and* with the driest ground [that is, there is no damp in that extent of it]. 10. Even *where* least upon the paths do cattle and beasts of burden step forth, and the fire of Aûharmazd, the sacred twigs[3] spread forth with righteousness, and the righteous man[4] *do least exist.*'

11. 'Creator of the material world! *thou* righteous *one!* how far from the fire? how far from the water? how far from the sacred twigs spread forth

---

[1] Which would be 42 feet (see Dd. XLIII, 5 n); but the phrase gvî*d* nâî (which, in Pahl.Vend.VII, 90, has become gvî*d* hanâ by misreading gvî*d*ŏ-aê, and then substituting Huz. hanâ for Pâz. aê) is merely an attempted translation of Av. vîbâzu, which latter appears to mean the 'two arms' outstretched, or a fathom. So the 'separate reed' should be understood as a longer kind of reed, equal to a fathom, instead of 4 feet 8 inches.

[2] See Dd. XLVIII, 19 n. L4 omits this clause altogether.

[3] See Dd. XLIII, 5 n.

[4] Any priest not engaged in the purification.

with righteousness? how far from a man of the righteous?'

12. And Aûharmazd spoke thus: 'Thirty steps[1] from the fire, thirty steps from the water, thirty steps from the sacred twigs spread forth with righteousness, and three steps[2] from the men of the righteous. 13. The cutting out for the first hole [for bull's urine][3], after the coming on of summer, is two finger-*breadths* in excavation; after the coming on of hail-fraught (sôngagân-hômand) winter *it* is as *it were* a cup of four finger-*breadths*[4]. 14. *So also* for the second hole, for the third hole, for the fourth hole, the fifth, *and* the sixth.'

'How much is *one* such hole from another hole[5]?'

'As much as one step onwards.'

---

[1] As the step is three feet (see § 15), and the foot, being fourteen finger-breadths (see Bd. XXVI, 3 n), may be taken as 10½ inches, these thirty steps would be nearly 79 English feet.

[2] That is, 7 feet 10½ inches. This diminution of distance enables a purifying priest to stand near enough to an unclean person to hand him the purifying liquid in a ladle tied to a stick (see §§ 40–42), without going within the furrows traced around the holes or ablution seats at the same distance of three steps (see §§ 21–23).

[3] That is, at which the unclean person is sprinkled with the urine (see §§ 48–116). The urine should be that of a bull, according to Vend. XIX, 70; but Vend. VIII, 35, 36 state that it may be that of cattle or draught oxen, generally, or even that of those who perform Khvêtûk-das (see p. 391). At the present time the term magh, which means 'a hole' in the Avesta, is applied to the stones which are used as ablution seats for squatting upon.

[4] The greater depth of the hole for catching the ablution droppings in the winter, would provide for the larger quantity of liquid that could not sink into the soil, or evaporate, during the tedious washing, owing to the soil and air being damper than in summer.

[5] The probable positions of these holes, and of the furrows enclosing them are shown upon the plan of the Bareshnûm Gâh on p. 435, which differs but little from the plan still in use.

15. 'What kind of one step?'

'Just like three feet.'

16. 'The cutting out of the three other holes [which are for water], (17) after the coming on of summer, is as much as two finger-*breadths* in excavation; after the coming on of hail-fraught winter *it* is as much as four finger-*breadths*.'

18. 'How much from those former *ones* [for bull's urine]?'

'As much as three steps.'

19. 'What kind of three steps?'

'As much as the steps *one* plants in walking with the steps he would take.'

20. 'What kind of walking with steps?'

'Just like nine feet.'

21. 'Thou shalt also plough up a furrow with the blade due to Shat*r*yôvair[1].'

22. 'How much from the holes?'

'As much as three steps.'

'What kind of three steps?'

'As much as *in* walking with the steps *one* would take *and* plant.'

23. 'How much is the walking with steps?'

'As much as nine feet.'

24. 'Then, afterwards, is the ploughing up of the twelve furrows. 25. *By* the ploughing up of three from among *them* three holes are separated within *them*. 26. Thou shalt plough up three from among *them with* six holes separated within. 27. Thou shalt plough up three from among *them with* nine holes separated within. 28. *And* thou shalt plough

[1] That is, made of metal, which is under the special protection of the archangel Shat*r*yôvair or Shatvaîrô (see Dd. XLVIII, 17 n).

Plan of Bareshnûm Gâh.

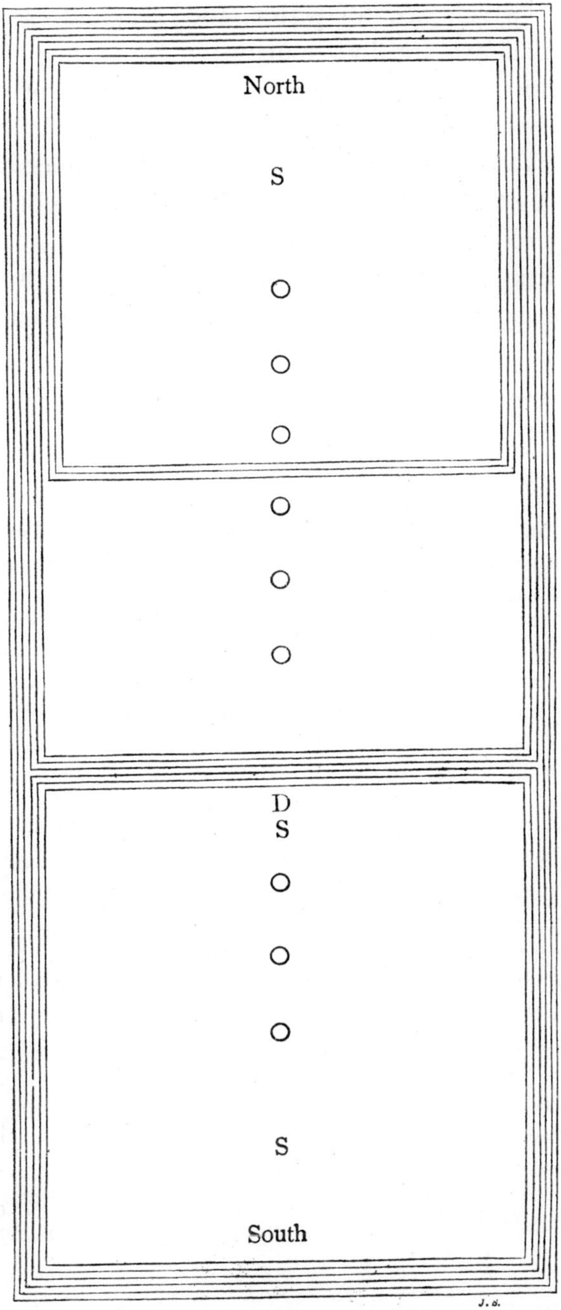

O, O, O, O, O, O, six northern holes, for bull's urine, one step apart.
O, O, O, three southern holes, for water, one step apart and three steps from the others.
S, S, S, three loads of stones on the three spaces of three steps.
D, place for collecting fifteen handfuls of dust for drying the body.

up three, within which are the [three] holes that are apart, [which are for water, and] beyond [*those* within, which are for bull's urine][1].

29. 'Thou shalt carry three loads of stones on to those spaces of nine feet[2], *as* an approach *to* the holes; (30) *or* potsherds, or knotty *and* massive *blocks*, or a *clod of the* earth of Vistâsp, or [a pot *or* something of] any hard earth whatever.

31. 'Afterwards, he who *has been* by the dead shall come to that approach, which is the approach to the holes. 32. Thereupon thou, O Zaratûst! hast to stand up more aside, by the furrows[3].

---

[1] The arrangement, here described, is that of six holes in a row, one step apart; then an interval of three steps, followed by three more holes, one step apart, in the same line. This row of nine holes, from north to south (see § 132, *e*), is surrounded by three furrows, the first six holes and the last three are both surrounded by a second series of three furrows, and the first three holes are surrounded by a third series of three furrows. And these furrows are not less than three steps from the holes in any place, except where they separate the three series of holes from each other. The object of the furrows, which are scored during the recitation of certain formulas (see § 132, *f*, *g*), is to prevent the fiend of corruption from forcing its way from the unclean person within the furrows to any other person outside them. And, as the fiend is supposed to be strongest at first, and to become gradually weakened by the progress of the purification (see § 119), the first three holes are surrounded by the strongest barrier of nine furrows.

[2] There were three such spaces, one between the furrows and the first hole, one between the sixth and seventh holes, and one between the last hole and the furrows (see the plan). It is not distinctly stated that these stones were to be distributed, as ablution seats, to each of the nine stations, as at present; but this was probably intended. At the present time an additional group of stones is placed outside the furrows, at the entrance to the north, as a station for the preliminary washing.

[3] That is, the priest is to stand outside, to the right (see § 132, *i*), but close to the furrows.

33. Then these words are to be murmured [*by thee*, that is]: "Praise to Spendarmad[1], the propitious!" 34. *And* he who *has been* by the dead shall speak in reply to it thus: "Praise to Spendarmad, the propitious!" 35. Then the fiend becomes disabled by every word [of each repetition]; (36) the smiting of the evil spirit, the wicked *one*, is owing to it; (37) the smiting of Aeshm[2], the impetuous assailant, is owing to it; (38) the smiting of the Mâzinîkân demons[3] is owing to it; (39) the smiting of all the demons is owing to it.

40. 'Afterwards, thou shalt sprinkle bull's urine upon *him* with an iron, or with a leaden, *ladle*. 41. *If* thou shalt sprinkle upon *him with a leaden one*[4], thou shalt strongly demand, O Zaratûst! the stem of a reed whose nine customary parts (pîsak) you have mentioned[5] [*as* nine knots]; (42) *and one* should tie that leaden *ladle* strongly on *its* foremost part[6].

43. 'He shall first wash over his hands [even to the elbows]. 44. When he does not wash over his hands, (45) he then makes all his own body impure [*and* polluted]. 46. When he shall have washed over his hands for three times, (47) then, when *thy* hands

---

[1] See p. 393, note 2. This exclamation is a Pahlavi version of a quotation from the Gâthas (Yas. XLVIII, 10, c).

[2] The demon of wrath (see Dd. XXXVII, 44).

[3] See Dd. XXXVII, 81. This passage (§§ 36–39) is quoted from Yas. XXVII, 2, LVI, xii, 5.

[4] These words are omitted in the Pahlavi text, but occur in the Avesta.

[5] Or, perhaps, 'murmured over' with prayers.

[6] This nine-knotted reed, or stick, must be so long that the ladle, tied to its end. can easily reach the unclean person at the holes, when the stick is held by the priest who stands outside the furrows.

shall have been washed over, (48) thou shalt sprinkle him on the front of the top of his head, [as far as the hair has grown.] 49. Then the fiend of corruption[1] rushes in front, upon *some* of the space between the brows of that man.

50. 'Thou shalt sprinkle in front, on *some* of the space between the brows of that man, [from the place where the hair has grown, as far as to the ears backwards, *and* both cheeks at the bottom.] 51. Then the fiend of corruption rushes upon the back of his head.

52. 'Thou shalt sprinkle on the back of his head, [from the place where the hair has grown, casting (stunak) one-fourth to the spine.] 53. Then the fiend of corruption rushes in front upon his jaws.

54. 'Thou shalt sprinkle in front, on his jaws, [both cheeks as far as to the ears backwards, casting one-fourth unto the throat.] 55. Then the fiend of corruption rushes upon his right ear.

56. 'Thou shalt sprinkle on his right ear. 57. Then the fiend of corruption rushes upon his left ear.

58. 'Thou shalt sprinkle on his left ear, [just as the ear is turned, casting one-fourth to the liquid[2].]

---

[1] The Nasûs fiend (see Dd. XVII, 7).

[2] The word, both here and in § 68, must be Av. âfs, 'water,' and not a Pâzand term for any part of the body, as any such term would be inadmissible in § 68. It would seem as if a smaller supply of liquid were requisite for the ears than for the other customary parts, so that a quarter of the supply is directed to be returned to the vessel holding the liquid. The remarks made by the Pahlavi translator, upon the sprinkling of the left-hand members of the body, are evidently intended also to apply, in nearly all cases, to the sprinkling of the right-hand members.

59. Then the fiend of corruption rushes upon his right shoulder.

60. 'Thou shalt sprinkle on his right shoulder. 61. Then the fiend of corruption rushes upon his left shoulder.

62. 'Thou shalt sprinkle on his left shoulder, [*on* the side in front, just as it is turned, even unto the elbow.] 63. Then the fiend of corruption rushes upon his right armpit.

64. 'Thou shalt sprinkle on his right armpit. 65. Then the fiend of corruption rushes upon his left armpit.

66. 'Thou shalt sprinkle on his left armpit, [as far as the hair has grown.] 67. Then the fiend of corruption rushes in front upon his chest.

68. 'Thou shalt sprinkle in front on his chest, [half the liquid to the shoulders, *and* half to the region of the throat, within three finger-*breadths* of the face[1].] 69. Then the fiend of corruption rushes upon his back.

70. 'Thou shalt sprinkle on his back, [from the slender *part* of the spine unto the anus.] 71. Then the fiend of corruption rushes upon his right nipple.

72. 'Thou shalt sprinkle on his right nipple. 73. Then the fiend of corruption rushes upon his left nipple.

74. 'Thou shalt sprinkle on his left nipple, [just as the nipple shall be turned; *and* those of women (zanagânŏ) are to be held up.] 75. Then the fiend of corruption rushes upon his right side.

76. 'Thou shalt sprinkle on his right side. 77. Then the fiend of corruption rushes upon his left side.

---

[1] Reading dîmak, but it may be gâmak (compare Pers. gâm, 'jaw'). L4 has gîmak.

78. 'Thou shalt sprinkle on his left side; [this, moreover, is because one specially recites for ever on *that* side.] 79. Then the fiend of corruption rushes upon his right hip[1].

80. 'Thou shalt sprinkle on his right hip. 81. Then the fiend of corruption rushes upon his left hip.

82. 'Thou shalt sprinkle on his left hip, [just as it is turned, as far as to the hollow[2] of it (gûyak-î valman) below the thigh.] 83. Then the fiend of corruption rushes upon his sexual part.

84. 'Thou shalt sprinkle on his sexual part. 85. If it be a male, thou shalt sprinkle behind it before*hand*, and in front of it afterwards; (86) and if it be a female, thou shalt sprinkle in front of it before*hand*, *and* behind it afterwards; [*on* this occasion half is for the front *and* half for behind, and it is rubbed in in front.] 87. Then the fiend of corruption rushes upon his right thigh.

88. 'Thou shalt sprinkle on his right thigh. 89. Then the fiend of corruption rushes upon his left thigh.

90. 'Thou shalt sprinkle on his left thigh, [from the prominence (gôhâk) below the thigh to the knee.] 91. Then the fiend of corruption rushes upon his right knee.

92. 'Thou shalt sprinkle on his right knee. 93. Then the fiend of corruption rushes upon his left knee.

---

[1] Reading srînak, as in Pahl. Vend. VIII, 178–182; but here the word is four times written sînak.

[2] Or, perhaps, 'prominence' is meant, as in § 90; although the two words gûyak and gôhâk are written differently, they refer probably to the same part.

94. 'Thou shalt sprinkle on his left knee, [above just as it is turned, *and* below the slender *part;* there are *some* who would say thus: "As much above it as below."] 95. Then the fiend of corruption rushes upon his right shin.

96. 'Thou shalt sprinkle on his right shin. 97. Then the fiend of corruption rushes upon his left shin.

98. 'Thou shalt sprinkle on his left shin, [from the knee unto the place where the leg *and* foot unite.] 99. Then the fiend of corruption rushes upon his right ankle[1].

100. 'Thou shalt sprinkle on his right ankle. 101. Then the fiend of corruption rushes upon his left ankle.

102. 'Thou shalt sprinkle on his left ankle, [just as the leg *and* foot unite, that is, while the ten toes are back to the ground.] 103. Then the fiend of corruption rushes upon his right instep.

104. 'Thou shalt sprinkle on his right instep. 105. Then the fiend of corruption rushes upon his left instep.

106. 'Thou shalt sprinkle on his left instep, [from the place where the leg *and* foot unite, to the end of his toes.] 107. Then the fiend of corruption turns dejected under the sole *of the foot, and* its likeness is as *it were* the wing of a fly's body.

108. 'The toes *being* held quite in union with the ground, his heel is held up from the ground. 109. Thou shalt sprinkle on his right sole. 110. Then the fiend of corruption rushes upon his left sole.

---

[1] The word zang means rather 'the lower part of the leg.'

111. 'Thou shalt sprinkle on his left sole. 112. Then the fiend of corruption turns dejected under the toes, *and* its likeness is as *it were* the wing of a fly.

113. 'The heel *being* held quite in union with the ground, his toes are held up from the ground. 114. Thou shalt sprinkle on his right toes. 115. Then the fiend of corruption rushes upon his left toes.

116. 'Thou shalt sprinkle on his left toes. 117. Then the fiend of corruption returns dejected to the northern quarter in the shape of a raging fly, bandy-legged, lean-hipped, illimitably spotted, so that spot is joined to spot, like the most tawdry[1] noxious creature, *and* most filthy.

118. 'Then these words are to be murmured, which are most triumphant *and* most healing[2]:—

'"As is the will of the patron spirit [as is the will of Aûha*r*ma*zd*], so should be the *earthly* master [so should be the high priest], owing to whatever are the duty *and* good works of righteousness; [that is, *he* is always to perform duty and good works as authoritatively as the will of Aûha*r*ma*zd*.] That which is the gift of good thought is the work of both existences [and the work] of Aûha*r*ma*zd*; [that is, the reward *and* recompense they give to good thought, they give also to him; there are *some* who would say thus: 'It is the possession of good thought.']

[1] Reading bô*g*-âkîntûm, 'most stuffed with ostentation,' as in L4. In AV. XVII, 12 the word can be read ba*z*ak-âyîntûm, 'most sin-accustomed.'

[2] Only the initial and final words of the Avesta of the following passages are given in the MSS. here, but they are given at length, with their Pahlavi translation, in Vend. VIII, 49–62, whence the Pahlavi version is here taken.

The sovereignty is given to Aûharmazd, [that is, Aûharmazd has made the ruler for himself,] who *has* given protection *and* nourishment to the poor, [that is, he would provide assistance *and* intercession for them.][1]

'"Who is given to me by thee, O Aûharmazd! *as* a protection? [when[2] I shall do duty *and* good works, who would provide me protection?]—when I am in custody of the malice of that wicked [Aharman, that is, he retains malice with me in *his* thoughts]—other than thy fire *and* good thought? [this I know, that they would do *so* on account of you; but, apart from you, who would provide me protection?] When in their employ I invoke righteousness, O Aûharmazd! [that is, I shall do duty *and* good works, who would provide me protection?] That which thou shalt proclaim to me *as* religion through a high-priest [this I say, that is, preach religion through a high-priest][3].

'"Who is the smiter with triumph, through this thy teaching of protection? [that is, so *far* as is declared by the revelation of scripture, who should inflict the punishment for sinners?] With clearness the superintendence (radîh) of the creation in both existences is to be taught to me, [that is, it is necessary for thee to give unto me the high-priesthood here *and* there[4].] The arrival of virtuous obedience (Srôsh), with good thought (Vohûman), is here,

[1] This paragraph is the Pahlavi version of the Ahunavar, or Yathâ-ahû-vairyô formula (see p. 385).

[2] Reading amat, instead of mûn, 'who,' (see Dd. LXII, 4 n.)

[3] This paragraph is the Pahlavi version of the Kem-nâ-mazdâ stanza of the Gâthas (Yas. XLV, 7).

[4] Both in this world and the next.

[that is, it is necessary for thee to give Vistâsp[1] unto me as assistance.] O Aûharmazd! [the arrival of] that *one* [is *according* to my wish], who is he *according* to the wish of every one, [*that* Sôshâns[2] that shall be necessary for every one, so that they *may* thereby convey away their misery, the misery *it* is possible he should convey away from every one.][3]

'"*Let us be* guarded from the most afflicting *one* [here, *and* apart from the sinners], O Aûharmazd *and* Spendarmad[4]! [that is, keep us away from the harm of the evil spirit!] Perish, thou demon fiend! [as I speak in front *of thee.*] Perish, thou race of the demons! [that is, their race is from that place.][5] Perish, thou *work* transformed by the demons [for uselessness]! Perish, thou *work* produced by the demons [*hereto*fore *and here*after! this produced without the sacred beings, and produced by them (the demons) even for uselessness]. Perish utterly, thou fiend! [that is, mayst thou become invisible!] Perish utterly, thou fiend! [that is, rush away from here, *and* mayst thou become invisible on any path!] Perish utterly and apart, thou fiend! [that is, stand not again on any path!] Thou shalt perish again to the north! [the path was mentioned thus: 'Go *in* the direction of the north!'] do not destroy the material world of righteousness[6]!"

[1] The king in the time of Zaratûst (see Dd. XXXVII, 36).

[2] The last of the future apostles (see Dd. II, 10).

[3] This paragraph is the Pahlavi version of a passage in the Gâthas (Yas. XLIII, 16, b–e).

[4] See p. 393, note 2.

[5] From hell, the place of the demons.

[6] It appears from what follows, in § 120, that the whole of the sprinklings and exorcisms, detailed in §§ 33–118, are to be repeated at each of the first six holes.

119. 'At the first hole the man becomes freer from the *fiend of* corruption, [that is, it shall depart a little from his body, like a flock when they disperse it.]

120. '*Then these words are to be murmured by thee, &c.* [*as in* §§ 33–118. *At*] *the second* [*hole, &c., as in* § 119. *And the same routine is to be followed at*] *the third, fourth, fifth, and sixth* [*holes*][1].

'Afterwards he shall sit—he who *has been* by the dead—within the precinct (*sitrâ*) of the holes[2] apart from those holes [which are for bull's urine]. 121. So much from that [of the previous *ones* for bull's urine] as four finger-*breadths*[3]. 122. They shall also dig up those full diggings up of this earth, [they should accomplish this well.] 123. They shall scrape together fifteen handfuls of the earth, [so that they shall quite dislodge the damp purely.][4] 124. And they shall remain about it the whole *period* from that *time* until *the time* when the hair on his head shall become dry, (125) *and* until *the time* when the wet earth on his body shall become dry.

126. 'Then he who *has been* by the dead shall come to that approach to those other holes [which are for water]. 127. At the first hole he shall then purify over his own body once with water. 128. At the second hole he shall then purify over his own

---

[1] This paragraph is omitted in the Pahlavi text, being merely given in the Avesta (for the sake of brevity) so far as the words are not included in the brackets.

[2] The three holes for washing with water.

[3] That is, three English inches south of the six furrows which separate the first six holes from the last three, at the point D on the plan.

[4] That is, the person undergoing purification shall be rubbed with dust until he is quite dry.

body twice with water. 129. At the third hole he shall then purify over his own body thrice with water.

130. 'Afterwards, he who is perfumed with sandarac (râsnŏ)[1], or benzoin, or aloes[2], or any other of the most odoriferous of plants, (131) shall then put on *his* clothes. 132. Then he who *has been* by the dead shall come to that approach, the approach to *his* abode[3].'

[*a*. The clothing is always *cleansed* by the Khshvash-m*a*unghô ("the six-months' *process*")[4].

b. Afarg[5] said two purifiers are requisite[6], and of the two he is suitable who has performed the ritual; thus they have been very unanimous; when he scores the furrow, washes that *unclean person* in the customary *places, and* utters the Avesta he has performed it; the other, when he has not performed *it*,

---

[1] Av. urvâsna (which is translated by Pahl. râsnŏ) is supposed, in India, to mean sandal-wood.

[2] These are supposed, in India, to be the two substances meant by the Av. vohû-gaona and vohû-kereti, which are merely transcribed by the Pahl. hû-gôn and hû-keret. The Avesta text adds a fourth perfume, named hadhâ naêpata, which is understood to mean the pomegranate bush, although that plant seems to yield no perfume.

[3] For the continuation of the instructions see § 133; the text being here interrupted by a long Pahlavi commentary on the whole of the foregoing description of the ceremony.

[4] This sentence is evidently incomplete in the Pahlavi text. The process is thus described in Pahl. Vend. VII, 36:—'If it be that *it* is woven, they shall wash *it* over six times with bull's urine, they shall scrape together six times on the earth *with it* [so that they quite dislodge its moisture purely], they shall wash *it* over six times with water, *and* they shall perfume over *it* six months at a window in the house.' For the Avesta version of this description, which is nearly the same, see Sls. II, 95 n.

[5] See Ep. I, v, 1.

[6] See Ep. I, vi, 4, II, ii, 7.

is unsuitable; when *there* shall also be one who is suitable[1] he fully solemnizes a Vendidâ*d* *service*, for this purpose, with a dedication (shnumanŏ) *to* Srôsh.

c. For every single person, at the least, one cup, alike of water and bull's urine, is to be set down *in* that place[2], and at the beginning of its consecration *it* is to be thoroughly inspected, and at the Vendidâ*d* *it* is to be thoroughly inspected[3]; afterwards, when it is covered, *it* is also well; the pebbles cast into *it*[4] they should carry back to the holy-water, there is no use *for them;* when thoroughly consecrated it is always suitable, until it becomes quite fetid[5].

d. For the avoidance of an unsecluded (agûbâl) menstruous *woman* nava vîbâzva drâ*g*ô ('the length of nine fathoms')[6] from her is necessary, when she stands nearest; in a wild spot the herbage is to be dug up[7]; when they shall make *the purifying place* in the town, and a path, or a stream, or a wall does not extend into it, it is suitable; and the cleanly plucking up of its small trees, extracting *them* in the daytime with *recitation of* the Avesta of Zaratû*s*t[8] —those which are thick not existing among the holes—is proper.

e. And every one who digs the holes, with whatever he digs, *and* whenever he digs, is suitable; four finger-*breadths* and two finger-*breadths*[9] is no matter;

---

[1] See Ep. I, vi, 7. [2] See Ep. I, vii, 1.

[3] L4 has '*it* is to be taken up,' by omitting the first letter of nikîri*s*nŏ.

[4] See Ep. I, vii, 16, II, iii, 12. [5] See Ep. I, viii, 1–6.

[6] See § 8. [7] See § 7.

[8] These twelve words do not occur in L4.

[9] See § 13.

each hole is at a minimum *distance* of three feet[1], at a maximum as much as *one* thoroughly purifies his body in; and *they* are to be formed in it from the north, and are to be dug in the direction towards its more southern side.

f. In the day*time* is the purifier's scoring of the furrows, and with a blade *they* are to be scored; with *the recital of* the Avesta[2] *they* are to be scored; in the day *they* are to be scored[3]; in that day *they* are to be scored, when a furrow is scored, three Ashem-vohûs[4], the Fravarânê[5], whatever period *of the day one* considers *it to be*, the dedication *to* Srôsh[6], and its *inward* prayer[7] are to be taken up *inwardly*.

g. *It* is also to be done inside it from the north, and its end is to be passed back at the end; *for* every single furrow *there* is one Yathâ-ahû-vairyô[8] at the least, and at the most as many as are possible for it; a furrow is not to be scored again for a furrow, until *it* is to be put into use; whenever it is fully disturbed *it* is to be scored again with *the recital of* its Avesta; when prepared for use *and one* scores *it* again it is no matter.

---

[1] See §§ 14, 15.

[2] The Ahunavar or Yathâ-ahû-vairyô (see § *g*).

[3] So in L4.

[4] See Dd. LXXIX, 1, note.

[5] That is, the profession of faith (Yas. I, 65), which is as follows:—'I will profess myself a Zarathustrian Mazda-worshipper, opposed to the demons *and* of the Ahura faith.' This is followed by the dedication to the period of the day, which is given for the first period only in Yas. I, 66, 67; the dedications for the other periods will be found in Gâh II–V, 1.

[6] Sîr. I, 17.

[7] See Dd. XL, 5, note. All the prayers here detailed are to be murmured merely as a preliminary spell, but while each furrow is being scored a further formula is to be recited (see § *g*).

[8] See pp. 385–386.

h. Once the outside of the body is to be made quite clean from the bodily refuse[1] of the world; *and* the hair *being* tied up—it is no use to cut the pubes (nihânŏ)—*he* is also to be brought into it (the precinct) from the north to the holes.

i. The purifier stands up on the right-hand side, and when he retains the *inward* prayer from scoring the furrows[2] it is proper; when not, the prayer to be taken *inwardly* by him—which is his utterance of Nemas*k*â yâ ârmaitis îzâ*k*â ('and the homage which is devotion and nourishment')[3]—is also that which is to be uttered *by the unclean person*; and when *he* is not able to speak, *it* is both times to be uttered for *him*.

j. And his hands are to be thoroughly washed three times, not in the inside; *as to* the other customary *parts* (pîsak) Afarg *has* said three times, not in the inside, *but* Mê*d*ôk-mâh[4] one time; also the water *and* bull's urine, such as are necessary for him, are to be conveyed on to him; and a portion (bahrak) is to be preserved for him *away* from the body, *and*, when anything comes upon him, a little bull's urine is to be dropped down upon him; likewise,

---

[1] See Dd. XLVIII, 19 n.

[2] That is, when he has not broken its spell by talking, since he began the scoring.

[3] These are the Avesta words from Yas. XLVIII, 10, c, of which the Pahlavi version is given in §§ 33, 34.

[4] Written Mê*d*yôk-mâh in Ep. I, v, 1. The statement here attributed to Mê*d*ôk-mâh is ascribed to Afarg in Ep. I, vi, 7, 9, II, ii, 6, but Afarg is there said to be 'the prior deponent,' as he is here; we should, therefore, probably transpose the 'three times' and 'one time' in our text; the blunder having originated from the frequent substitution of hanâ for aê in Pahlavi, both meaning 'this,' while aê also means 'one' and is the cipher for '3.'

any customary *part*, while *being* washed by him, is to be preserved from that which is not washed; when it comes upon it, it is improper.

k. When a drop of water (âv yûgakŏ-1) shall remain upon *him*, *his* hand is to be thoroughly rubbed over it; when at the same hole and he becomes doubtful as to a customary *part*[1], when he knows *which*, *it* is to be washed by him again, and from that onwards *they* are always to be washed again by him; when he does not know *which*, the beginning of *the washing at* the hole is to be done again by him, and when he comes unto that which *he did* before, when he knows *it*, *he* is also to go again to that after it, from his doing again of the beginning of *the washing at* the hole; when he becomes doubtful as to the hole, he is to go back to that which is not doubtful.

l. And when they go from hole to hole, the dog[2] is to be held once, the Avesta[3] of the purifier is to be spoken, and it is to be done by him thus:—When he arrives at the place, *it* is done by him; when not, the head is to be done thoroughly—there are *some* who would say thus: 'In the same hole the head is to be done thoroughly'—and all four feet of the dog are to be put by him into the hole; he is also to sit down within four finger-*breadths*[4], and the Pa*nk*adasa zemô ha*n*kanayen ('fifteen *times* of earth they shall

[1] That is, when he is doubtful which he washed last.

[2] The dog is not mentioned in the Avesta account of the Bareshnûm in Vend. IX, but it is ordered to be brought before the unclean person in another such account in Vend. VIII, 120, 123. The use of the dog is that its sight or touch is supposed to destroy or drive away the Nasû*s*, or fiend of corruption.

[3] The exorcism in § 118.

[4] See § 121.

scrape together')[1] are to be well completed by him, *it* is also to be thoroughly done by him, and *he* is to be fully guarded while he properly *and* thoroughly well perseveres.

m. And, after it, he is to go unto the holes for water; the different times with water are just like the different holes for bull's urine, except holding the dog; the dog, too, works for *him* inside.

n. When he seeks for it, *it*[2] is to be thoroughly warmed *for* him; when he hungers for it, bread is to be given to him; when *the necessity of* making water arises, something is to be held unto him; when, on account of his imperfect strength (va*d* zôrîh), *he* is quite unable to wash, some one is to sit down inside with him; when *he* is only just[3] washed, *he* is to come into his position therein before, the *inward* prayer is to be spoken out by him, and the *inward* prayer is to be again offered by him, his customary *parts* are also washed, and are to be considered as washed.

o. When he shall keep on for three washings[4], though not clean, it is not improper; when he does not attain three washings, it is not proper; when the enclosure is not to be formed to the north[5], it is not proper; when *one* shall not solemnize the Vendidâ*d service*[6], it is not proper.

p. When the purifier shall not have performed the ritual, it is not proper; when the purifier is not a man, it is not proper.

---

[1] The Avesta version of § 123.

[2] The water, apparently.

[3] Perhaps it should be *k*and tâk, 'several times,' instead of *k*îgûn tâk, 'only just.'

[4] See §§ 130, 140, 144. [5] See § *e*. [6] See § *b*.

q. When he shall not wash on the customary *parts*, it is not proper; when he does not utter the Avesta, it is not proper; and when the dog[1] is not held, it is not proper; when *there* is no digging of the holes, it is not proper; when he does not perform the Pa*n*kadasa zemô ha*n*kanayen ('fifteen *times* of earth they shall scrape together')[2], it is not proper.

r. When *it* is not the purifier *who* scores the furrows, *and* he does not score *them* with a blade[3], nor does he score *them* with *the recitation of* the Avesta, nor does he score *them* in the day*time*, it is not proper.

s. When he shall see *anything* impure in the hole, it is not proper; when they shall cause rain *to come* within a hole for bull's urine, it is not proper; when night shall come in upon him, it is not proper; when in everything *there* is suitableness, but as to one thing doubt arises, through that suitableness it is not proper.]

133. '*He*[4] is to sit down in the place of the secluded (armê*s*tânŏ)[5], within the precinct (*s*it*r*â) of *his* abode, apart from the other Ma*zd*a-worshippers. 134. He shall not come with authorization to fire, nor to water, nor to earth, nor to animals, nor to plants, nor to a righteous man, nor to a righteous

[1] See § *l*. [2] See § 123. [3] See § *f*.

[4] He who has been by the dead, as stated in § 132, in connection with which this sentence is to be read; the foregoing §§ *a–s* being interpolated by the Pahlavi translators.

[5] The original meaning of armê*s*t was probably 'most stationary,' as it is a term applied to water in tanks, helpless cripples, and insane people, as well as to unclean persons who have to remain apart from their friends (see Sls. II, 98 n).

woman, (135) at all from that *time,* until *the time* when his three nights shall fully elapse.

136. 'After those three nights he shall wash over *his* body, and *his* clothes are purified over in such a way *as* with bull's urine and also with water. 137. He shall sit in the place of the secluded, within the precinct of *his* abode, apart from the other Maz*d*a-worshippers. 138. He shall not come with authorization to fire, *&c.* [just as *has been* written *in* § 134], (139) at all from that *time,* until *the time* when his six nights shall fully elapse.

140. '*After those six nights*[1] he shall wash over *his* body, and *his* clothes *are purified* over *in such a way as* with bull's urine and also with water. 141–143. He shall sit in the place of the secluded [just as *has been* written *in* §§ 133–135] *until the time when his nine nights shall fully elapse.*

144. 'Then, after the nine nights, he shall wash over *his* body, *and his* clothes *are purified over in such a way as with bull's urine and also with water.* 145. Then he shall come with authorization unto fire, unto water, unto earth, unto animals, unto plants, unto a righteous man, unto a righteous woman.'

Besides the above fully detailed description of the Bareshnûm ceremony we find two other accounts of the rite, in the Vendidâ*d*. Of these the most detailed is contained in Vend. VIII, 117–228, which mentions the use of the dog[2], the nine holes, the washing with bull's urine and water, and all the

---

[1] The MSS. omit several words, when sentences are repeated, for the sake of brevity.

[2] See § *l* above.

detail of driving the fiend of corruption from one part of the body to another (by sprinkling with 'the good waters') till it flies away to the north as in Vend. IX, 117. But it omits the description of the purifier, the dimensions of the purifying place, the scoring of the furrows, the placing of the stones, the exorcism[1], the seclusion for nine nights, and all the washings after the first day.

The other account, which is much shorter, is given in Vend. XIX, 67–84. It specifies that the urine must be that of a young bull, and that the purifier must score a furrow; it mentions the recitation of a hundred Ashem-vohûs and two hundred Yathâ-ahû-vairyôs, four washings with bull's urine and two with water, nine nights' exposure, followed by attention to the fire and fumigation, when the man clothes himself while paying homage to the sacred beings, and is clean; but no other details are given.

[1] That is, the exorcism is not found in the Pahlavi version, but is introduced in the Vendidâ*d* sâdah in an abbreviated form, possibly copied from Vend. IX, 118.

V. Finding a Corpse in the Wilderness.

The controversy between Mânûs*k*îhar and his brother, Zâ*d*-sparam, of which the Epistles of Mânûs*k*îhar are the only portion extant, turned chiefly upon the meaning to be attached to Vend. VIII, 271–299[1], and whether the mode of purification therein detailed was a sufficient substitute, or merely a preparation, for the Bareshnûm ceremony. The following is a translation of the Pahlavi version of this passage[2]:—

Pahl. Vend. VIII, 271. 'O creator! how are those men purified, O righteous Aûha*r*ma*zd*! who shall stand by a corpse, in a distant place, upon a wild spot[3]?'

272. And Aûha*r*ma*zd* spoke thus: 'They are purified, O righteous Zaratû*s*t!'

273. 'But when so? [that is, how will *such a one* become clean?]'

274. 'If a corpse-eating dog, or a corpse-eating bird, *has* attacked that corpse, (275) *the man* shall then purify over his own body with bull's urine, (276) thirty times by washing forwards [*with* the bull's urine], *and* thirty times by washing over[4], [and

[1] See Sacred Books of the East, vol. iv, pp. 116–118.

[2] Subject to the same observations as those detailed in p. 431 n.

[3] Reading pavan va*s*kar, but the MSS., by omitting a stroke, have pavan *s*ikar, 'on the chase.'

[4] So here, but 'washing backwards' in § 279; and in Ep. II, iv, 2 we find 'upwards' and 'downwards,' instead of 'forwards' and 'backwards.' The Pahlavi translators were evidently doubtful whether the Av. upasnât*e*ê (see Ep. II, iii, 2) meant 'washing over, backwards, or downwards.'

his hand shall rub over it.] 277. Of the topmost *part* of him is the washing over, [that is, the washing of his head is that regarding which *there* is a mention through this study-causing (hûshkar) exclamation.][1]

278. 'If a corpse-eating dog, or a corpse-eating bird, *has* not attacked that corpse, (279) *he shall purify* fifteen times by washing forwards, *and* fifteen times by washing backwards, [and *his* hand shall rub over it.]

280. 'He shall run the first mile (hâsar)[2]. 281. He shall then run forwards, [when the Pa*nk*adasa ("fifteen *times*") shall be performed by him.] 282. *And* when he shall thus stop opposite any one whomsoever of the material existence[3], he shall be prepared with a loud issue of words, (283) thus[4]: "I have thus stood close by the body of him who is dead; I am no wisher *for it* by thought, I am no wisher *for it* by word, I am no wisher *for it* by deed, [that is, *it* is not possible for me *to be* as *though* washed.] 284. It demands purification for me, [that is, wash me thoroughly!]" 285. When he runs, the first he shall reach, (286) if they do not grant him purification, share one-third of that deed of his, [that is, of all that sin, not possible for him *to bear*, except when they shall perform *his purification*, one *part* in three is theirs at *its* origin.]

287. 'He runs the second mile [while he runs for

---

[1] Implying that the Pahlavi translators had found the use of Av. aghrya for 'head' rather perplexing.

[2] The hâsar was 'a thousand steps of the two feet' (see Bd. XXVI, 1, note), and was, therefore, about an English mile.

[3] That is, any human being.

[4] See Ep. I, ii, 10.

it]. 288. He runs, *and* a second time he reaches *people*. 289. If they do not grant him purification, (290) they share a half[1] of that deed of his, [that is, of all that sin, not possible for him *to bear*, except when they shall perform *his purification*, as *it were* a half is even for them at *its* origin.]

291. 'He shall run the third mile [while he runs for *it*]. 292. When he runs, the third he shall reach, (293) if they do not grant him purification, share all[2] that deed of his, [that is, all that sin which *it* is not possible for him *to bear*, except when they shall perform *his purification*, is ever *theirs* at *its* origin.]

294. 'He shall then run forwards[3]. 295. He shall thus stop opposite *some people* of the next house, village, tribe, *or* district, *and* he shall be prepared with a loud issue of words, (296) thus: "I have thus stood close by the body of him who is dead; (297) I am no wisher *for it* by thought, I am no wisher *for it* by word, I am no wisher *for it* by deed, [that is, *it* is not possible *to bear* without washing.] 298. It demands purification for me, [that is, wash me thoroughly!]" 299. If they do not grant him purification, he shall then purify over his own body with bull's urine, *and* also with water; thus he shall be thoroughly purified over[4].'

[*a*. He shall go three miles; it is not allowable to walk back to *his* district, until he *has* fully striven

[1] That is, half of the two-thirds remaining with him, or one-third of the whole original trespass.

[2] That is, all the remaining one-third of the original trespass.

[3] See Ep. II, iii, 3.

[4] What follows is a commentary, by the Pahlavi translators, on the whole passage.

with three persons, and all that sin, not possible for him *to bear*, except when they shall perform *his purification*, is theirs at *its* origin.

b. When thus thoroughly washed by him*self*, his duty even then is the work frakairi frakerenao*d*, vâstrê verezyôi*d* ('he should accomplish with perseverance, he should cultivate in the pastures[1]'); there are *some* who would say thus: 'He is always for the performance of work, and abstinence from the ceremonies of others is for him[2].']

[1] Quoted from Vend. XIX, 140, where the words 'sheep's food *and* food for oxen' are added.

[2] A person so purified by himself, after vainly seeking a proper purifier, is, therefore, only fit for the ordinary labours of life, and must avoid all religious celebrations till properly purified by the Bareshnûm ceremony. This was the opinion of Mânû*sk*îhar, but it is based upon a Pahlavi commentary, and not upon the Avesta text, which is not clear upon this point.

INDEX.

OBSERVATIONS.

1. The references in this index are to the pages of the introduction and appendix, and to the chapters and sections of the translations; the chapters being denoted by the larger ciphers, or by roman type.

2. References to passages which contain special information are given in parentheses, when the reference is not the first one.

3. Though different forms of the same name may occur in the translations, only one form is usually given in the index, to which the references to all forms are attached; except when the forms differ so much as to require to be widely separated in the index.

4. Pâzand forms are printed in italics, as their orthography is usually corrupt. In all such italicised names any letters which would elsewhere be italic are printed in roman type.

5. Abbreviations used are:—Ap. for Appendix; AV. for Ar*d*â-Vîrâf; Av. for Avesta word; Byt. for Bahman Ya*s*t; com. for commentator; Cor. for Corrections; Dd. for Dâ*d*istân-î-Dînîk; Dk. for Dînka*rd*; Dr. for Doctor; Ep. for Epistle; ins. for inscription; lun. man. for lunar mansion; m. for mountain; meas. for measure; Mkh. for Mainyô-î Khar*d*; n for foot-note; Pahl. for Pahlavi; Pers. for Persian; Prof. for Professor; r. for river; Riv. for Rivâyat; Sans. for Sanskrit word; trans. for translation; Vend. for Vendidâ*d*; Visp. for Vispara*d*; Yas. for Yasna.

INDEX.

CORRECTIONS.

P. 66, line 15; p. 67, l. 7; for 'Mitrô' read 'Mit*r*ô.'

P. 108, lines 1, 3, for 'the *Supreme* Being' and 'the Being' read 'God (yêdatô),' and cancel note 1.

P. 109, note 2, add 'Malkôs has also been read Markûs and traced to Av. mahrkû*s*ô (see Fragment VIII, 2 in Westergaard's Zend-Avesta, p. 334), which appears to be the title of some demon, regarding whom very little can be ascertained from the text that mentions him.'

P. 143, l. 12; 145, l. 6; 150, note 6; 252, l. 6; 289, note 2; 318, ll. 26, 27; 346, l. 24; for 'Âtûr' and 'Âtûrô' read 'Âtû*r*' and 'Âtû*r*ô.'

The following emendations depend upon the meaning to be attached to the word vâspôharak, or vâspûharak, which in Mkh. I, 7 was traced to Pers. bâ, 'with,' and sipihrah, 'sphere, world, universe,' and supposed to mean 'world-renowned,' being rendered by vikhyâtimat in Sanskrit. The objections to this etymology are that Pers. bâ is Pahl. a*v*âk (not vâ), which is nearly always replaced by Huz. levatman, and that vâspûhar appears to be the correct form of the word vaspûr, which explains the Huz. barbêtâ, literally 'son of the house' in the Pahlavi Farhang (p. 9, ed. H.); the latter word having been the highest title of the Persian nobility, probably confined to the heads of seven families (see Nöldeke's Geschichte der Perser und Araber zur Zeit der Sasaniden, pp. 71, 501). Such nobles are called barbêtân in the Hâ*g*îâbâd inscription, line 6, and vâspûharakan in the Naq*s*-i Rustam inscription, line 6; they may perhaps be styled 'princes,' and their title, vâspûhar, may be traced to the ancient Persian equivalent of Av. vîsô puthra (Vend. VII, 114), literally 'son of the village or borough.' It may be noted, however, that the word 'sphere' does really occur in a form very similar to this title, in the word aspiharakânîkîhâ, 'as regards the spheres,' in Dd. 69, 4.

P. 78, ll. 11-13, read 'But those who are the more princely (vâspûharakânîktar) producers of the renovation are said to be seven . . .'

P. 91, ll. 11, 12, read '. . . and he made the princes (vâspûharakânîhâ) contented.'

P. 172, ll. 26, 27, read '. . . a minder of the princes of the religion (dîn-vâspûharakânŏ), the angels, and *with* pure thoughts . . .'

P. 262, ll. 15, 16, read '. . . and its position is most princely (vâspû-harakânîktar).'

P. 281, ll. 17, 18, read 'On account of the princeliness (vâspûhara-kânîh) of the good *people* of Khvanîras . . .'

P. 289, ll. 14, 15, read '. . . I *am* more applauding the princes (vâspû-harakânŏ-zâhtar) about the property of the profession . . .'

P. 306, ll. 23, 24, read '. . . to keep in use the equal measure *which is* more *the custom* of his own superiors (nafsman vâspûhara-kântar).'

Transliteration of Oriental Alphabets adopted for the Translations of the Sacred Books of the East.

CONSONANTS.	MISSIONARY ALPHABET. I Class.	II Class.	III Class.	Sanskrit.	Zend.	Pehlevi.	Persian.	Arabic.	Hebrew.	Chinese.
Gutturales.										
1 Tenuis	k	...	....	क	𐬐	[illegible]	ك	ك	כּ	k
2 " aspirata	kh	...	....	ख	𐬑	[illegible]	...	...	כ	kh
3 Media	g	...	....	ग	𐬔	[illegible]	گ	...	גּ	...
4 " aspirata	gh	...	....	घ	𐬖	[illegible]	...	...	ג	...
5 Gutturo-labialis	q	...	....	...	....	...	ق	ق	ק	...
6 Nasalis	ṅ (ng)	...	....	ङ	{𐬧 (ng) / 𐬣 (N)}	...	...	...	...	...
7 Spiritus asper	h	...	....	ह	𐬵 (𐬓 *hv*)	[illegible]	ه	ه	ה	h, hs
8 " lenis	’	...	....	...	....	...	ا	ا	א	...
9 " asper faucalis	‘h	...	....	...	....	...	ح	ح	ח	...
10 " lenis faucalis	’h	...	....	...	....	...	ع	ع	ע	...
11 " asper fricatus	...	*‘h*	....	...	....	...	خ	خ	ח	...
12 " lenis fricatus	...	*’h*	....	...	....	...	...	...	...	...
Gutturales modificatae (palatales, &c.)										
13 Tenuis	...	*k*	....	च	𐬗	[illegible]	چ	...	...	*k*
14 " aspirata	...	*kh*	....	छ	....	...	...	...	...	*kh*
15 Media	...	*g*	....	ज	𐬘	[illegible]	ج	ج	...	...
16 " aspirata	...	*gh*	....	झ	....	...	ژ	ژ	...	...
17 " Nasalis	...	*ñ*	....	ञ	....	...	...	...	...	...

CONSONANTS (*continued*).	MISSIONARY ALPHABET. I Class.	II Class.	III Class.	Sanskrit.	Zend.	Pehlevi.	Persian.	Arabic.	Hebrew.	Chinese.
18 Semivocalis	y	. . .	. . . .	य	𐬫 (init. [illegible])	[illegible]	ي	ي	י	y
19 Spiritus asper	. . .	(ẏ)	. . . .	. . .	. . . .	. . .	. . .	. . .	. . .	. . .
20 „ lenis	. . .	(ẏ)	. . . .	. . .	. . . .	. . .	. . .	. . .	. . .	. . .
21 „ asper assibilatus . .	. . .	*s*	. . . .	श	𐬴	[illegible]	ش	ش	. . .	. . .
22 „ lenis assibilatus . .	. . .	*z*	. . . .	. . .	𐬲	[illegible]	ژ	. . .	. . .	*z*
Dentales.										
23 Tenuis	t	. . .	. . . .	त	𐬙	[illegible]	ت	ت	תּ	t
24 „ aspirata	th	. . .	. . . .	थ	𐬚	. . .	. . .	. . .	ת	th
25 „ assibilata	. . .	. . .	TH	. . .	. . . .	. . .	ث	ث	. . .	. . .
26 Media	d	. . .	. . . .	द	𐬛	[illegible]	د	د	דּ	. . .
27 „ aspirata	dh	. . .	. . . .	ध	𐬜	. . .	. . .	. . .	ד	. . .
28 „ assibilata	. . .	. . .	DH	. . .	. . . .	. . .	ذ	ذ	. . .	. . .
29 Nasalis	n	. . .	. . . .	न	𐬥	[illegible]	ن	ن	נ	n
30 Semivocalis	l	. . .	. . . .	ल	. . . .	[illegible]	ل	ل	ל	l
31 „ mollis 1	. . .	*l*	. . . .	ळ	. . . .	. . .	. . .	. . .	. . .	. . .
32 „ mollis 2	. . .	. . .	L	. . .	. . . .	. . .	. . .	. . .	. . .	. . .
33 Spiritus asper 1	s	. . .	. . . .	स	𐬯	[illegible]	س (ث)	س	שׁ	s
34 „ asper 2	. . .	. . .	s (ʃ)	. . .	. . . .	. . .	. . .	. . .	ס	. . .
35 „ lenis	z	. . .	. . . .	. . .	𐬰	[illegible]	ز (ذ)	ز	ז	z
36 „ asperrimus 1	. . .	. . .	z (ʒ)	. . .	. . . .	. . .	ص	ص	צ	ʒ, ʒh
37 „ asperrimus 2	. . .	. . .	ẓ (ʒ̣)	. . .	. . . .	. . .	ض	. . .	. . .	. . .

Dentales modificatae (linguales, &c.)										
38 Tenuis	...	*t*	....	ट	....	...	ط	ط	ט	...
39 „ aspirata	...	*th*	....	ठ	....	...	ظ	ظ	...	...
40 Media	...	*d*	....	ड	[illegible]	[illegible]	...	...	...	...
41 „ aspirata	...	*dh*	....	ढ	....	...	...	ض	...	...
42 Nasalis	...	*n*	....	ण	[illegible]	...	...	...	...	...
43 Semivocalis	r	...	....	र	[illegible]	[illegible]	ر	ر	ר	...
44 „ fricata	...	*r*	....	...	....	...	...	...	...	*r*
45 „ diacritica	...	...	R	...	....	...	...	...	...	...
46 Spiritus asper	sh	...	....	ष	[illegible]	[illegible]	...	...	...	sh
47 „ lenis	zh	...	....	...	....	...	...	...	...	...
Labiales.										
48 Tenuis	p	...	....	प	[illegible]	[illegible]	پ	...	פּ	p
49 „ aspirata	ph	...	....	फ	....	...	...	...	פ	ph
50 Media	b	...	....	ब	[illegible]	[illegible]	ب	ب	בּ	...
51 „ aspirata	bh	...	....	भ	....	...	...	...	ב	...
52 Tenuissima	...	*p*	....	...	....	...	...	...	...	...
53 Nasalis	m	...	....	म	[illegible]	[illegible]	م	م	מ	m
54 Semivocalis	w	...	....	...	[illegible]	...	...	...	...	w
55 „ aspirata	hw	...	....	...	....	...	...	...	...	...
56 Spiritus asper	f	...	....	...	[illegible]	[illegible]	ف	ف	...	f
57 lenis	v	...	....	व	»	[illegible]	و	و	ו	...
58 Anusvâra	...	*m*	....	अं	[illegible] ã	...	...	...	...	...
59 Visarga	...	*h*	....	अः	....	...	...	...	...	...

VOWELS.	MISSIONARY ALPHABET. I Class.	II Class.	III Class.	Sanskrit.	Zend.	Pehlevi.	Persian.	Arabic.	Hebrew.	Chinese.
1 Neutralis	0	...	....	...	....	...	...	...	ְ	ă
2 Laryngo-palatalis	ĕ	...	....	...	....	...	...	...	...	...
3 „ labialis	ŏ	...	....	...	....	𐭠 fin.	...	...	...	...
4 Gutturalis brevis	a	...	....	अ	𐬀	𐭠 init.	َ	َ	ַ	a
5 „ longa	â	(*a*)	....	आ	𐬁	𐭠	ـَا	ـَا	ָ	â
6 Palatalis brevis	i	...	....	इ	𐬌	...	ِ	ِ	ִ	i
7 „ longa	î	(*i*)	....	ई	𐬍	𐭩	ـِي	ـِي	ִי	î
8 Dentalis brevis	*li*	...	....	ऌ	....	...	...	...	...	...
9 „ longa	*lî*	...	....	ॡ	....	...	...	...	...	...
10 Lingualis brevis	*ri*	...	....	ऋ	....	...	...	...	...	...
11 „ longa	*rî*	...	....	ॠ	....	...	...	...	...	...
12 Labialis brevis	u	...	....	उ	𐬎	...	ُ	ُ	ֻ	u
13 „ longa	û	(*u*)	....	ऊ	𐬏	𐭥	ـُو	ـُو	וּ	û
14 Gutturo-palatalis brevis	e	...	....	...	𐬈 (e) 𐬉 (*e*)	...	...	...	ֶ	e
15 „ longa	ê (ai)	(*e*)	....	ए	𐬊, 𐬋	𐭩	...	...	ֵ	ê
16 Diphthongus gutturo-palatalis	âi	(*ai*)	....	ऐ	....	...	ـَیْ	ـَيْ	...	âi
17 „ „	ei (ĕi)	...	....	...	....	...	...	...	...	ei, êi
18 „ „	oi (ŏu)	...	....	...	....	...	...	...	...	...
19 Gutturo-labialis brevis	o	...	....	...	𐬊	...	...	...	ָ	o
20 „ longa	ô (au)	(*o*)	....	ओ	𐬋	𐭥	...	...	וֹ	...
21 Diphthongus gutturo-labialis	âu	(*au*)	....	औ	𐬈𐬎 (*au*)	...	ـَوْ	ـَوْ	...	âu
22 „ „	eu (ĕu)	...	....	...	....	...	...	...	...	...
23 „ „	ou (ŏu)	...	....	...	....	...	...	...	...	...
24 Gutturalis fracta	ä	...	....	...	....	...	...	...	...	...
25 Palatalis fracta	ï	...	....	...	....	...	...	...	...	...
26 Labialis fracta	ü	...	....	...	....	...	...	...	...	ü
27 Gutturo-labialis fracta	ö	...	....	...	....	...	...	...	...	...